DEVOL™

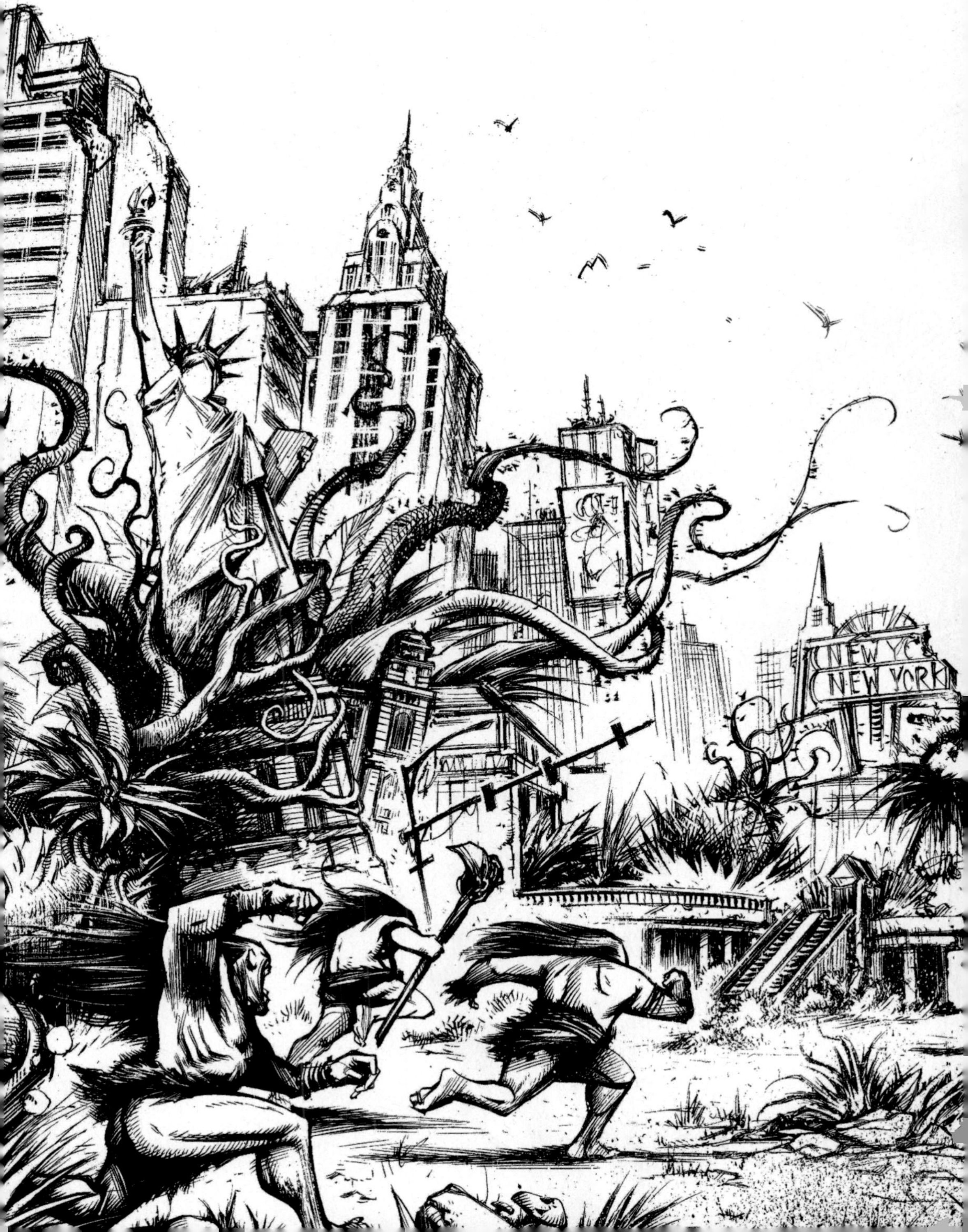
NEW YC
NEW YORK

DƎVOLUTION

writer
RICK REMENDER

artist
JONATHAN WAYSHAK

colorist
JORDAN BOYD

letterer
RUS WOOTON

collection cover artist
JAE LEE

collection cover colorist
JUNE CHUNG

collection designer
GEOFF HARKINS

editor
JOSEPH RYBANDT

DYNAMITE®

Nick Barrucci, CEO / Publisher
Juan Collado, President / COO

Joe Rybandt, Executive Editor
Matt Idelson, Senior Editor
Rachel Pinnelas, Associate Editor
Anthony Marques, Assistant Editor
Kevin Ketner, Editorial Assistant

Jason Ullmeyer, Art Director
Geoff Harkins, Senior Graphic Designer
Cathleen Heard, Graphic Designer
Alexis Persson, Production Artist

Chris Caniano, Digital Associate
Rachel Kilbury, Digital Assistant

Brandon Dante Primavera, V.P. of IT and Operations
Rich Young, Director of Business Development

Alan Payne, V.P of Sales & Marketing
Keith Davidsen, Marketing Director
Pat O'Connell, Sales Manager

Online at **www.DYNAMITE.com** | On Facebook **/Dynamitecomics**
Instagram **/Dynamitecomics** | On Tumblr **dynamitecomics.tumblr.com**
On Twitter **@dynamitecomics** | On YouTube **/Dynamitecomics**

PEFC Certified
Printed on paper from
sustainably managed
forests and controlled
sources
PEFC/01-31-106   www.pefc.org

First Printing   ISBN-13: 978-1-5241-0028-5   10 9 8 7 6 5 4 3 2 1

DEVOLUTION™, Volume 1, First printing. Contains materials originally published in DEVOLUTION™, Volume 1, #1-5. Published by Dynamite Entertainment. 113 Gaither Dr., STE 205, Mt. Laurel, NJ 08054. DEVOLUTION is ™ & © 2016 Dynamite Characters,llc. and Rick Remender. DYNAMITE, DYNAMITE ENTERTAINMENT and its logo are ® & © 2016 Dynamite. All rights reserved. All names, charac-ters, events, and locales in this publication are entirely fictional. Any resemblance to actual persons (living or dead), events or places, without satiric intent, is coincidental. No portion of this book may be reproduced by any means (digital or print) without the written permission of Dynamite Entertainment except for review pur-poses. The scanning, uploading and distribution of this book via the Internet or via any other means without the permission of the publisher is illegal and punishable by law. Please purchase only authorized electronic editions, and do not participate in or encourage electronic piracy of copyrighted materials. Printed in Canada.

For media rights, foreign rights, promotions, licensing, and advertising: marketing@dynamite.com

Issue 1 Cover by JAE LEE With Colors by JUNE CHUNG

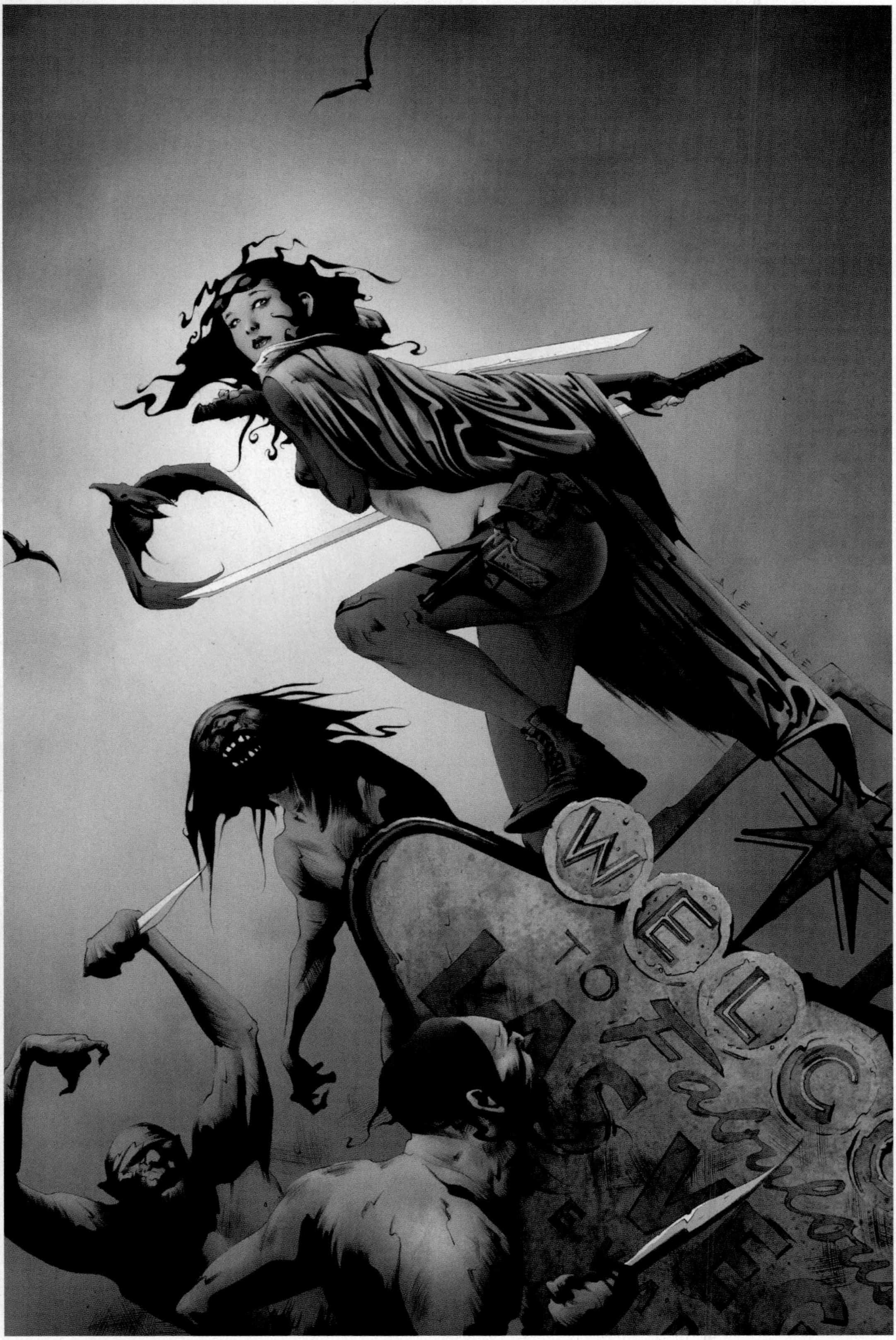
WELCO
TO

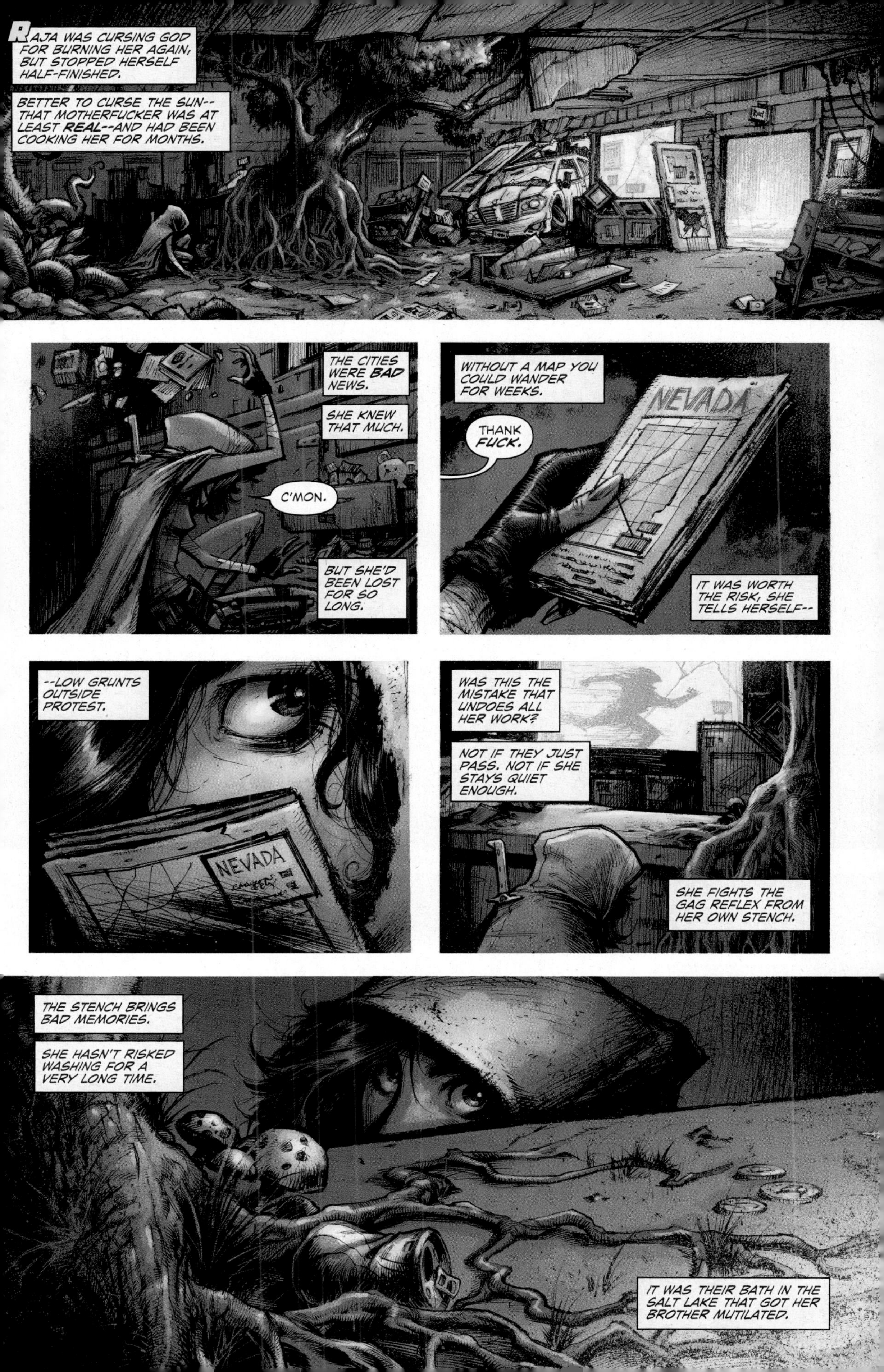
RAJA WAS CURSING GOD FOR BURNING HER AGAIN, BUT STOPPED HERSELF HALF-FINISHED.
BETTER TO CURSE THE SUN-- THAT MOTHERFUCKER WAS AT LEAST REAL--AND HAD BEEN COOKING HER FOR MONTHS.
THE CITIES WERE BAD NEWS.
SHE KNEW THAT MUCH.
C'MON.
BUT SHE'D BEEN LOST FOR SO LONG.
WITHOUT A MAP YOU COULD WANDER FOR WEEKS.
NEVADA
THANK FUCK.
IT WAS WORTH THE RISK, SHE TELLS HERSELF--
--LOW GRUNTS OUTSIDE PROTEST.
NEVADA
WAS THIS THE MISTAKE THAT UNDOES ALL HER WORK?
NOT IF THEY JUST PASS. NOT IF SHE STAYS QUIET ENOUGH.
SHE FIGHTS THE GAG REFLEX FROM HER OWN STENCH.
THE STENCH BRINGS BAD MEMORIES.
SHE HASN'T RISKED WASHING FOR A VERY LONG TIME.
IT WAS THEIR BATH IN THE SALT LAKE THAT GOT HER BROTHER MUTILATED.

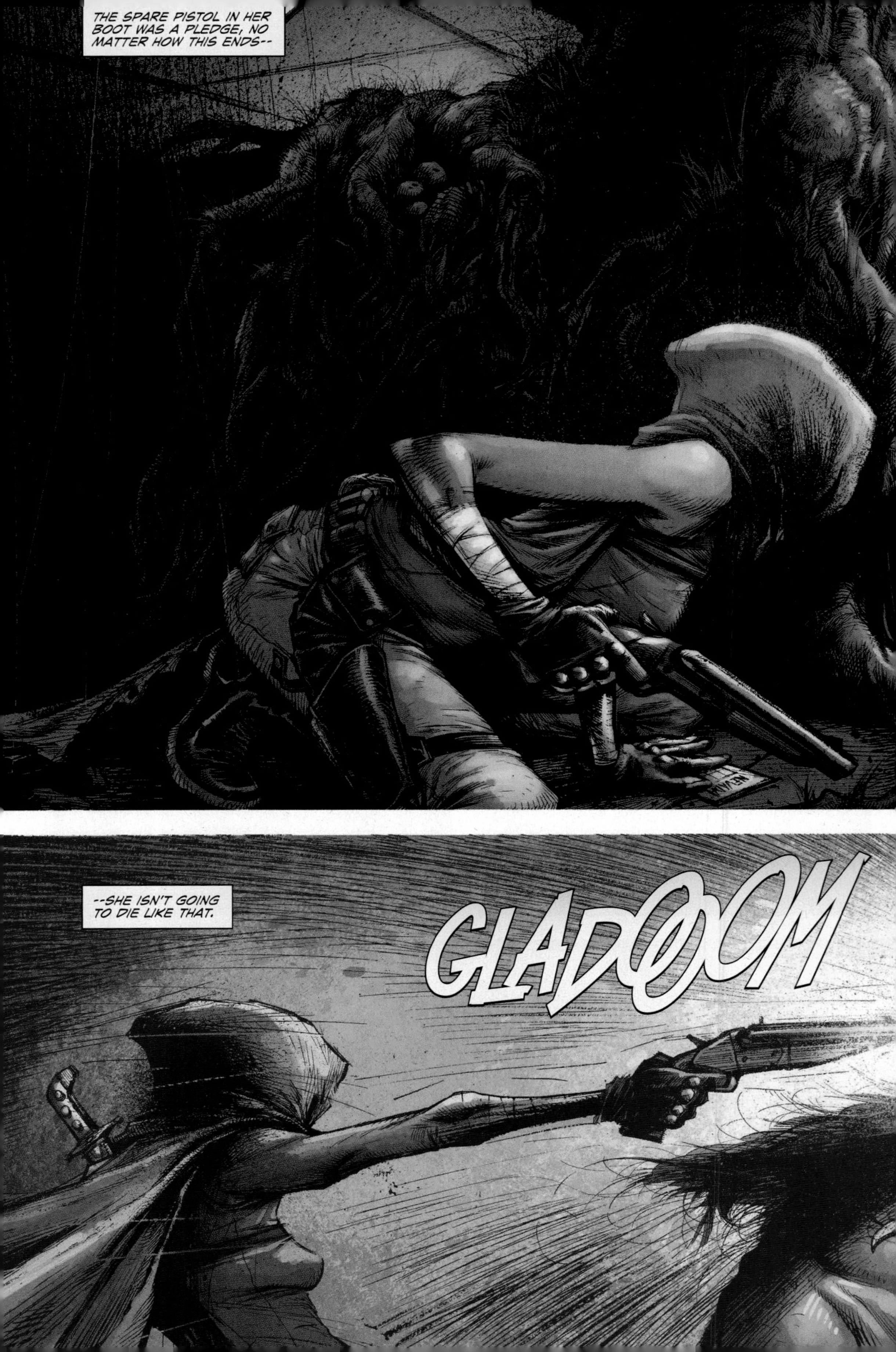
THE SPARE PISTOL IN HER BOOT WAS A PLEDGE, NO MATTER HOW THIS ENDS--
--SHE ISN'T GOING TO DIE LIKE THAT.
GLADOOOM

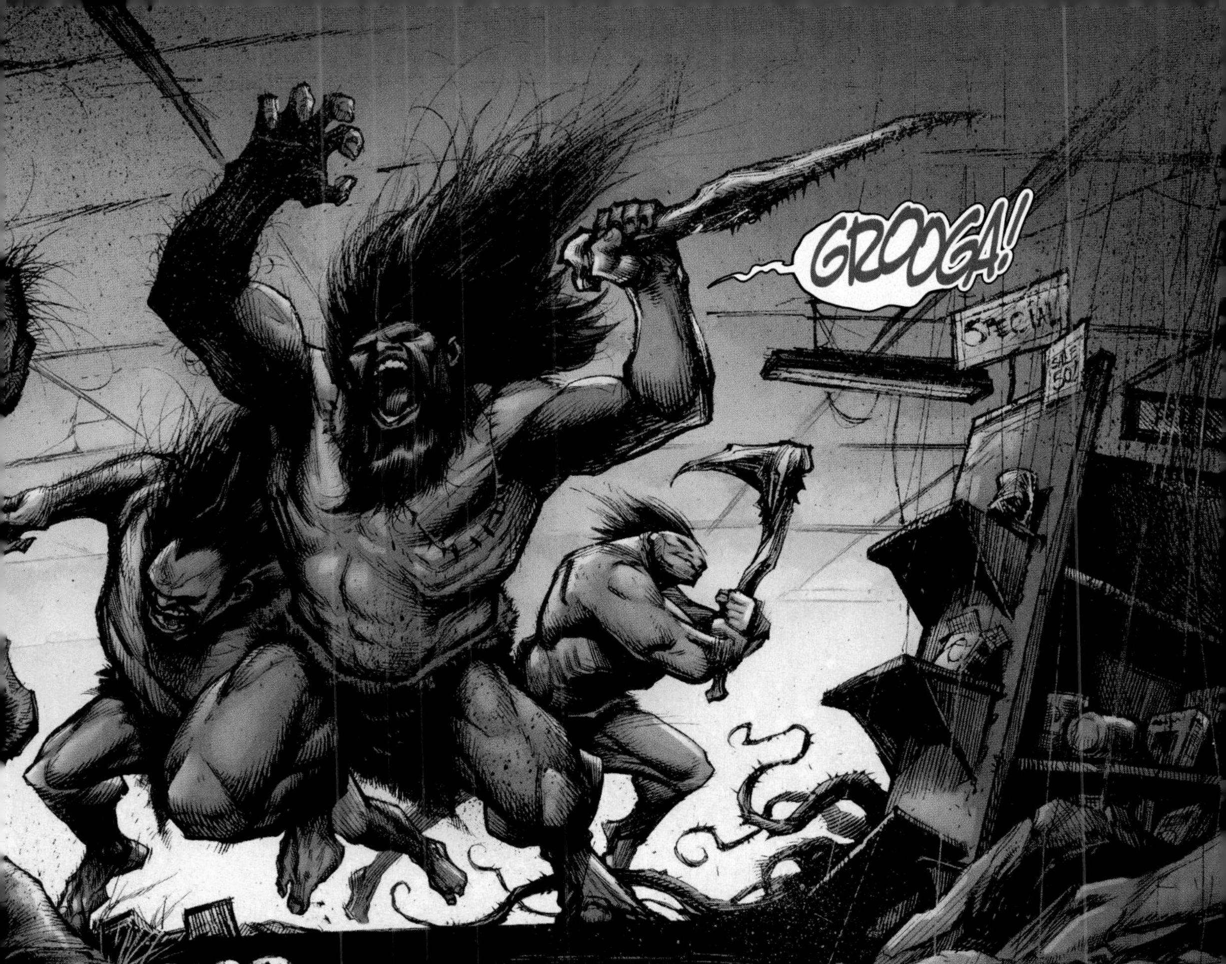
GROOGA!

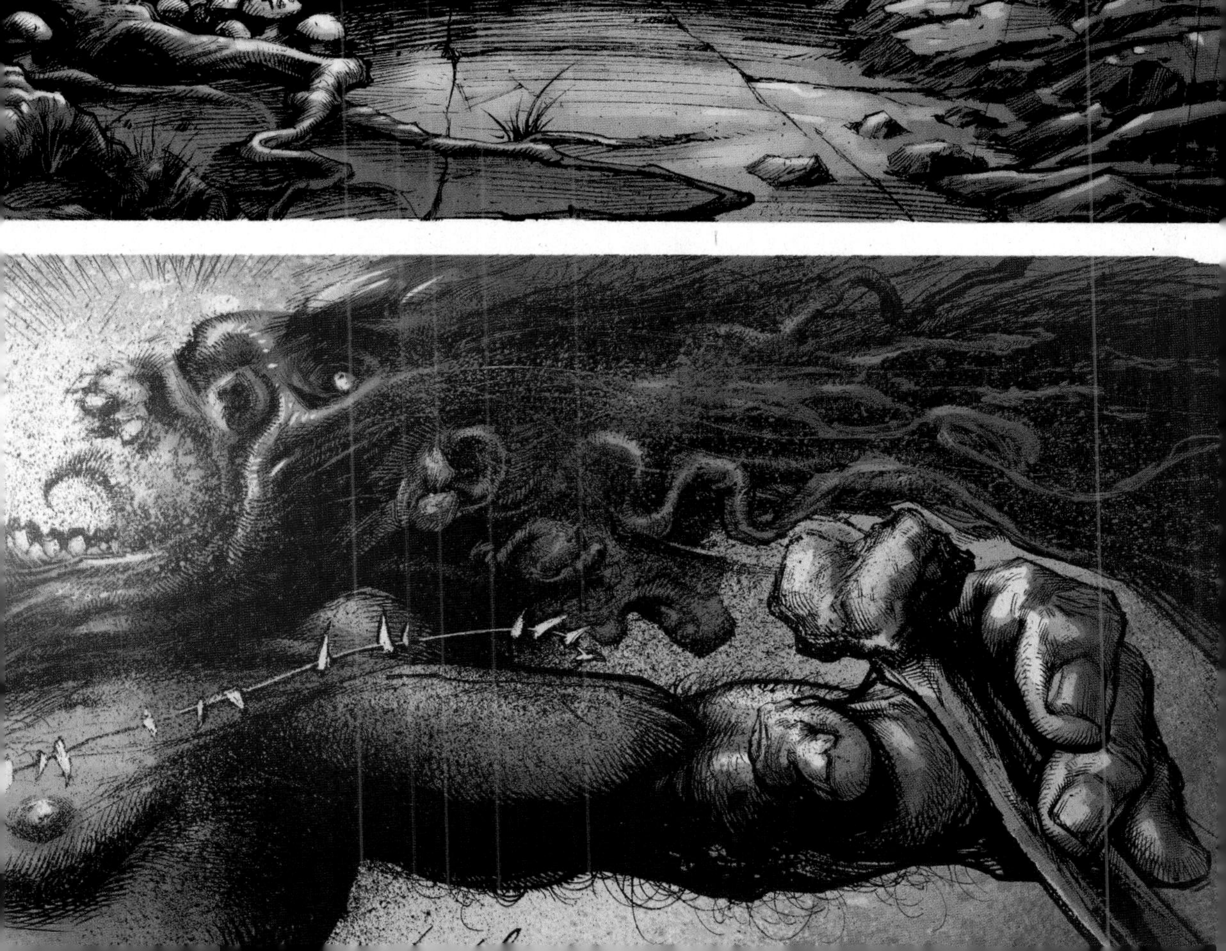

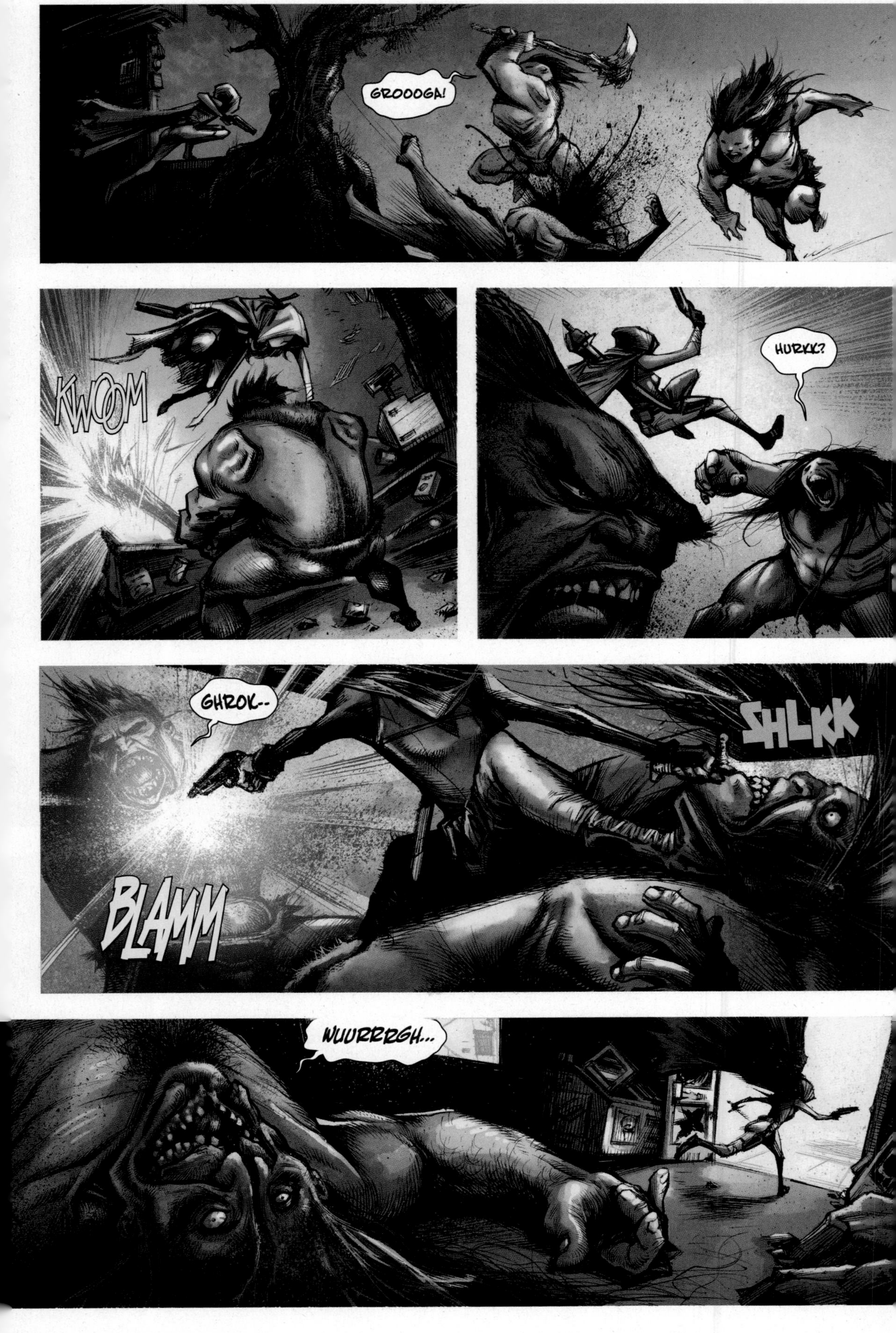
GROOOGA!
KWOOM
HURKK?
GHROK--
SHLKK
BLAMM
WUURRRGH...

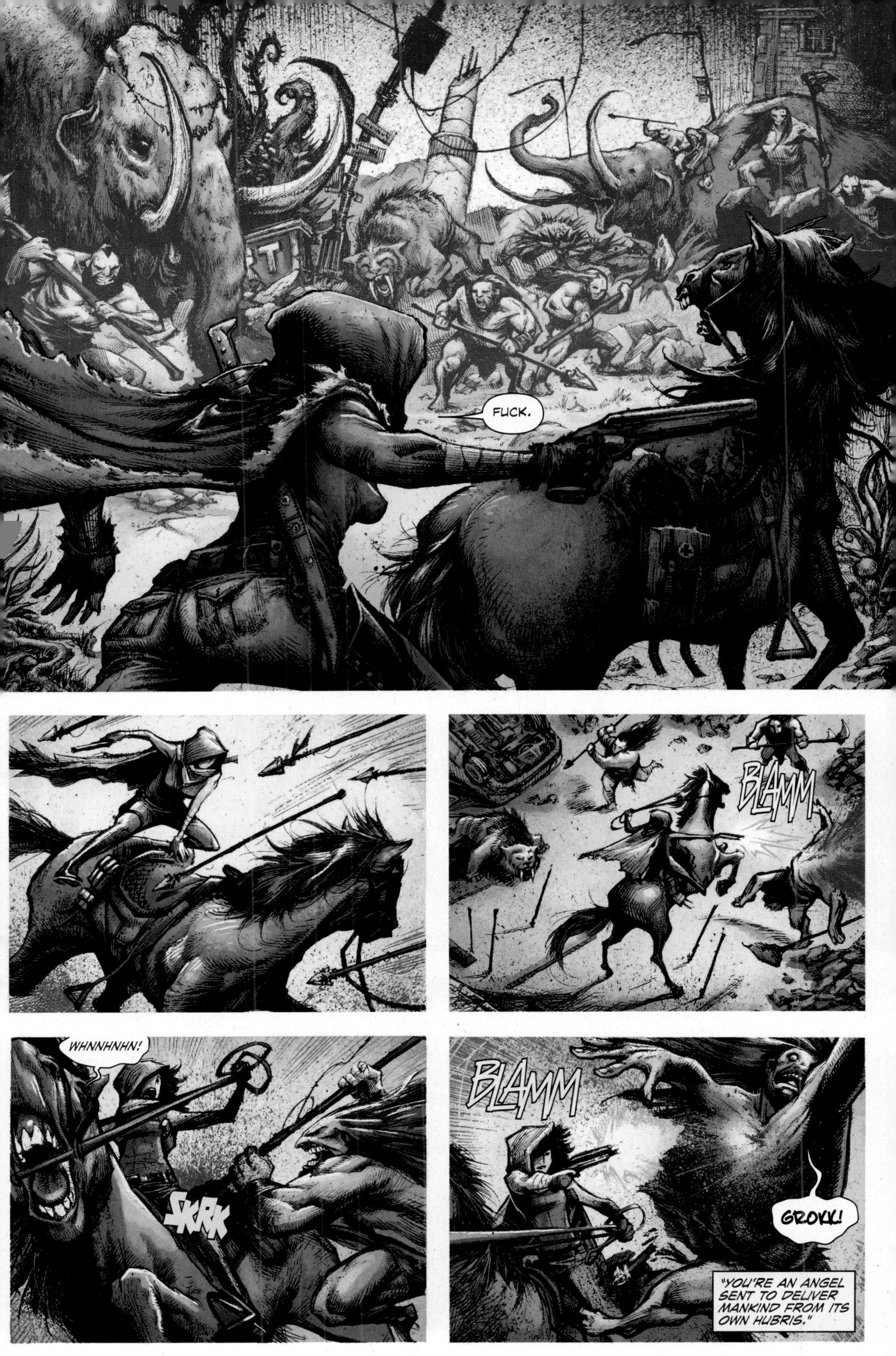
FUCK.
BLAMM
WHNNHNHN!
SKRK
BLAMM
GROKK!
"YOU'RE AN ANGEL SENT TO DELIVER MANKIND FROM ITS OWN HUBRIS."

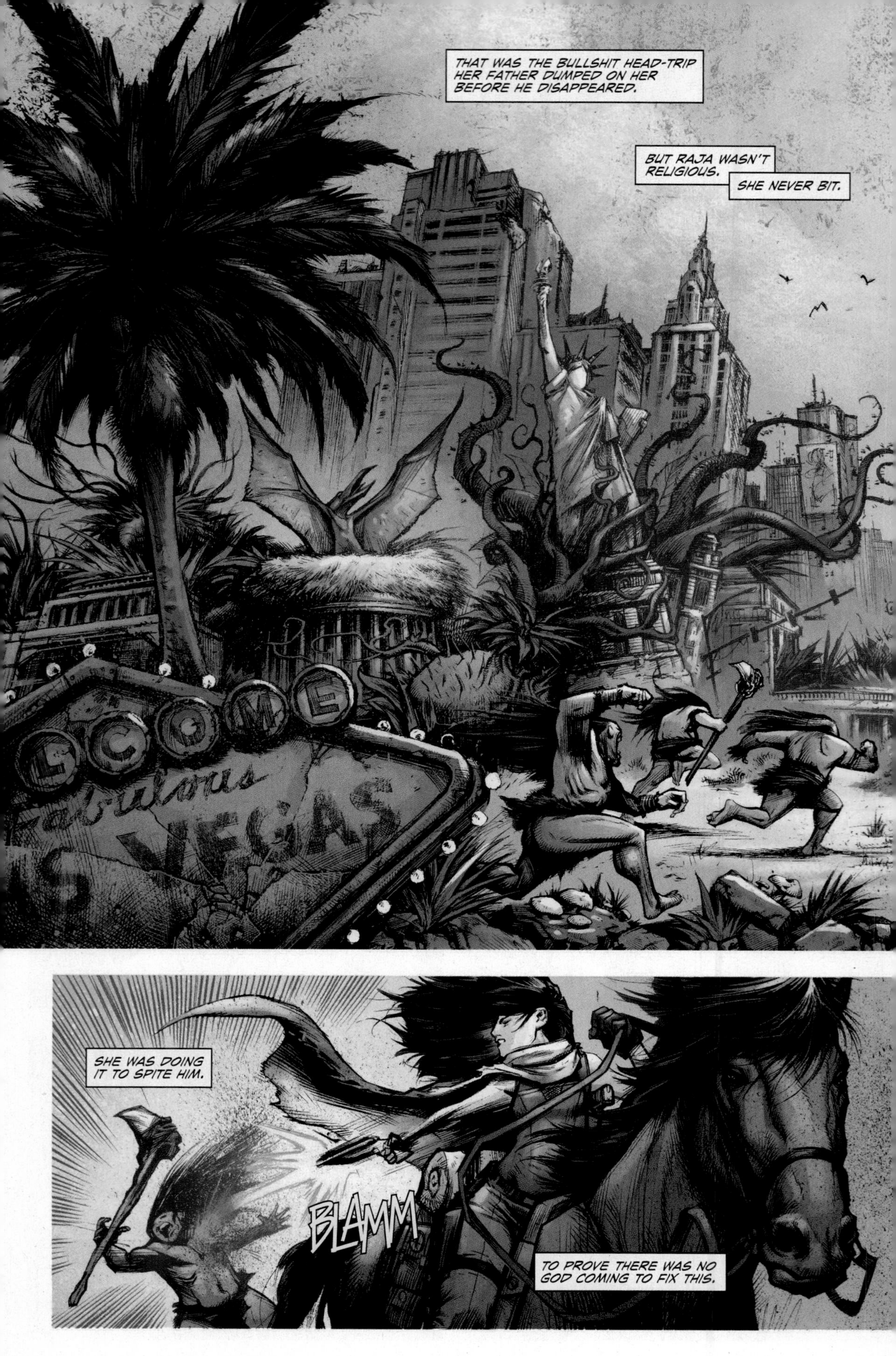
THAT WAS THE BULLSHIT HEAD-TRIP HER FATHER DUMPED ON HER BEFORE HE DISAPPEARED.
BUT RAJA WASN'T RELIGIOUS.
SHE NEVER BIT.
SHE WAS DOING IT TO SPITE HIM.
BLAMM
TO PROVE THERE WAS NO GOD COMING TO FIX THIS.

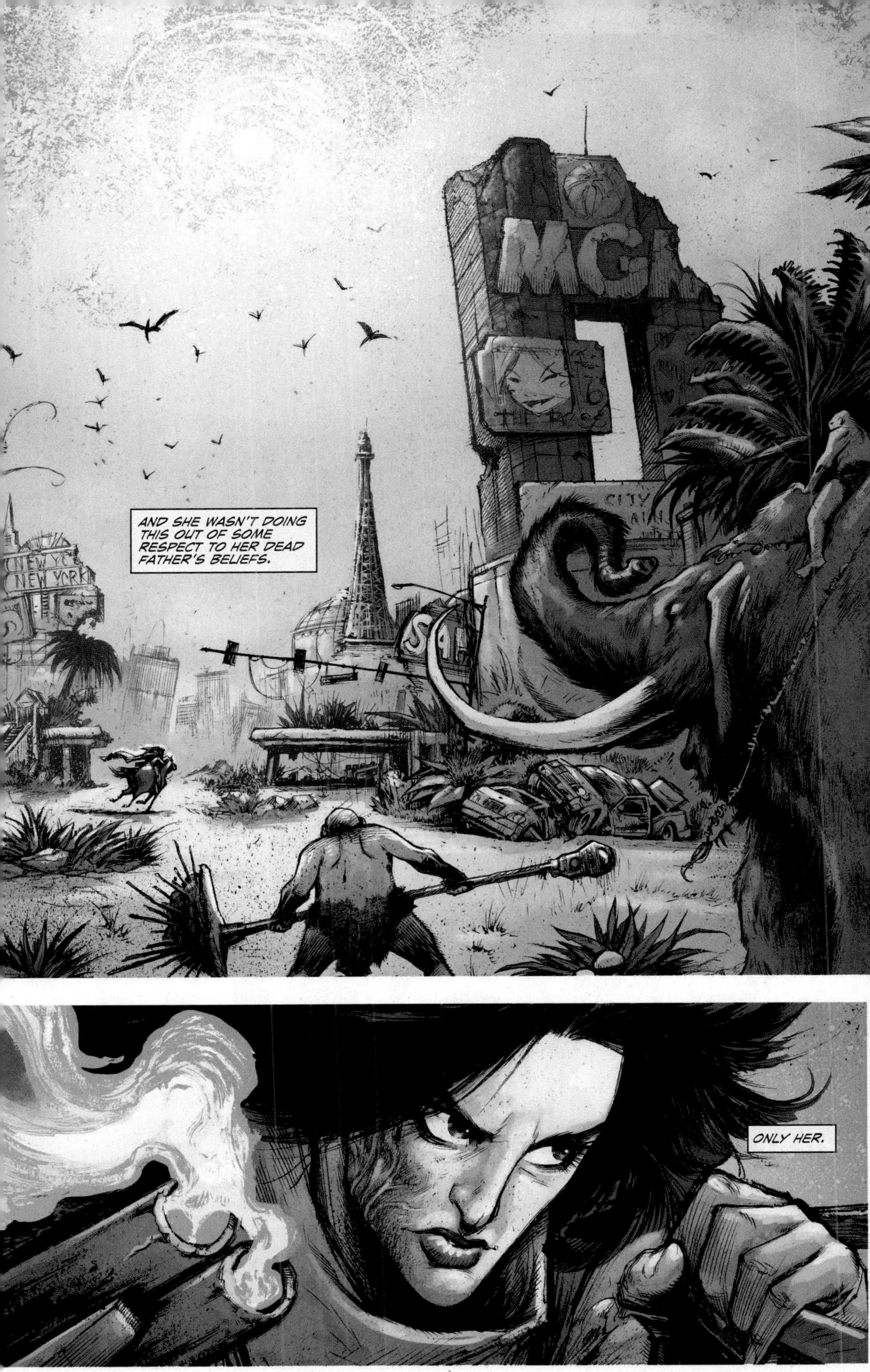
AND SHE WASN'T DOING THIS OUT OF SOME RESPECT TO HER DEAD FATHER'S BELIEFS.
ONLY HER.

DEVOLUTION

RICK REMENDER
WRITER

JONATHAN WAYSHAK
ARTIST

JORDAN BOYD
COLORIST

RUS WOOTON
LETTERER

JOSEPH RYBANDT
EDITOR

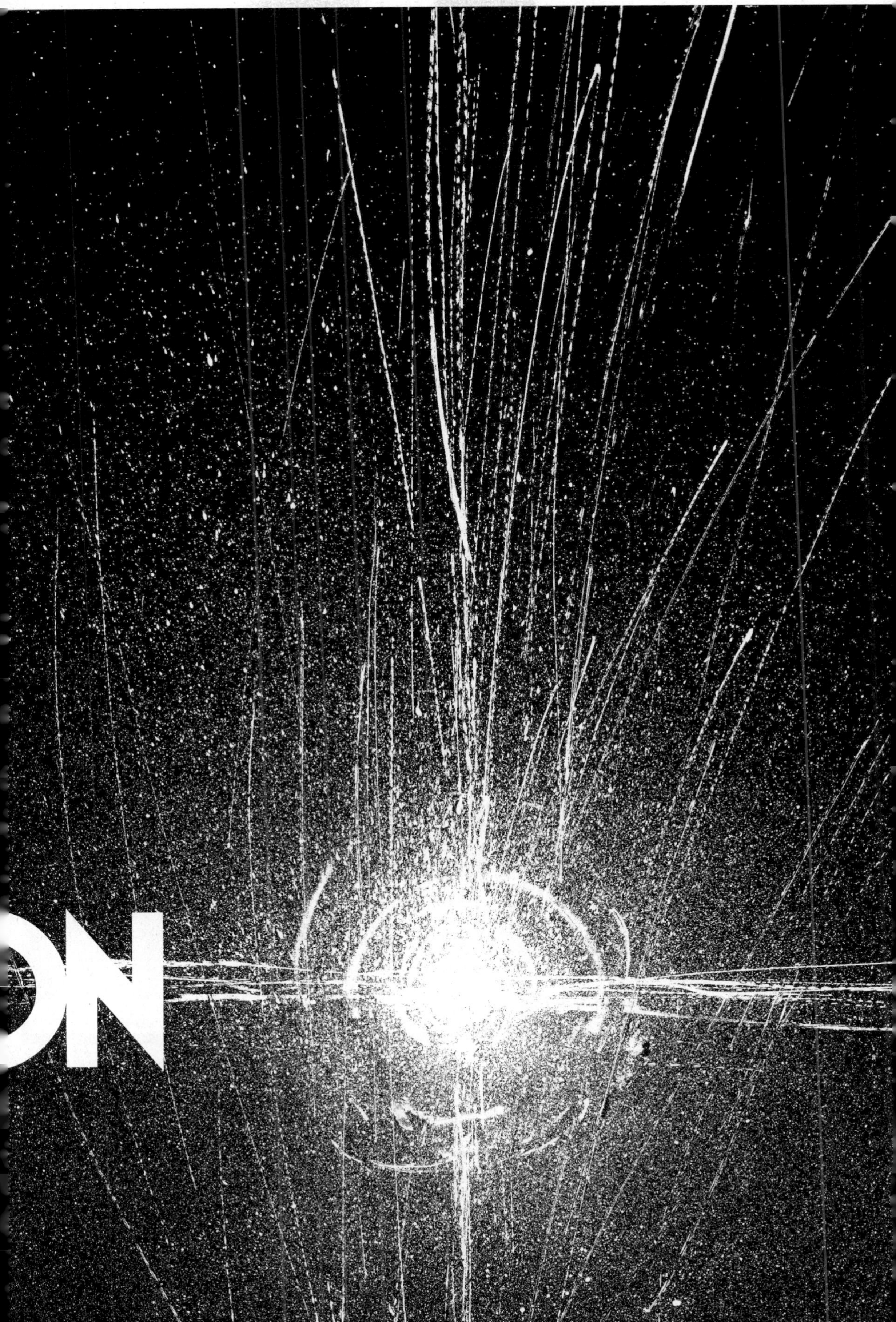
ON

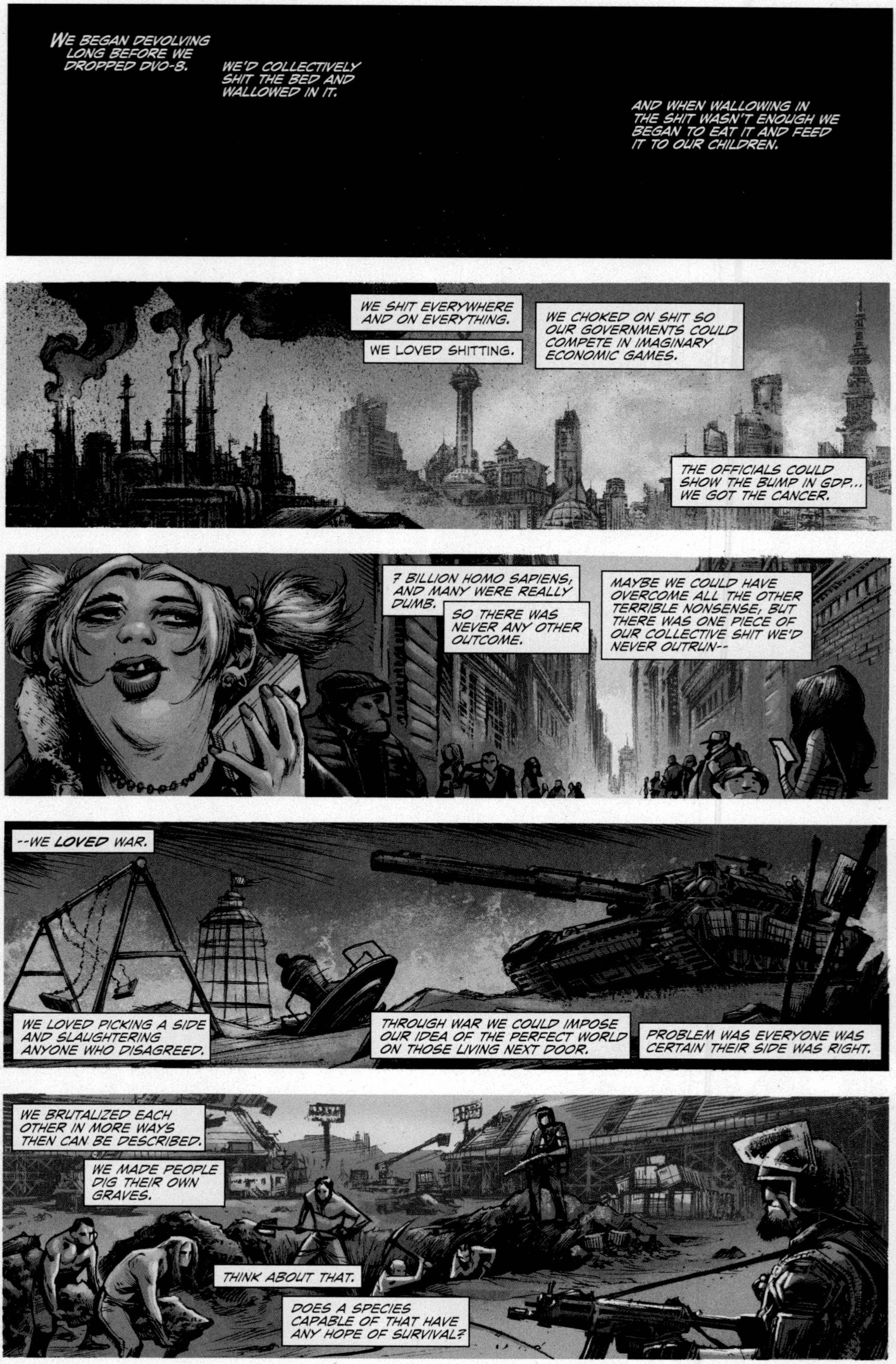
WE BEGAN DEVOLVING LONG BEFORE WE DROPPED DVO-8.
WE'D COLLECTIVELY SHIT THE BED AND WALLOWED IN IT.
AND WHEN WALLOWING IN THE SHIT WASN'T ENOUGH WE BEGAN TO EAT IT AND FEED IT TO OUR CHILDREN.
WE SHIT EVERYWHERE AND ON EVERYTHING.
WE LOVED SHITTING.
WE CHOKED ON SHIT SO OUR GOVERNMENTS COULD COMPETE IN IMAGINARY ECONOMIC GAMES.
THE OFFICIALS COULD SHOW THE BUMP IN GDP... WE GOT THE CANCER.
7 BILLION HOMO SAPIENS, AND MANY WERE REALLY DUMB.
SO THERE WAS NEVER ANY OTHER OUTCOME.
MAYBE WE COULD HAVE OVERCOME ALL THE OTHER TERRIBLE NONSENSE, BUT THERE WAS ONE PIECE OF OUR COLLECTIVE SHIT WE'D NEVER OUTRUN--
--WE LOVED WAR.
WE LOVED PICKING A SIDE AND SLAUGHTERING ANYONE WHO DISAGREED.
THROUGH WAR WE COULD IMPOSE OUR IDEA OF THE PERFECT WORLD ON THOSE LIVING NEXT DOOR.
PROBLEM WAS EVERYONE WAS CERTAIN THEIR SIDE WAS RIGHT.
WE BRUTALIZED EACH OTHER IN MORE WAYS THEN CAN BE DESCRIBED.
WE MADE PEOPLE DIG THEIR OWN GRAVES.
THINK ABOUT THAT.
DOES A SPECIES CAPABLE OF THAT HAVE ANY HOPE OF SURVIVAL?

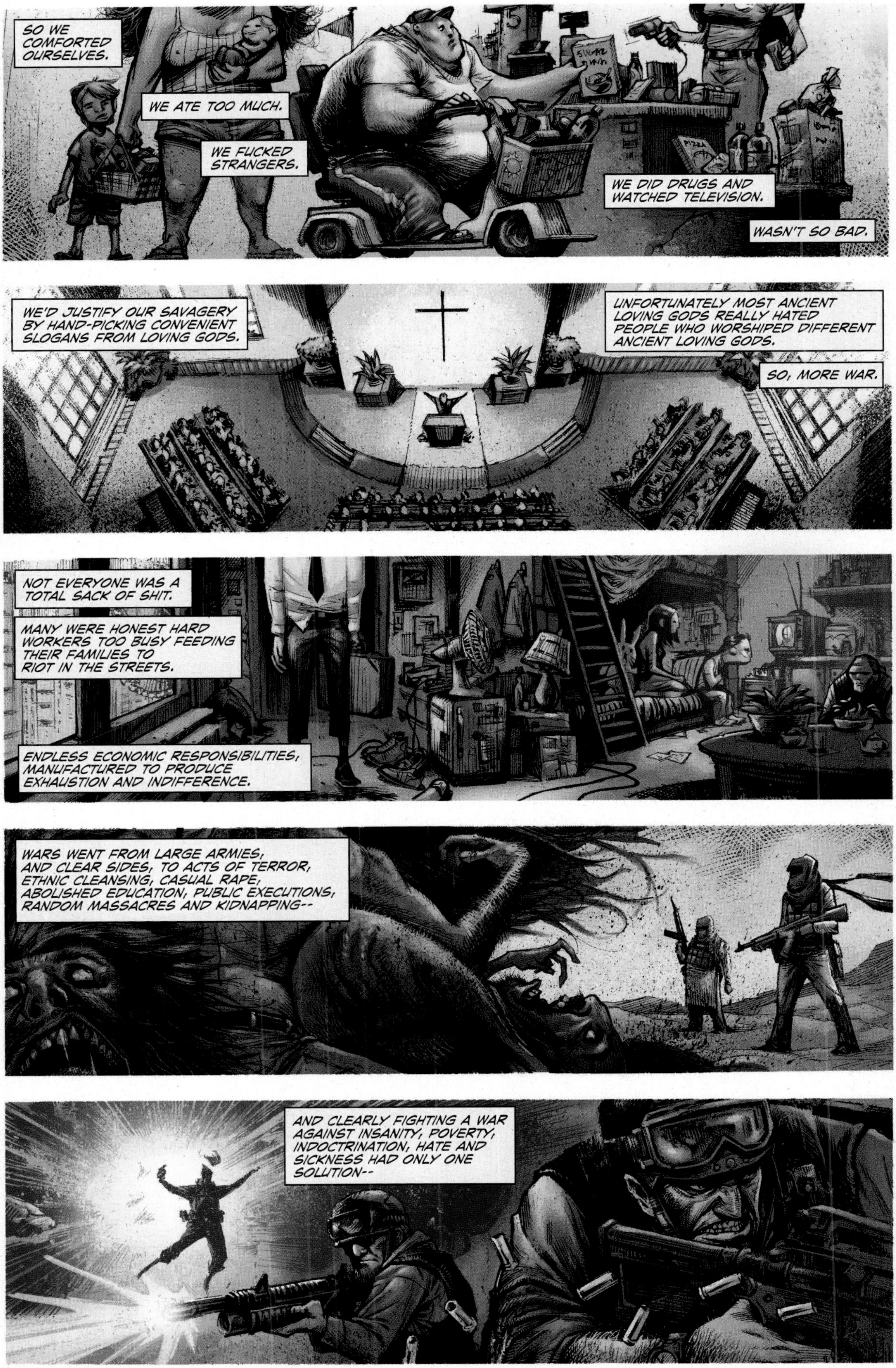
SO WE COMFORTED OURSELVES.
WE ATE TOO MUCH.
WE FUCKED STRANGERS.
WE DID DRUGS AND WATCHED TELEVISION.
WASN'T SO BAD.
WE'D JUSTIFY OUR SAVAGERY BY HAND-PICKING CONVENIENT SLOGANS FROM LOVING GODS.
UNFORTUNATELY MOST ANCIENT LOVING GODS REALLY HATED PEOPLE WHO WORSHIPED DIFFERENT ANCIENT LOVING GODS.
SO, MORE WAR.
NOT EVERYONE WAS A TOTAL SACK OF SHIT.
MANY WERE HONEST HARD WORKERS TOO BUSY FEEDING THEIR FAMILIES TO RIOT IN THE STREETS.
ENDLESS ECONOMIC RESPONSIBILITIES, MANUFACTURED TO PRODUCE EXHAUSTION AND INDIFFERENCE.
WARS WENT FROM LARGE ARMIES, AND CLEAR SIDES, TO ACTS OF TERROR, ETHNIC CLEANSING, CASUAL RAPE, ABOLISHED EDUCATION, PUBLIC EXECUTIONS, RANDOM MASSACRES AND KIDNAPPING--
AND CLEARLY FIGHTING A WAR AGAINST INSANITY, POVERTY, INDOCTRINATION, HATE AND SICKNESS HAD ONLY ONE SOLUTION--

--THEY DROPPED A BOMB IN THE MIDDLE OF THE MESS.

BUT, STILL, THE WAR WENT ON.

POLITICIANS DEBATED FOR MONTHS BEFORE REACHING A CONCLUSION.

IT WAS CLEAR TO THEM ALL, IN SECRET MEETINGS OF COURSE, THAT THE STEM OF THE PROBLEM WAS RELIGION--

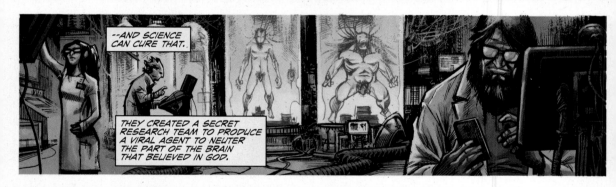

--AND SCIENCE CAN CURE THAT.

THEY CREATED A SECRET RESEARCH TEAM TO PRODUCE A VIRAL AGENT TO NEUTER THE PART OF THE BRAIN THAT BELIEVED IN GOD.

AN INTERNATIONAL COALITION OF SCIENTISTS DEVISED THE AGENT, NAMED DVO-8, WHICH WOULD ISOLATE THE PART OF THE BRAIN ASSOCIATED WITH BELIEF AND DEVOLVE IT, SHRINKING IT AWAY TO NOTHING.

TURNING OFF THE RECIPIENTS' BELIEF IN GOD.

OF COURSE THERE WERE SIDE EFFECTS, BUT NOTHING SEVERE ENOUGH TO PRECLUDE ITS USE IN A FEW TESTS.

A BAND OF MARINES WERE INOCULATED AND SET OUT TO GIVE THE DING-DONG SERUM A RUN.

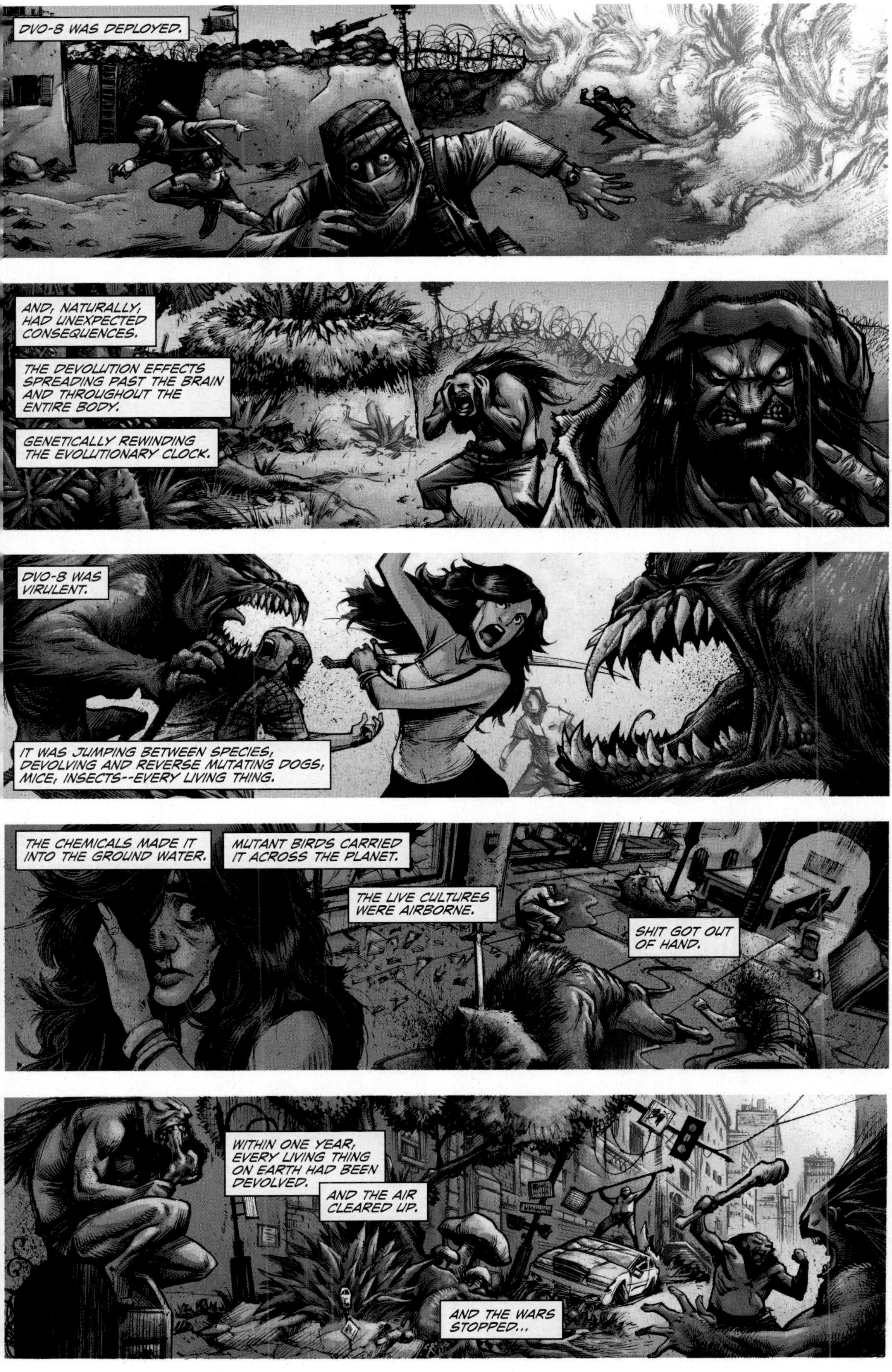
DVO-8 WAS DEPLOYED.
AND, NATURALLY, HAD UNEXPECTED CONSEQUENCES.
THE DEVOLUTION EFFECTS SPREADING PAST THE BRAIN AND THROUGHOUT THE ENTIRE BODY.
GENETICALLY REWINDING THE EVOLUTIONARY CLOCK.
DVO-8 WAS VIRULENT.
IT WAS JUMPING BETWEEN SPECIES, DEVOLVING AND REVERSE MUTATING DOGS, MICE; INSECTS--EVERY LIVING THING.
THE CHEMICALS MADE IT INTO THE GROUND WATER.
MUTANT BIRDS CARRIED IT ACROSS THE PLANET.
THE LIVE CULTURES WERE AIRBORNE.
SHIT GOT OUT OF HAND.
WITHIN ONE YEAR, EVERY LIVING THING ON EARTH HAD BEEN DEVOLVED.
AND THE AIR CLEARED UP.
AND THE WARS STOPPED...

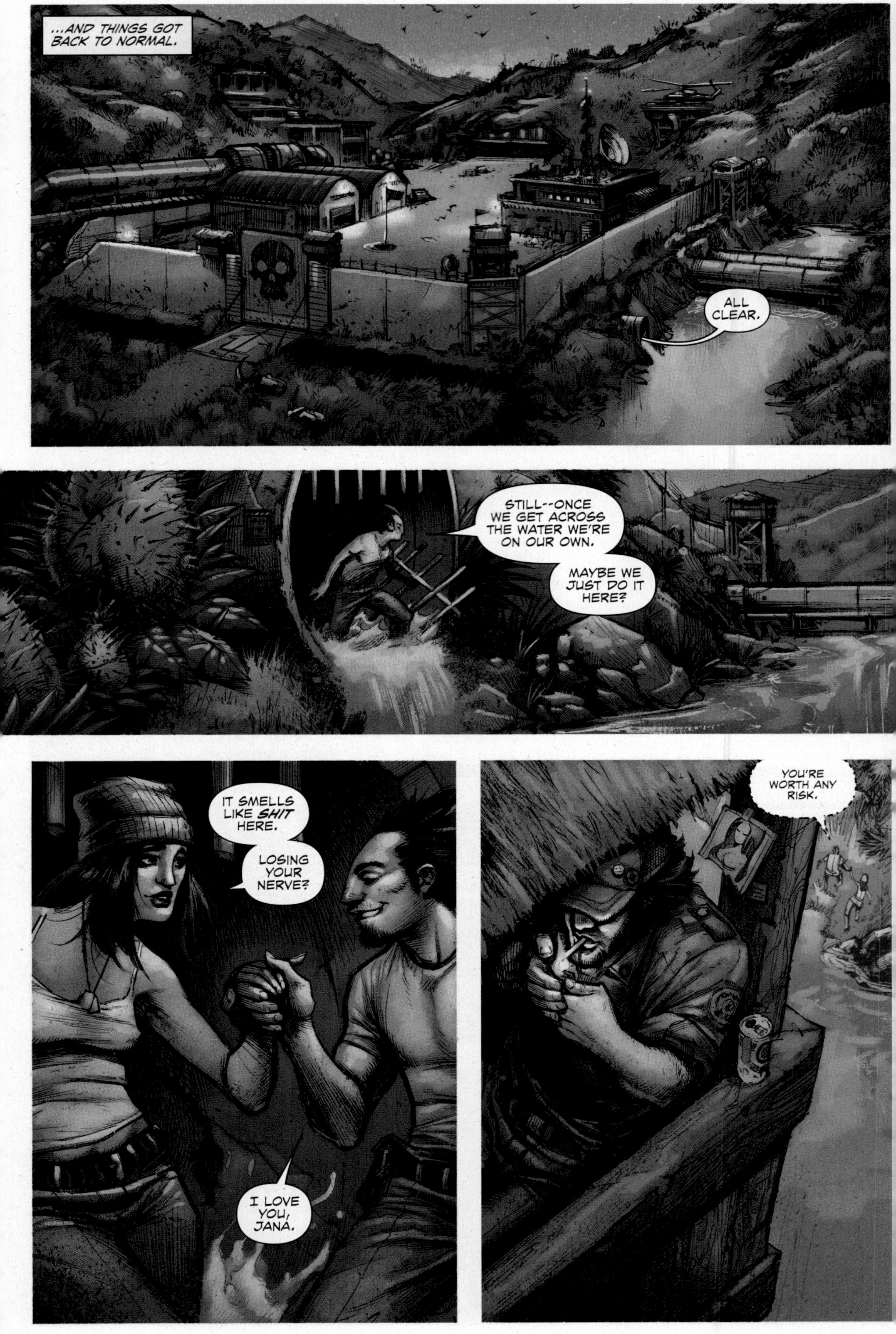
...AND THINGS GOT BACK TO NORMAL.
ALL CLEAR.
STILL--ONCE WE GET ACROSS THE WATER WE'RE ON OUR OWN.
MAYBE WE JUST DO IT HERE?
IT SMELLS LIKE *SHIT* HERE.
LOSING YOUR NERVE?
I LOVE YOU, JANA.
YOU'RE WORTH ANY RISK.

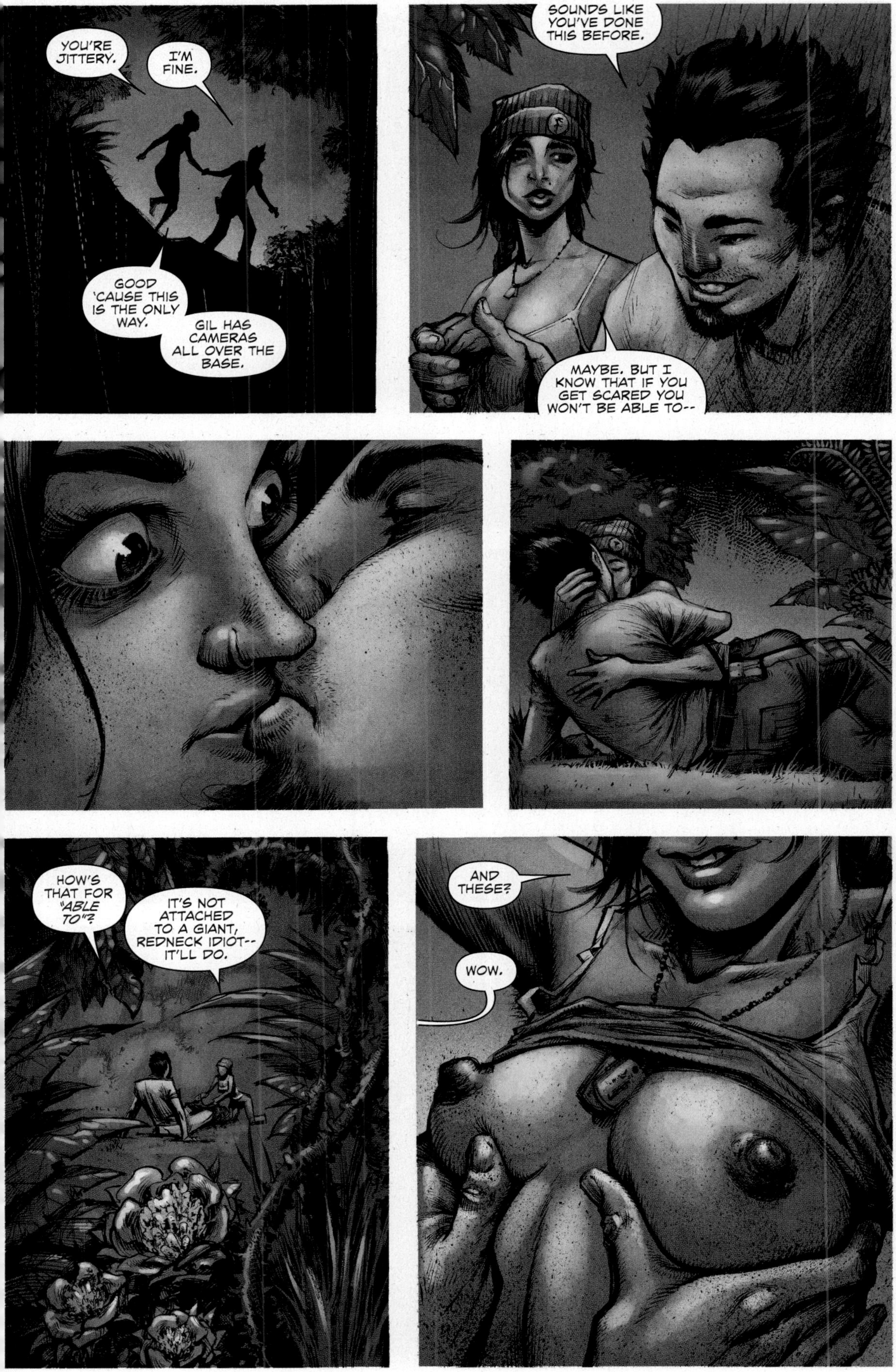
YOU'RE JITTERY.
I'M FINE.
GOOD 'CAUSE THIS IS THE ONLY WAY.
GIL HAS CAMERAS ALL OVER THE BASE.
SOUNDS LIKE YOU'VE DONE THIS BEFORE.
MAYBE. BUT I KNOW THAT IF YOU GET SCARED YOU WON'T BE ABLE TO--
HOW'S THAT FOR *"ABLE TO"*?
IT'S NOT ATTACHED TO A GIANT, REDNECK IDIOT-- IT'LL DO.
AND THESE?
WOW.

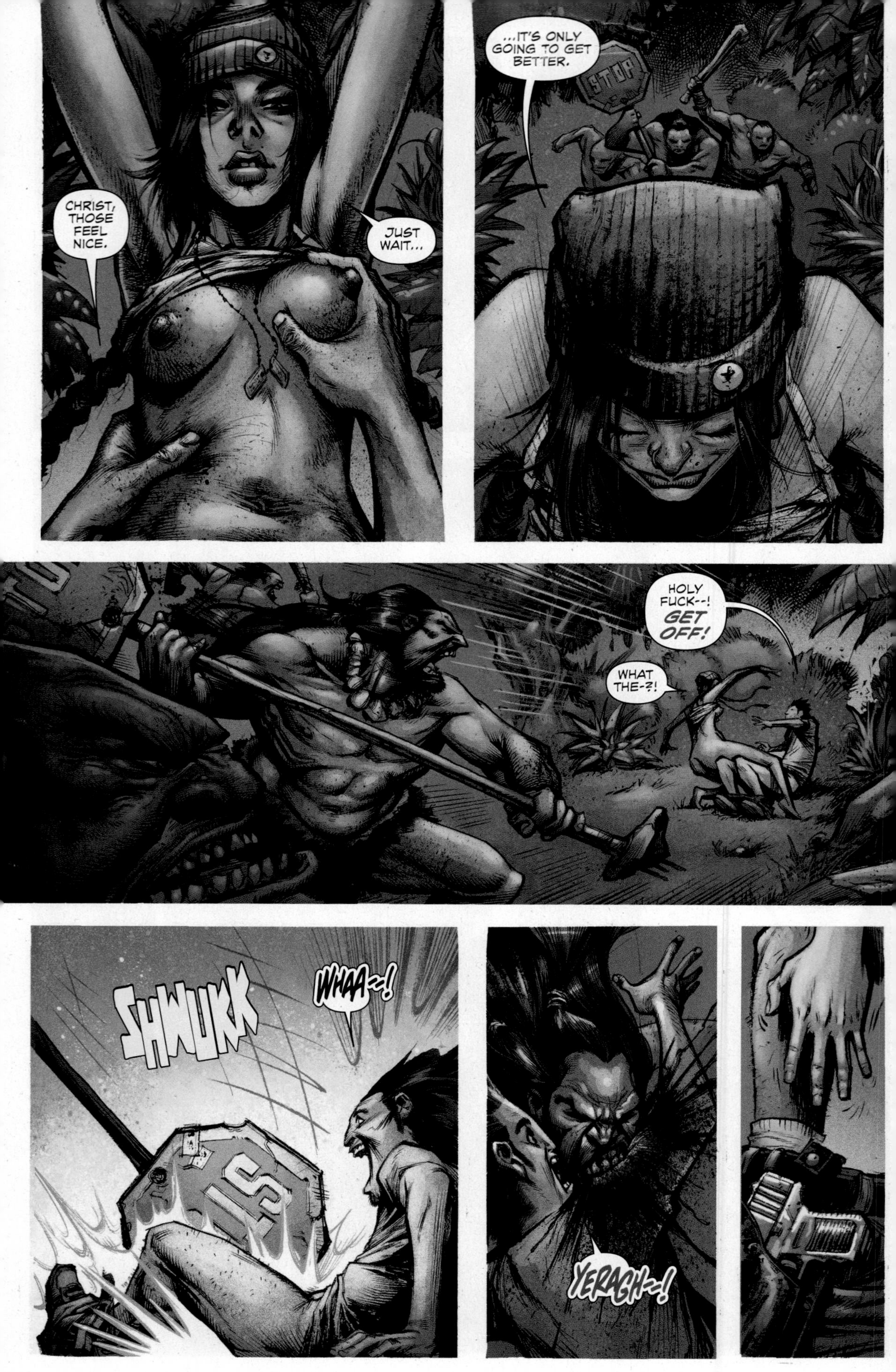
CHRIST, THOSE FEEL NICE.
JUST WAIT...
...IT'S ONLY GOING TO GET BETTER.
STOP
HOLY FUCK--! GET OFF!
WHAT THE-?!
SHWUKK
WHAA--!
YERAGH--!

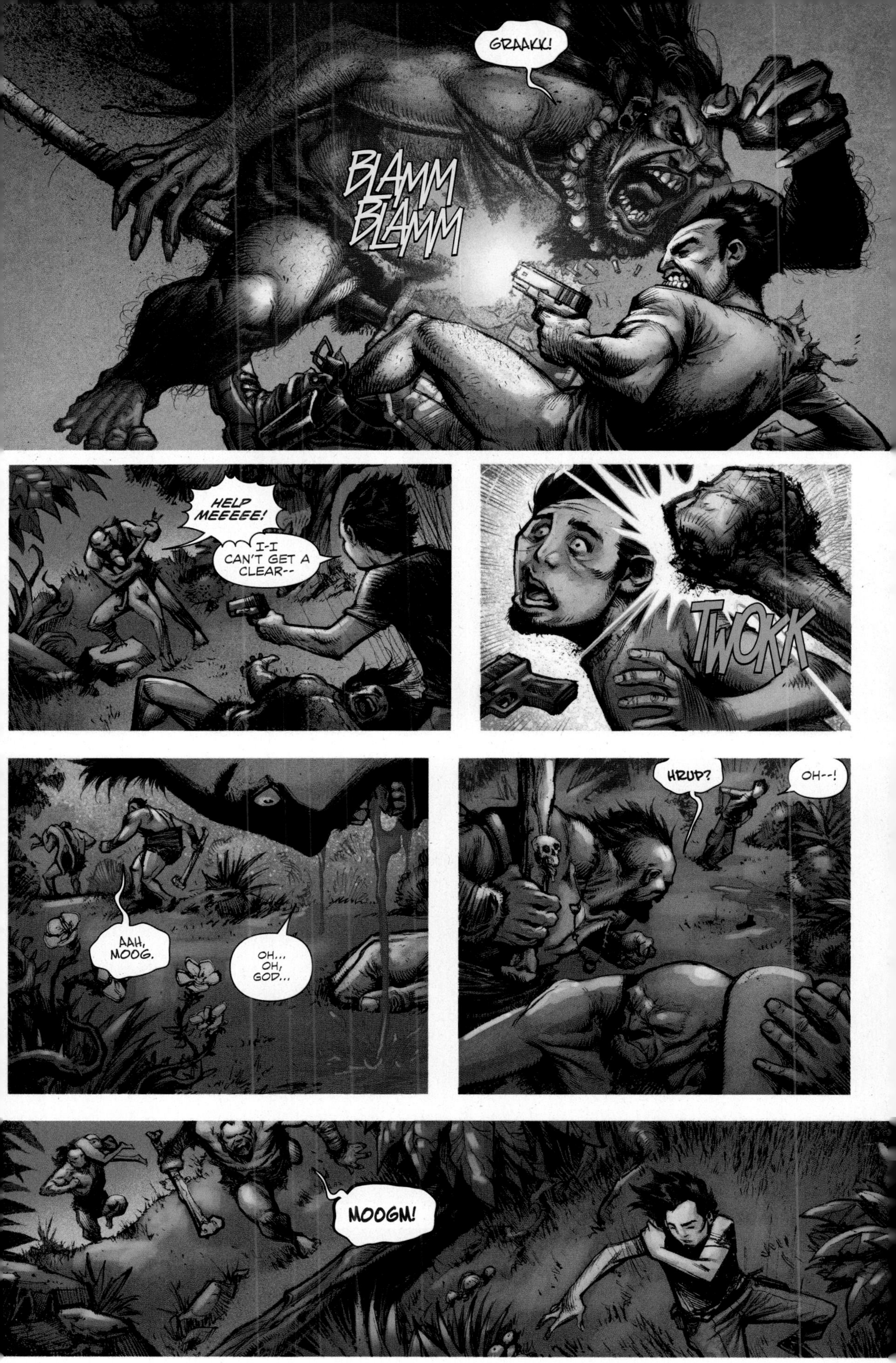
GRAAKK!
BLAMM BLAMM
HELP MEEEEE!
I-I CAN'T GET A CLEAR--
TWOKK
AAH, MOOG.
OH... OH, GOD...
HRUP?
OH--!
MOOGM!

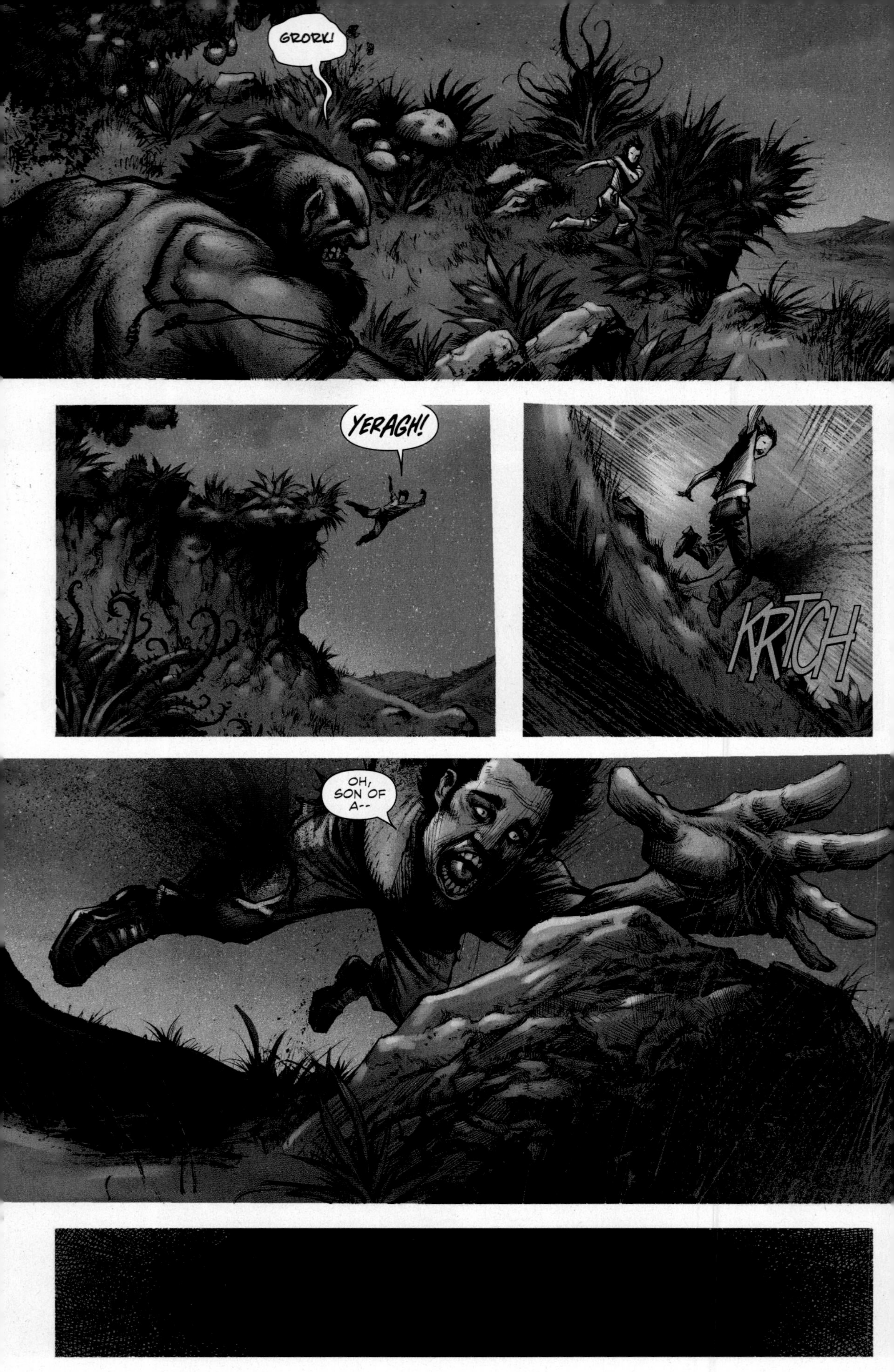
GRORK!
YERAGH!
KRTCH
OH, SON OF A--

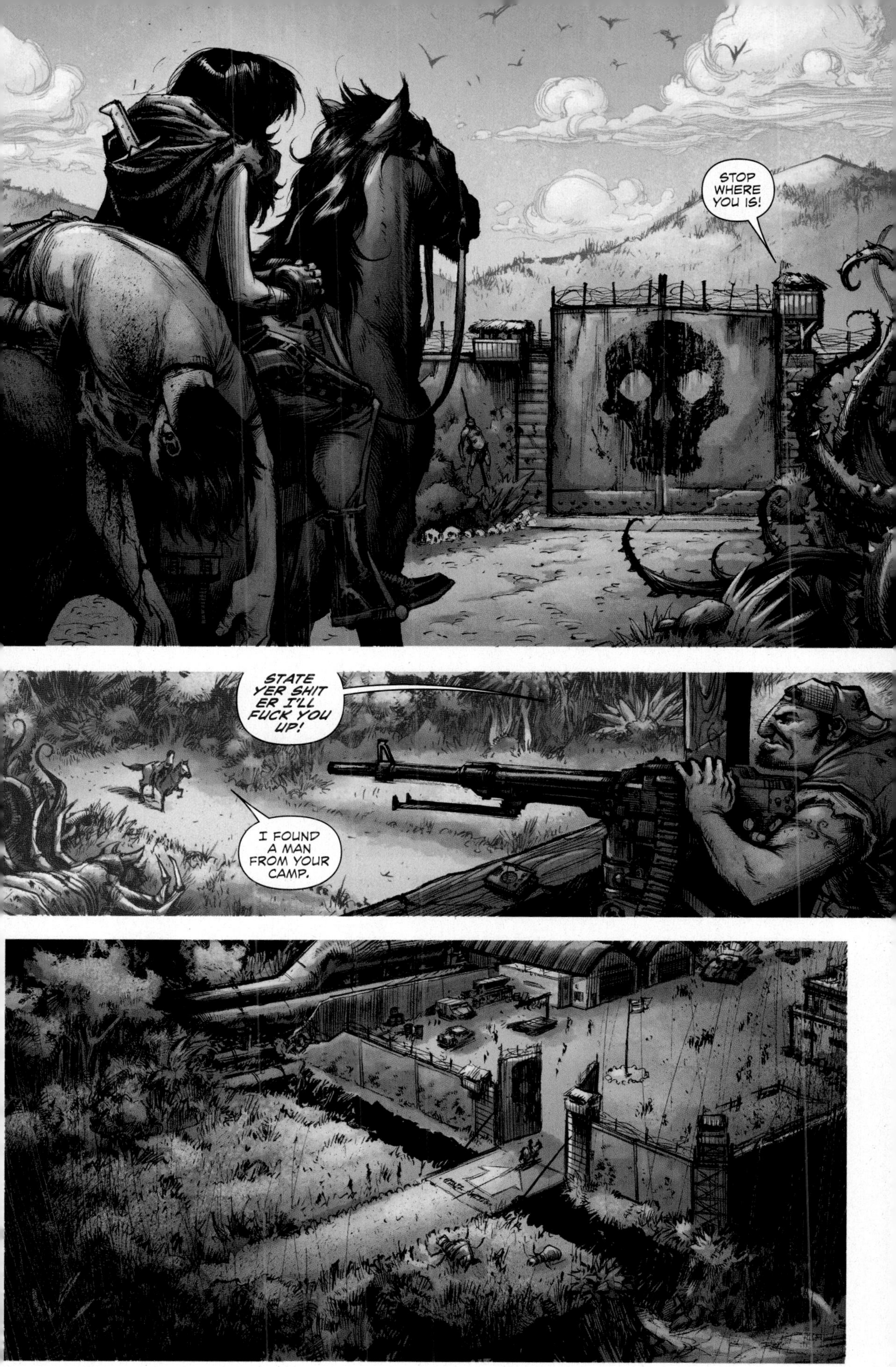
STOP WHERE YOU IS!
STATE YER SHIT ER I'LL FUCK YOU UP!
I FOUND A MAN FROM YOUR CAMP.

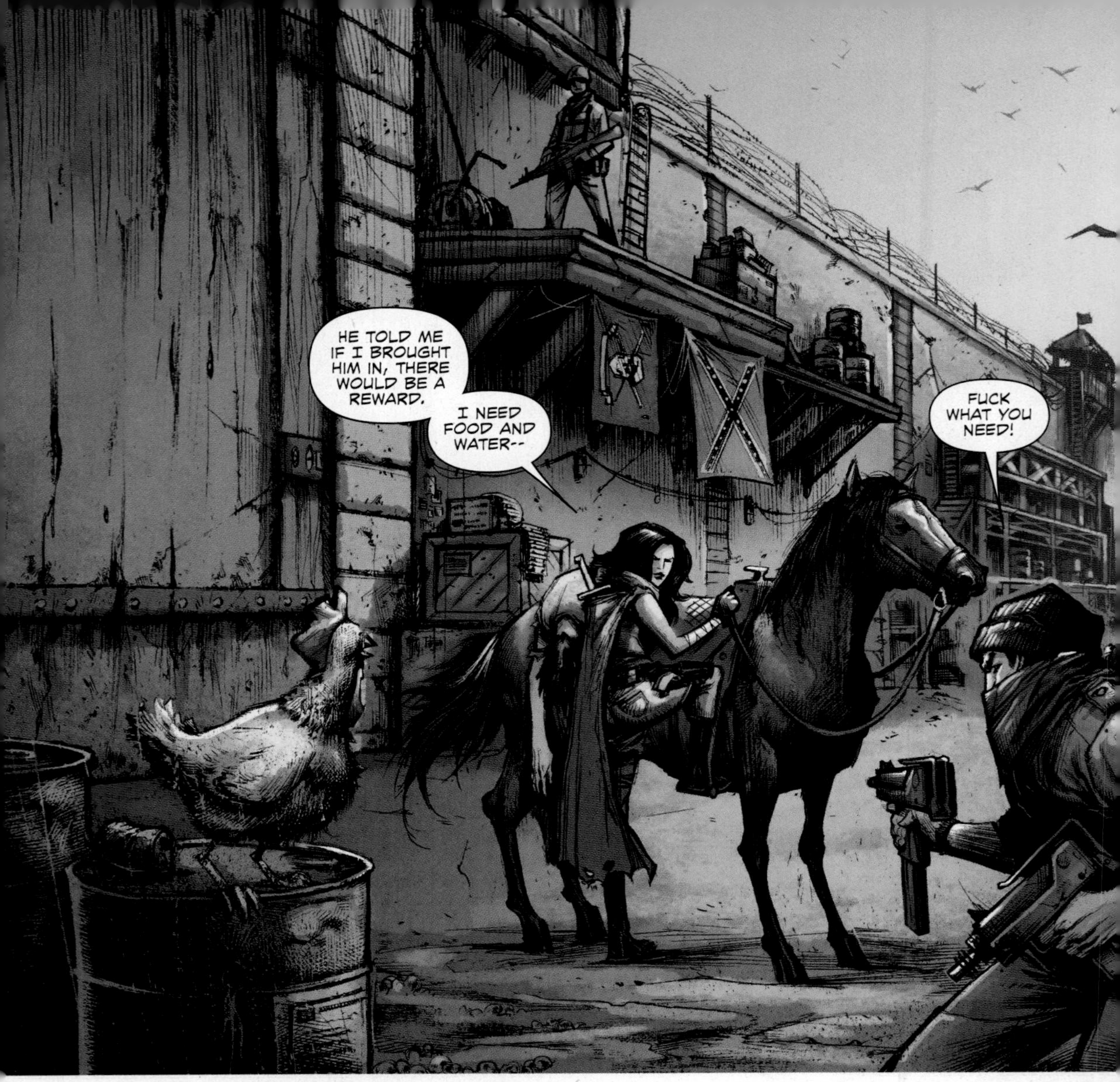
HE TOLD ME IF I BROUGHT HIM IN, THERE WOULD BE A REWARD.
I NEED FOOD AND WATER--
FUCK WHAT YOU NEED!

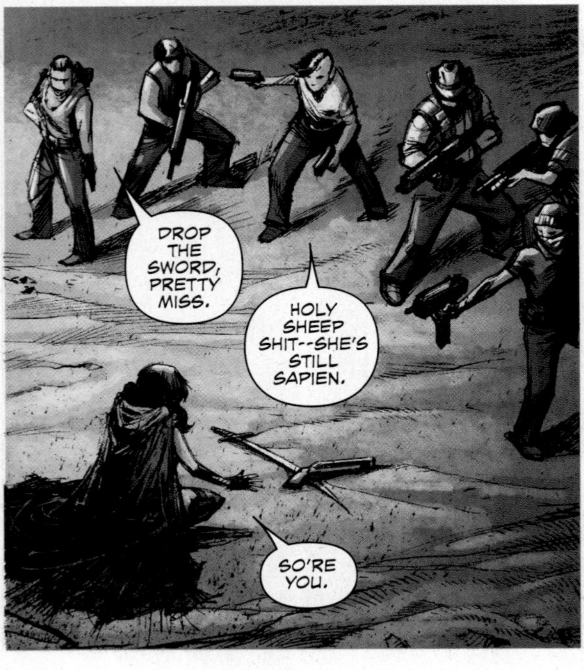
DROP THE SWORD, PRETTY MISS.
HOLY SHEEP SHIT--SHE'S STILL SAPIEN.
SO'RE YOU.

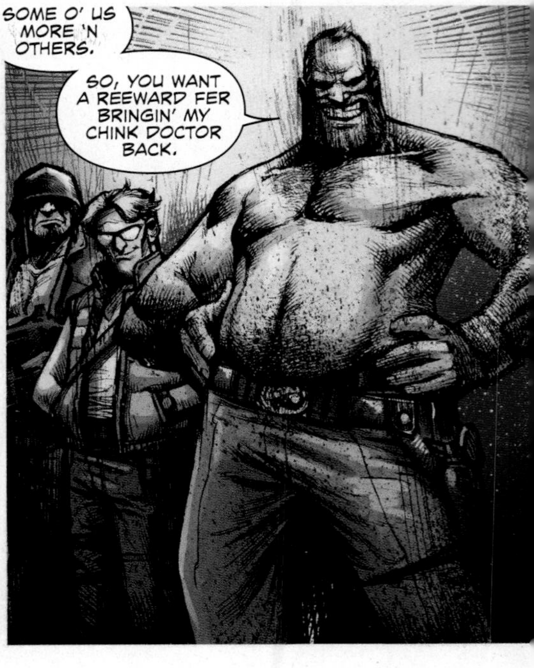
SOME O' US MORE 'N OTHERS.
SO, YOU WANT A REEWARD FER BRINGIN' MY CHINK DOCTOR BACK.

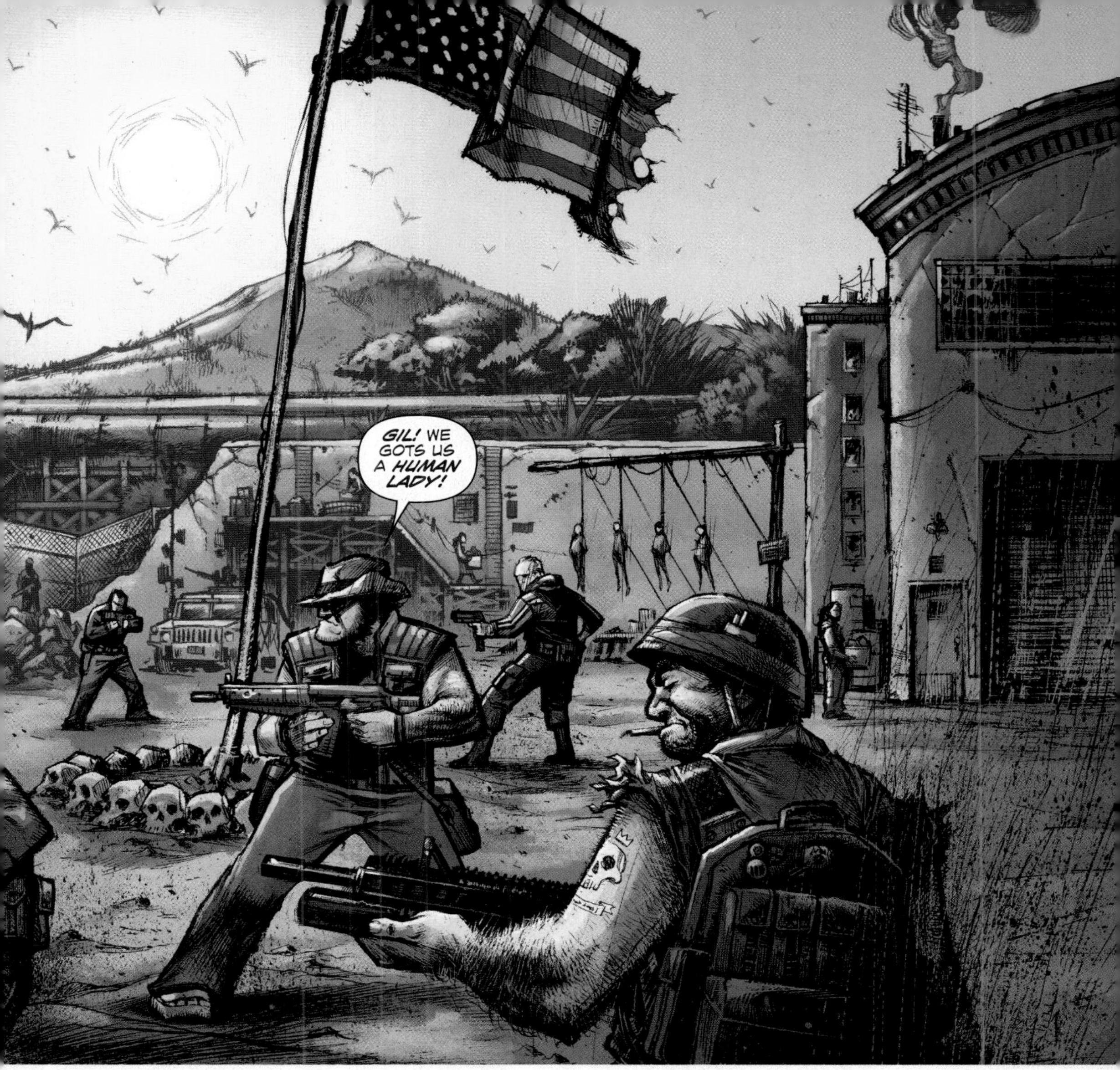
GIL! WE GOTS US A HUMAN LADY!

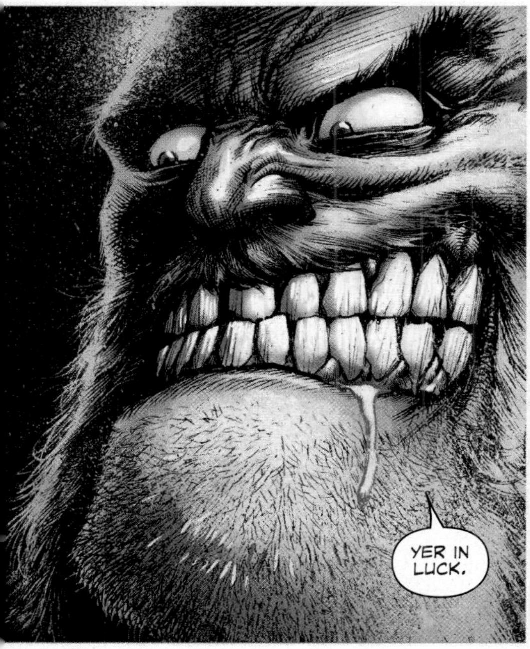
YER IN LUCK.

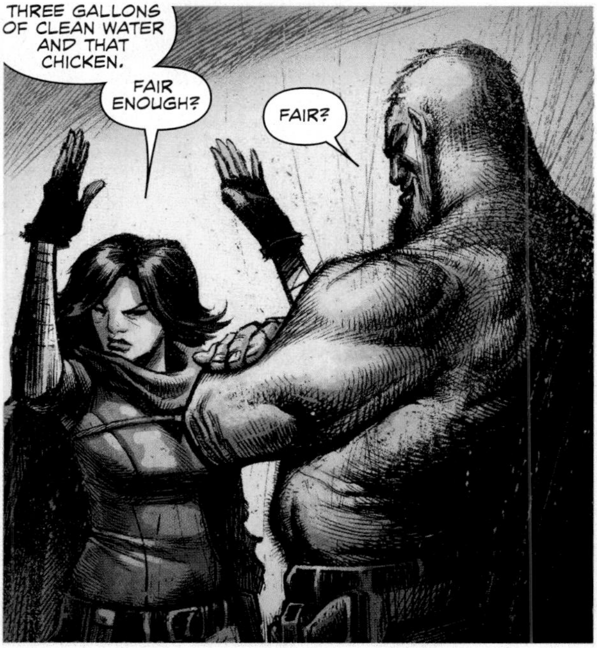
THREE GALLONS OF CLEAN WATER AND THAT CHICKEN.
FAIR ENOUGH?
FAIR?

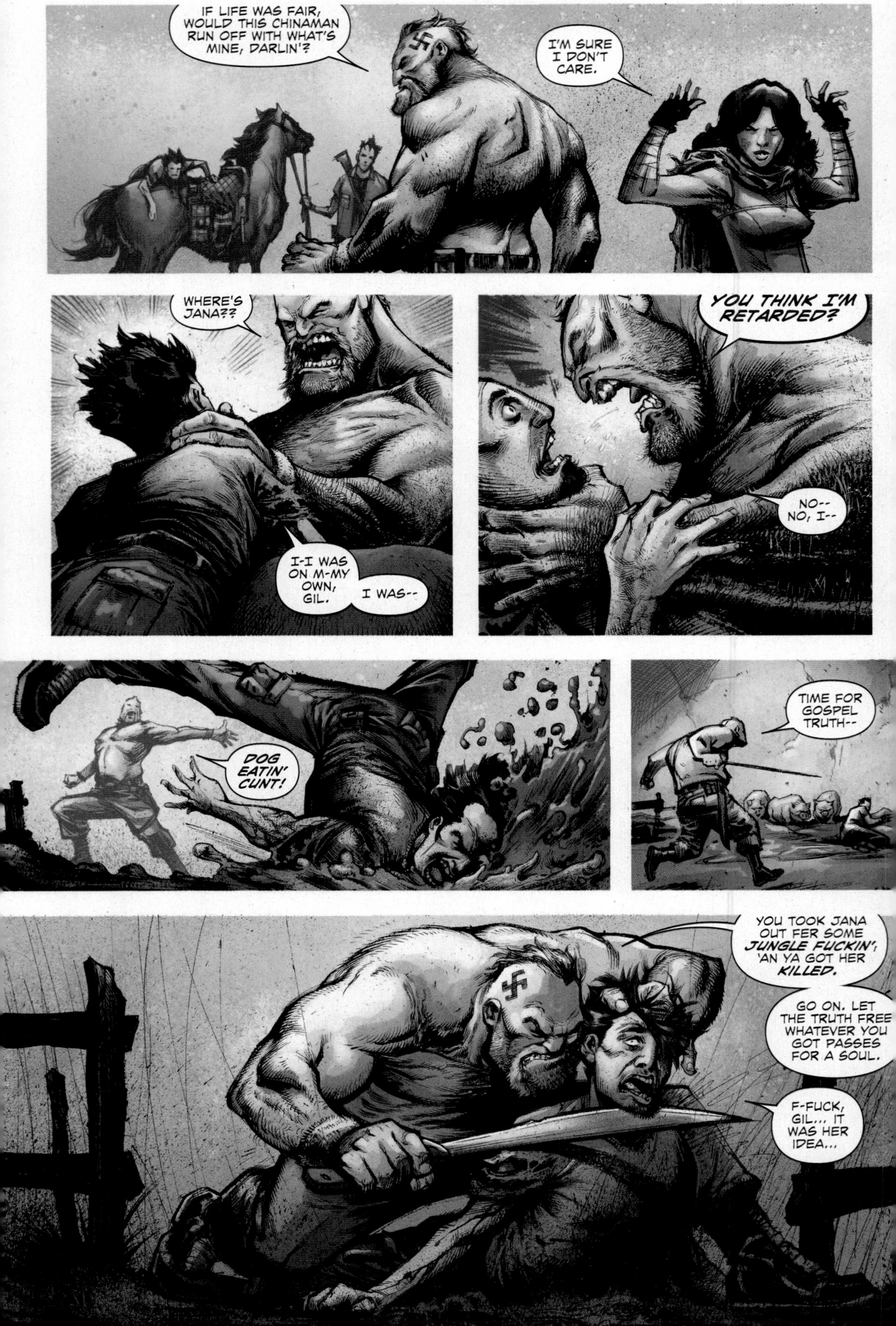

IF LIFE WAS FAIR, WOULD THIS CHINAMAN RUN OFF WITH WHAT'S MINE, DARLIN'?
I'M SURE I DON'T CARE.
WHERE'S JANA??
I-I WAS ON M-MY OWN, GIL.
I WAS--
YOU THINK I'M RETARDED?
NO-- NO, I--
DOG EATIN' CUNT!
TIME FOR GOSPEL TRUTH--
YOU TOOK JANA OUT FER SOME JUNGLE FUCKIN', 'AN YA GOT HER KILLED.
GO ON. LET THE TRUTH FREE WHATEVER YOU GOT PASSES FOR A SOUL.
F-FUCK, GIL... IT WAS HER IDEA...

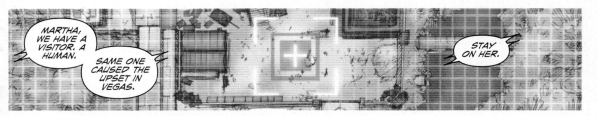

MARTHA, WE HAVE A VISITOR. A HUMAN.

SAME ONE CAUSED THE UPSET IN VEGAS.

STAY ON HER.

GUESS THERE'S AN UPSHOT. SCOTT GOT ONE OL' LADY KILLED-- BROUGHT ME A NEW LADY.

STILL SAPIEN, TOO.

I LIKE TO MARRY YOU. YOU WANT TO MARRY? THAT'S WHY YOU COME HERE IS IT?

IF YOU LOOKIN' FER A BIG TIME ALABAMA PARTY MACHINE YER IN LUCK!

THERE'S A REVOLUTION AGENT IN SAN FRANCISCO.

IN THE LAB THAT MADE THE DVO-8. I'M ON MY WAY THERE. TO SAVE HUMANITY.

I CAME ONLY TO DELIVER THIS MAN TO TRADE FOR FOOD.

AIN'T NO SAVIN' HUMANITY-- STOP TALKIN', STUPID.

RUNNIN' YER STUPID MOUTH!

DAMN IT, GIL--

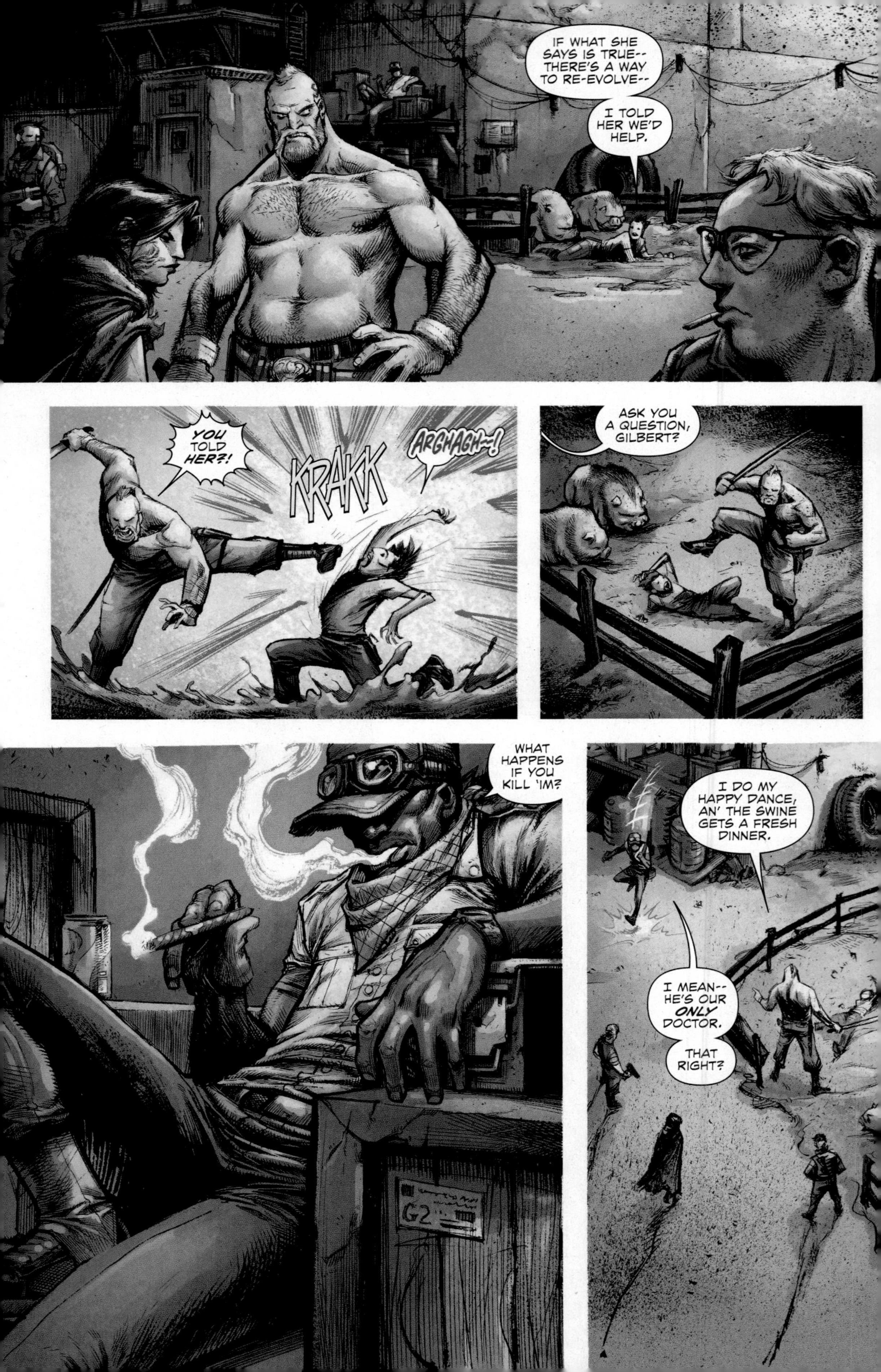

IF WHAT SHE SAYS IS TRUE-- THERE'S A WAY TO RE-EVOLVE--
I TOLD HER WE'D HELP.
YOU TOLD HER?!
KRAKK
ARGHAGH--!
ASK YOU A QUESTION, GILBERT?
WHAT HAPPENS IF YOU KILL 'IM?
I DO MY HAPPY DANCE, AN' THE SWINE GETS A FRESH DINNER.
I MEAN-- HE'S OUR ONLY DOCTOR.
THAT RIGHT?

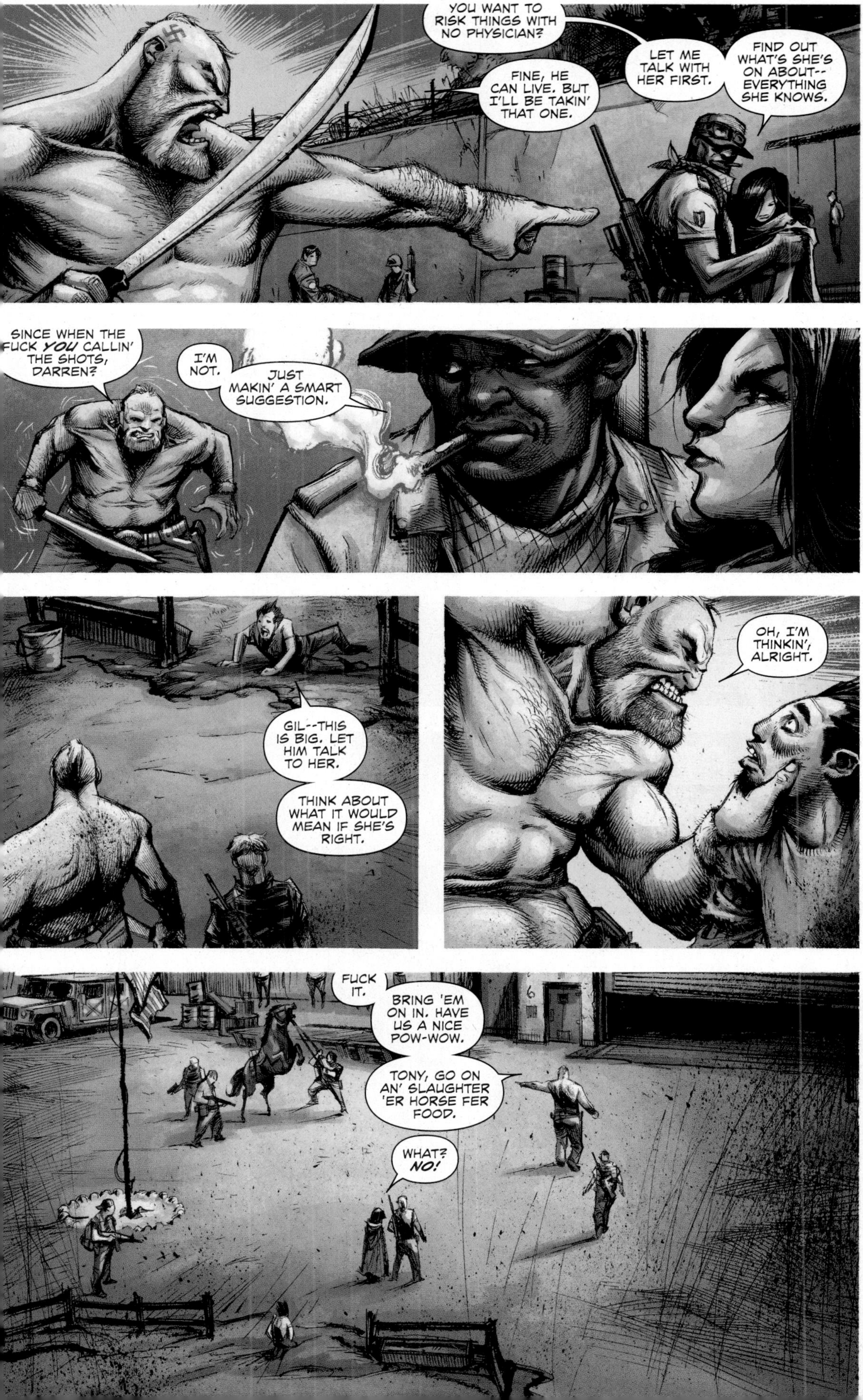
YOU WANT TO RISK THINGS WITH NO PHYSICIAN?
FINE, HE CAN LIVE. BUT I'LL BE TAKIN' THAT ONE.
LET ME TALK WITH HER FIRST.
FIND OUT WHAT'S SHE'S ON ABOUT-- EVERYTHING SHE KNOWS.
SINCE WHEN THE FUCK YOU CALLIN' THE SHOTS, DARREN?
I'M NOT.
JUST MAKIN' A SMART SUGGESTION.
GIL--THIS IS BIG. LET HIM TALK TO HER.
THINK ABOUT WHAT IT WOULD MEAN IF SHE'S RIGHT.
OH, I'M THINKIN', ALRIGHT.
FUCK IT.
BRING 'EM ON IN. HAVE US A NICE POW-WOW.
TONY, GO ON AN' SLAUGHTER 'ER HORSE FER FOOD.
WHAT? NO!

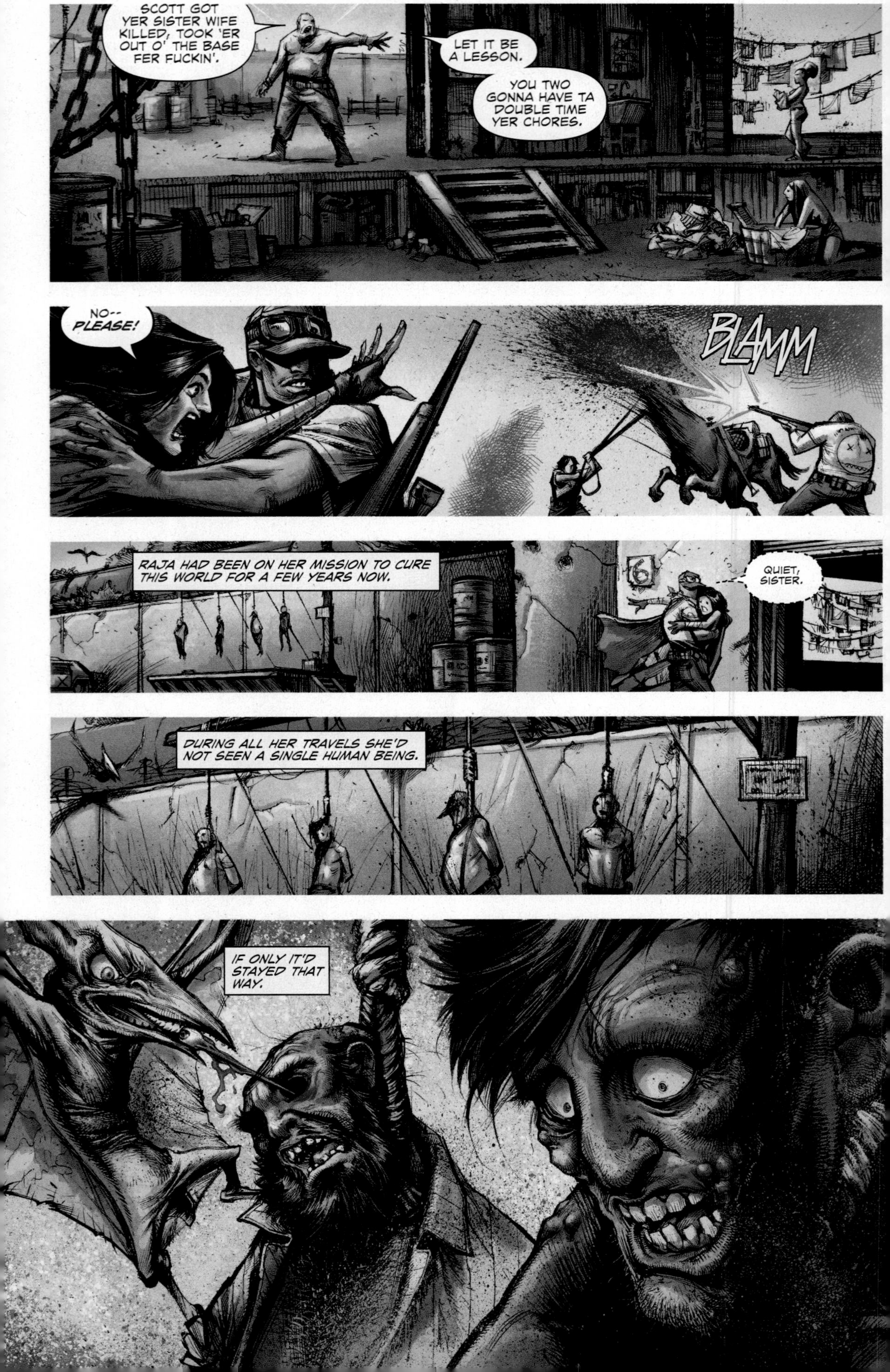

SCOTT GOT YER SISTER WIFE KILLED, TOOK 'ER OUT O' THE BASE FER FUCKIN'.
LET IT BE A LESSON.
YOU TWO GONNA HAVE TA DOUBLE TIME YER CHORES.
NO-- PLEASE!
BLAMM
RAJA HAD BEEN ON HER MISSION TO CURE THIS WORLD FOR A FEW YEARS NOW.
QUIET, SISTER.
DURING ALL HER TRAVELS SHE'D NOT SEEN A SINGLE HUMAN BEING.
IF ONLY IT'D STAYED THAT WAY.

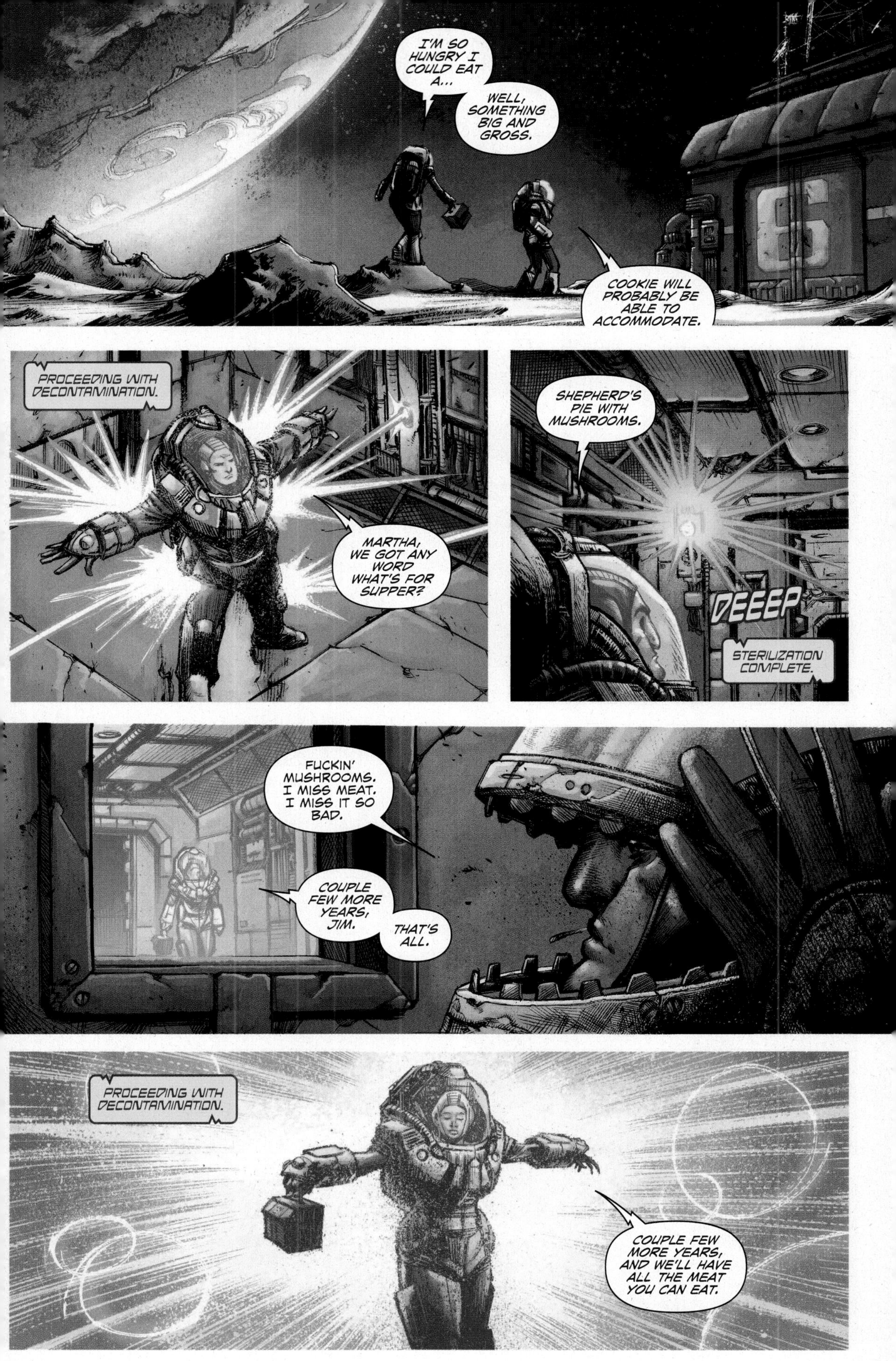
I'M SO HUNGRY I COULD EAT A...
WELL, SOMETHING BIG AND GROSS.
COOKIE WILL PROBABLY BE ABLE TO ACCOMMODATE.
PROCEEDING WITH DECONTAMINATION.
MARTHA, WE GOT ANY WORD WHAT'S FOR SUPPER?
SHEPHERD'S PIE WITH MUSHROOMS.
DEEEP
STERILIZATION COMPLETE.
FUCKIN' MUSHROOMS. I MISS MEAT. I MISS IT SO BAD.
COUPLE FEW MORE YEARS, JIM.
THAT'S ALL.
PROCEEDING WITH DECONTAMINATION.
COUPLE FEW MORE YEARS, AND WE'LL HAVE ALL THE MEAT YOU CAN EAT.

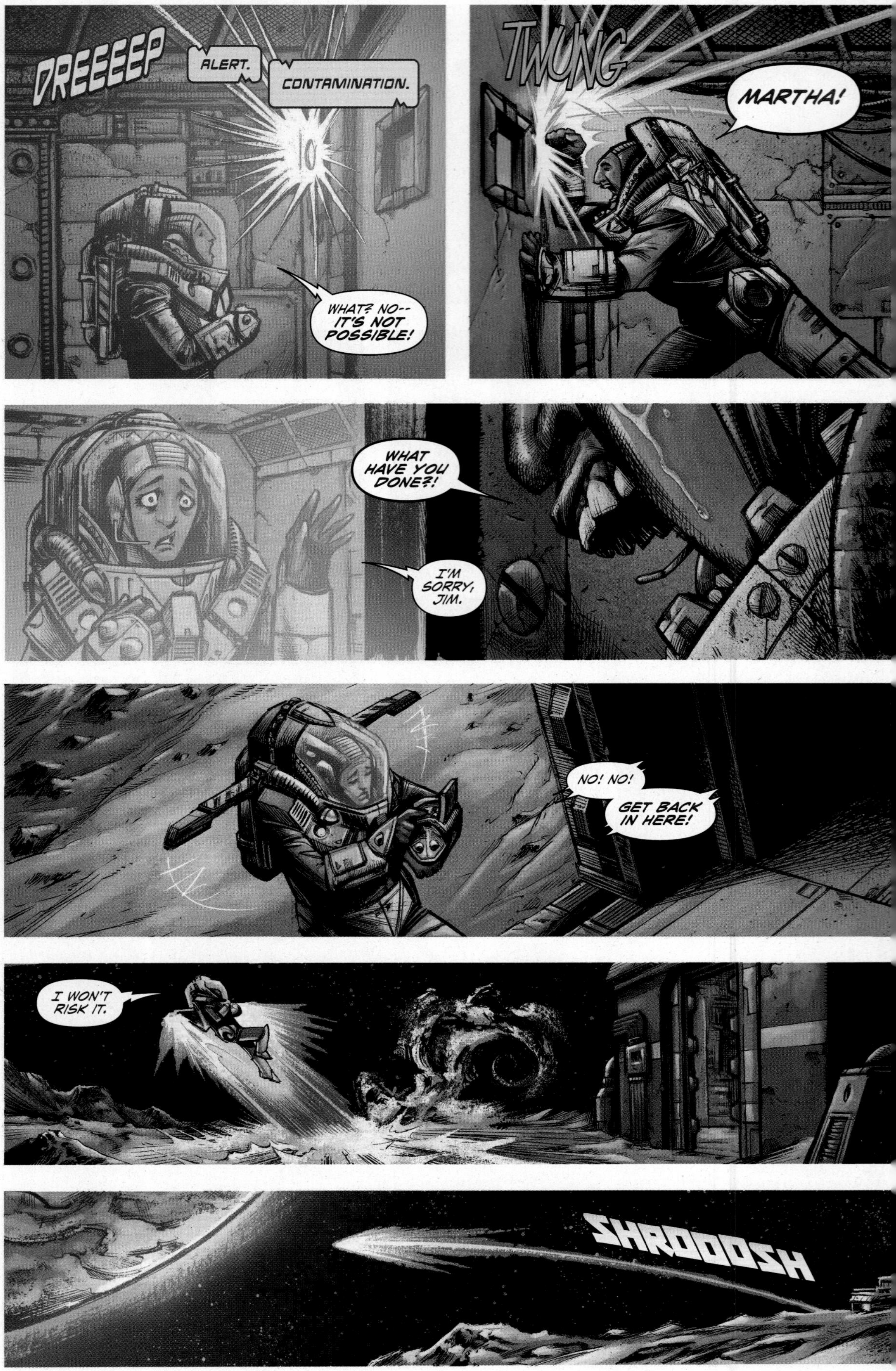
DREEEEP
ALERT.
CONTAMINATION.
WHAT? NO-- IT'S NOT POSSIBLE!
TWUNG
MARTHA!
WHAT HAVE YOU DONE?!
I'M SORRY, JIM.
NO! NO!
GET BACK IN HERE!
I WON'T RISK IT.
SHROOOSH

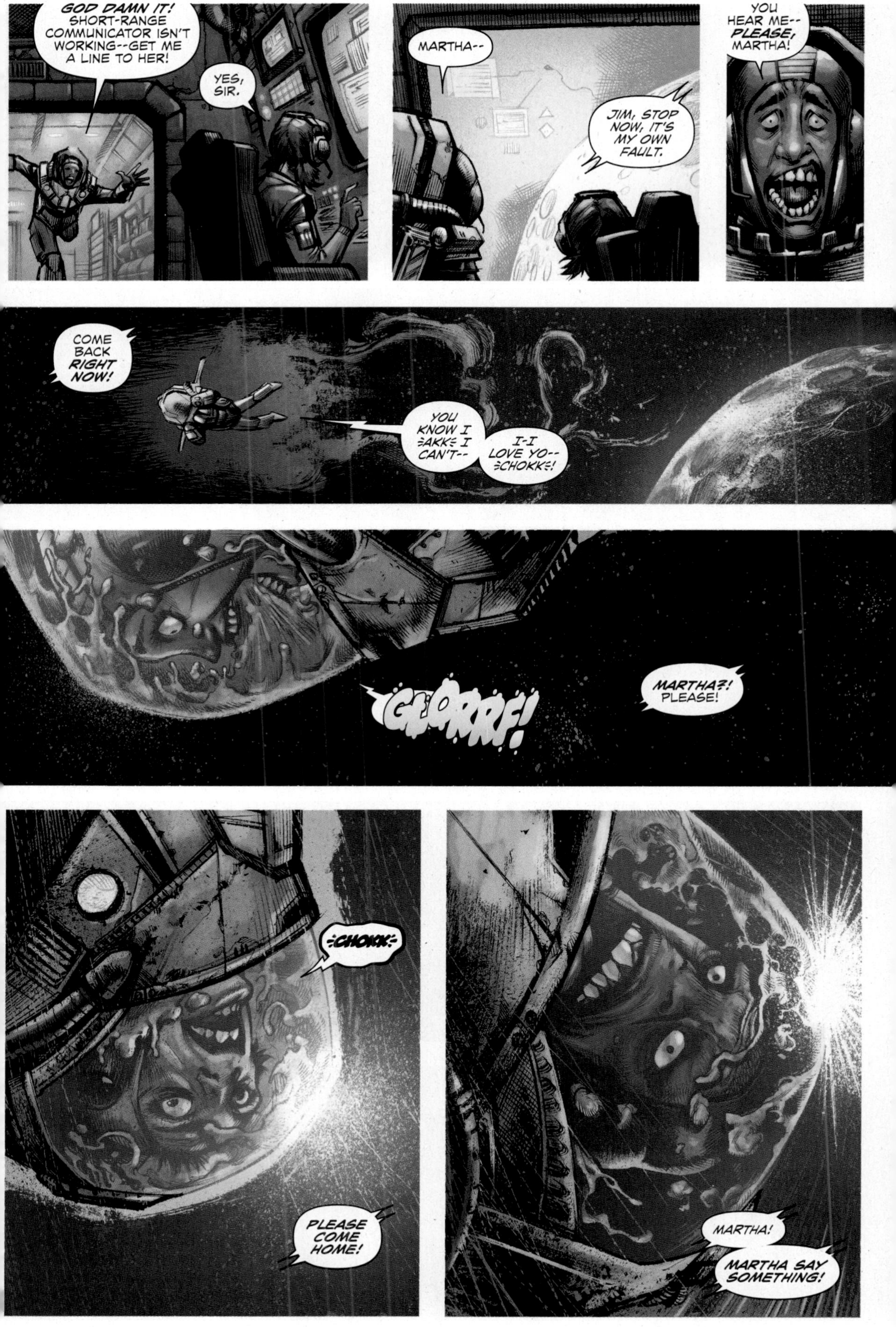
GOD DAMN IT! SHORT-RANGE COMMUNICATOR ISN'T WORKING--GET ME A LINE TO HER!
YES, SIR.
MARTHA--
JIM, STOP NOW, IT'S MY OWN FAULT.
YOU HEAR ME-- PLEASE, MARTHA!
COME BACK RIGHT NOW!
YOU KNOW I AKK I CAN'T--
I-I LOVE YO-- CHOKK!
GLORRF!
MARTHA?! PLEASE!
CHOKK
PLEASE COME HOME!
MARTHA!
MARTHA SAY SOMETHING!

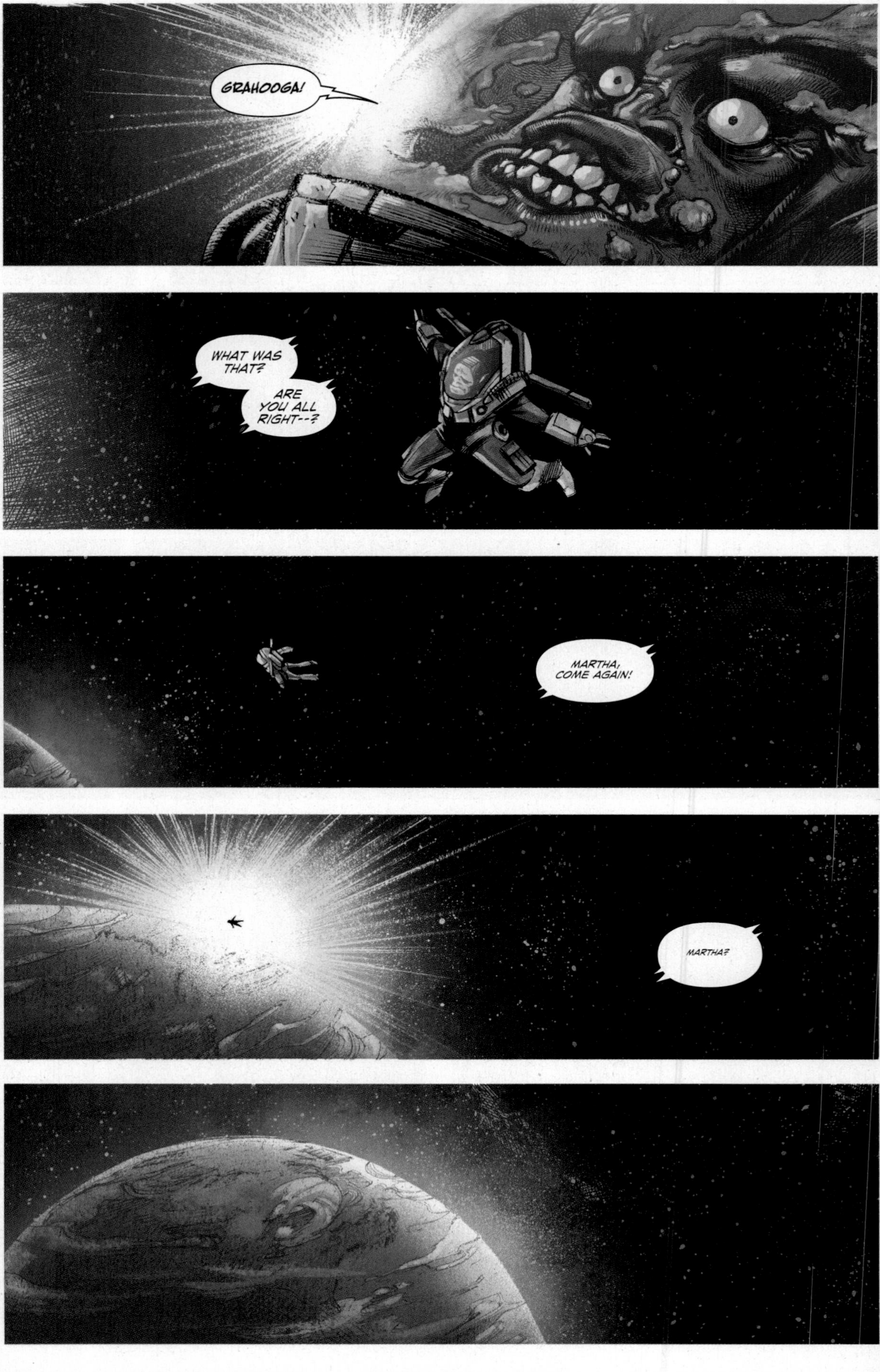
GRAHOOGA!
WHAT WAS THAT?
ARE YOU ALL RIGHT--?
MARTHA, COME AGAIN!
MARTHA?

Issue 2 Cover by JAE LEE With Colors by JUNE CHUNG

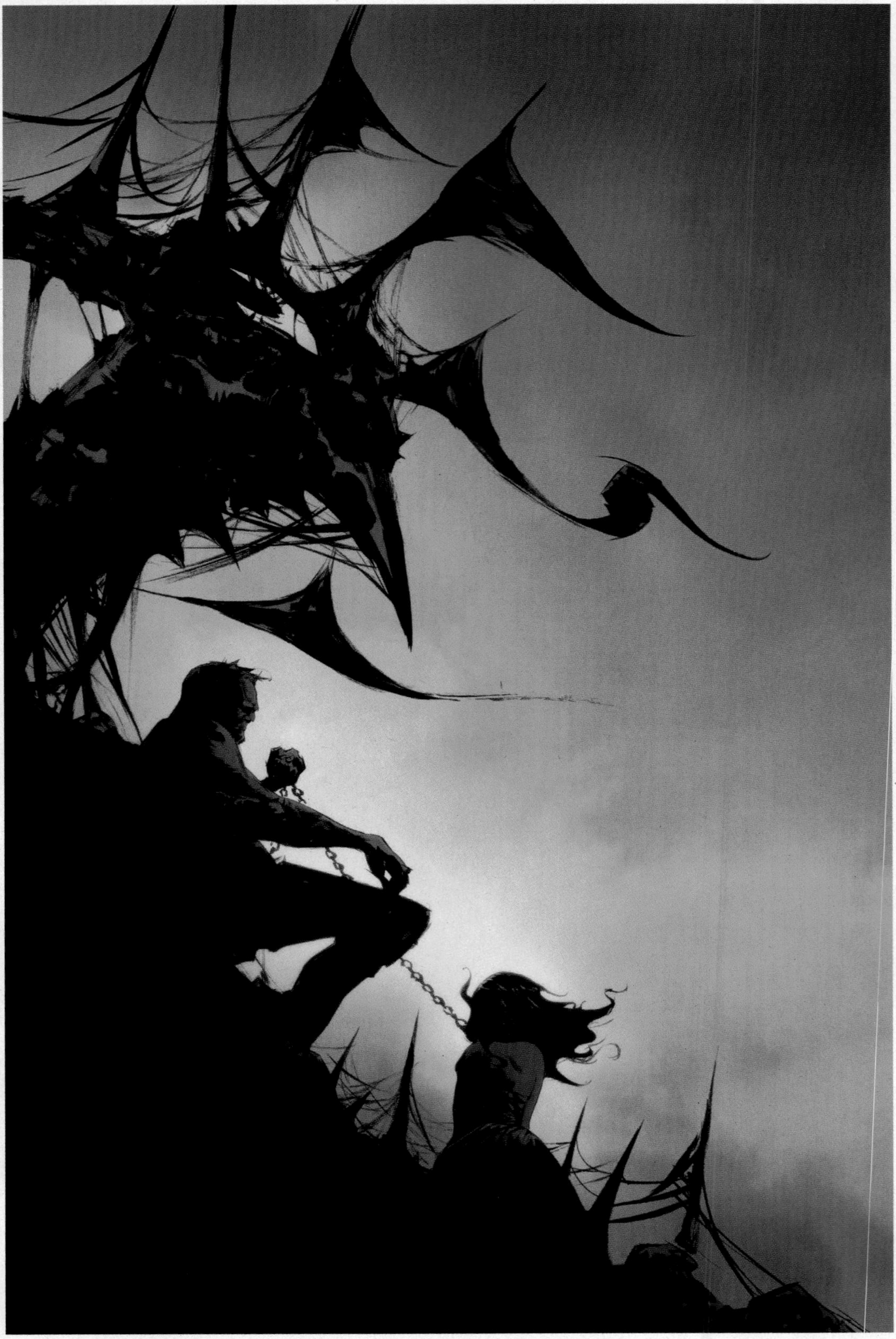

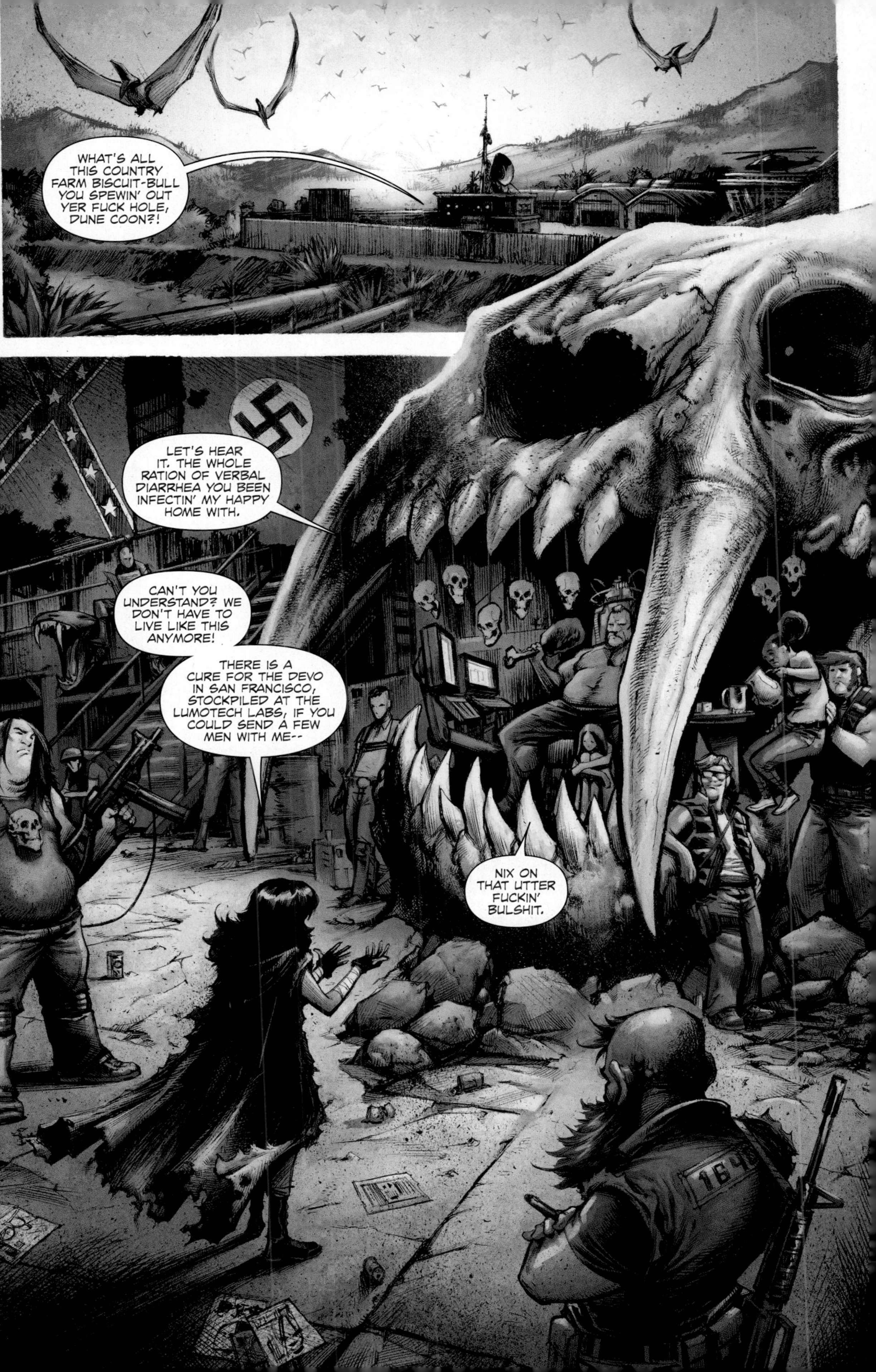
WHAT'S ALL THIS COUNTRY FARM BISCUIT-BULL YOU SPEWIN' OUT YER FUCK HOLE, DUNE COON?!
LET'S HEAR IT. THE WHOLE RATION OF VERBAL DIARRHEA YOU BEEN INFECTIN' MY HAPPY HOME WITH.
CAN'T YOU UNDERSTAND? WE DON'T HAVE TO LIVE LIKE THIS ANYMORE!
THERE IS A CURE FOR THE DEVO IN SAN FRANCISCO, STOCKPILED AT THE LUMOTECH LABS, IF YOU COULD SEND A FEW MEN WITH ME--
NIX ON THAT UTTER FUCKIN' BULSHIT.

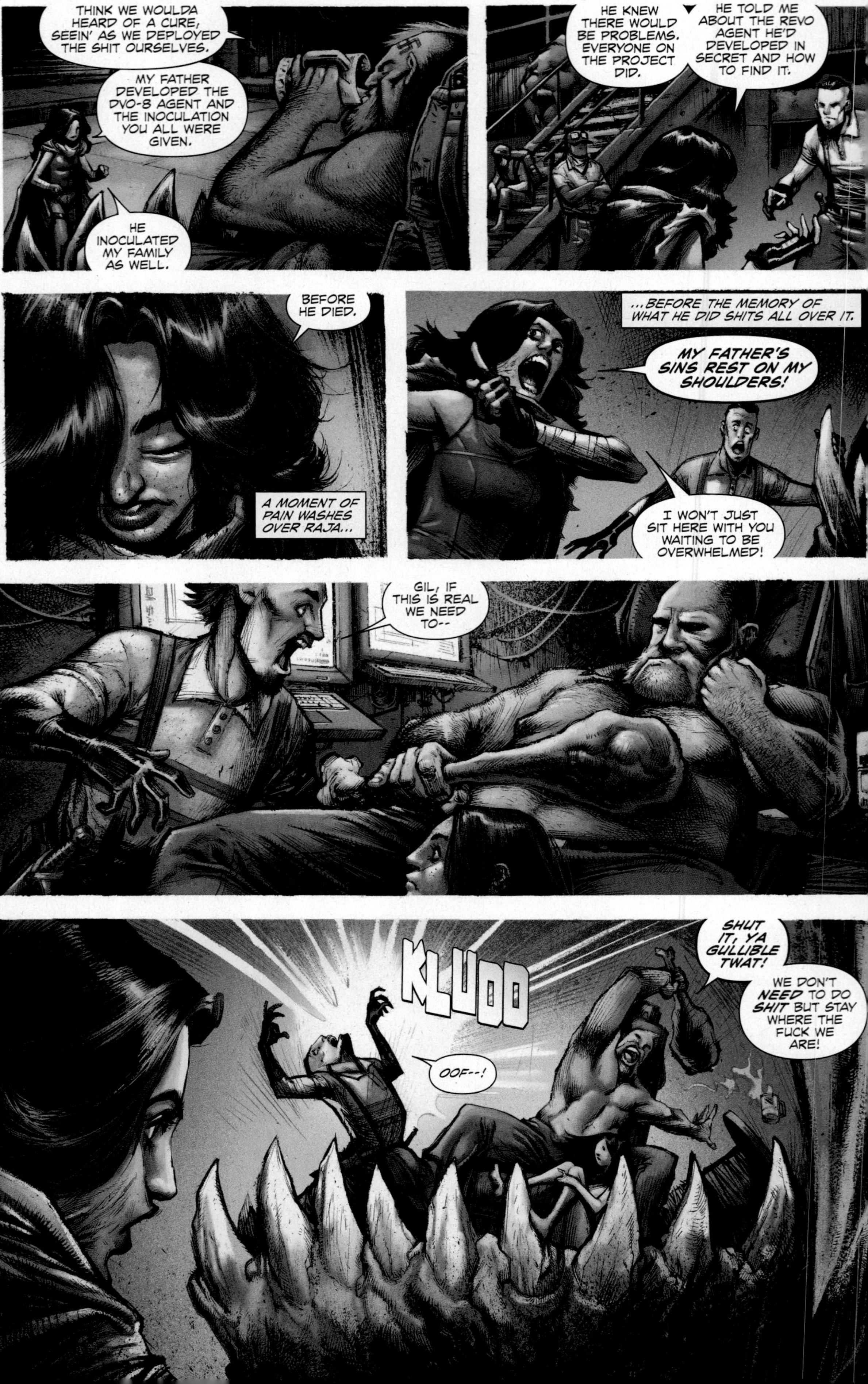
THINK WE WOULDA HEARD OF A CURE, SEEIN' AS WE DEPLOYED THE SHIT OURSELVES.
MY FATHER DEVELOPED THE DVO-8 AGENT AND THE INOCULATION YOU ALL WERE GIVEN.
HE INOCULATED MY FAMILY AS WELL.
HE KNEW THERE WOULD BE PROBLEMS. EVERYONE ON THE PROJECT DID.
HE TOLD ME ABOUT THE REVO AGENT HE'D DEVELOPED IN SECRET AND HOW TO FIND IT.
BEFORE HE DIED.
A MOMENT OF PAIN WASHES OVER RAJA...
...BEFORE THE MEMORY OF WHAT HE DID SHITS ALL OVER IT.
MY FATHER'S SINS REST ON MY SHOULDERS!
I WON'T JUST SIT HERE WITH YOU WAITING TO BE OVERWHELMED!
GIL, IF THIS IS REAL WE NEED TO--
KLUDD
OOF--!
SHUT IT, YA GULLIBLE TWAT!
WE DON'T NEED TO DO SHIT BUT STAY WHERE THE FUCK WE ARE!

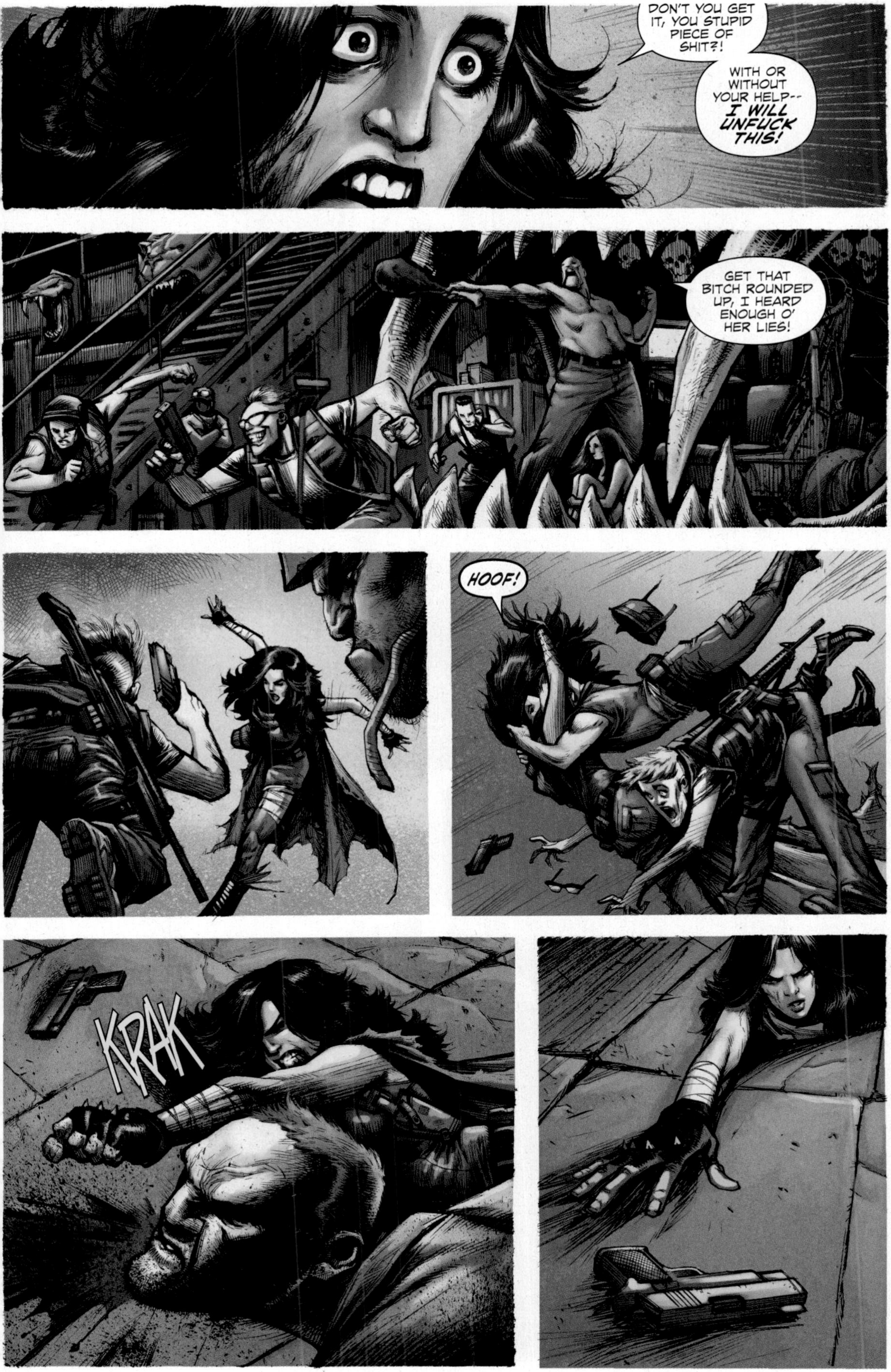
DON'T YOU GET IT, YOU STUPID PIECE OF SHIT?!
WITH OR WITHOUT YOUR HELP-- I WILL UNFUCK THIS!
GET THAT BITCH ROUNDED UP, I HEARD ENOUGH O' HER LIES!
HOOF!
KRAK

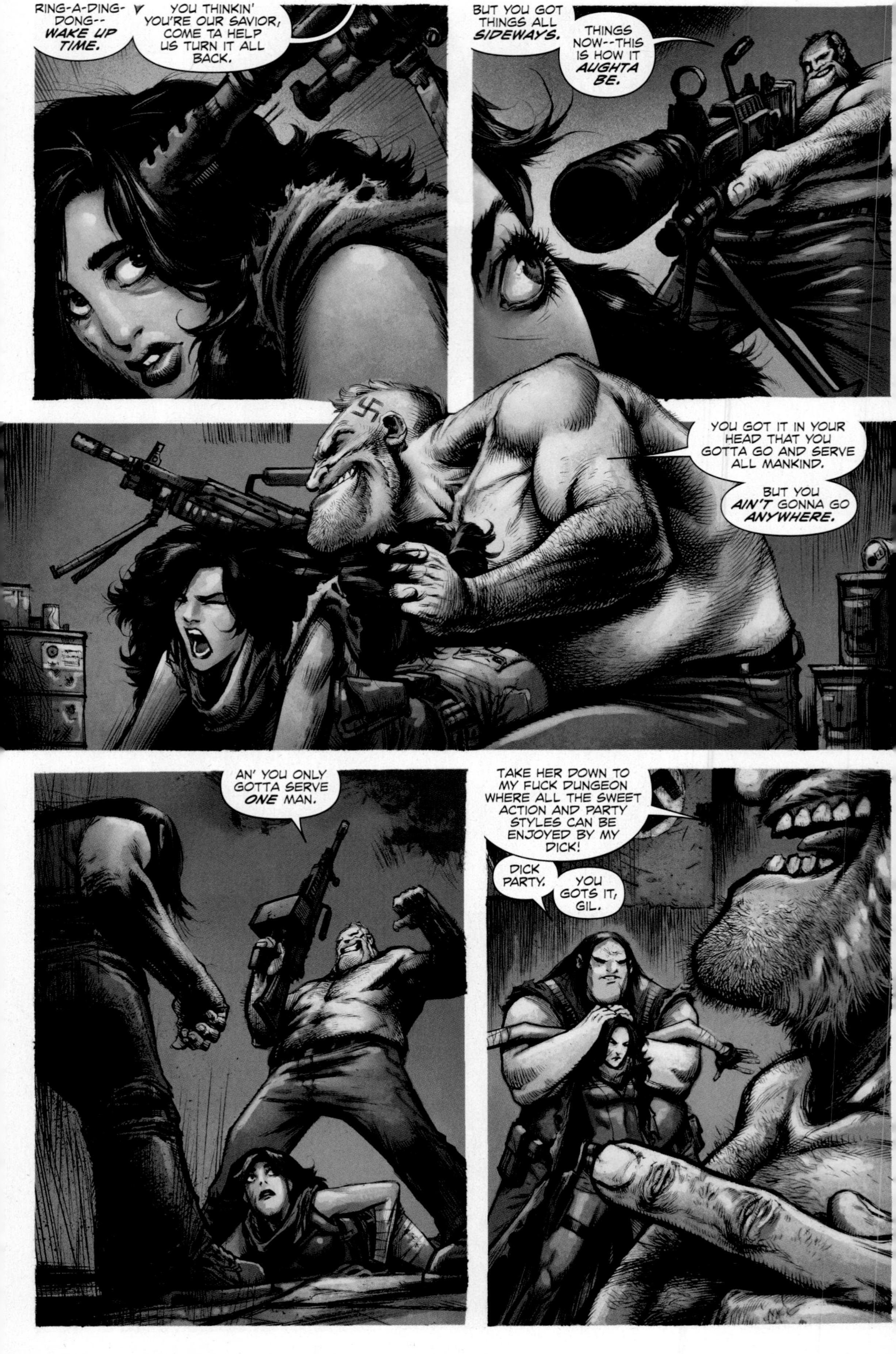
RING-A-DING-DONG-- WAKE UP TIME.
YOU THINKIN' YOU'RE OUR SAVIOR, COME TA HELP US TURN IT ALL BACK.
BUT YOU GOT THINGS ALL SIDEWAYS.
THINGS NOW--THIS IS HOW IT AUGHTA BE.
YOU GOT IT IN YOUR HEAD THAT YOU GOTTA GO AND SERVE ALL MANKIND.
BUT YOU AIN'T GONNA GO ANYWHERE.
AN' YOU ONLY GOTTA SERVE ONE MAN.
TAKE HER DOWN TO MY FUCK DUNGEON WHERE ALL THE SWEET ACTION AND PARTY STYLES CAN BE ENJOYED BY MY DICK!
DICK PARTY.
YOU GOTS IT, GIL.

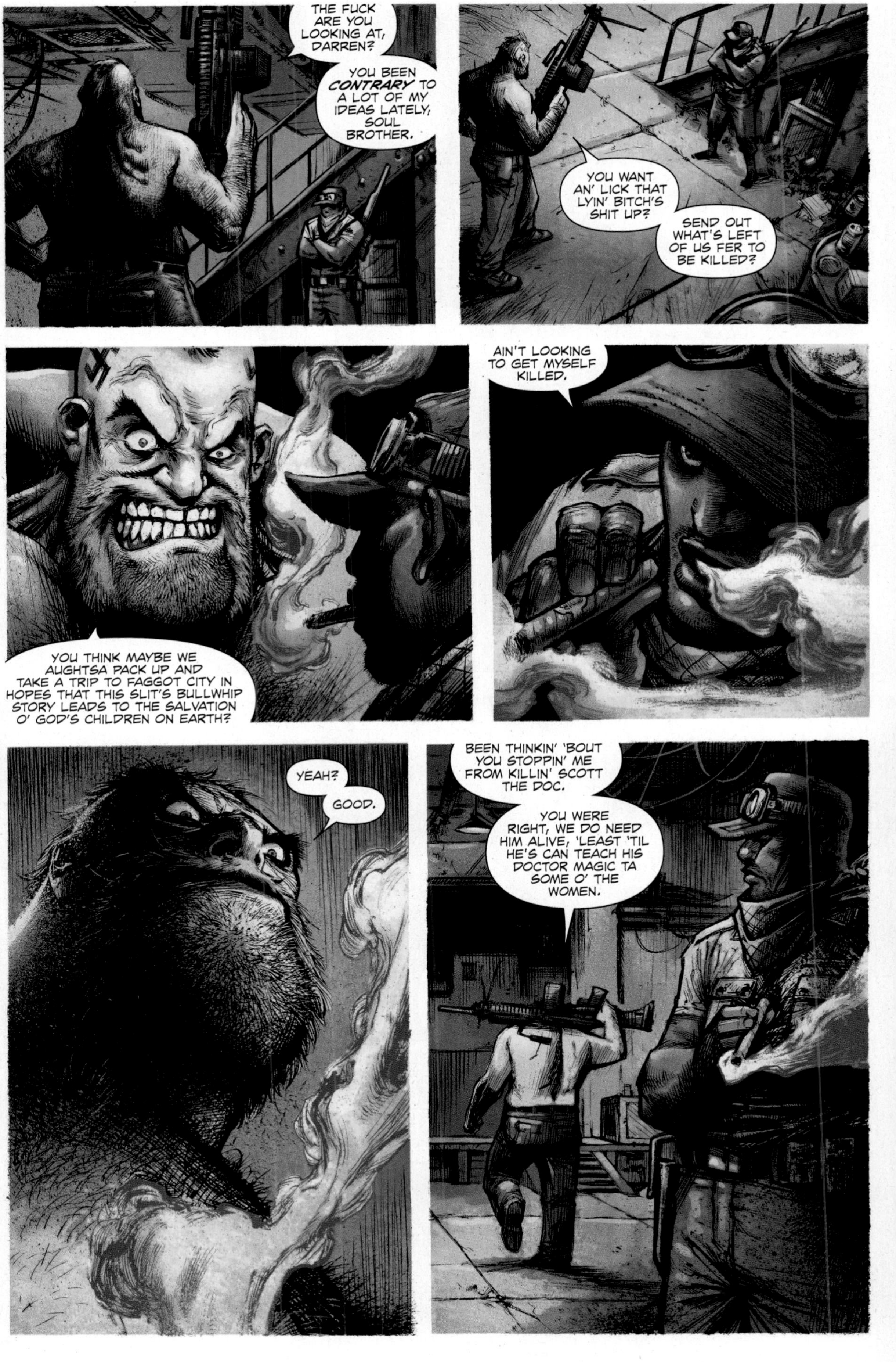
THE FUCK ARE YOU LOOKING AT, DARREN?
YOU BEEN CONTRARY TO A LOT OF MY IDEAS LATELY, SOUL BROTHER.
YOU WANT AN' LICK THAT LYIN' BITCH'S SHIT UP?
SEND OUT WHAT'S LEFT OF US FER TO BE KILLED?
YOU THINK MAYBE WE AUGHTSA PACK UP AND TAKE A TRIP TO FAGGOT CITY IN HOPES THAT THIS SLIT'S BULLWHIP STORY LEADS TO THE SALVATION O' GOD'S CHILDREN ON EARTH?
AIN'T LOOKING TO GET MYSELF KILLED.
YEAH?
GOOD.
BEEN THINKIN' 'BOUT YOU STOPPIN' ME FROM KILLIN' SCOTT THE DOC.
YOU WERE RIGHT, WE DO NEED HIM ALIVE, 'LEAST 'TIL HE'S CAN TEACH HIS DOCTOR MAGIC TA SOME O' THE WOMEN.

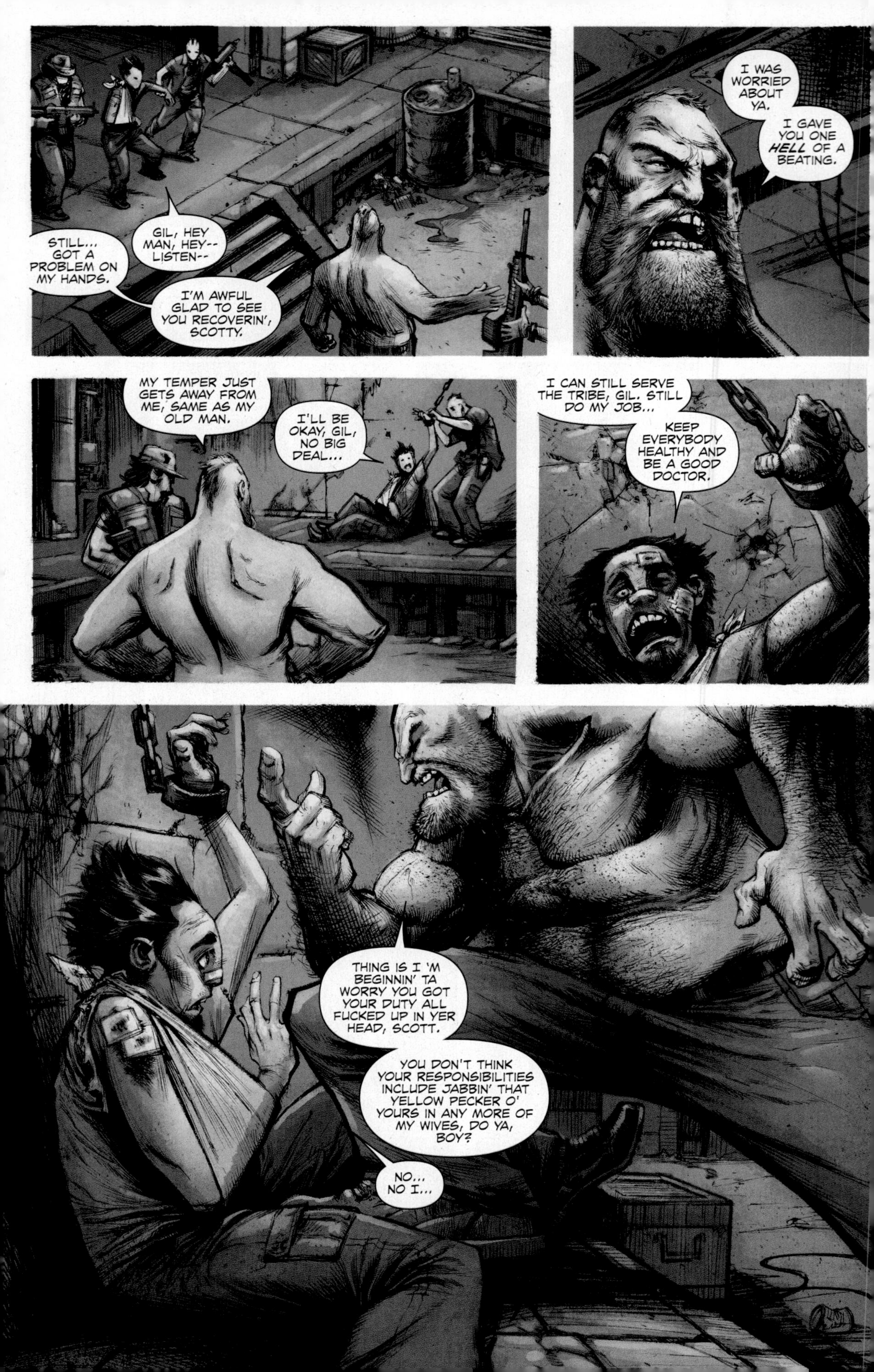

STILL... GOT A PROBLEM ON MY HANDS.
GIL, HEY MAN, HEY-- LISTEN--
I'M AWFUL GLAD TO SEE YOU RECOVERIN', SCOTTY.
I WAS WORRIED ABOUT YA.
I GAVE YOU ONE **HELL** OF A BEATING.
MY TEMPER JUST GETS AWAY FROM ME, SAME AS MY OLD MAN.
I'LL BE OKAY, GIL, NO BIG DEAL...
I CAN STILL SERVE THE TRIBE, GIL. STILL DO MY JOB...
KEEP EVERYBODY HEALTHY AND BE A GOOD DOCTOR.
THING IS I 'M BEGINNIN' TA WORRY YOU GOT YOUR DUTY ALL FUCKED UP IN YER HEAD, SCOTT.
YOU DON'T THINK YOUR RESPONSIBILITIES INCLUDE JABBIN' THAT YELLOW PECKER O' YOURS IN ANY MORE OF MY WIVES, DO YA, BOY?
NO... NO I...

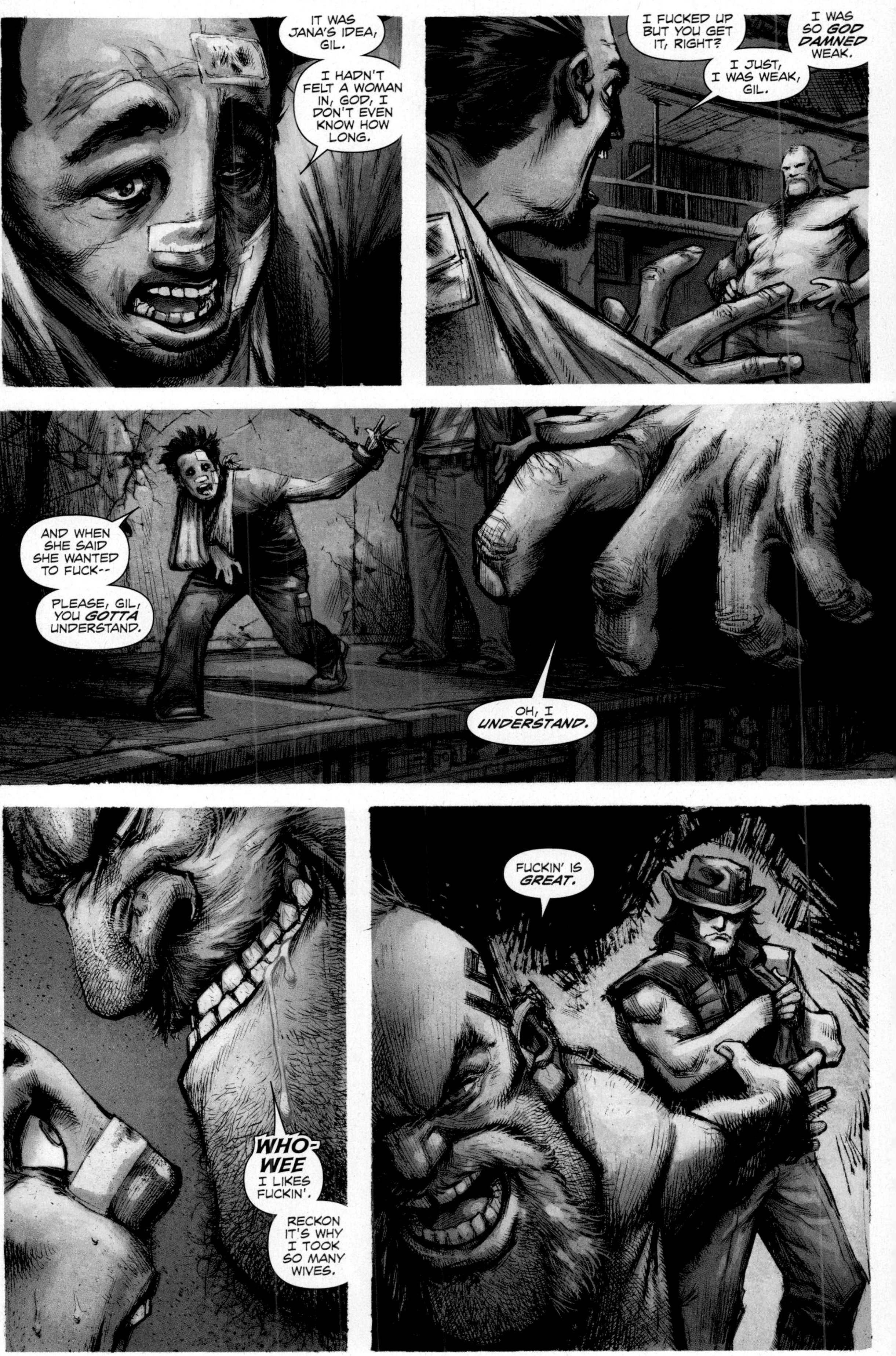
IT WAS JANA'S IDEA, GIL.
I HADN'T FELT A WOMAN IN, GOD, I DON'T EVEN KNOW HOW LONG.
I FUCKED UP BUT YOU GET IT, RIGHT?
I JUST, I WAS WEAK, GIL.
I WAS SO GOD DAMNED WEAK.
AND WHEN SHE SAID SHE WANTED TO FUCK--
PLEASE, GIL, YOU GOTTA UNDERSTAND.
OH, I UNDERSTAND.
WHO-WEE I LIKES FUCKIN'.
RECKON IT'S WHY I TOOK SO MANY WIVES.
FUCKIN' IS GREAT.

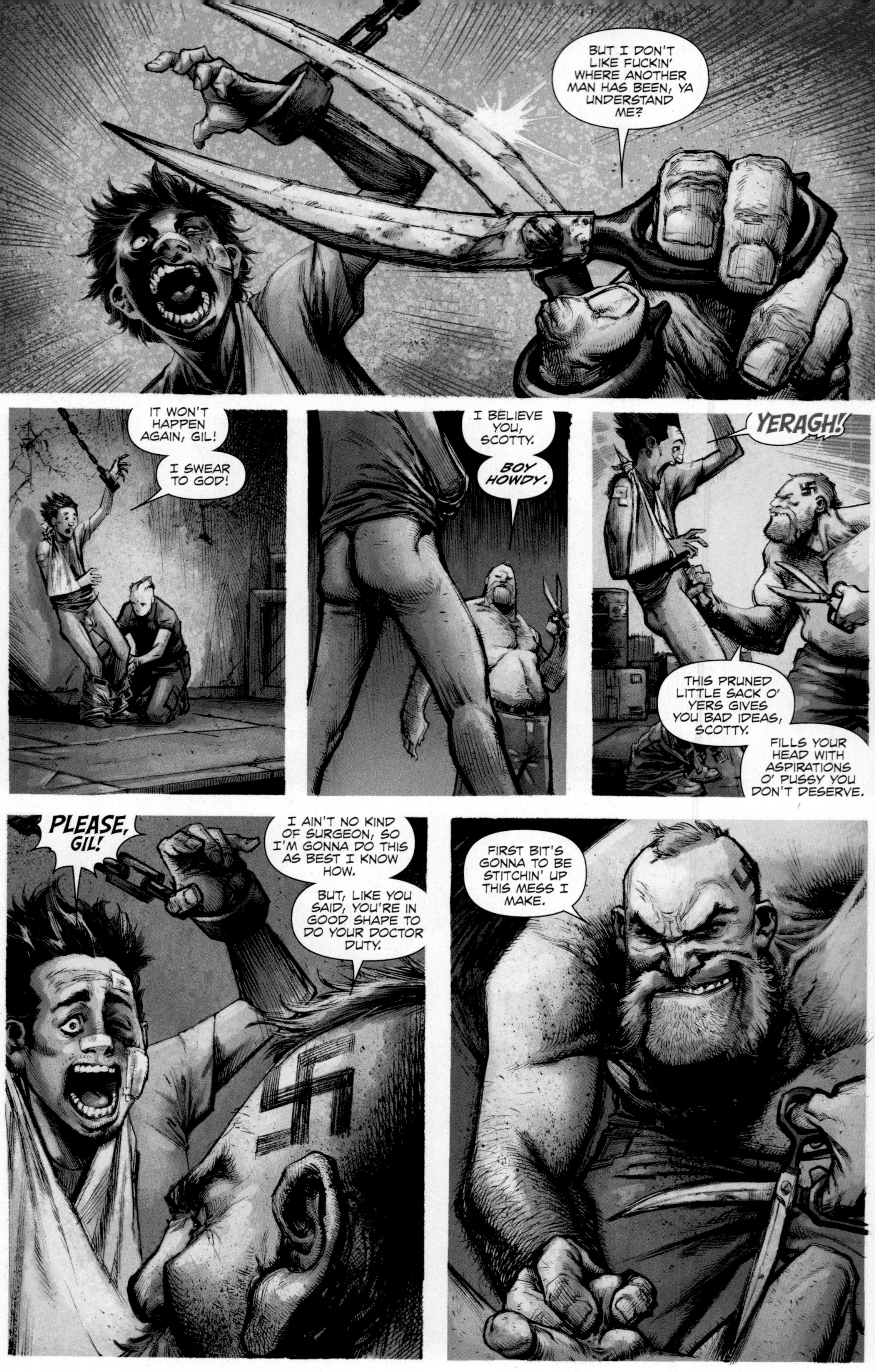

BUT I DON'T LIKE FUCKIN' WHERE ANOTHER MAN HAS BEEN, YA UNDERSTAND ME?
IT WON'T HAPPEN AGAIN, GIL!
I SWEAR TO GOD!
I BELIEVE YOU, SCOTTY.
BOY HOWDY.
YERAGH!
THIS PRUNED LITTLE SACK O' YERS GIVES YOU BAD IDEAS, SCOTTY.
FILLS YOUR HEAD WITH ASPIRATIONS O' PUSSY YOU DON'T DESERVE.
PLEASE, GIL!
I AIN'T NO KIND OF SURGEON, SO I'M GONNA DO THIS AS BEST I KNOW HOW.
BUT, LIKE YOU SAID, YOU'RE IN GOOD SHAPE TO DO YOUR DOCTOR DUTY.
FIRST BIT'S GONNA TO BE STITCHIN' UP THIS MESS I MAKE.

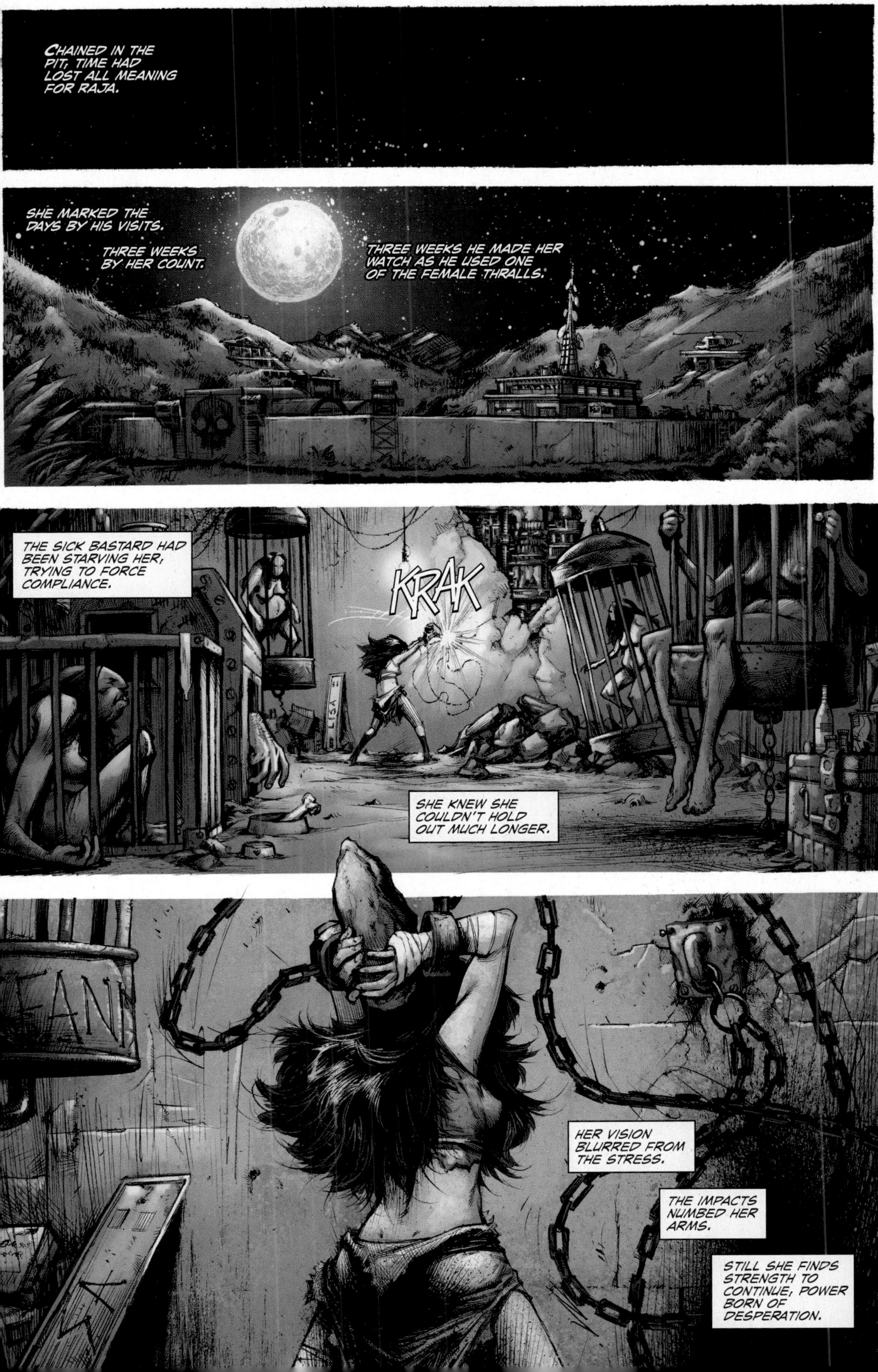
CHAINED IN THE PIT, TIME HAD LOST ALL MEANING FOR RAJA.
SHE MARKED THE DAYS BY HIS VISITS.
THREE WEEKS BY HER COUNT.
THREE WEEKS HE MADE HER WATCH AS HE USED ONE OF THE FEMALE THRALLS.
THE SICK BASTARD HAD BEEN STARVING HER, TRYING TO FORCE COMPLIANCE.
KRAK
LISA
SHE KNEW SHE COULDN'T HOLD OUT MUCH LONGER.
HER VISION BLURRED FROM THE STRESS.
THE IMPACTS NUMBED HER ARMS.
STILL SHE FINDS STRENGTH TO CONTINUE, POWER BORN OF DESPERATION.

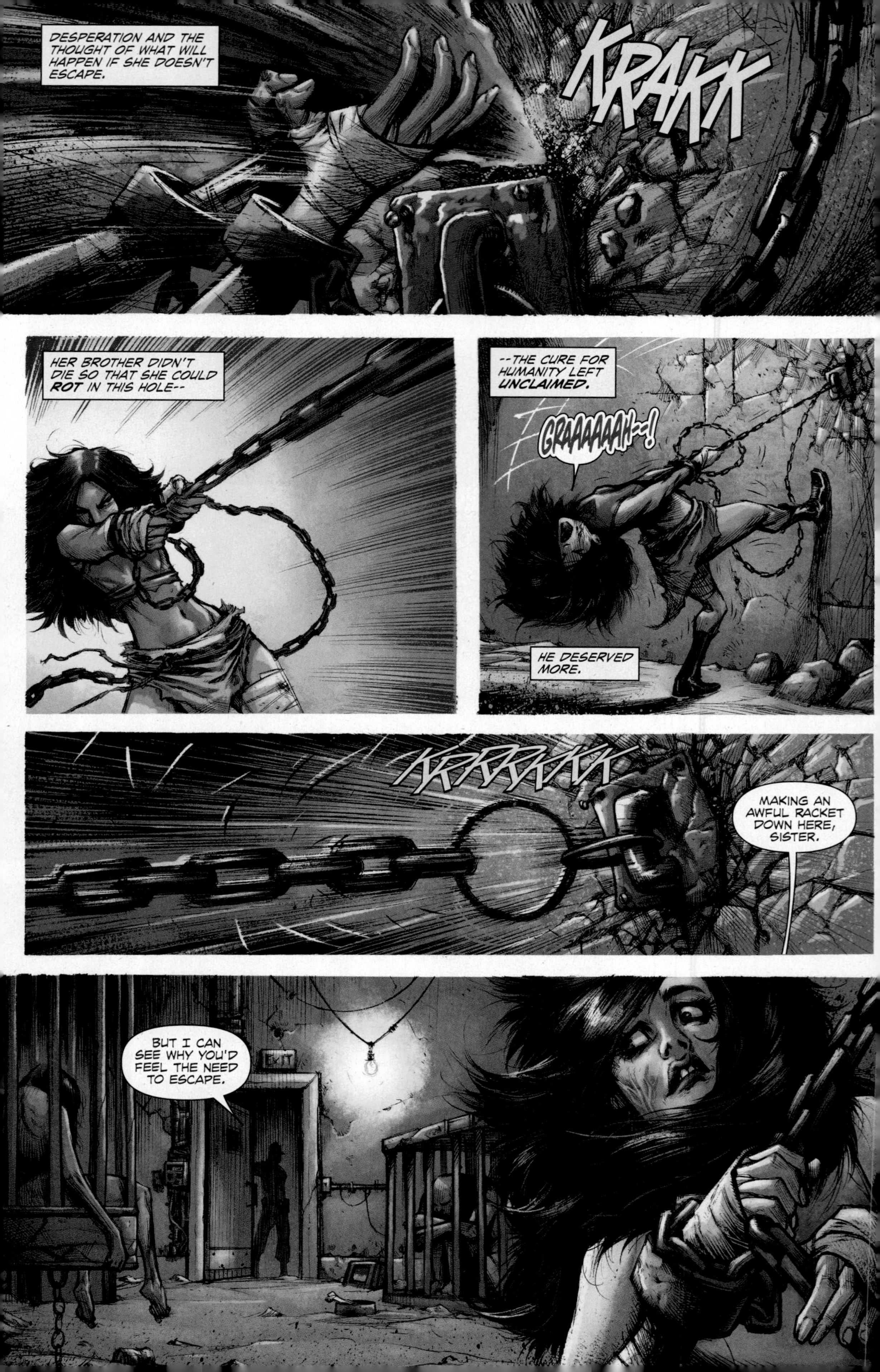
DESPERATION AND THE THOUGHT OF WHAT WILL HAPPEN IF SHE DOESN'T ESCAPE.
KRAKK
HER BROTHER DIDN'T DIE SO THAT SHE COULD ROT IN THIS HOLE--
--THE CURE FOR HUMANITY LEFT UNCLAIMED.
GRAAAAAAH--!
HE DESERVED MORE.
KRKRKKKK
MAKING AN AWFUL RACKET DOWN HERE, SISTER.
BUT I CAN SEE WHY YOU'D FEEL THE NEED TO ESCAPE.
EXIT

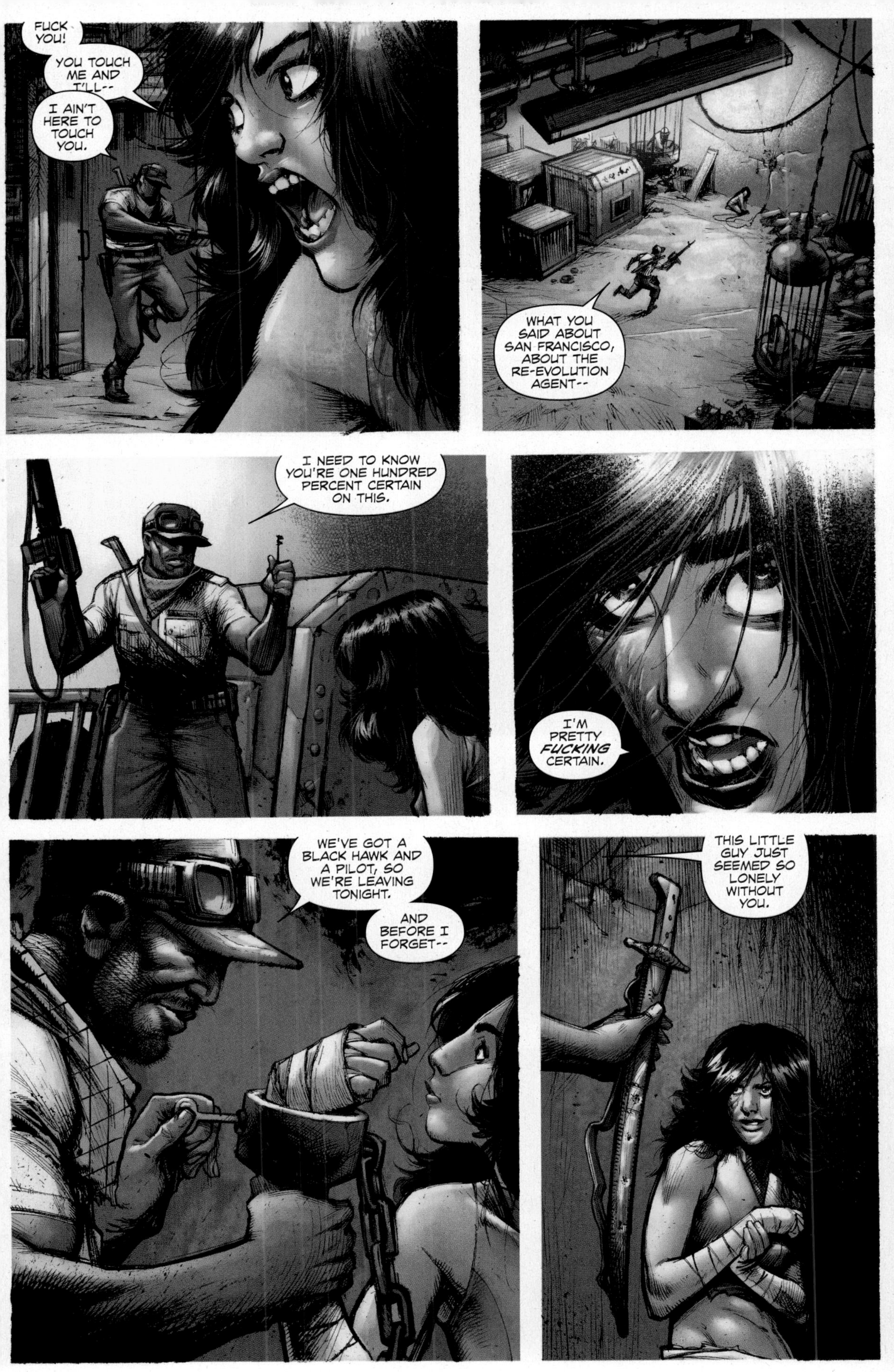
FUCK YOU!
YOU TOUCH ME AND I'LL--
I AIN'T HERE TO TOUCH YOU.
WHAT YOU SAID ABOUT SAN FRANCISCO, ABOUT THE RE-EVOLUTION AGENT--
I NEED TO KNOW YOU'RE ONE HUNDRED PERCENT CERTAIN ON THIS.
I'M PRETTY *FUCKING* CERTAIN.
WE'VE GOT A BLACK HAWK AND A PILOT, SO WE'RE LEAVING TONIGHT.
AND BEFORE I FORGET--
THIS LITTLE GUY JUST SEEMED SO LONELY WITHOUT YOU.

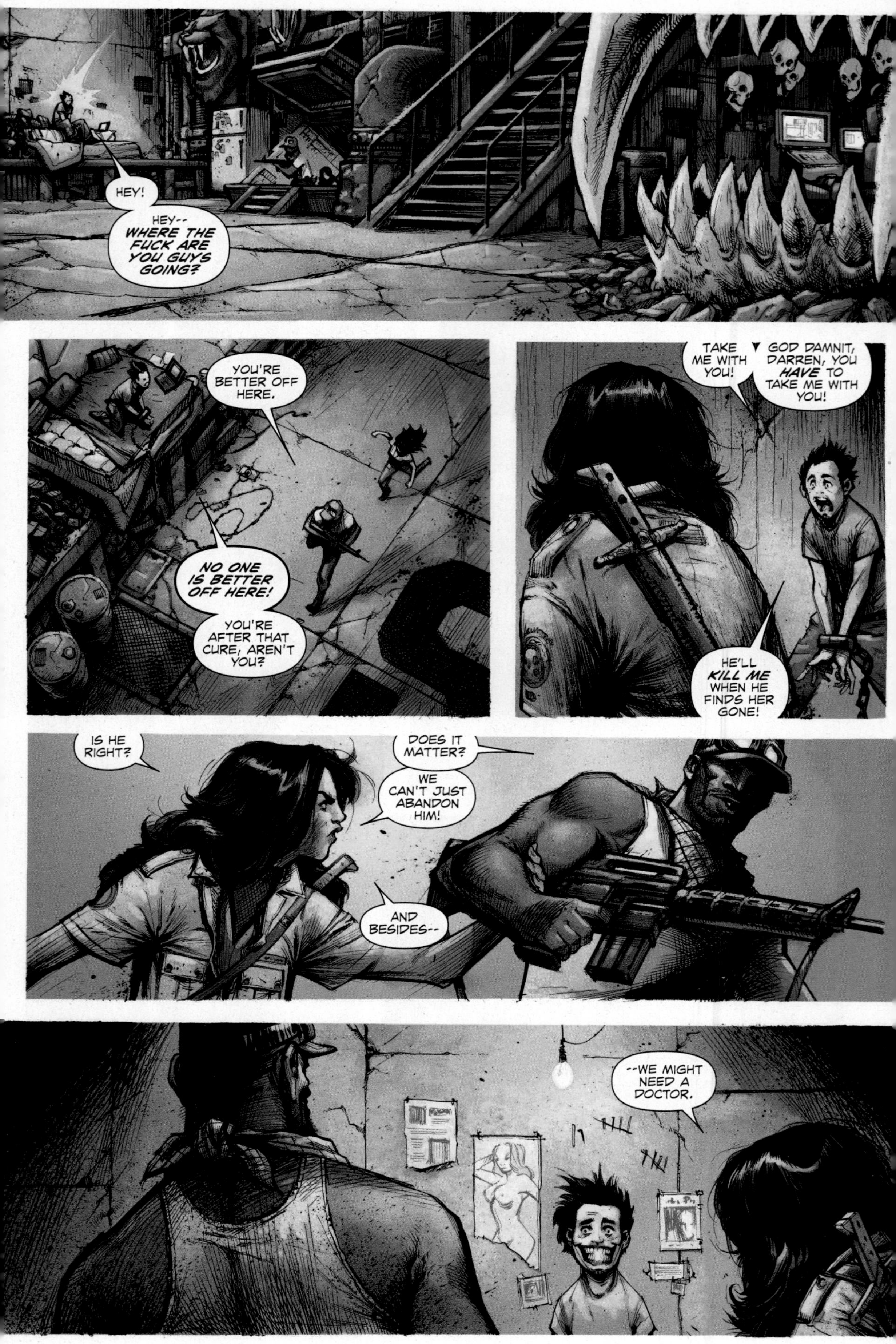

HEY!
HEY-- WHERE THE FUCK ARE YOU GUYS GOING?
YOU'RE BETTER OFF HERE.
NO ONE IS BETTER OFF HERE!
YOU'RE AFTER THAT CURE, AREN'T YOU?
TAKE ME WITH YOU!
GOD DAMNIT, DARREN, YOU HAVE TO TAKE ME WITH YOU!
HE'LL KILL ME WHEN HE FINDS HER GONE!
IS HE RIGHT?
DOES IT MATTER?
WE CAN'T JUST ABANDON HIM!
AND BESIDES--
--WE MIGHT NEED A DOCTOR.

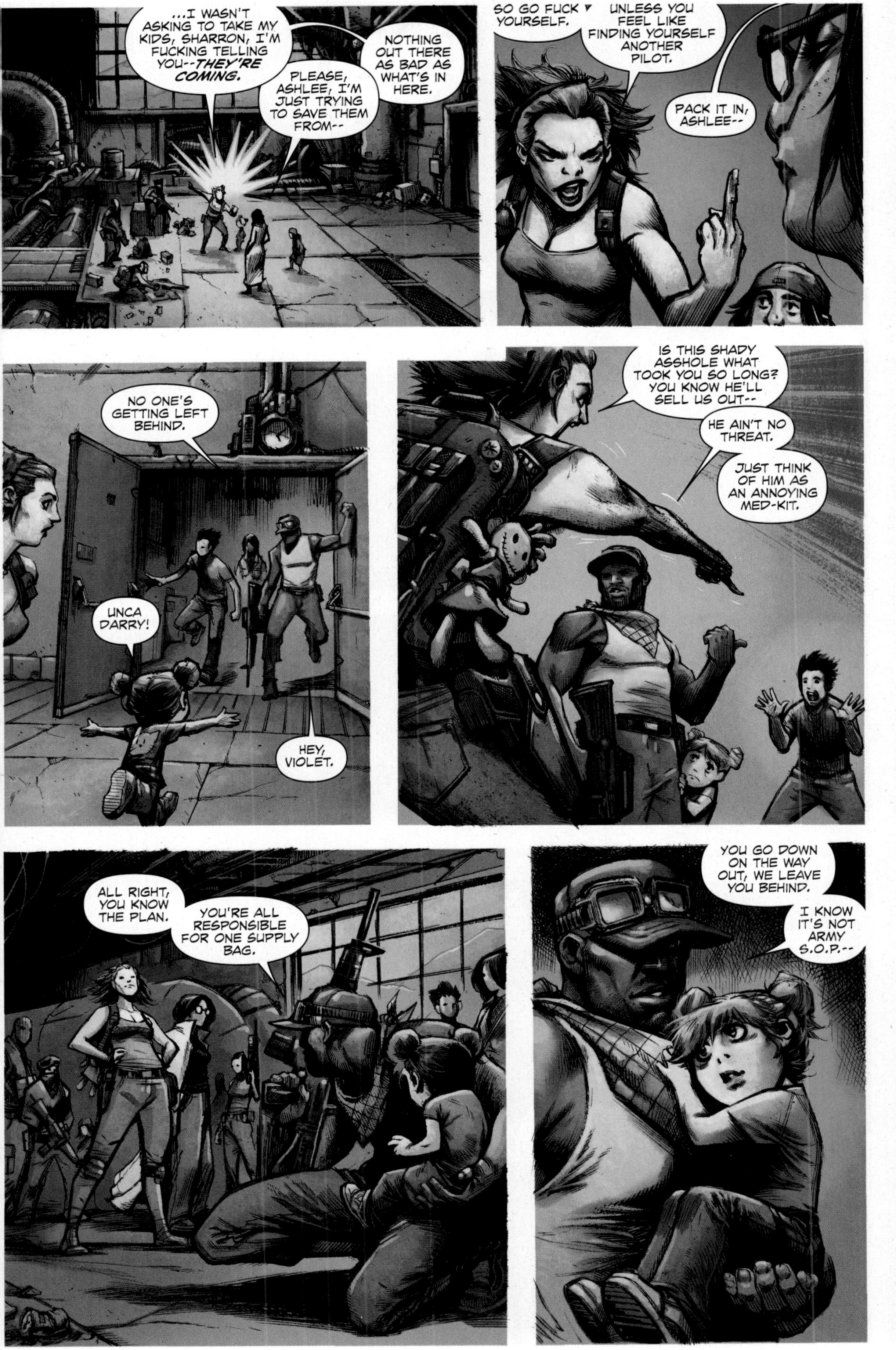
...I WASN'T ASKING TO TAKE MY KIDS, SHARRON, I'M FUCKING TELLING YOU--*THEY'RE COMING.*
PLEASE, ASHLEE, I'M JUST TRYING TO SAVE THEM FROM--
NOTHING OUT THERE AS BAD AS WHAT'S IN HERE.
SO GO FUCK YOURSELF.
UNLESS YOU FEEL LIKE FINDING YOURSELF ANOTHER PILOT.
PACK IT IN, ASHLEE--
NO ONE'S GETTING LEFT BEHIND.
UNCA DARRY!
HEY, VIOLET.
IS THIS SHADY ASSHOLE WHAT TOOK YOU SO LONG? YOU KNOW HE'LL SELL US OUT--
HE AIN'T NO THREAT.
JUST THINK OF HIM AS AN ANNOYING MED-KIT.
ALL RIGHT, YOU KNOW THE PLAN.
YOU'RE ALL RESPONSIBLE FOR ONE SUPPLY BAG.
YOU GO DOWN ON THE WAY OUT, WE LEAVE YOU BEHIND.
I KNOW IT'S NOT ARMY S.O.P.--

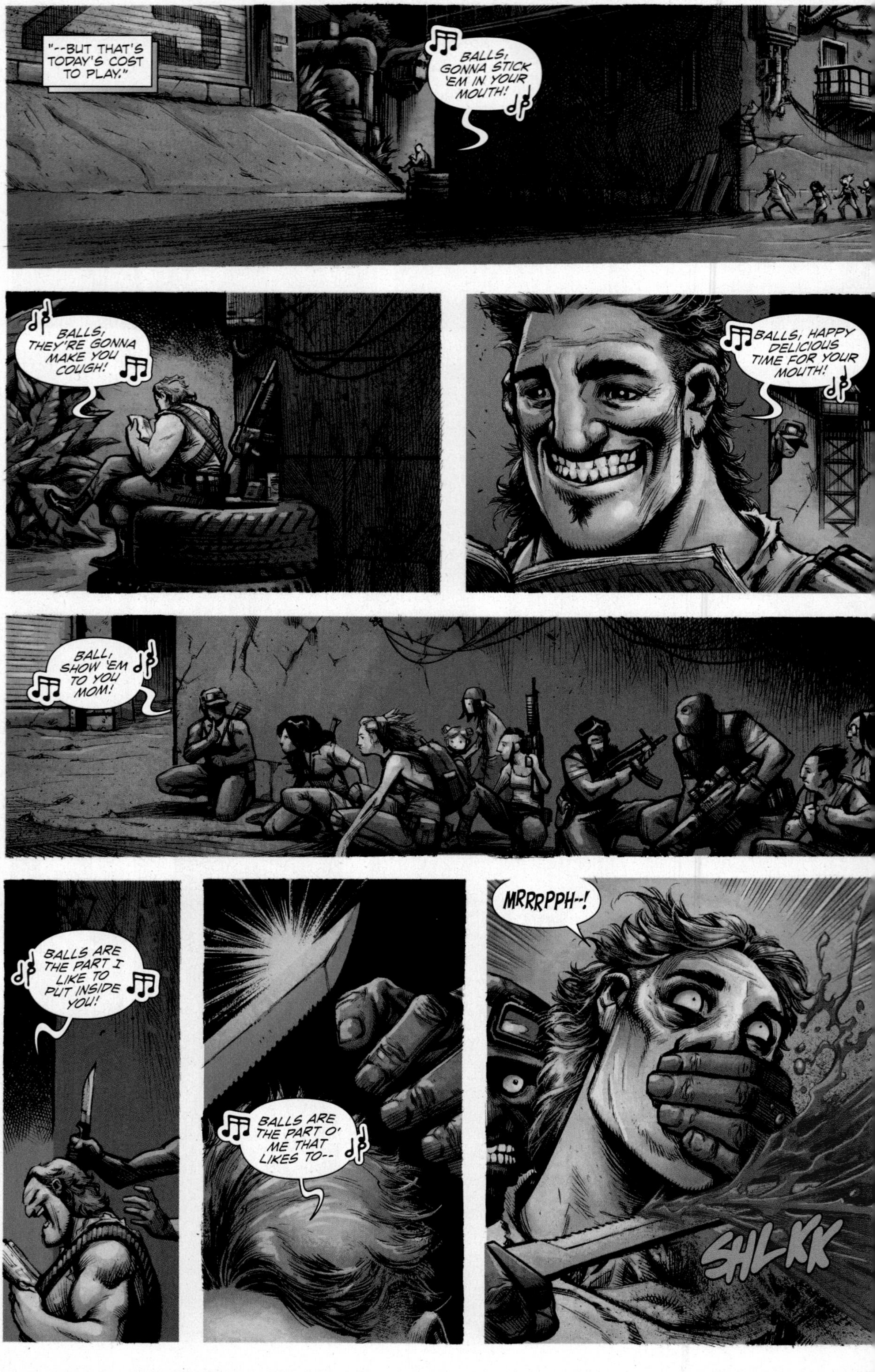
"--BUT THAT'S TODAY'S COST TO PLAY."
BALLS, GONNA STICK 'EM IN YOUR MOUTH!
BALLS, THEY'RE GONNA MAKE YOU COUGH!
BALLS, HAPPY DELICIOUS TIME FOR YOUR MOUTH!
BALL, SHOW 'EM TO YOU MOM!
BALLS ARE THE PART I LIKE TO PUT INSIDE YOU!
BALLS ARE THE PART O' ME THAT LIKES TO--
MRRRPPH--!
SHLKK

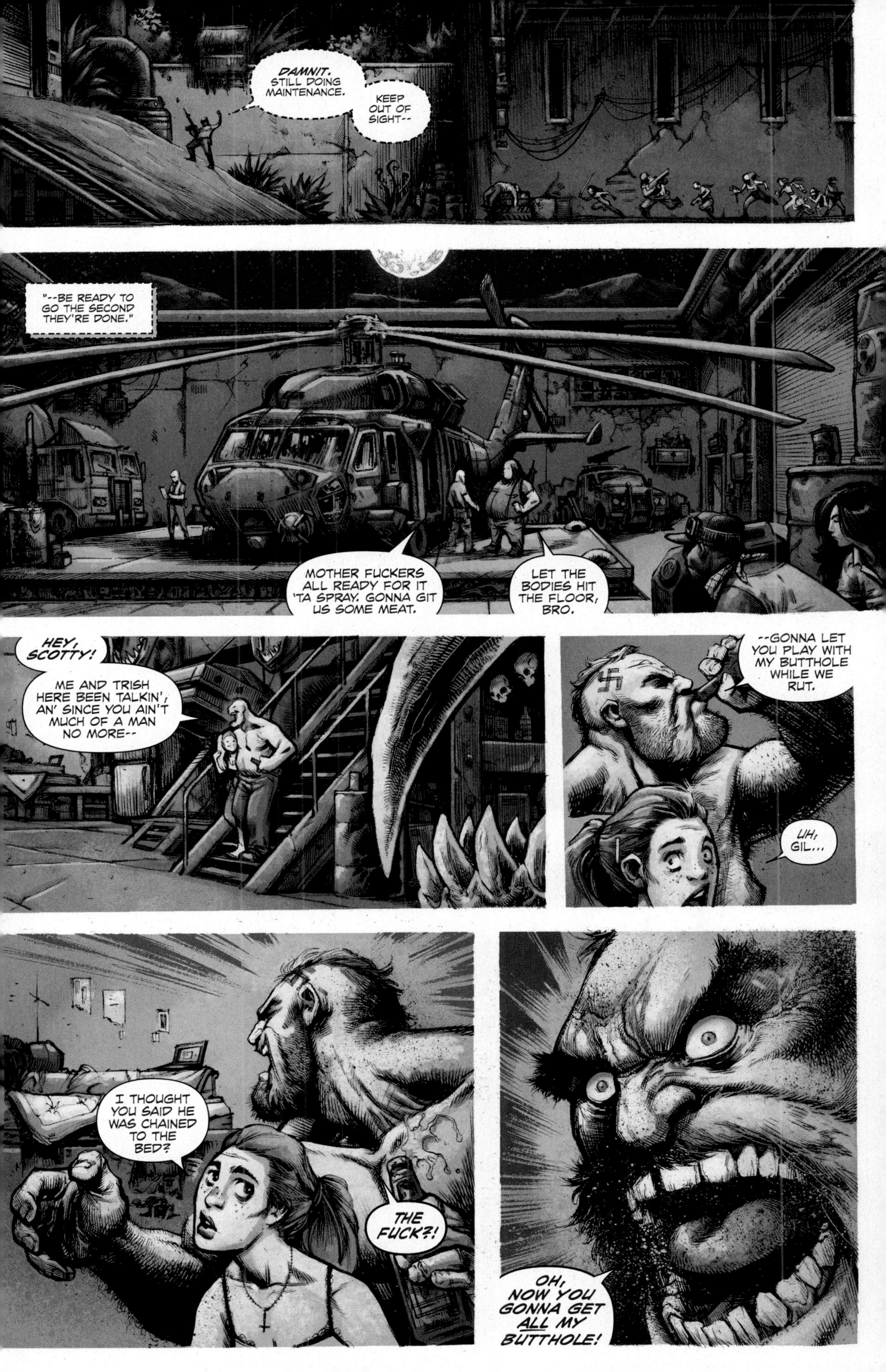
DAMNIT. STILL DOING MAINTENANCE.
KEEP OUT OF SIGHT--
"--BE READY TO GO THE SECOND THEY'RE DONE."
MOTHER FUCKERS ALL READY FOR IT 'TA SPRAY. GONNA GIT US SOME MEAT.
LET THE BODIES HIT THE FLOOR, BRO.
HEY, SCOTTY!
ME AND TRISH HERE BEEN TALKIN', AN' SINCE YOU AIN'T MUCH OF A MAN NO MORE--
--GONNA LET YOU PLAY WITH MY BUTTHOLE WHILE WE RUT.
UH, GIL...
I THOUGHT YOU SAID HE WAS CHAINED TO THE BED?
THE FUCK?!
OH, NOW YOU GONNA GET ALL MY BUTTHOLE!

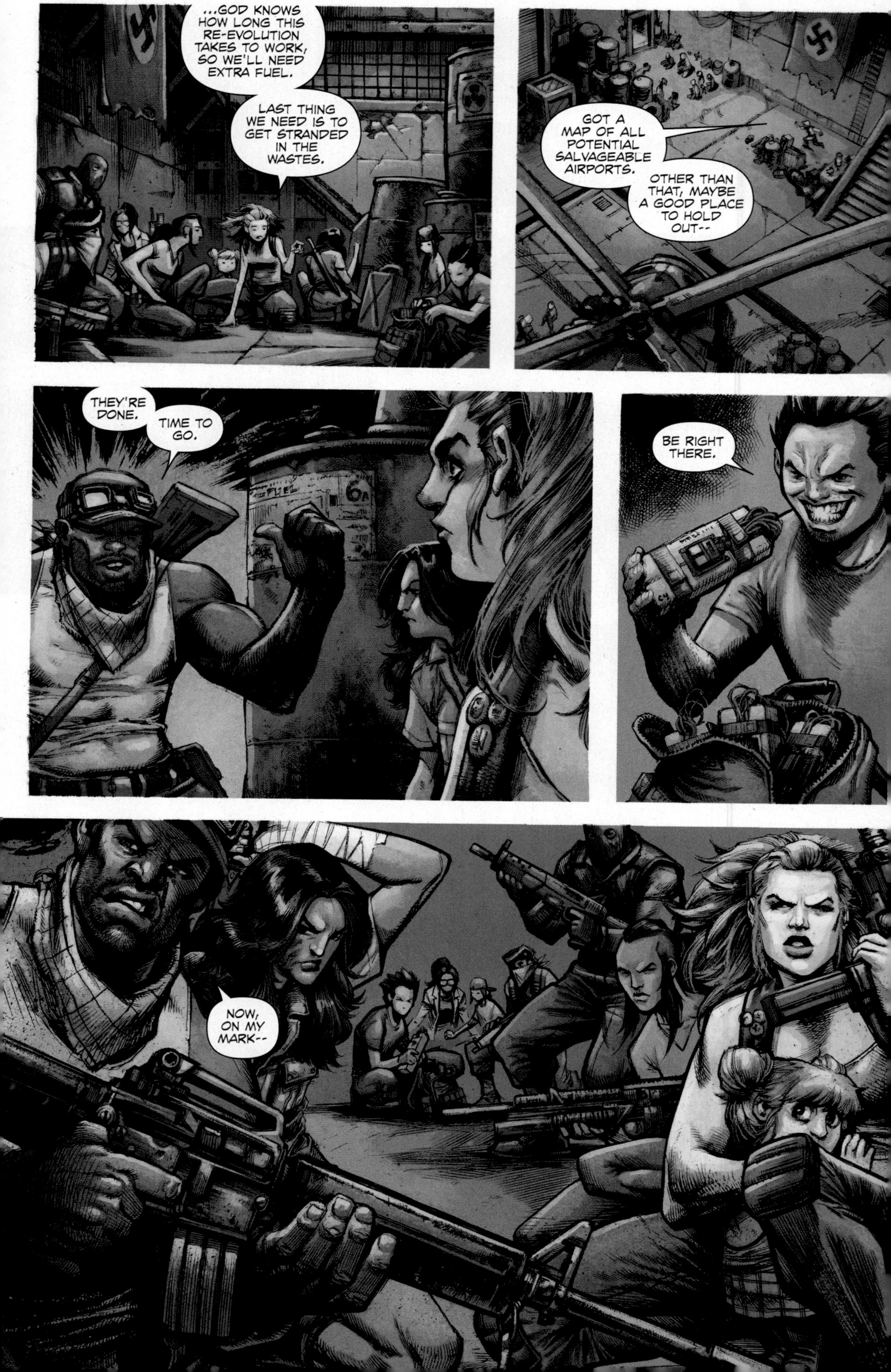
...GOD KNOWS HOW LONG THIS RE-EVOLUTION TAKES TO WORK, SO WE'LL NEED EXTRA FUEL.
LAST THING WE NEED IS TO GET STRANDED IN THE WASTES.
GOT A MAP OF ALL POTENTIAL SALVAGEABLE AIRPORTS.
OTHER THAN THAT, MAYBE A GOOD PLACE TO HOLD OUT--
THEY'RE DONE.
TIME TO GO.
BE RIGHT THERE.
NOW, ON MY MARK--

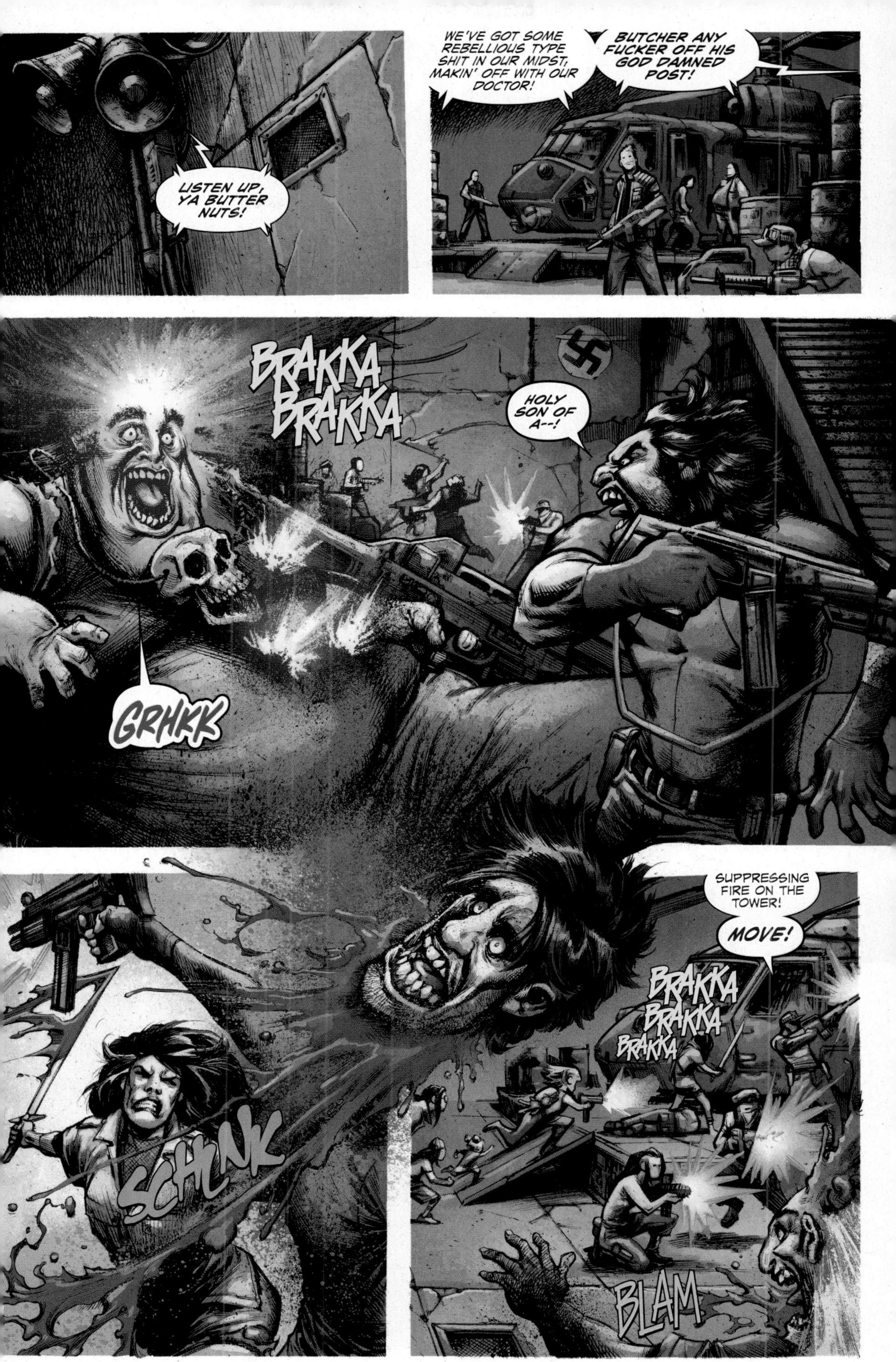
LISTEN UP, YA BUTTER NUTS!
WE'VE GOT SOME REBELLIOUS TYPE SHIT IN OUR MIDST, MAKIN' OFF WITH OUR DOCTOR!
BUTCHER ANY FUCKER OFF HIS GOD DAMNED POST!
BRAKKA BRAKKA
HOLY SON OF A--!
GRHKK
SUPPRESSING FIRE ON THE TOWER!
MOVE!
BRAKKA BRAKKA BRAKKA
SCHLNK
BLAM

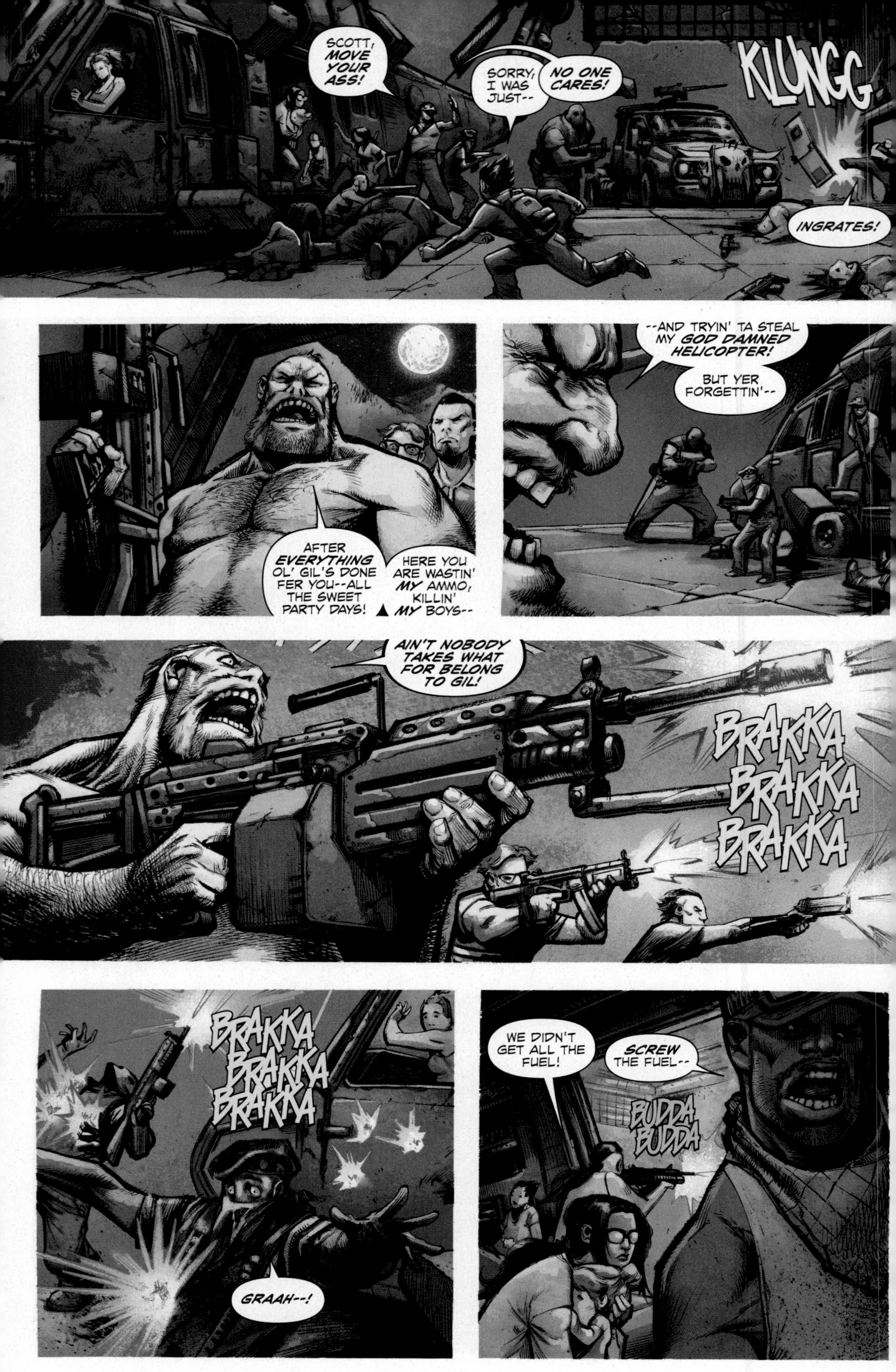
SCOTT, MOVE YOUR ASS!
SORRY, I WAS JUST--
NO ONE CARES!
KLUNGG
INGRATES!
AFTER EVERYTHING OL' GIL'S DONE FER YOU--ALL THE SWEET PARTY DAYS!
HERE YOU ARE WASTIN' MY AMMO, KILLIN' MY BOYS--
--AND TRYIN' TA STEAL MY GOD DAMNED HELICOPTER!
BUT YER FORGETTIN'--
AIN'T NOBODY TAKES WHAT FOR BELONG TO GIL!
BRAKKA BRAKKA BRAKKA
BRAKKA BRAKKA BRAKKA
GRAAH--!
WE DIDN'T GET ALL THE FUEL!
SCREW THE FUEL--
BUDDA BUDDA

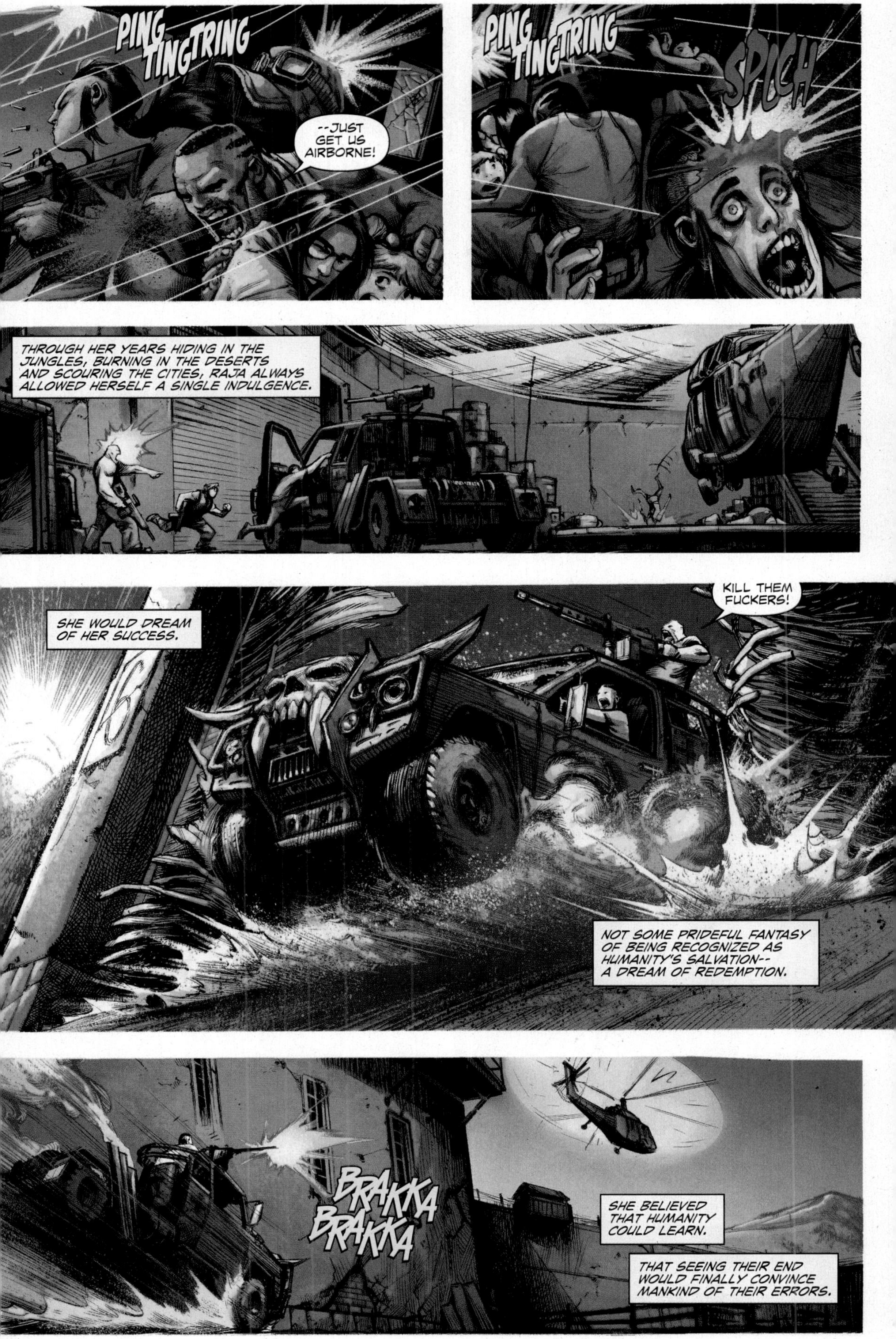
PING
TINGTRING
--JUST GET US AIRBORNE!
PING
TINGTRING
SPLCH
THROUGH HER YEARS HIDING IN THE JUNGLES, BURNING IN THE DESERTS AND SCOURING THE CITIES, RAJA ALWAYS ALLOWED HERSELF A SINGLE INDULGENCE.
SHE WOULD DREAM OF HER SUCCESS.
KILL THEM FUCKERS!
NOT SOME PRIDEFUL FANTASY OF BEING RECOGNIZED AS HUMANITY'S SALVATION-- A DREAM OF REDEMPTION.
BRAKKA
BRAKKA
SHE BELIEVED THAT HUMANITY COULD LEARN.
THAT SEEING THEIR END WOULD FINALLY CONVINCE MANKIND OF THEIR ERRORS.

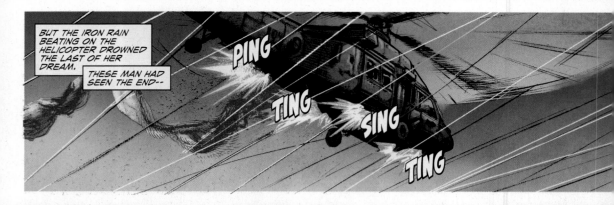

BUT THE IRON RAIN BEATING ON THE HELICOPTER DROWNED THE LAST OF HER DREAM.

THESE MAN HAD SEEN THE END--

PING

TING

SING

TING

--AND THEY WALLOWED IN IT.

THE OLD PAINS HAD SURVIVED.

THE LUST FOR DOMINANCE--

BRAKKA BRAKKA BRAKKA

THE HATE.

GET DOWN!

HE'S CUTTING US UP--WE'RE NOT GETTING OUT OF HERE!

THOSE MEN SHOULD HAVE KILLED GIL THE MOMENT THEY SAW WHAT HE WAS--

DAMNIT, CAN'T ANY OF YOU DO SOMETHING?!

NOW OR NEVER...

--INSTEAD, THEY WORSHIPED THE SAVAGERY.

WHAT WAS IT THAT DRIVES HUMANS TO SUCH EVIL?

-DREEP-

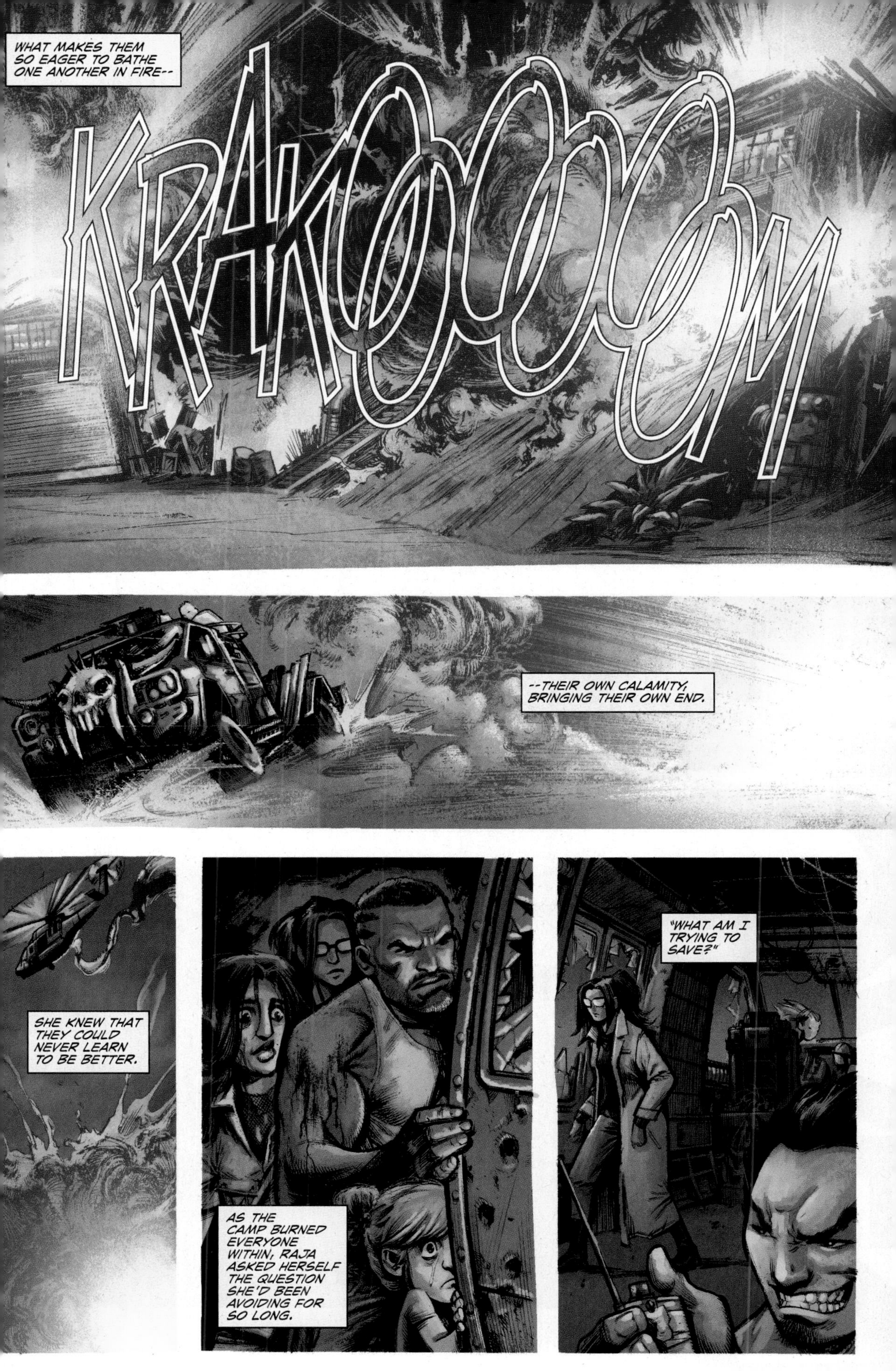
WHAT MAKES THEM SO EAGER TO BATHE ONE ANOTHER IN FIRE--
KRAKOOOOOM
--THEIR OWN CALAMITY, BRINGING THEIR OWN END.
SHE KNEW THAT THEY COULD NEVER LEARN TO BE BETTER.
AS THE CAMP BURNED EVERYONE WITHIN, RAJA ASKED HERSELF THE QUESTION SHE'D BEEN AVOIDING FOR SO LONG.
"WHAT AM I TRYING TO SAVE?"

Issue 3 Cover by JAE LEE With Colors by JUNE CHUNG

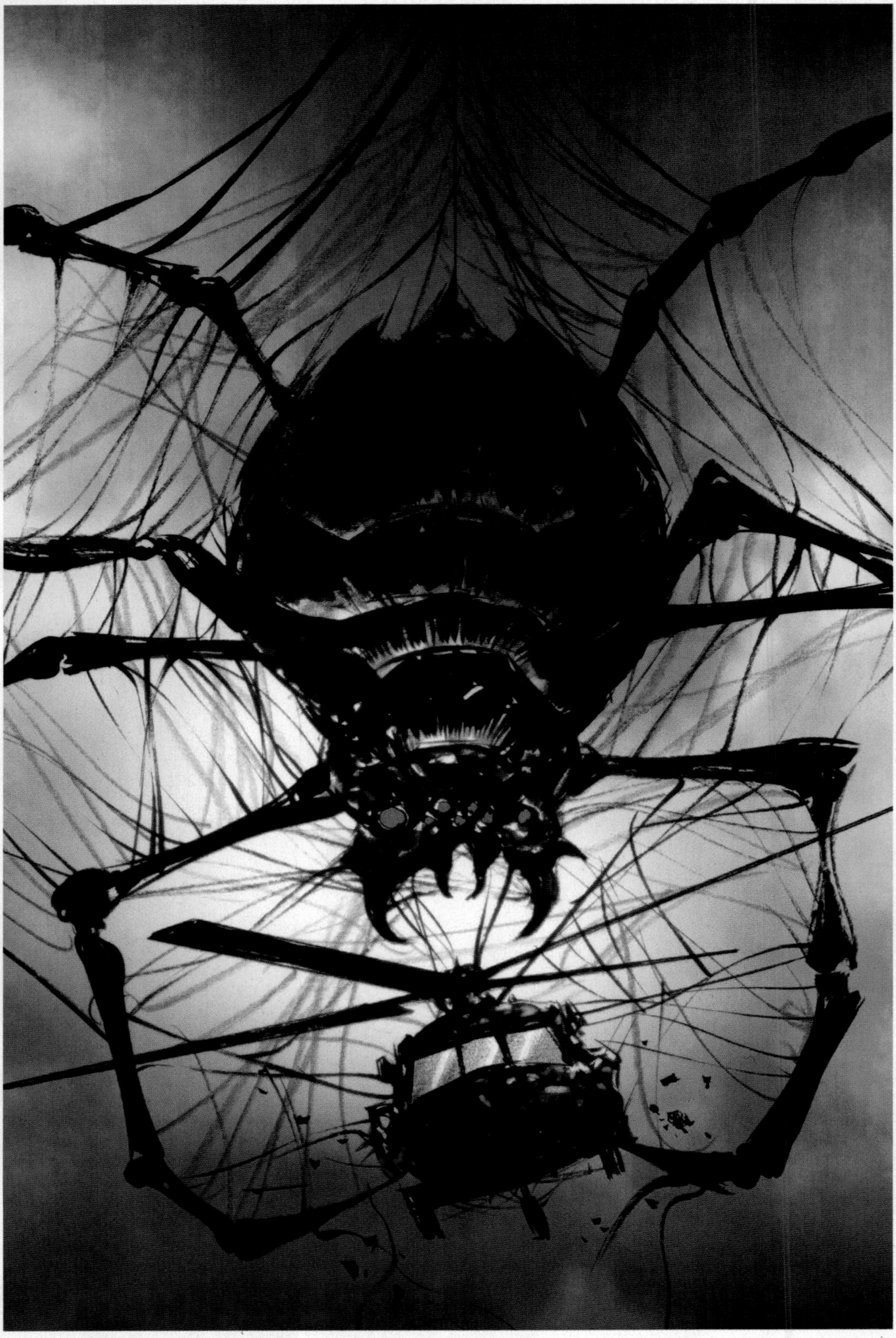

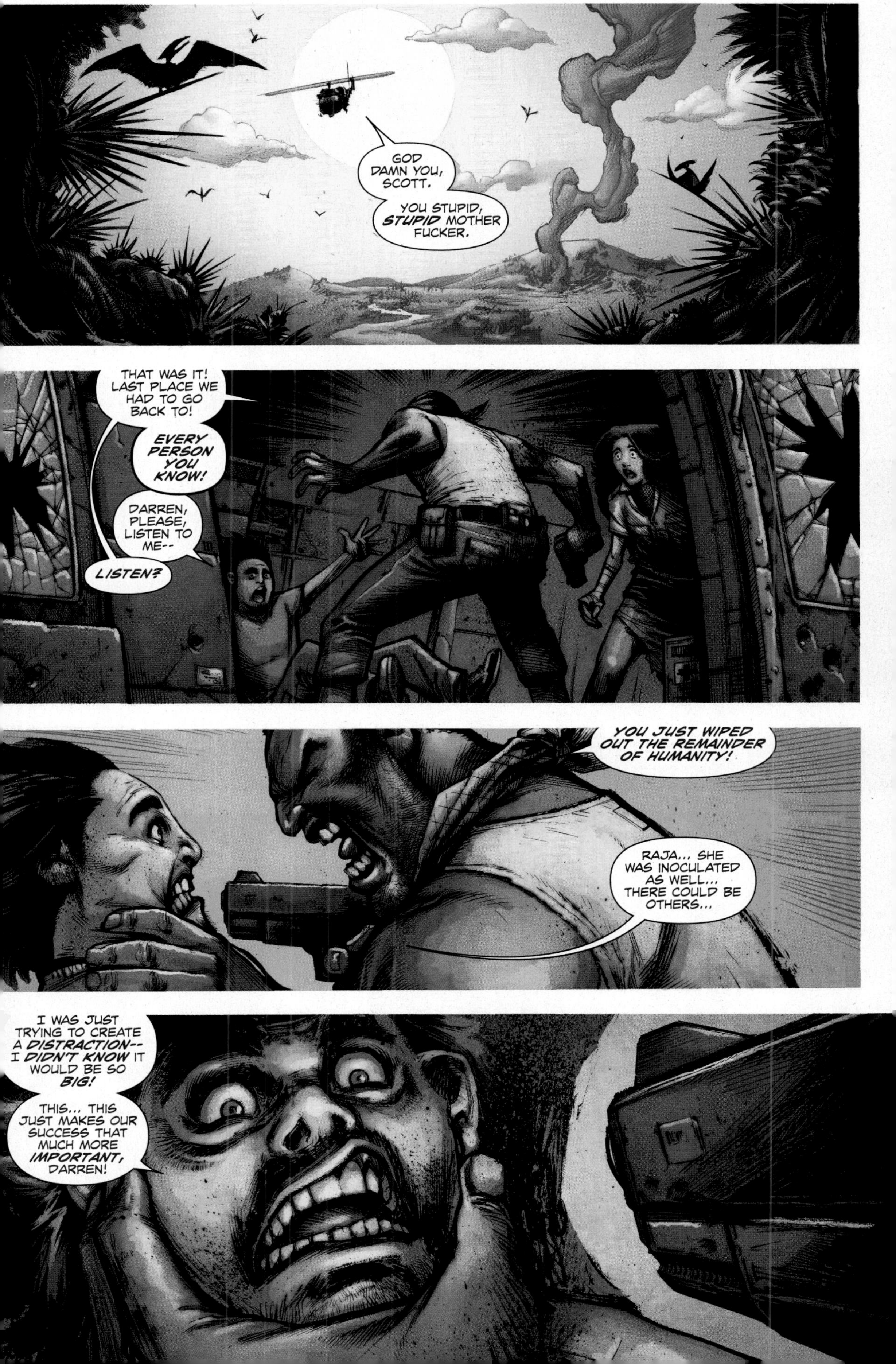
GOD DAMN YOU, SCOTT.
YOU STUPID, STUPID MOTHER FUCKER.
THAT WAS IT! LAST PLACE WE HAD TO GO BACK TO!
EVERY PERSON YOU KNOW!
DARREN, PLEASE, LISTEN TO ME--
LISTEN?
YOU JUST WIPED OUT THE REMAINDER OF HUMANITY!
RAJA... SHE WAS INOCULATED AS WELL... THERE COULD BE OTHERS...
I WAS JUST TRYING TO CREATE A DISTRACTION-- I DIDN'T KNOW IT WOULD BE SO BIG!
THIS... THIS JUST MAKES OUR SUCCESS THAT MUCH MORE IMPORTANT, DARREN!

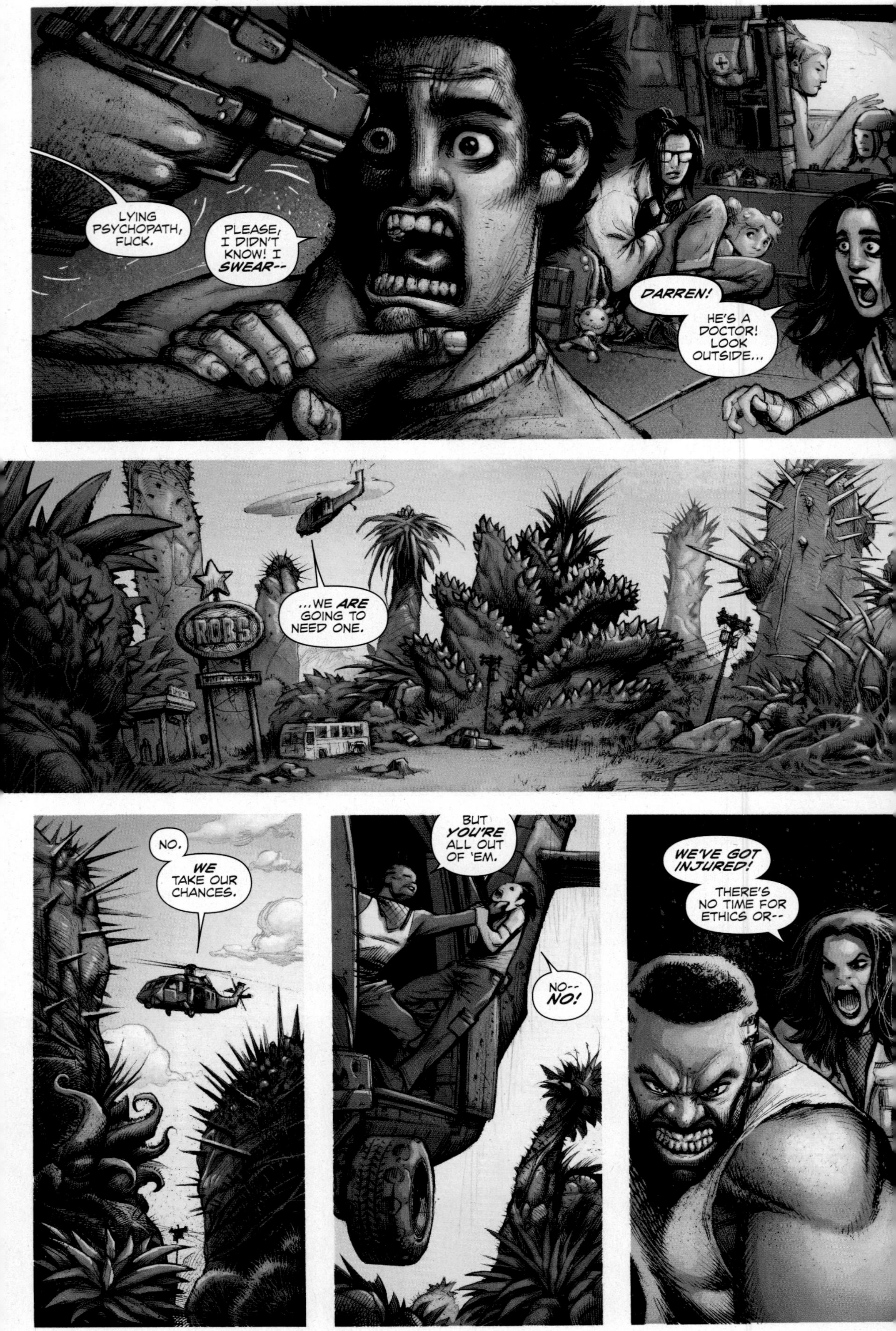
LYING PSYCHOPATH, FUCK.
PLEASE, I DIDN'T KNOW! I SWEAR--
DARREN!
HE'S A DOCTOR! LOOK OUTSIDE...
...WE ARE GOING TO NEED ONE.
ROBS
NO.
WE TAKE OUR CHANCES.
BUT YOU'RE ALL OUT OF 'EM.
NO-- NO!
WE'VE GOT INJURED!
THERE'S NO TIME FOR ETHICS OR--

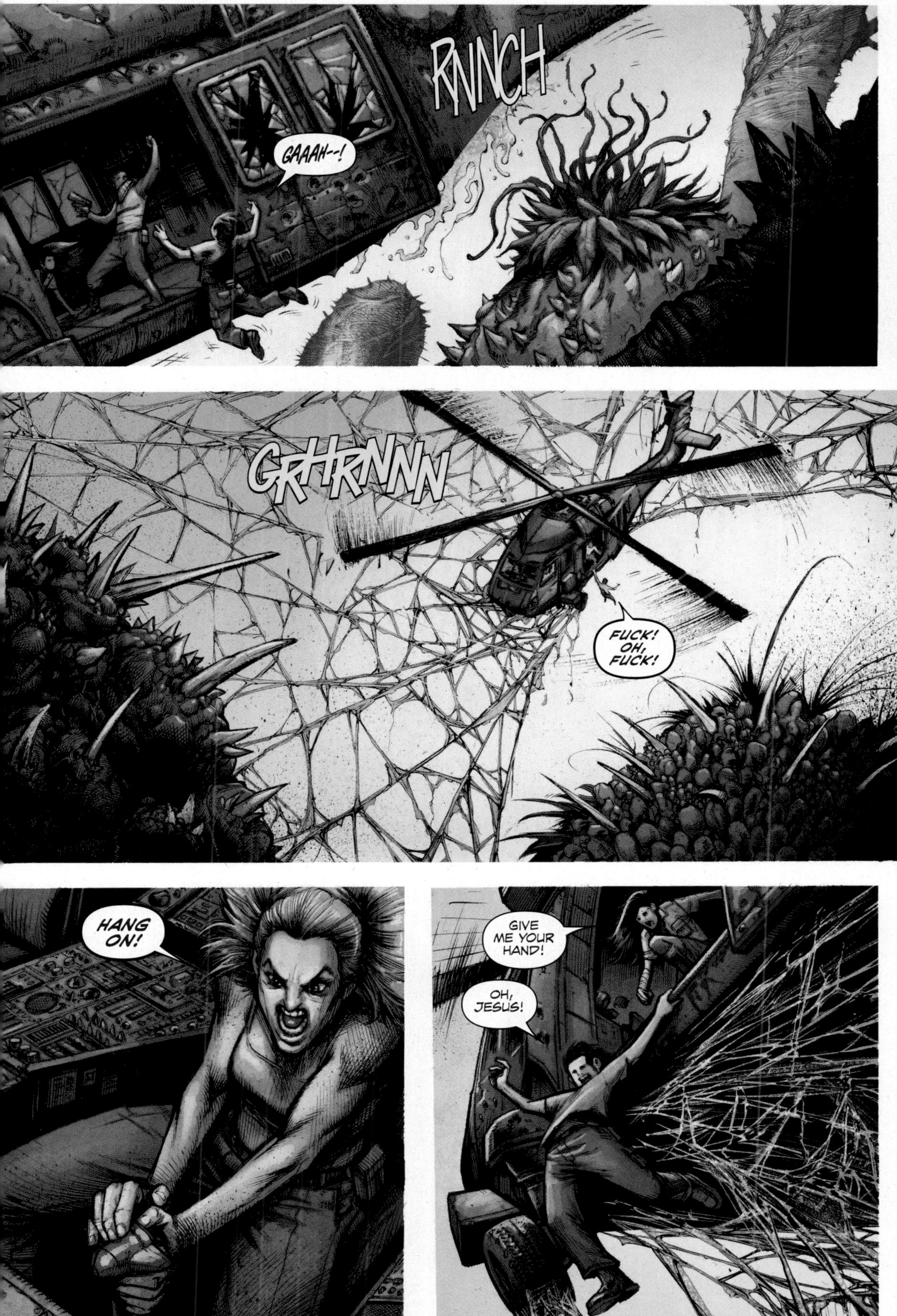
RNNCH
GAAAH--!
GRHRNNN
FUCK! OH, FUCK!
HANG ON!
GIVE ME YOUR HAND!
OH, JESUS!

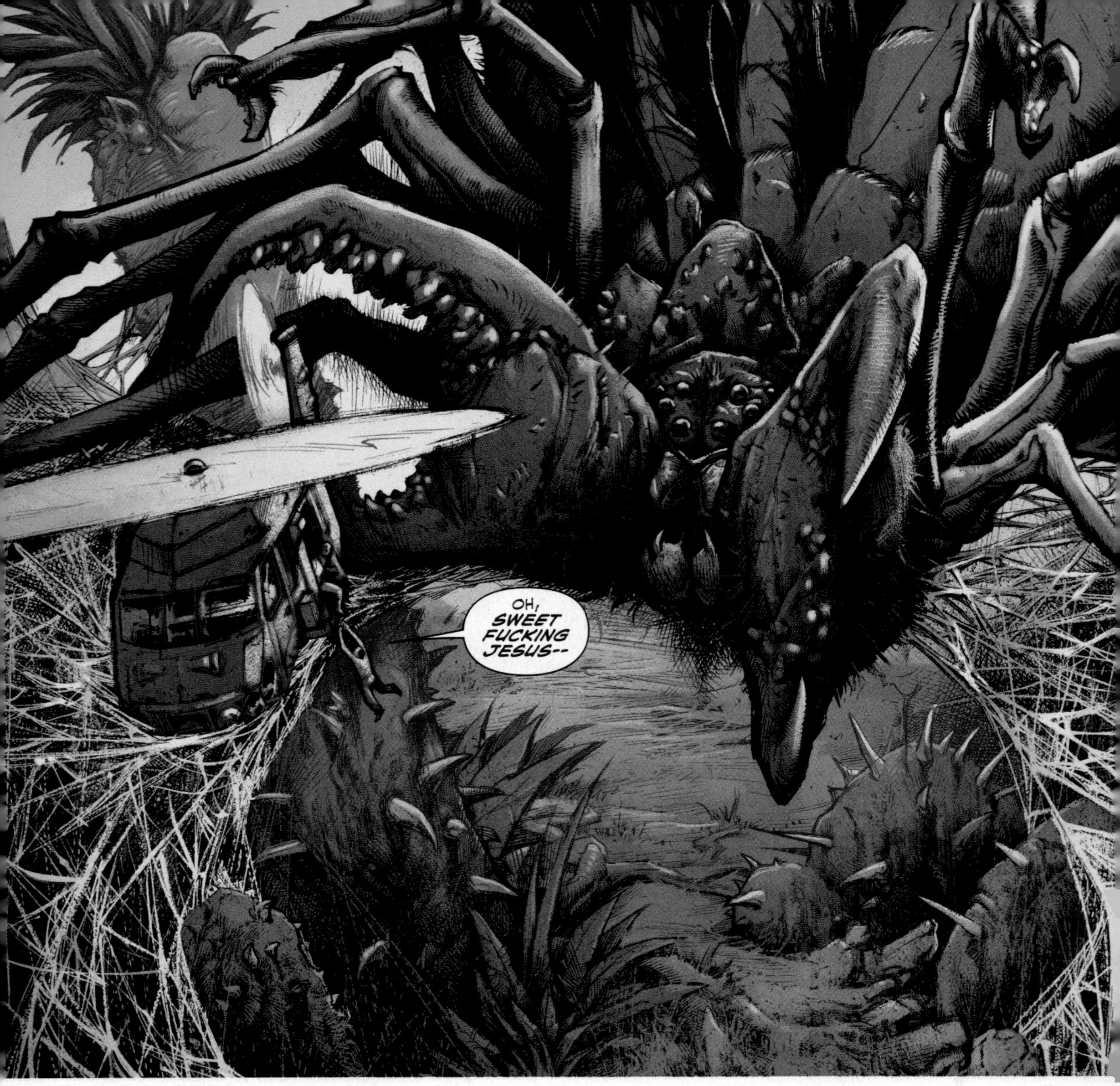
OH, SWEET FUCKING JESUS--

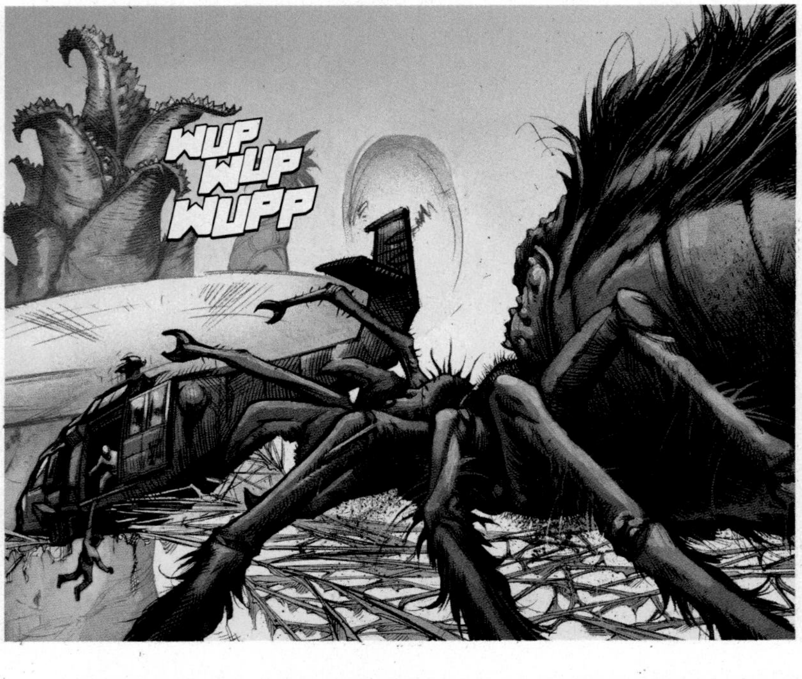
WUP WUP WUPP

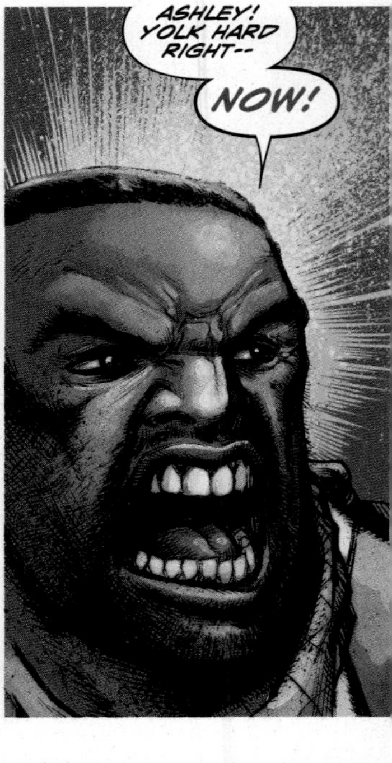
ASHLEY! YOLK HARD RIGHT--
NOW!

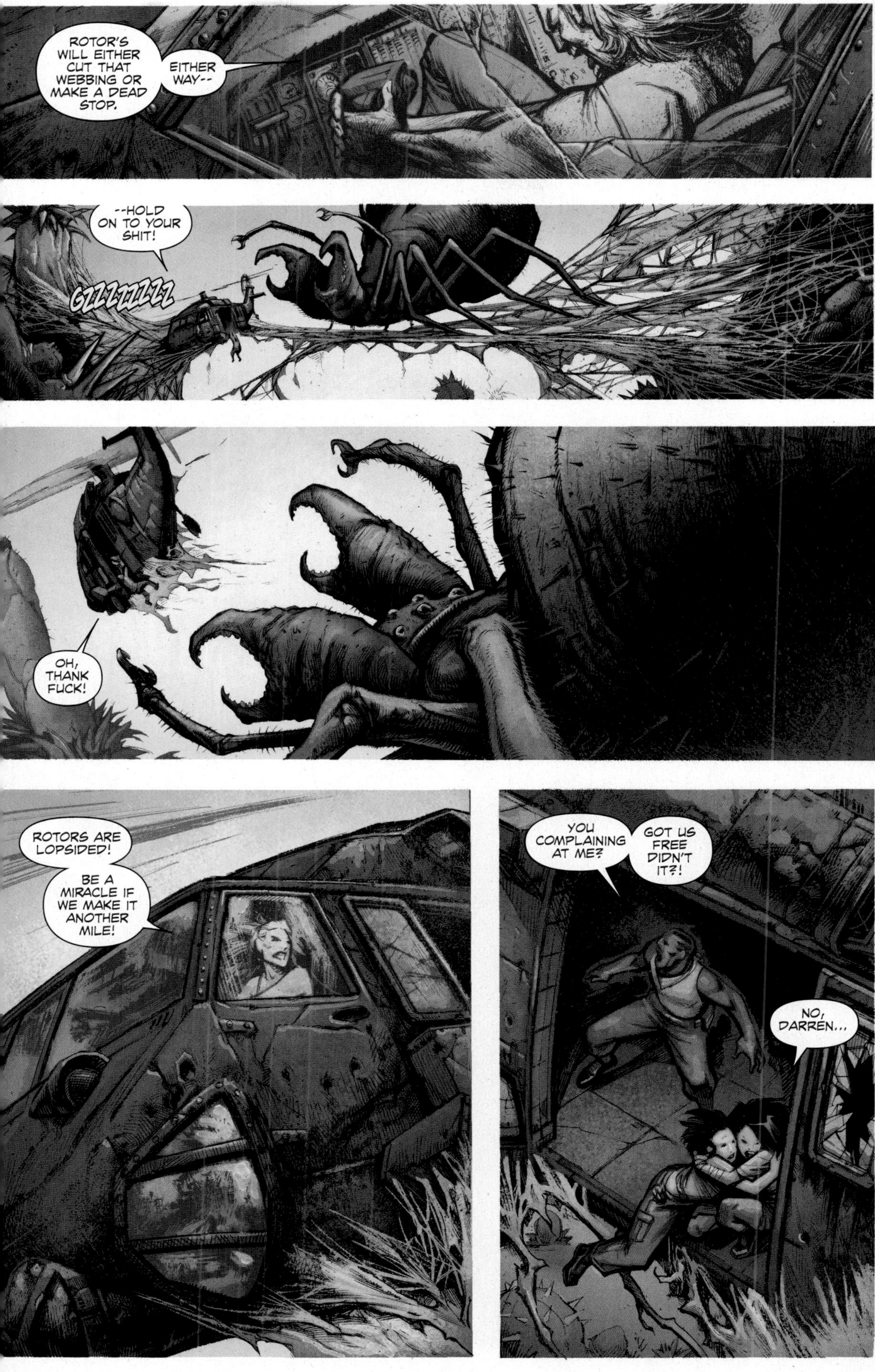
ROTOR'S WILL EITHER CUT THAT WEBBING OR MAKE A DEAD STOP.
EITHER WAY--
--HOLD ON TO YOUR SHIT!
GZZZZZZZZ
OH, THANK FUCK!
ROTORS ARE LOPSIDED!
BE A MIRACLE IF WE MAKE IT ANOTHER MILE!
YOU COMPLAINING AT ME?
GOT US FREE DIDN'T IT?!
NO, DARREN...

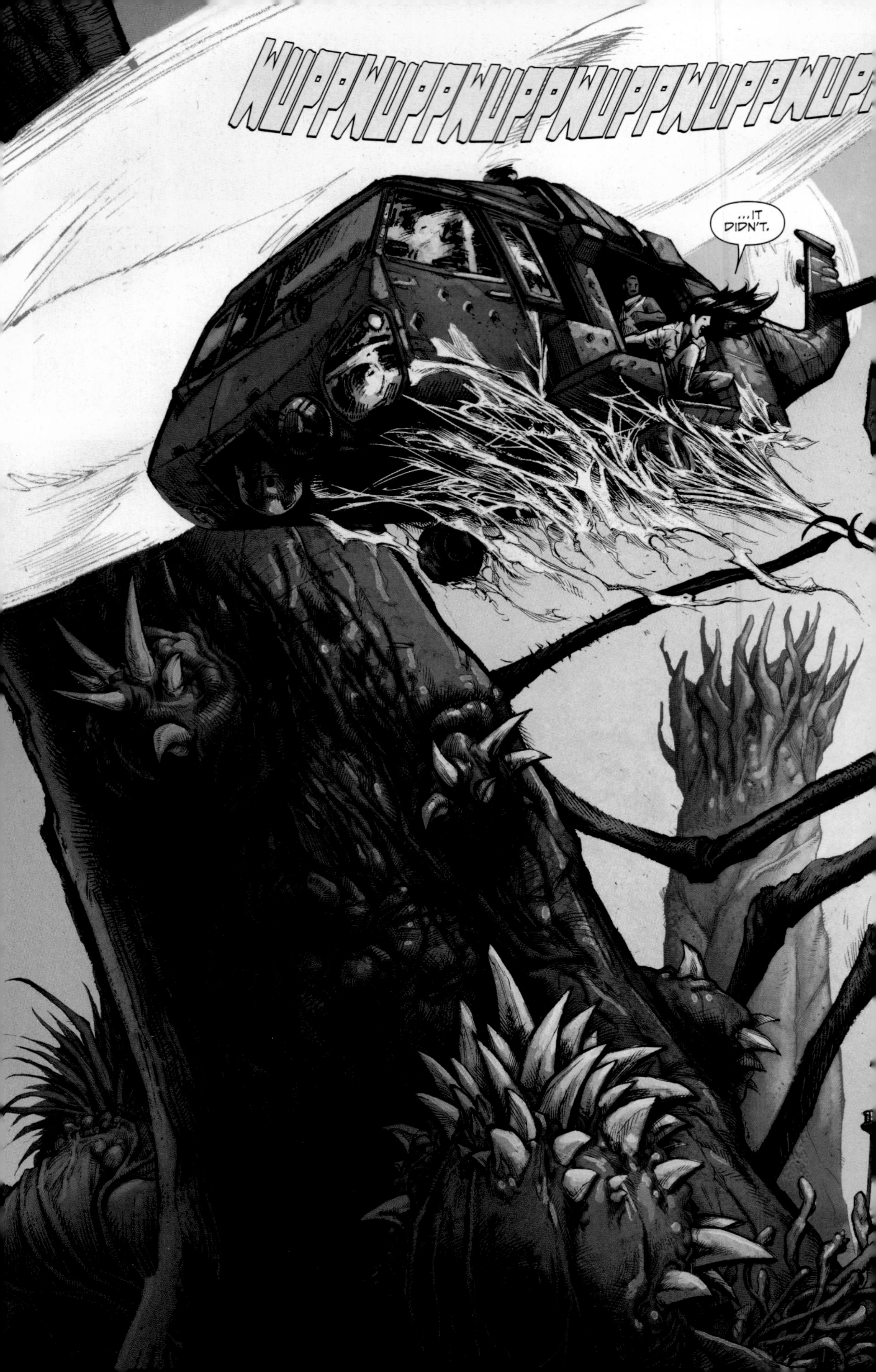
WUPPWUPPWUPPWUPPWUPPWUPP
...IT DIDN'T.

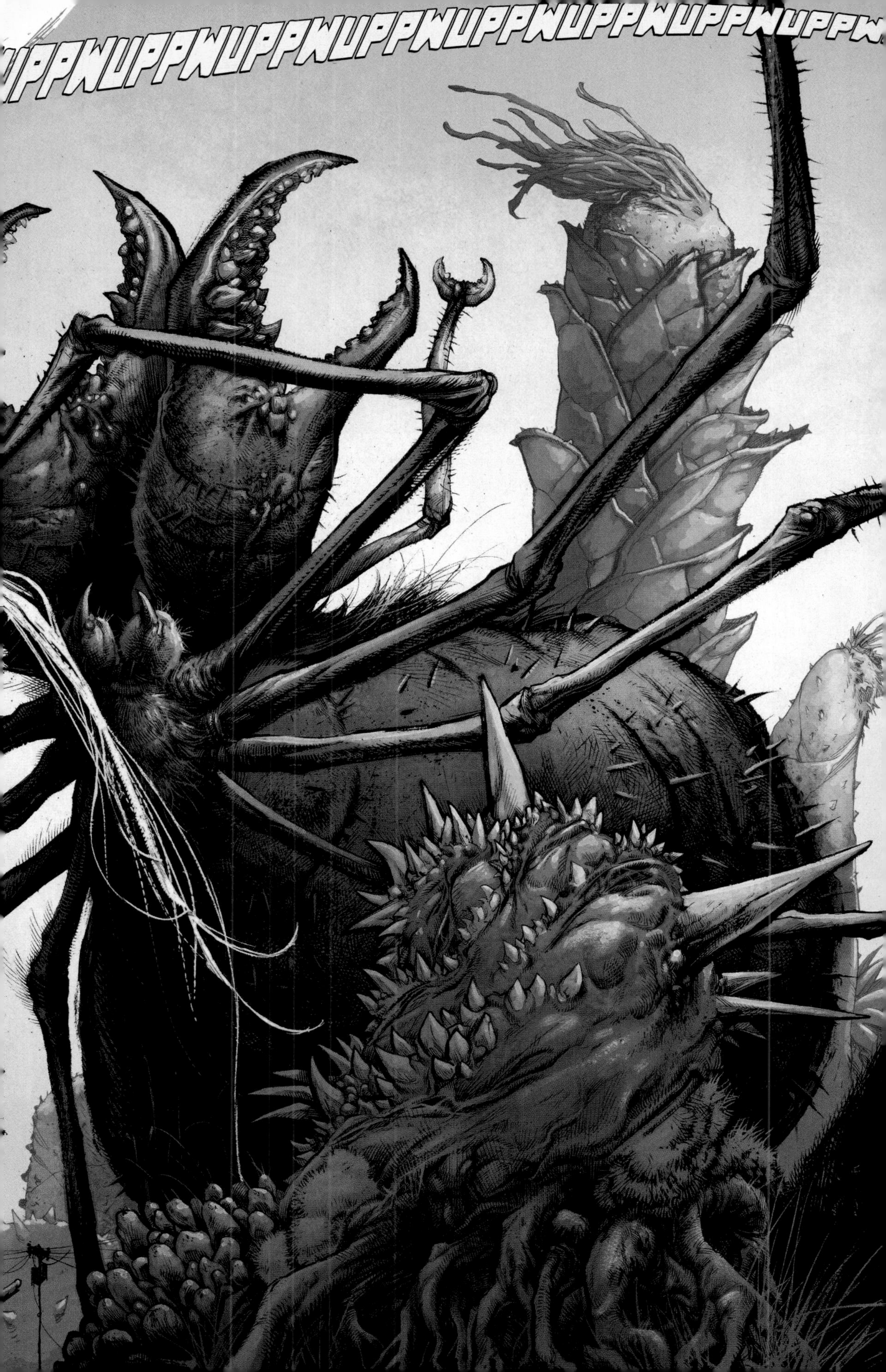
IPPWUPPWUPPWUPPWUPPWUPPWUPPW

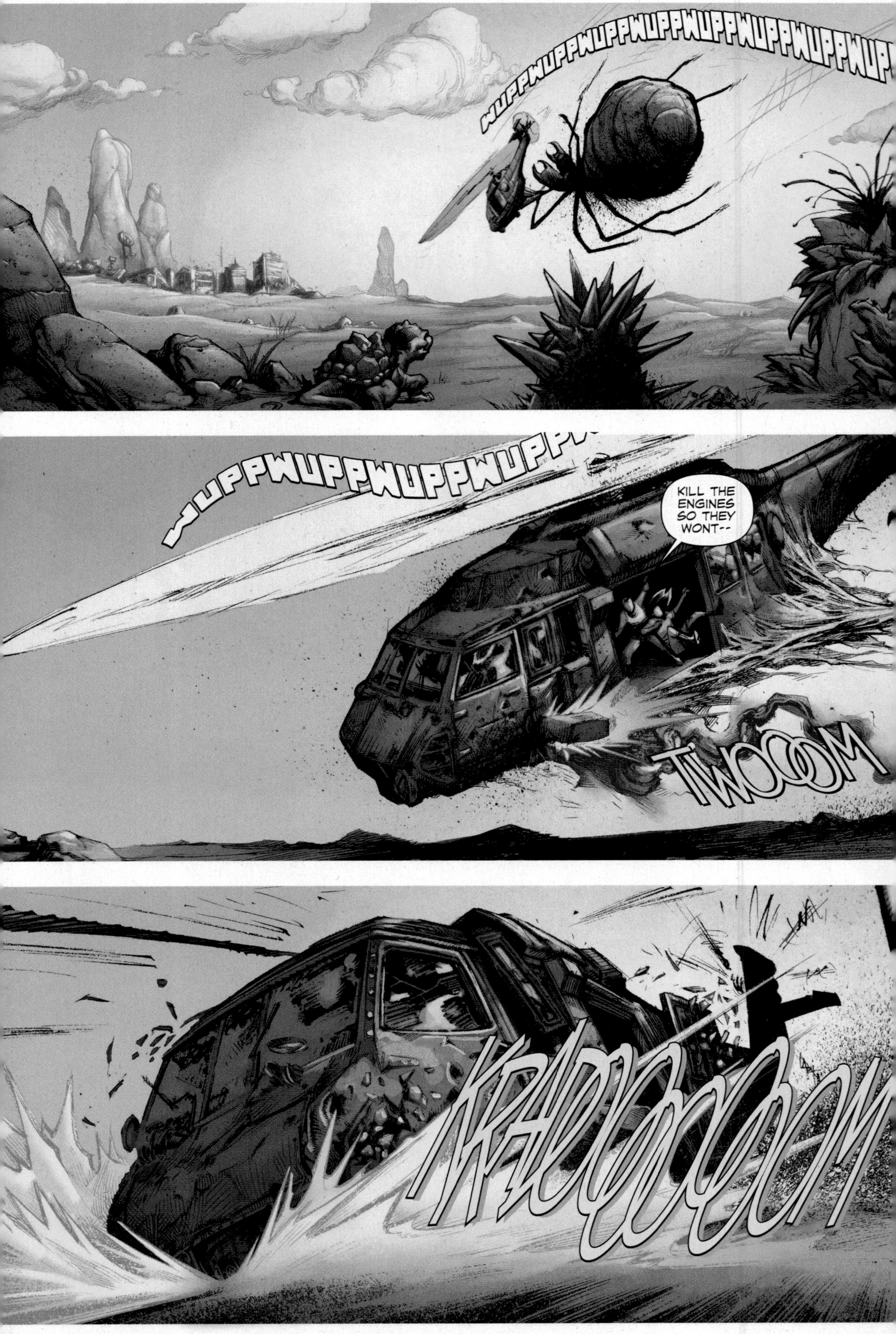
KILL THE ENGINES SO THEY WONT--

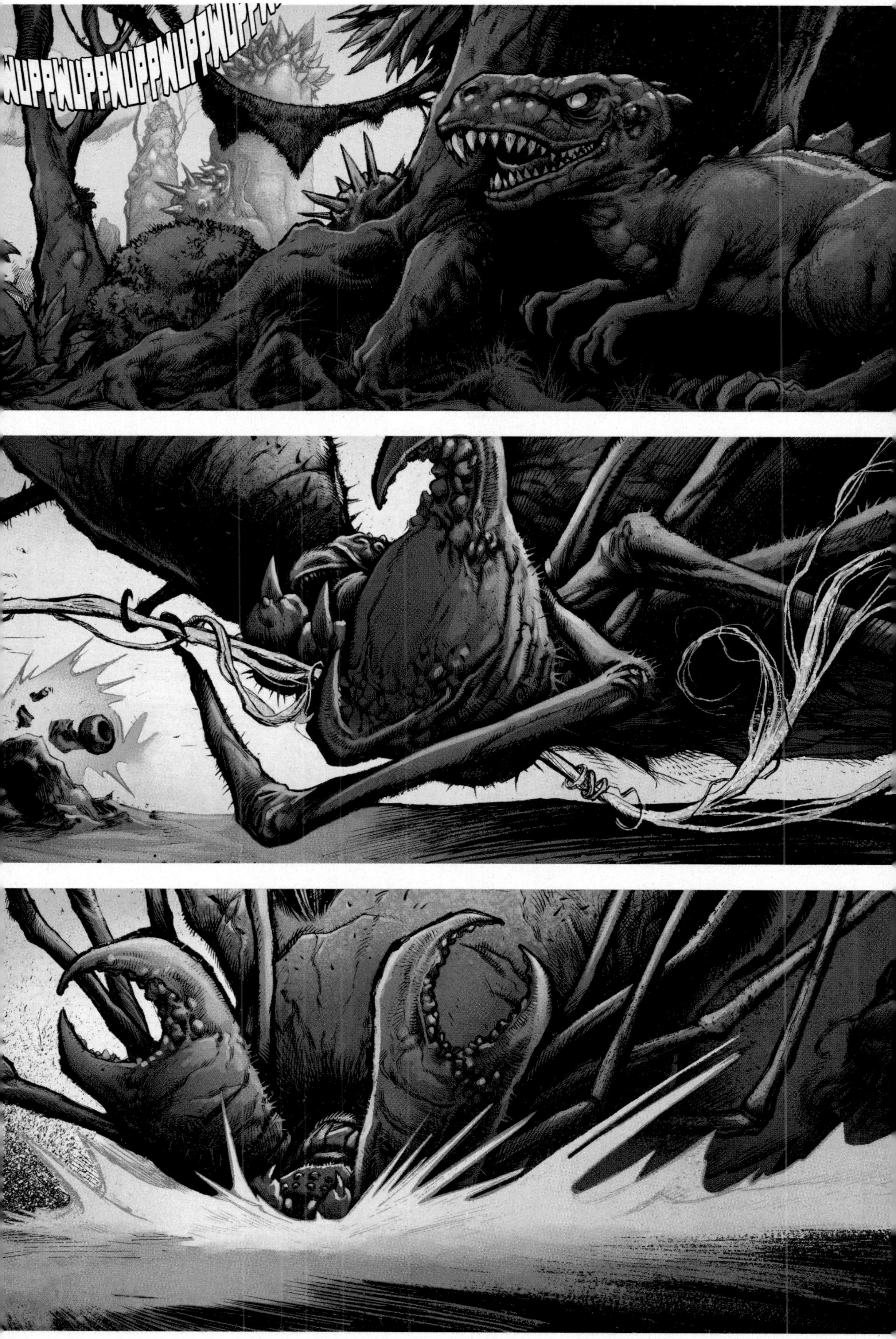
WUPPWUPPWUPPWUPPWUP

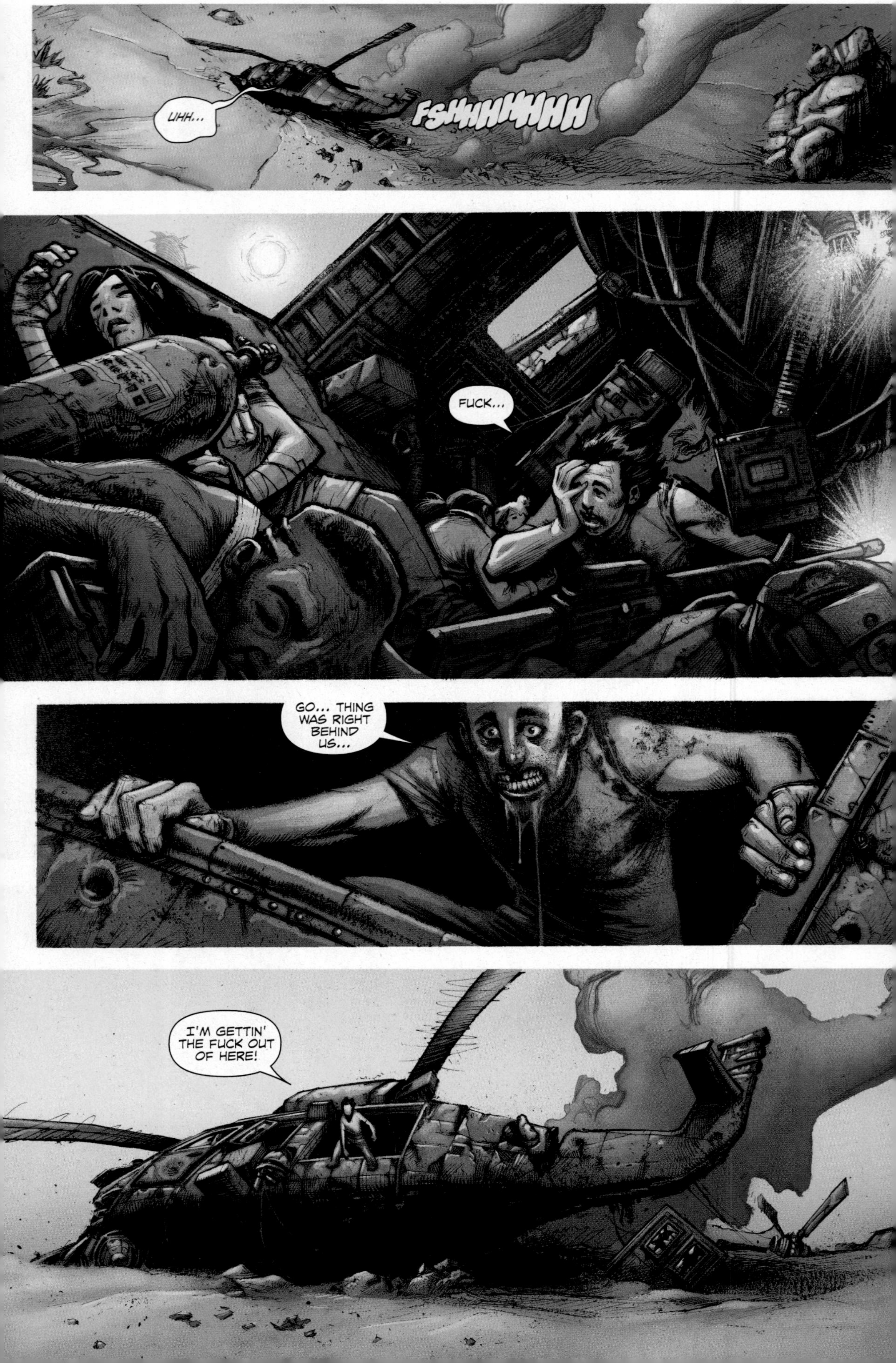
UHH...
FSHHHHHHHH
FUCK...
GO... THING WAS RIGHT BEHIND US...
I'M GETTIN' THE FUCK OUT OF HERE!

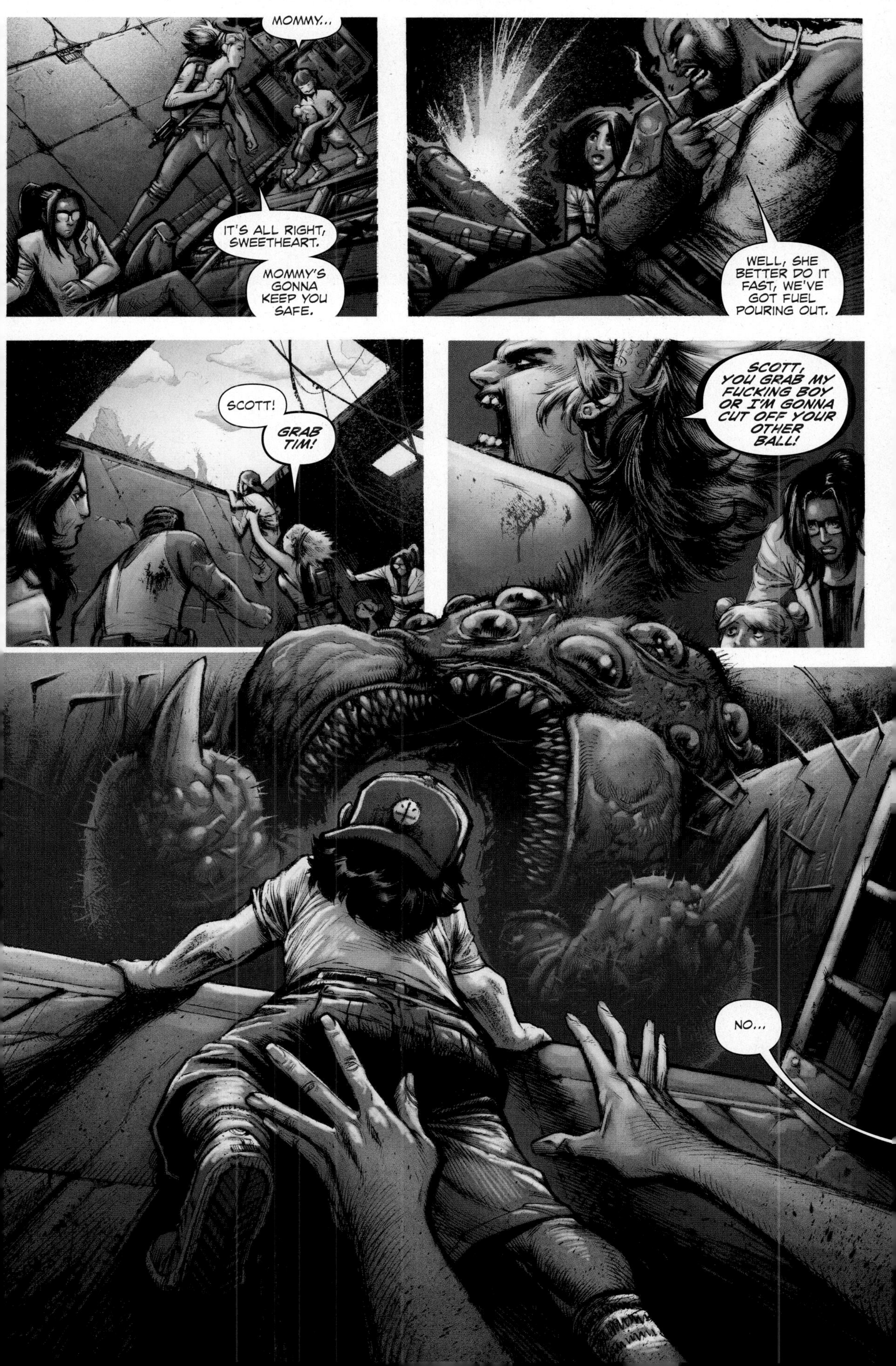
MOMMY...
IT'S ALL RIGHT, SWEETHEART.
MOMMY'S GONNA KEEP YOU SAFE.
WELL, SHE BETTER DO IT FAST, WE'VE GOT FUEL POURING OUT.
SCOTT!
GRAB TIM!
SCOTT, YOU GRAB MY FUCKING BOY OR I'M GONNA CUT OFF YOUR OTHER BALL!
NO...

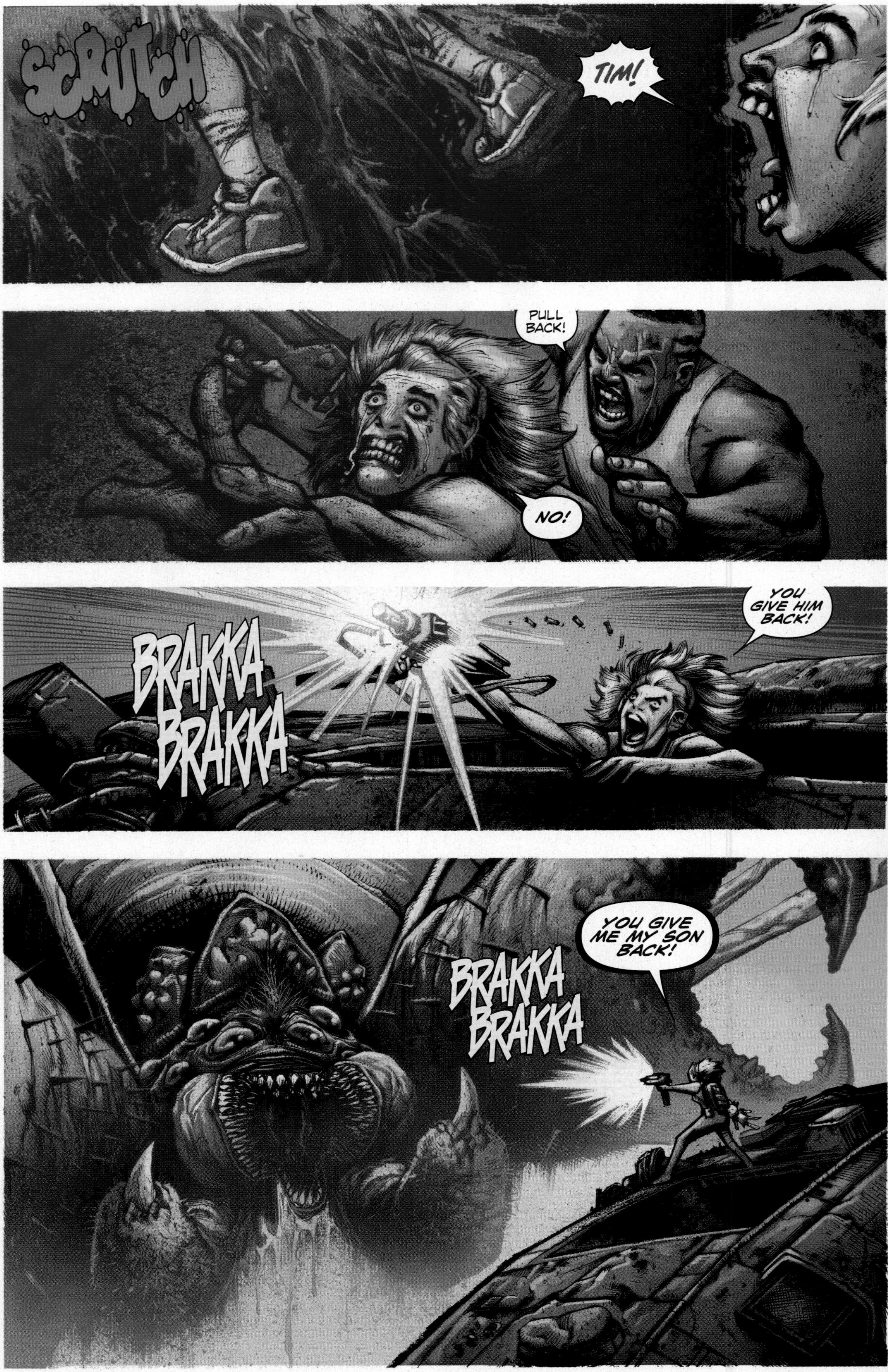
SCRUTCH
TIM!
PULL BACK!
NO!
BRAKKA BRAKKA
YOU GIVE HIM BACK!
YOU GIVE ME MY SON BACK!
BRAKKA BRAKKA

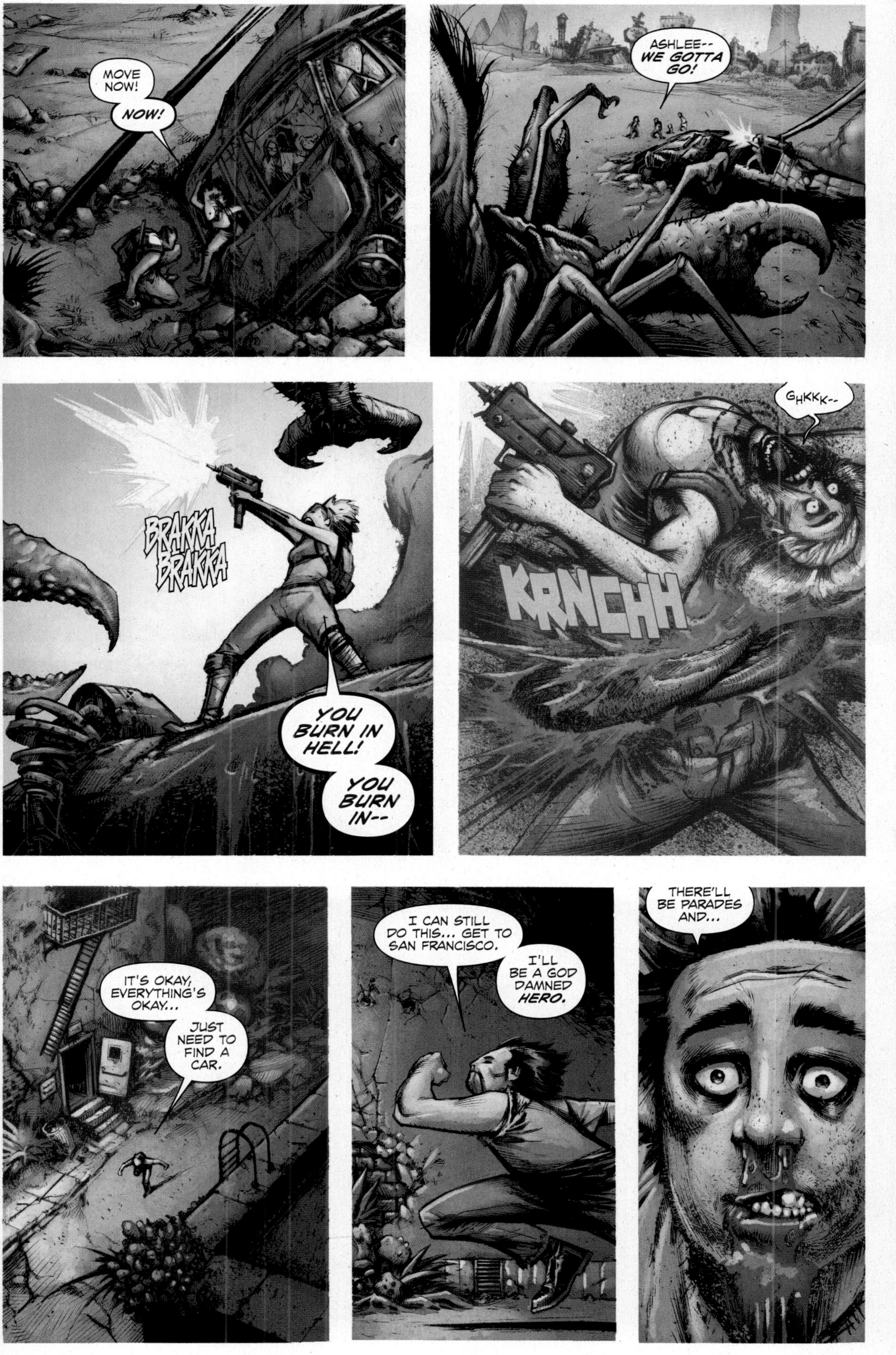
MOVE NOW!
NOW!
ASHLEE-- WE GOTTA GO!
BRAKKA BRAKKA
YOU BURN IN HELL!
YOU BURN IN--
GHKKK--
KRNCHH
IT'S OKAY, EVERYTHING'S OKAY...
JUST NEED TO FIND A CAR.
I CAN STILL DO THIS... GET TO SAN FRANCISCO.
I'LL BE A GOD DAMNED HERO.
THERE'LL BE PARADES AND...

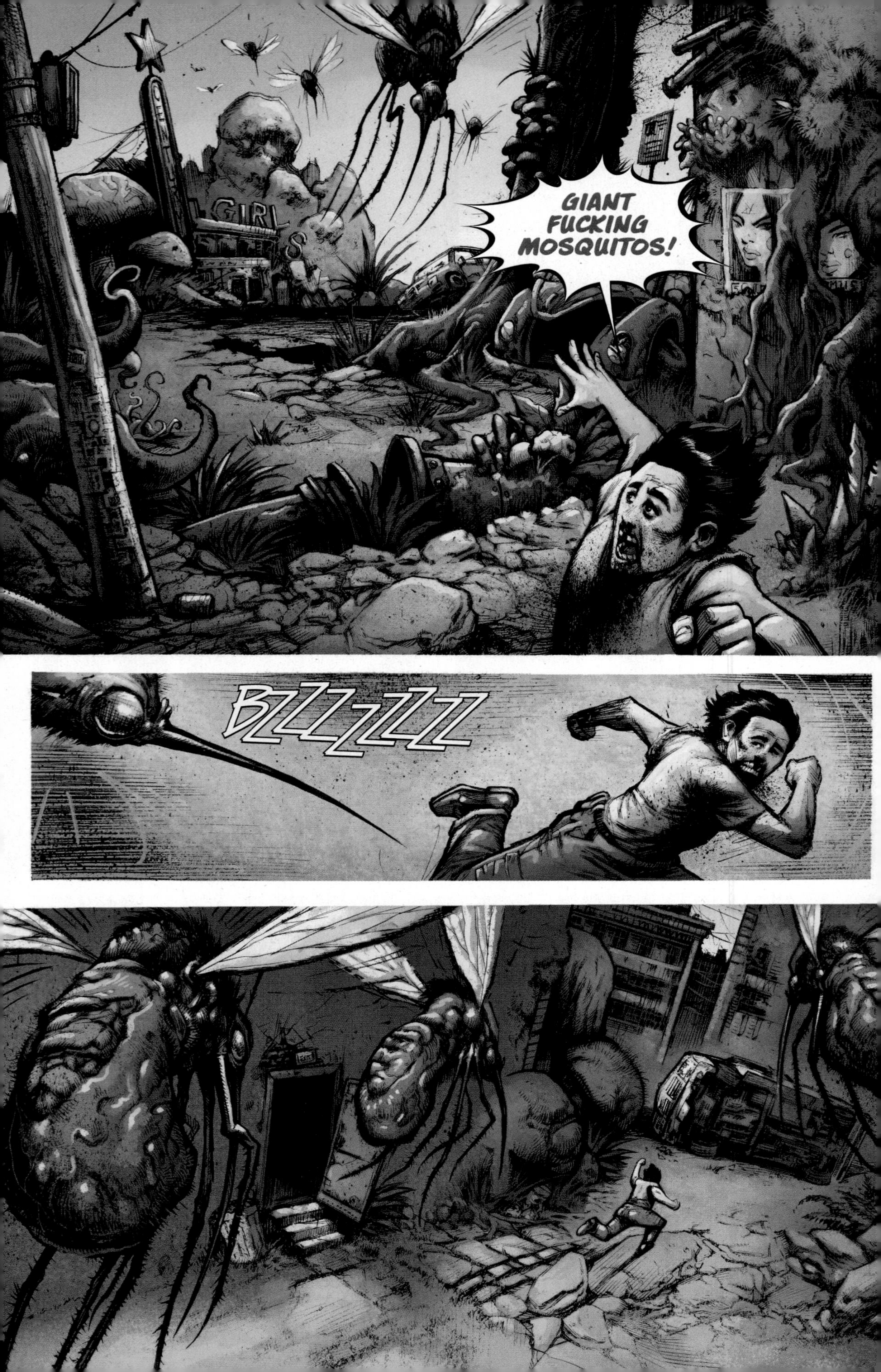
GIRLS
GIANT FUCKING MOSQUITOS!
BZZZZZZZ

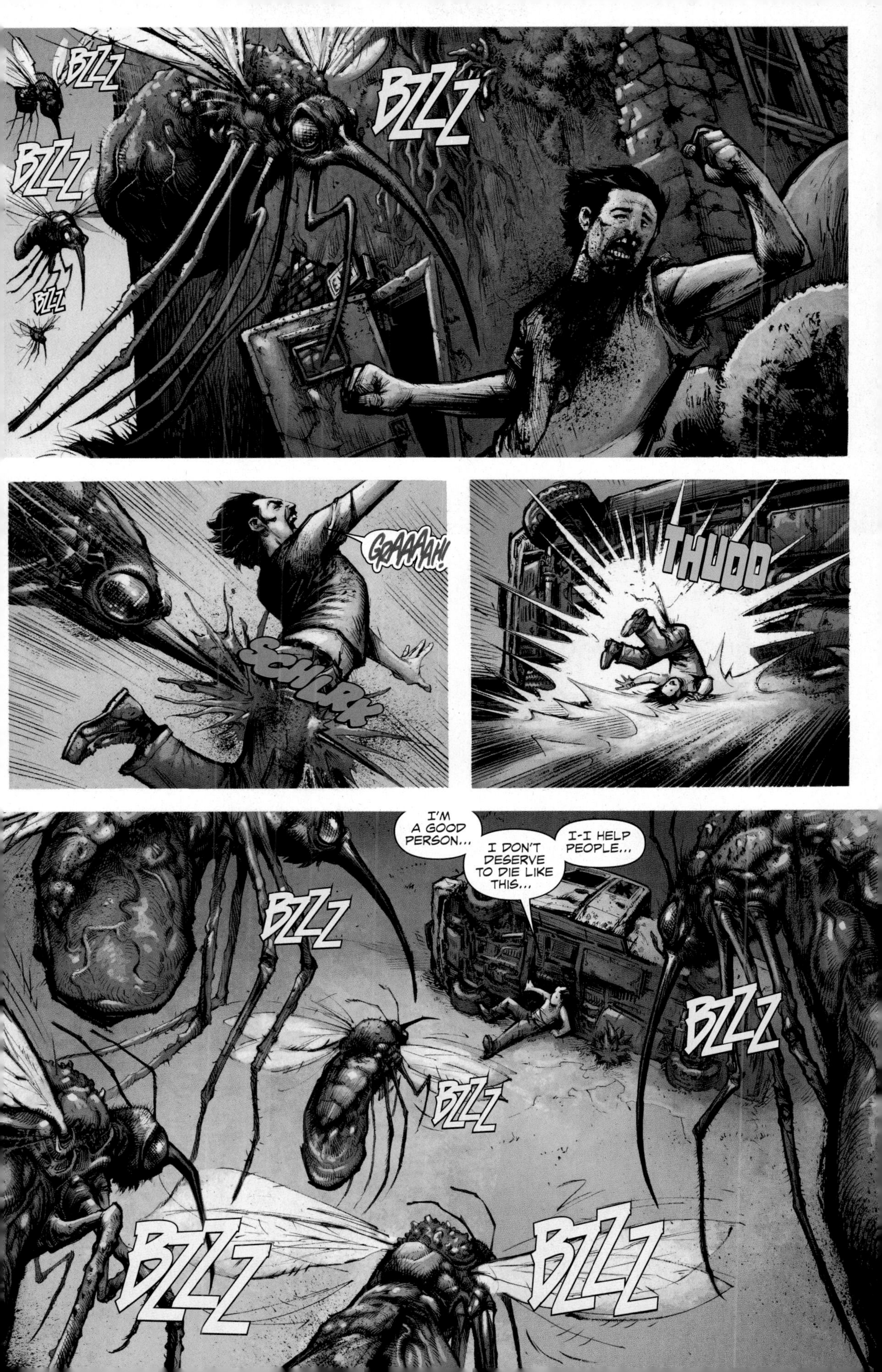
BZZZ
BZZZ
BZZZ
BZZ
GRAAAAH!
SCHLRK
THUDD
I'M A GOOD PERSON...
I DON'T DESERVE TO DIE LIKE THIS...
I-I HELP PEOPLE...
BZZZ
BZZZ
BZZZ
BZZZ
BZZZ

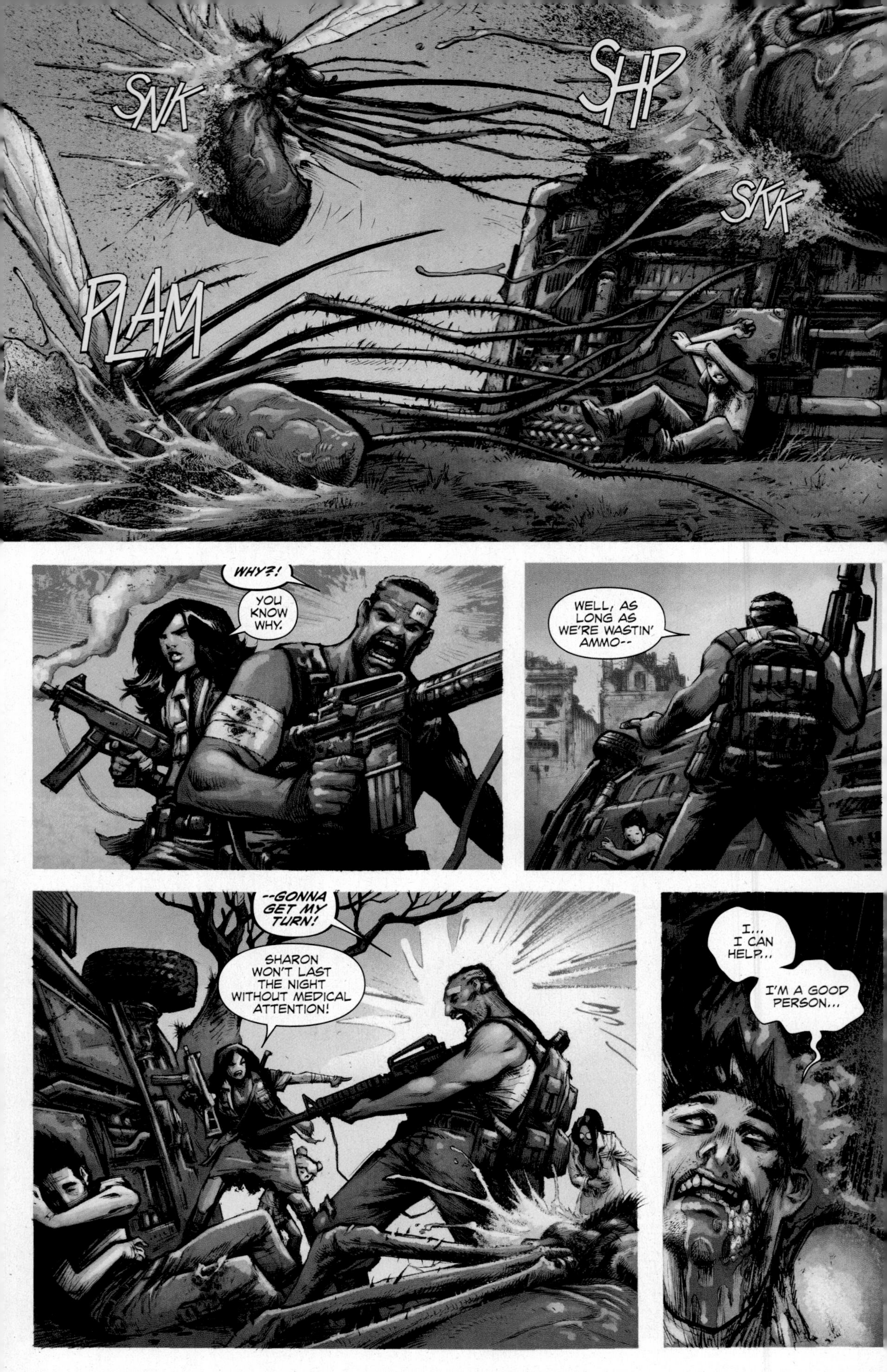

SNK
SHP
SKK
PLAM
WHY?!
YOU KNOW WHY.
WELL, AS LONG AS WE'RE WASTIN' AMMO--
--GONNA GET MY TURN!
SHARON WON'T LAST THE NIGHT WITHOUT MEDICAL ATTENTION!
I... I CAN HELP...
I'M A GOOD PERSON...

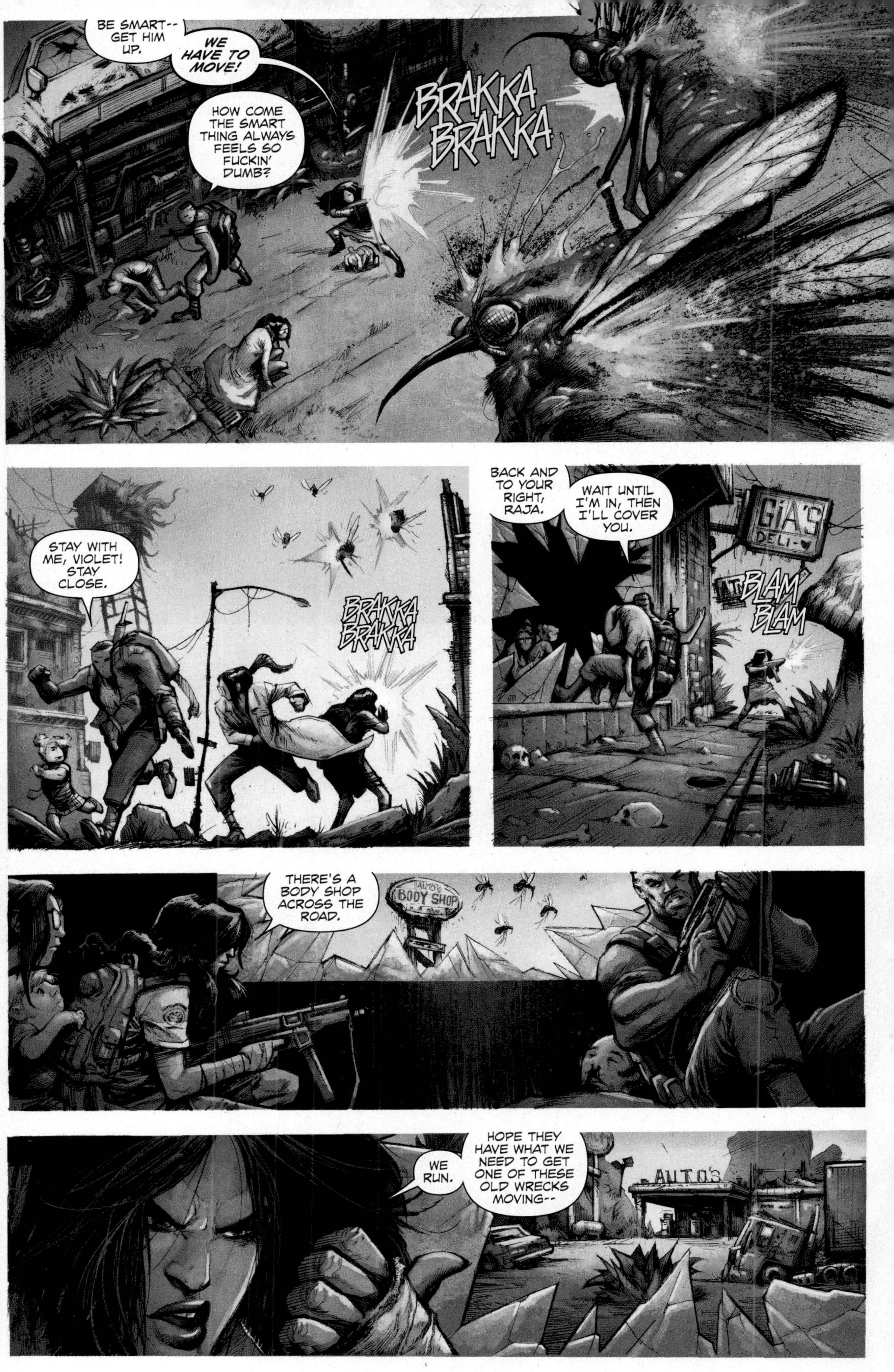
BE SMART--GET HIM UP.
WE HAVE TO MOVE!
HOW COME THE SMART THING ALWAYS FEELS SO FUCKIN' DUMB?
BRAKKA BRAKKA
STAY WITH ME, VIOLET! STAY CLOSE.
BRAKKA BRAKKA
BACK AND TO YOUR RIGHT, RAJA.
WAIT UNTIL I'M IN, THEN I'LL COVER YOU.
GIA'S DELI
BLAM BLAM
THERE'S A BODY SHOP ACROSS THE ROAD.
BODY SHOP
WE RUN.
HOPE THEY HAVE WHAT WE NEED TO GET ONE OF THESE OLD WRECKS MOVING--
AUTO'S

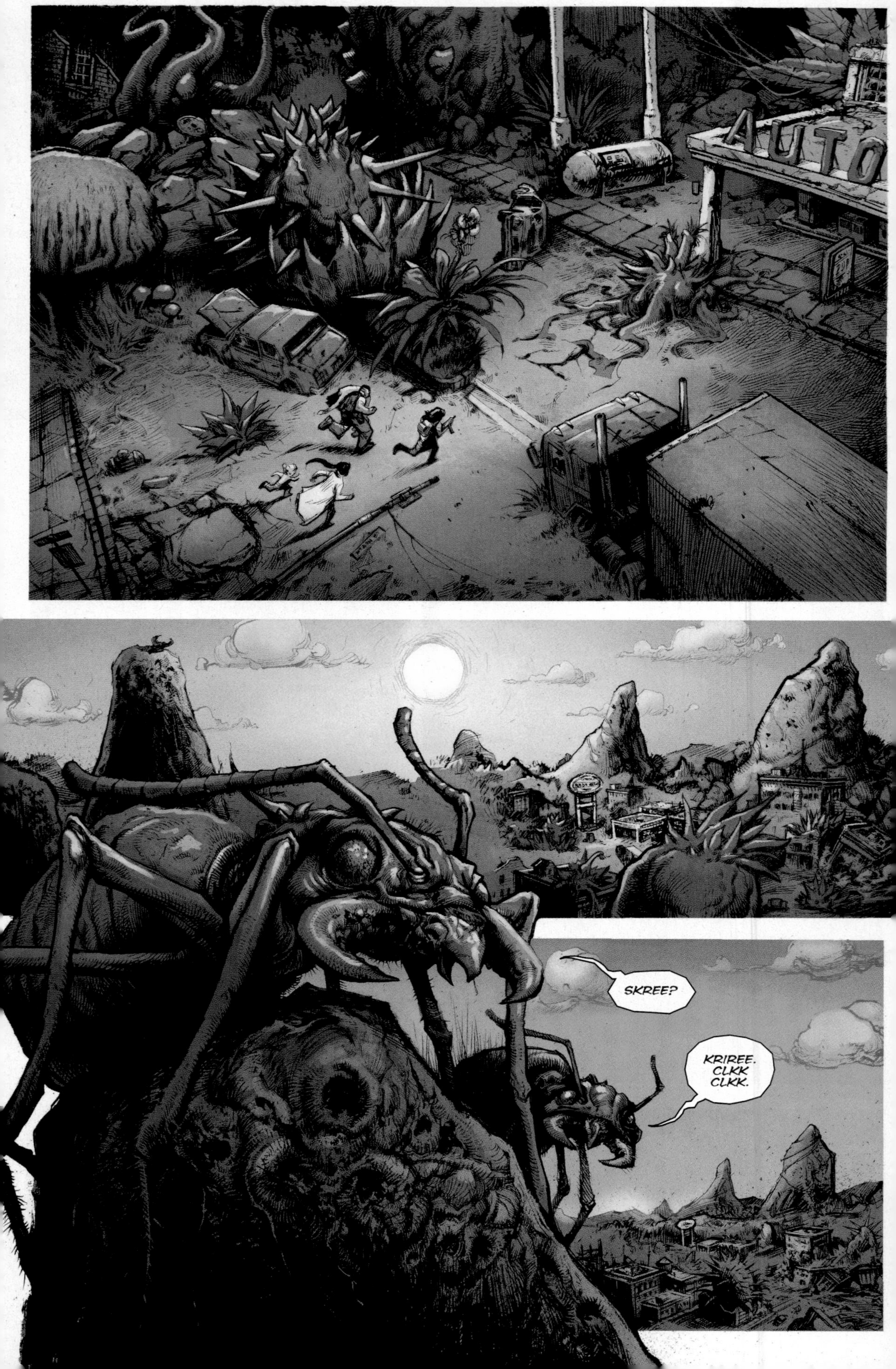
SKREE?
KRIREE. CLKK CLKK.

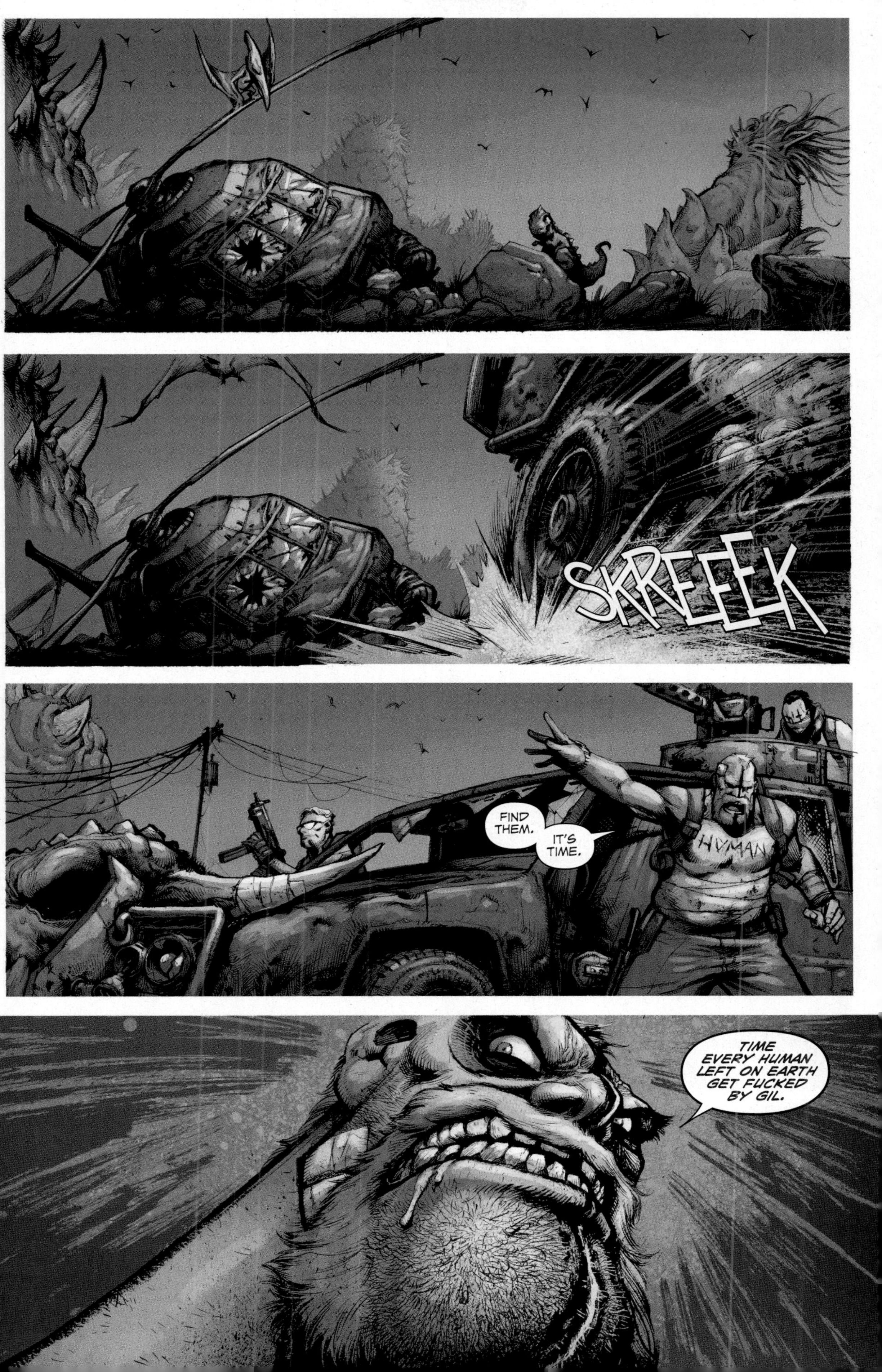
SKREEEK
FIND THEM.
IT'S TIME.
TIME EVERY HUMAN LEFT ON EARTH GET FUCKED BY GIL.

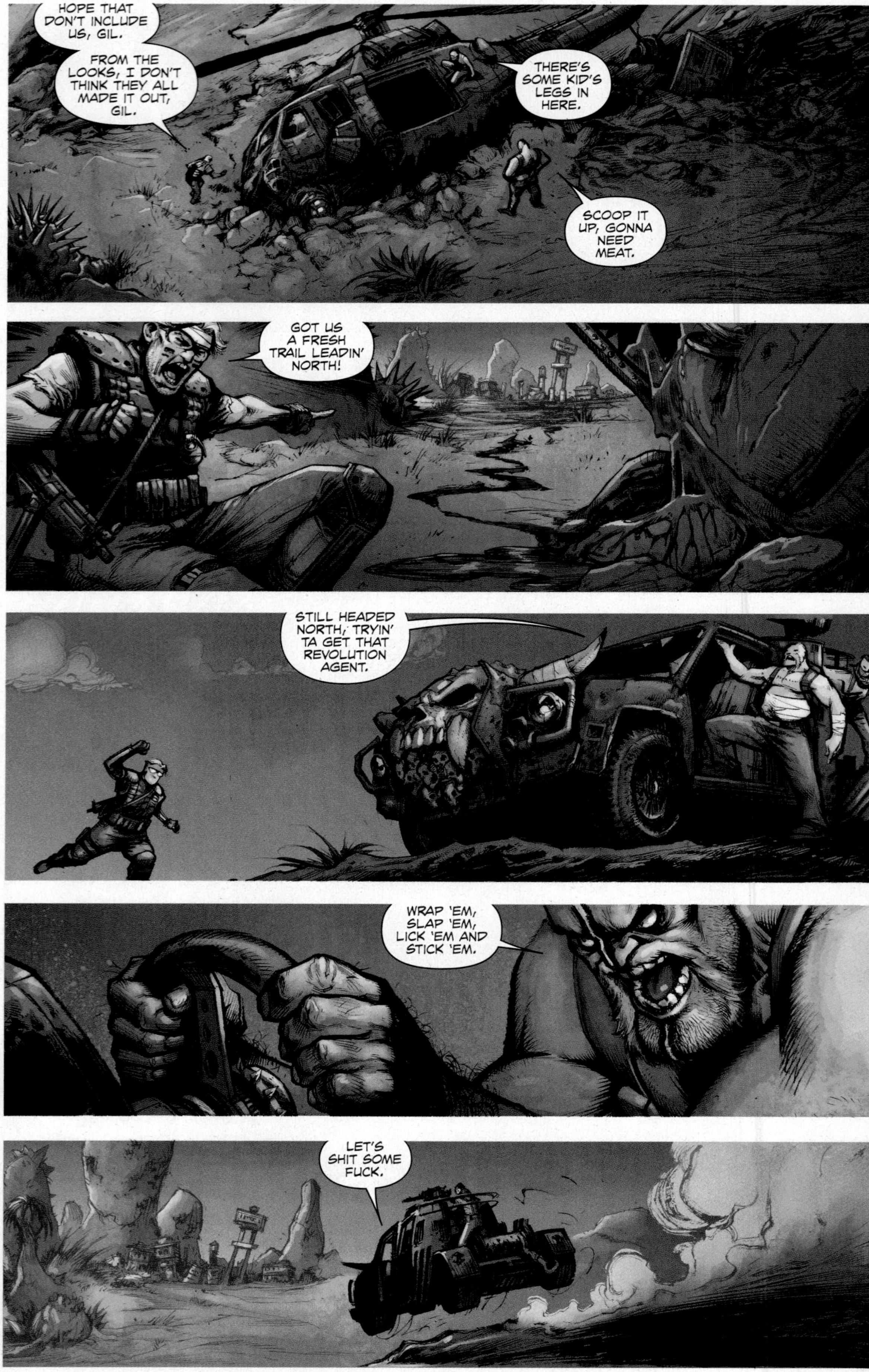
HOPE THAT DON'T INCLUDE US, GIL.
FROM THE LOOKS, I DON'T THINK THEY ALL MADE IT OUT, GIL.
THERE'S SOME KID'S LEGS IN HERE.
SCOOP IT UP, GONNA NEED MEAT.
GOT US A FRESH TRAIL LEADIN' NORTH!
STILL HEADED NORTH, TRYIN' TA GET THAT REVOLUTION AGENT.
WRAP 'EM, SLAP 'EM, LICK 'EM AND STICK 'EM.
LET'S SHIT SOME FUCK.

Issue 4 Cover by JAE LEE With Colors by JUNE CHUNG

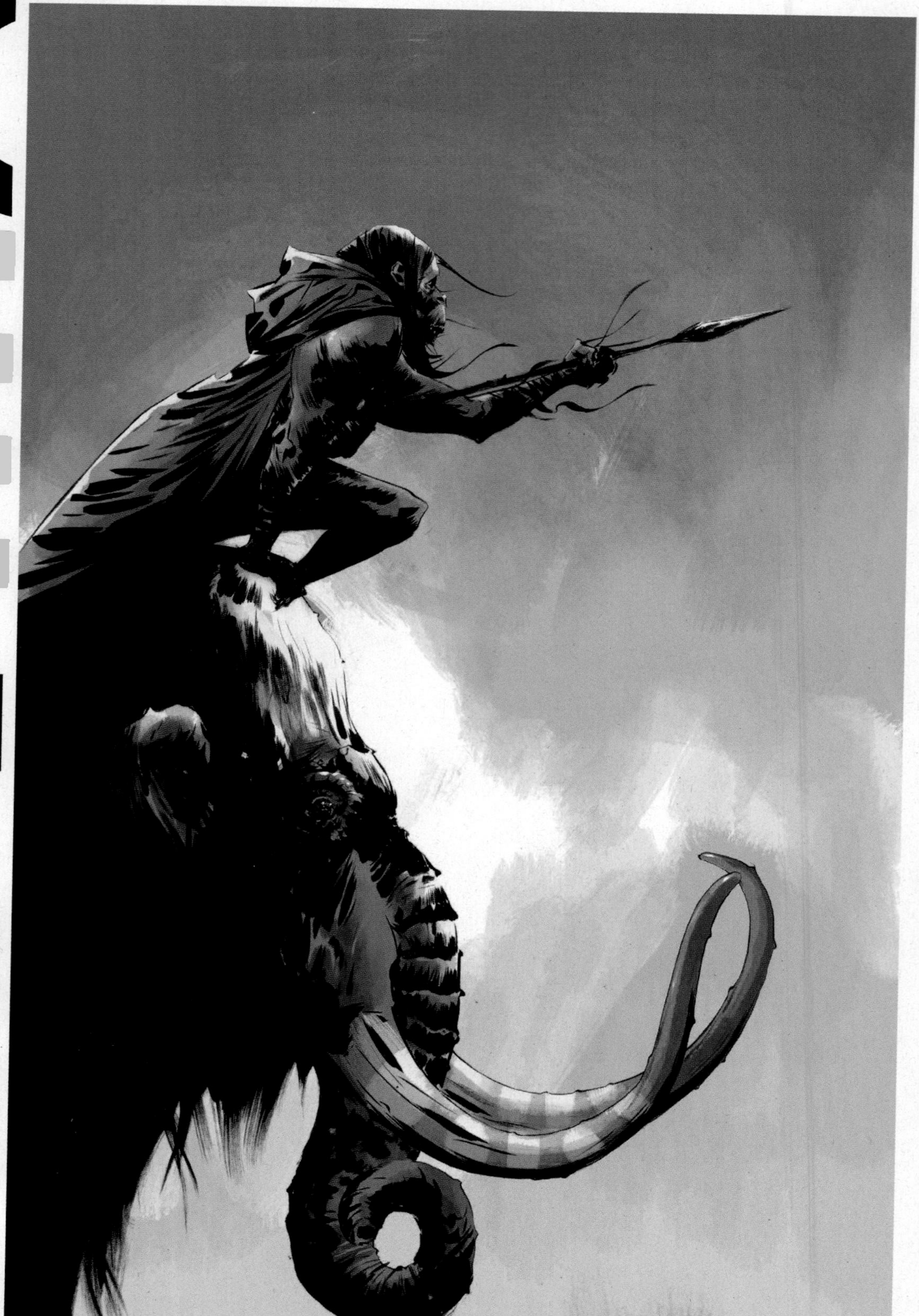

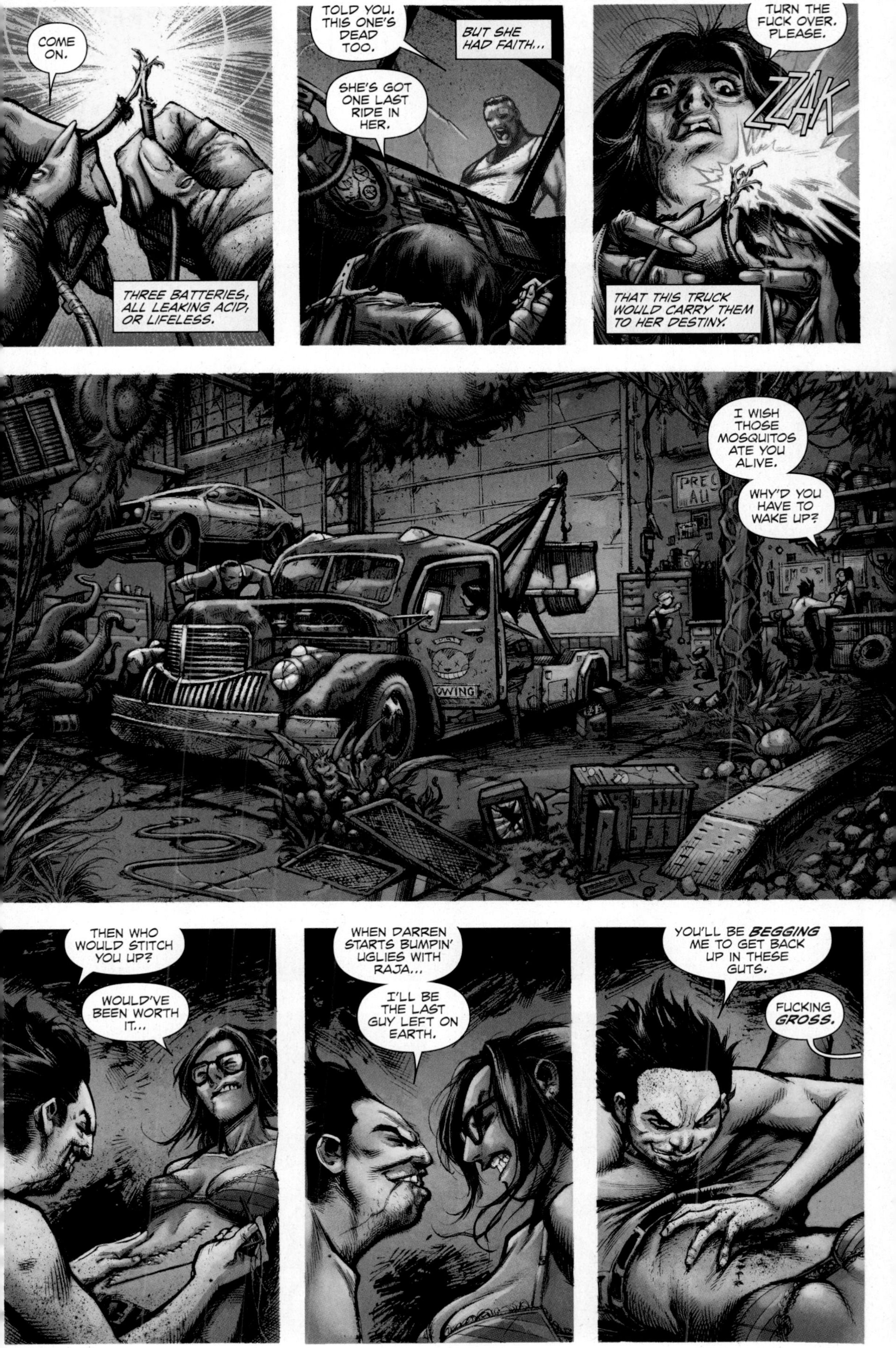
COME ON.
THREE BATTERIES, ALL LEAKING ACID, OR LIFELESS.
TOLD YOU. THIS ONE'S DEAD TOO.
BUT SHE HAD FAITH...
SHE'S GOT ONE LAST RIDE IN HER.
TURN THE FUCK OVER. PLEASE.
ZZAK
THAT THIS TRUCK WOULD CARRY THEM TO HER DESTINY.
I WISH THOSE MOSQUITOS ATE YOU ALIVE.
WHY'D YOU HAVE TO WAKE UP?
TOWING
THEN WHO WOULD STITCH YOU UP?
WOULD'VE BEEN WORTH IT...
WHEN DARREN STARTS BUMPIN' UGLIES WITH RAJA...
I'LL BE THE LAST GUY LEFT ON EARTH.
YOU'LL BE *BEGGING* ME TO GET BACK UP IN THESE GUTS.
FUCKING *GROSS.*

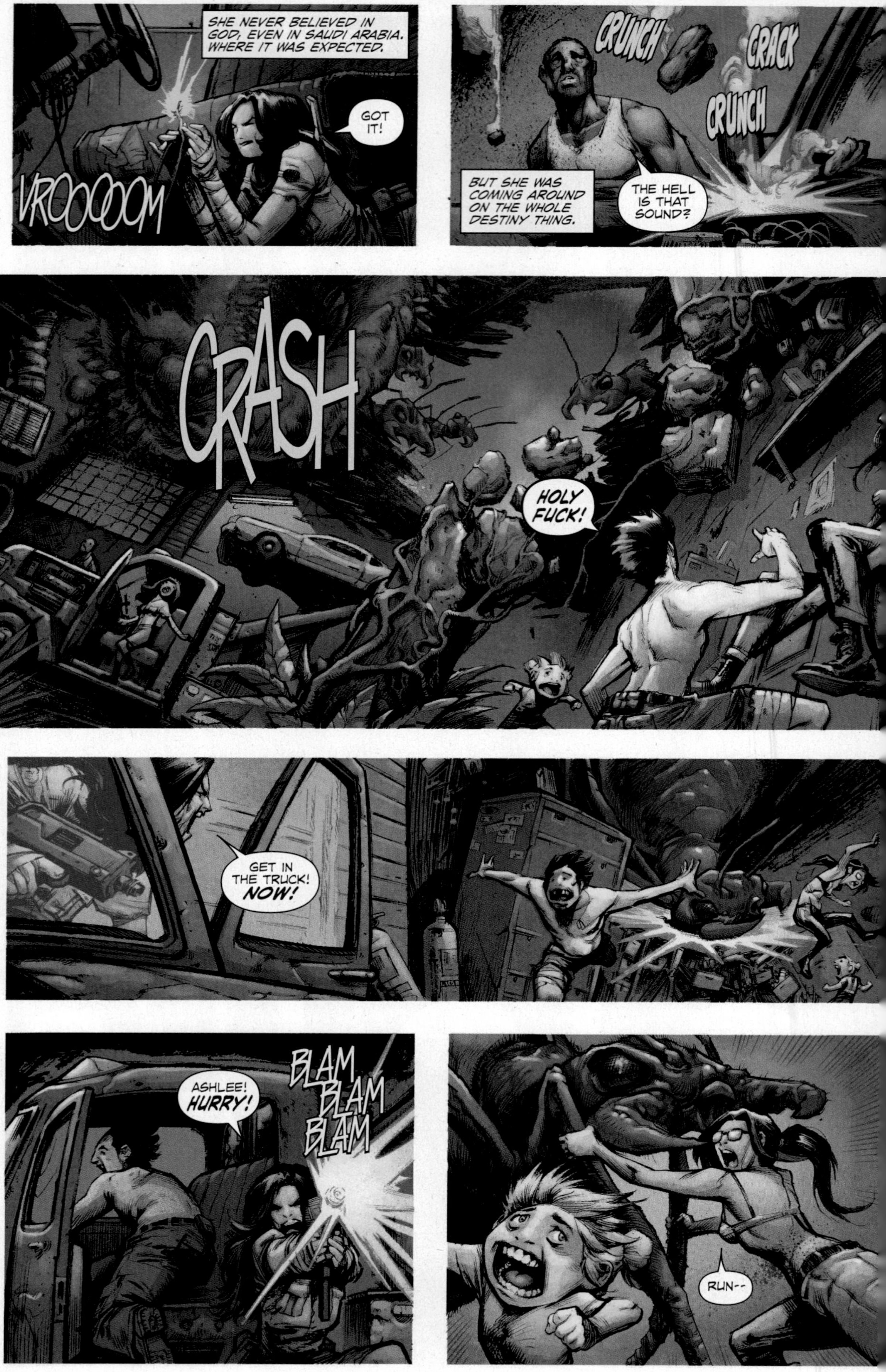
SHE NEVER BELIEVED IN GOD, EVEN IN SAUDI ARABIA. WHERE IT WAS EXPECTED.
GOT IT!
VROOOOOOM
CRUNCH
CRACK
CRUNCH
BUT SHE WAS COMING AROUND ON THE WHOLE DESTINY THING.
THE HELL IS THAT SOUND?
CRASH
HOLY FUCK!
GET IN THE TRUCK! NOW!
ASHLEE! HURRY!
BLAM BLAM BLAM
RUN--

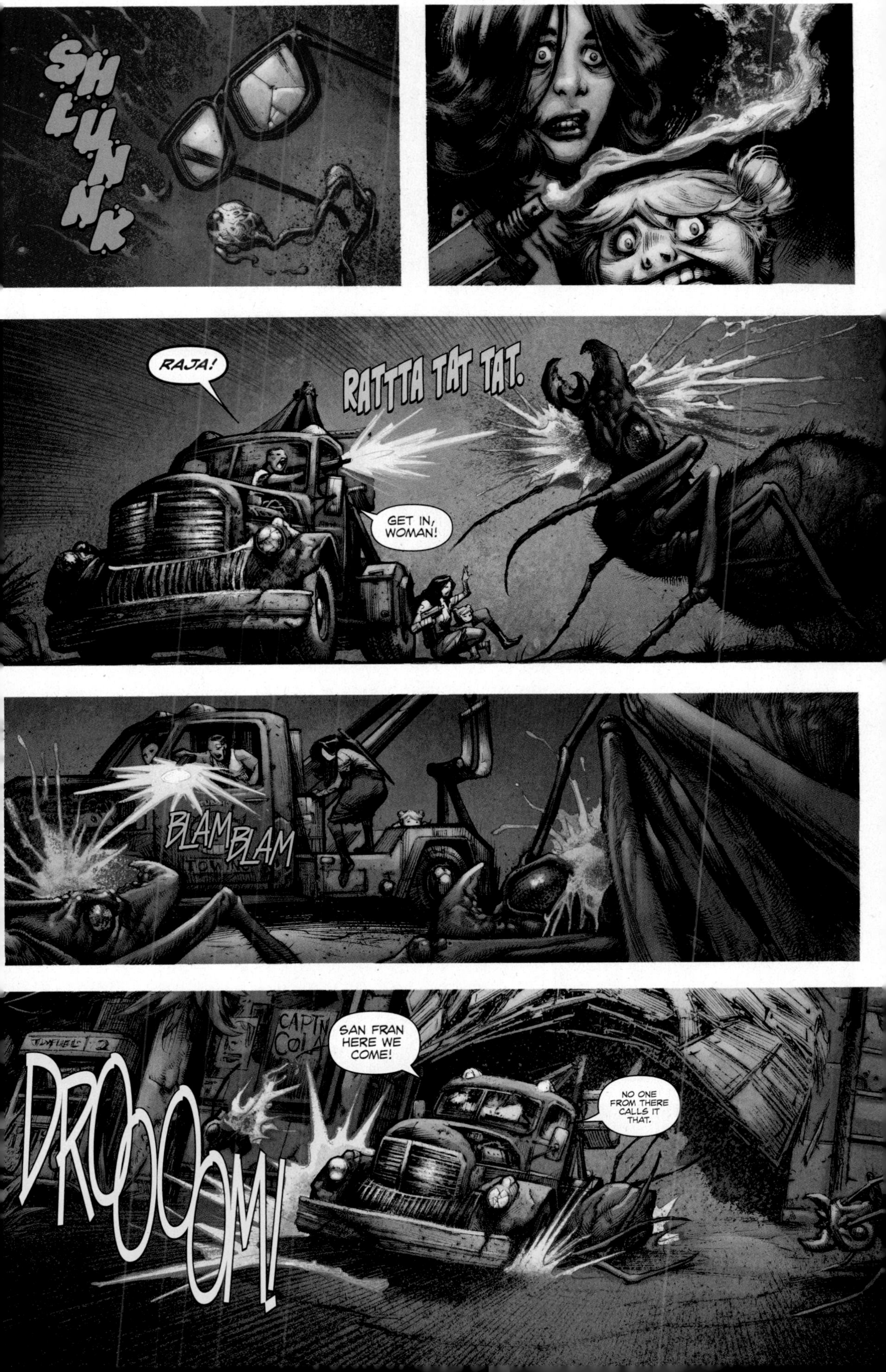
SHLUNNK
RAJA!
RATTTA TAT TAT.
GET IN, WOMAN!
BLAM BLAM
DROOOOOM!
SAN FRAN HERE WE COME!
NO ONE FROM THERE CALLS IT THAT.

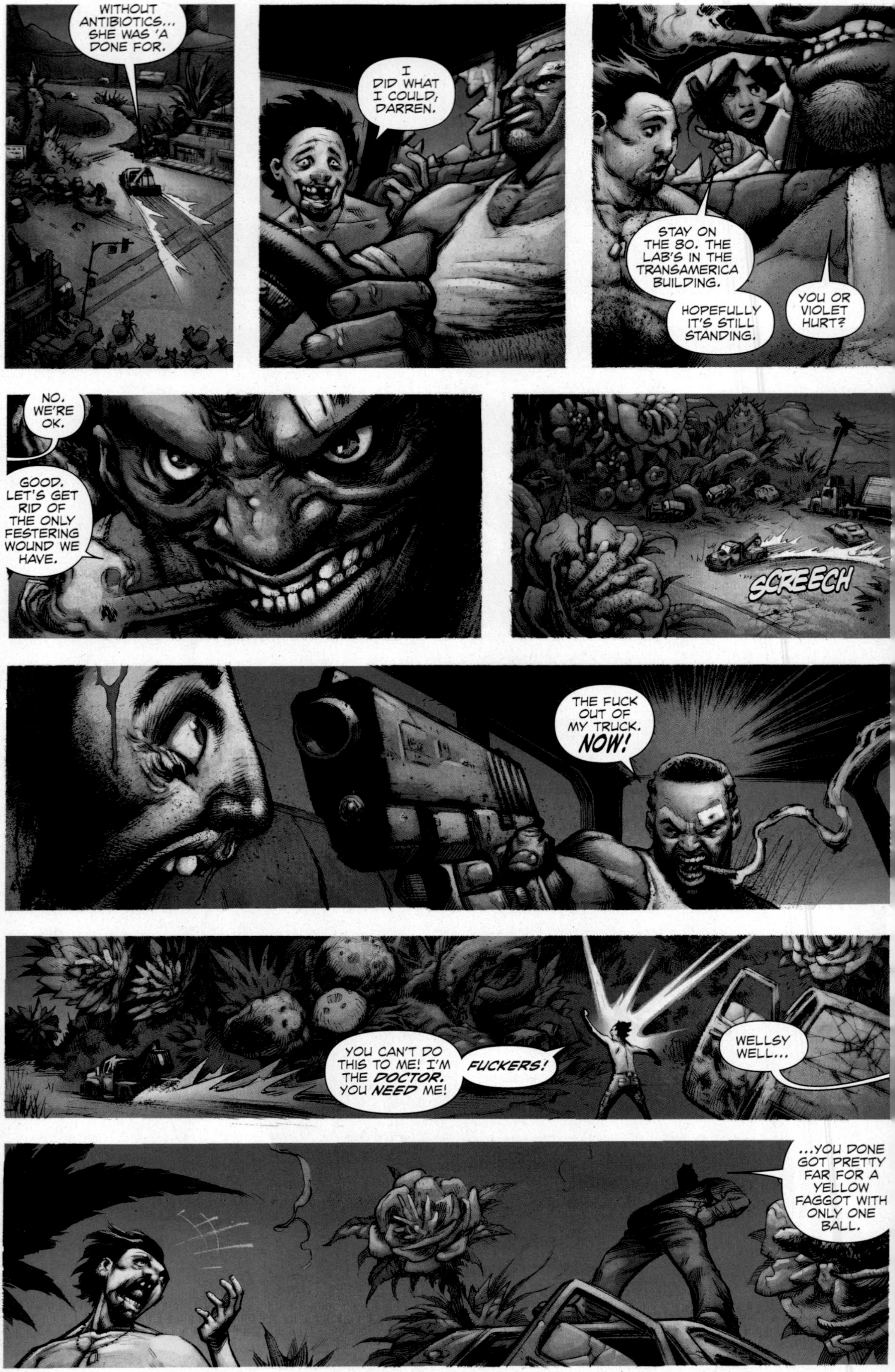
WITHOUT ANTIBIOTICS... SHE WAS 'A DONE FOR.
I DID WHAT I COULD, DARREN.
STAY ON THE 80. THE LAB'S IN THE TRANSAMERICA BUILDING.
HOPEFULLY IT'S STILL STANDING.
YOU OR VIOLET HURT?
NO. WE'RE OK.
GOOD. LET'S GET RID OF THE ONLY FESTERING WOUND WE HAVE.
SCREECH
THE FUCK OUT OF MY TRUCK. NOW!
YOU CAN'T DO THIS TO ME! I'M THE DOCTOR. YOU NEED ME!
FUCKERS!
WELLSY WELL...
...YOU DONE GOT PRETTY FAR FOR A YELLOW FAGGOT WITH ONLY ONE BALL.

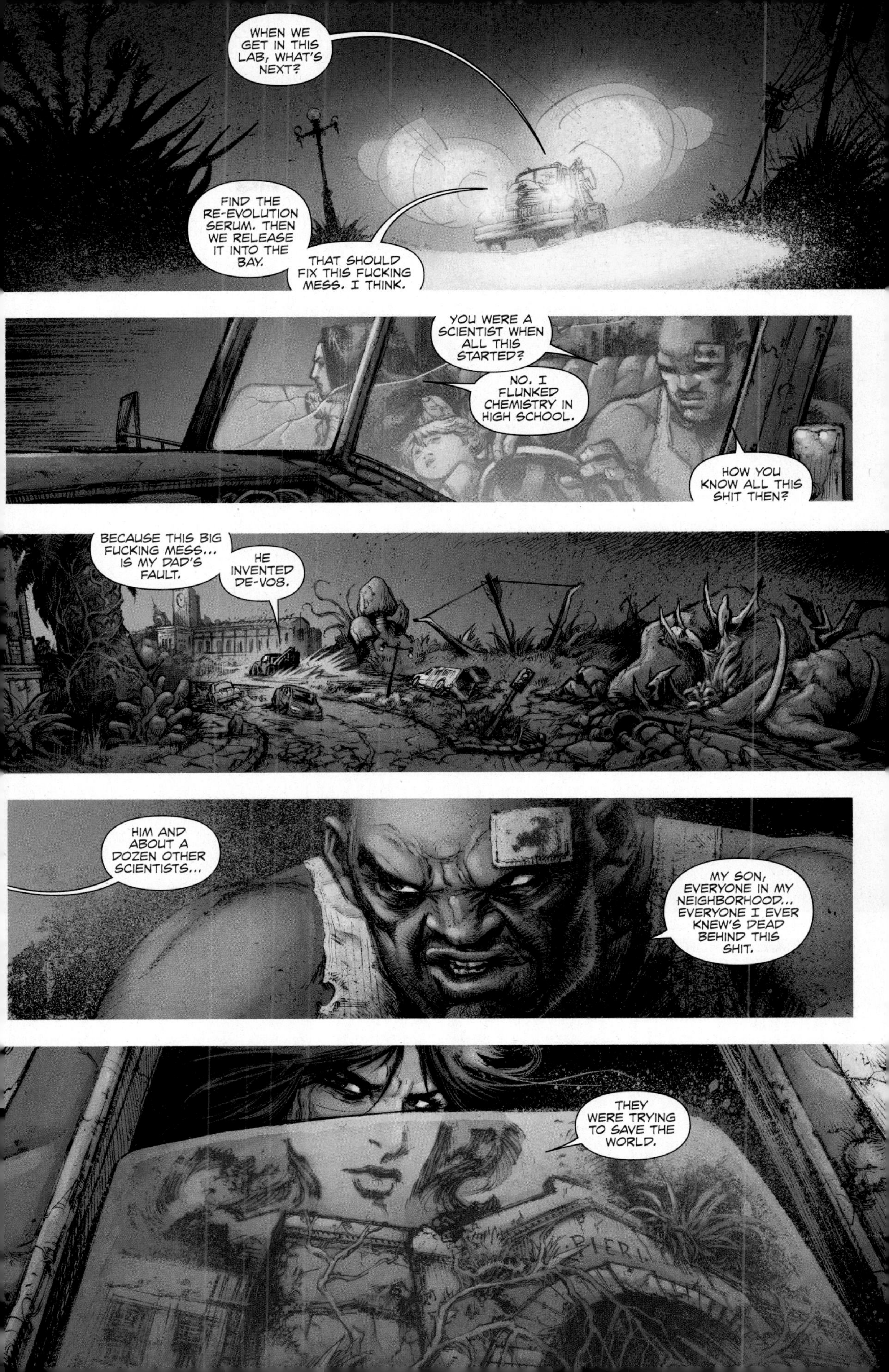
WHEN WE GET IN THIS LAB, WHAT'S NEXT?
FIND THE RE-EVOLUTION SERUM. THEN WE RELEASE IT INTO THE BAY.
THAT SHOULD FIX THIS FUCKING MESS. I THINK.
YOU WERE A SCIENTIST WHEN ALL THIS STARTED?
NO. I FLUNKED CHEMISTRY IN HIGH SCHOOL.
HOW YOU KNOW ALL THIS SHIT THEN?
BECAUSE THIS BIG FUCKING MESS... IS MY DAD'S FAULT.
HE INVENTED DE-VO8.
HIM AND ABOUT A DOZEN OTHER SCIENTISTS...
MY SON, EVERYONE IN MY NEIGHBORHOOD... EVERYONE I EVER KNEW'S DEAD BEHIND THIS SHIT.
THEY WERE TRYING TO SAVE THE WORLD.

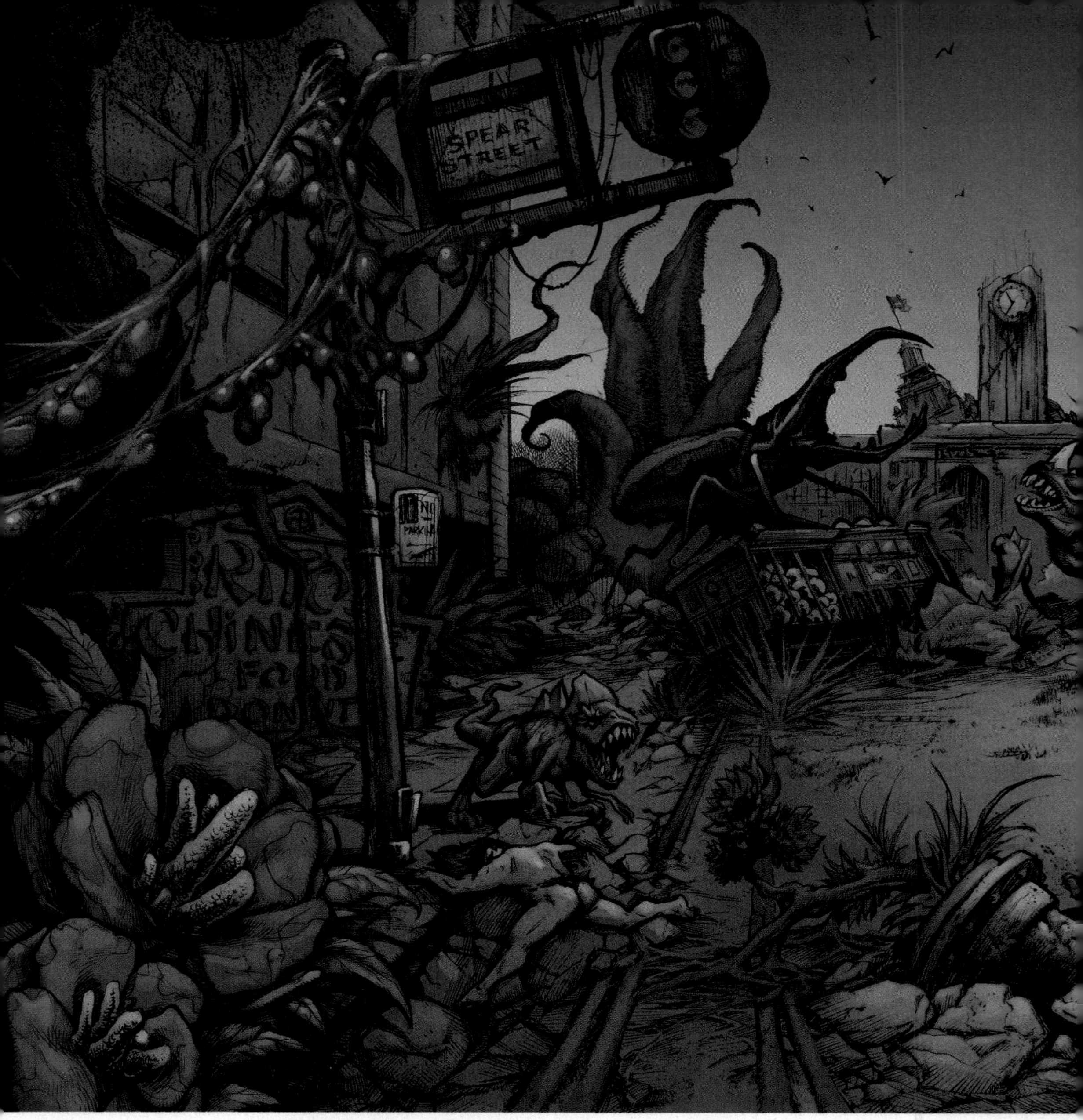
SPEAR STREET

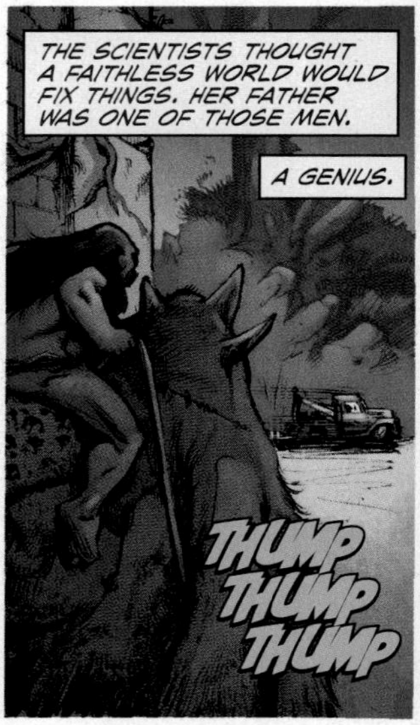
THE SCIENTISTS THOUGHT A FAITHLESS WORLD WOULD FIX THINGS. HER FATHER WAS ONE OF THOSE MEN.
A GENIUS.
THUMP THUMP THUMP

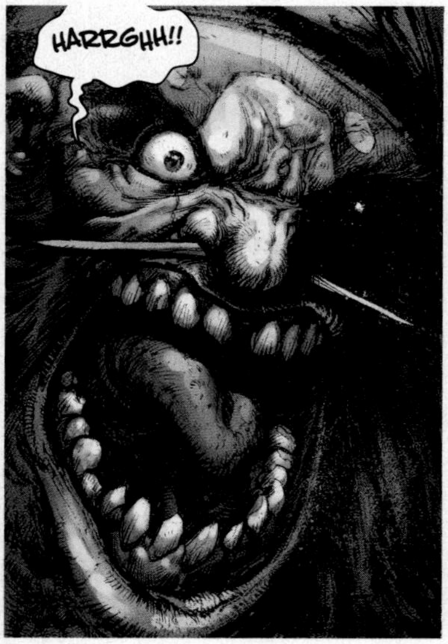
HARRGHH!!

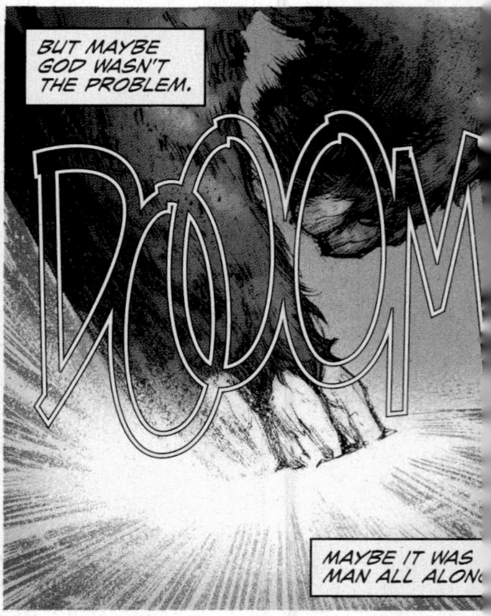
BUT MAYBE GOD WASN'T THE PROBLEM.
DOOOM
MAYBE IT WAS MAN ALL ALON

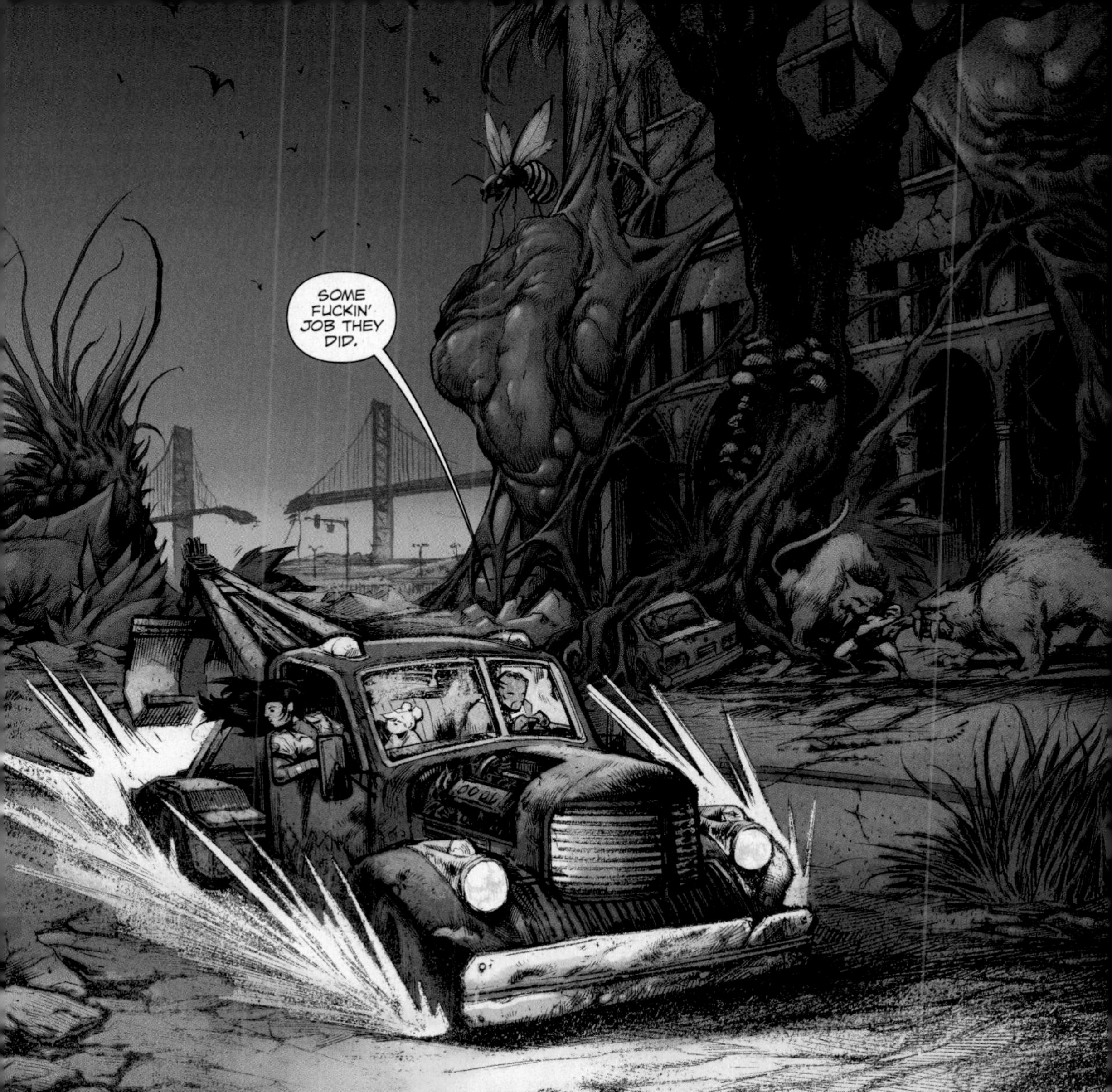
SOME FUCKIN' JOB THEY DID.

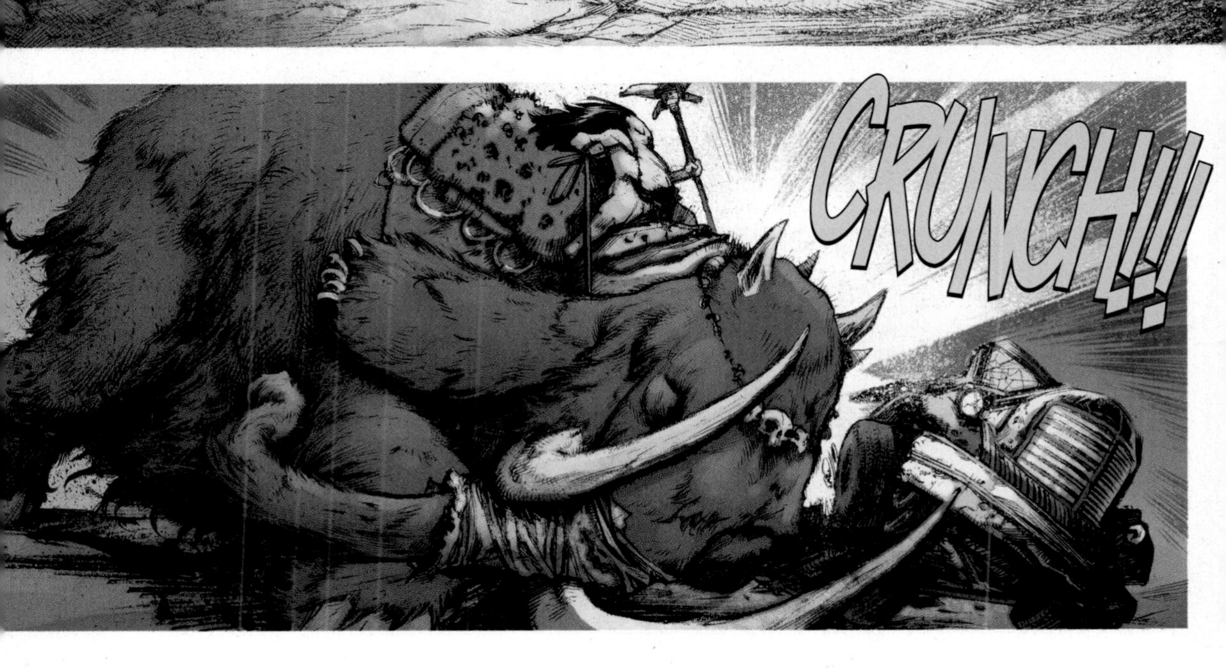
CRUNCH!!!

HUGH NAFF?

SHUNK!

DUMB QUESTION, BUT YOU OK, SWEETHEART?

I'M OK.

STAY CLOSE, OK?

THAT'S MY BRAVE GIRL.

SSSSSSSSSSSSSS

VIOLET!

RIIIIP

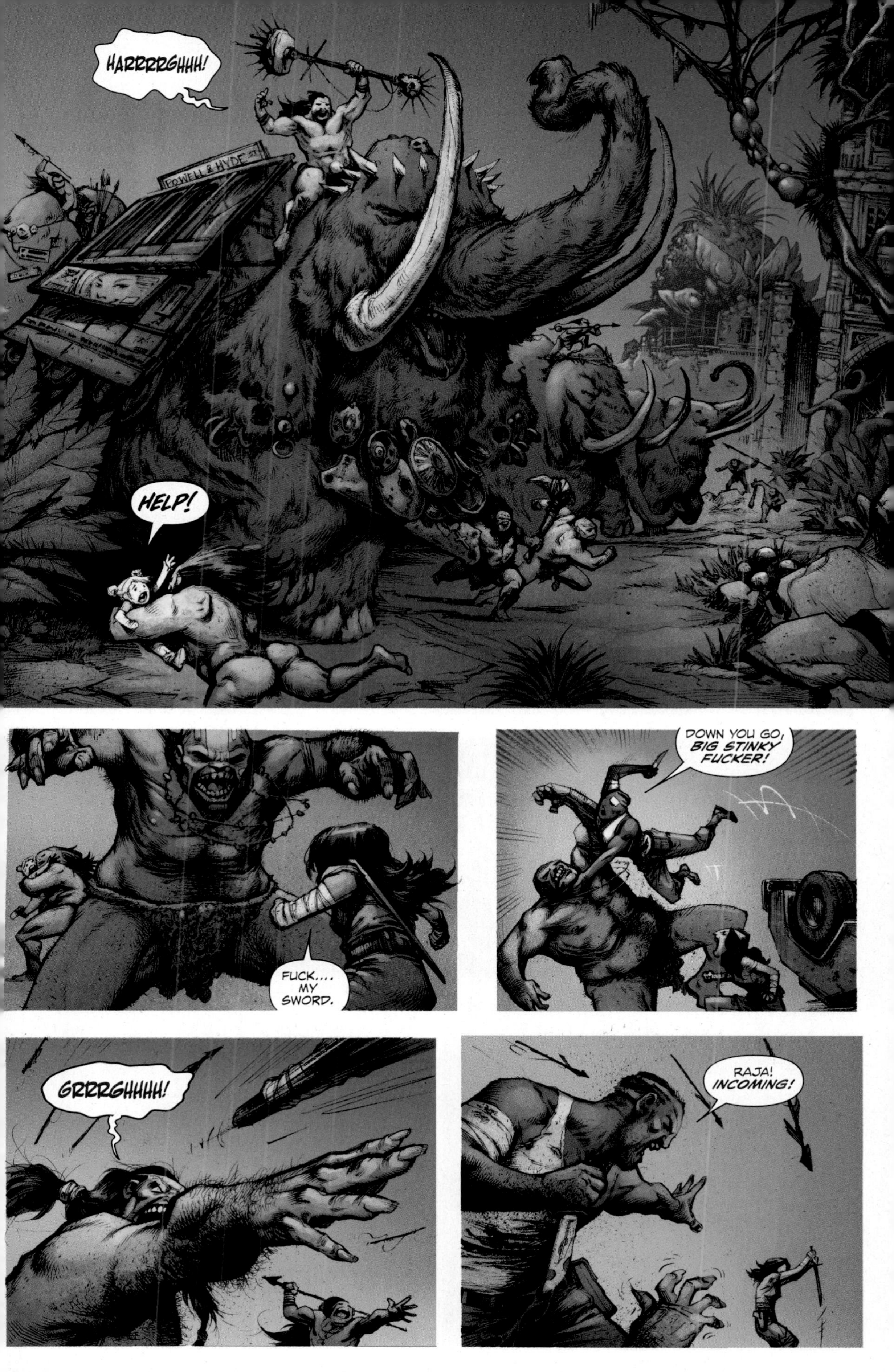
HARRRRGHHH!
POWELL & HYDE
HELP!
FUCK.... MY SWORD.
DOWN YOU GO, BIG STINKY FUCKER!
GRRRGHHHH!
RAJA! INCOMING!

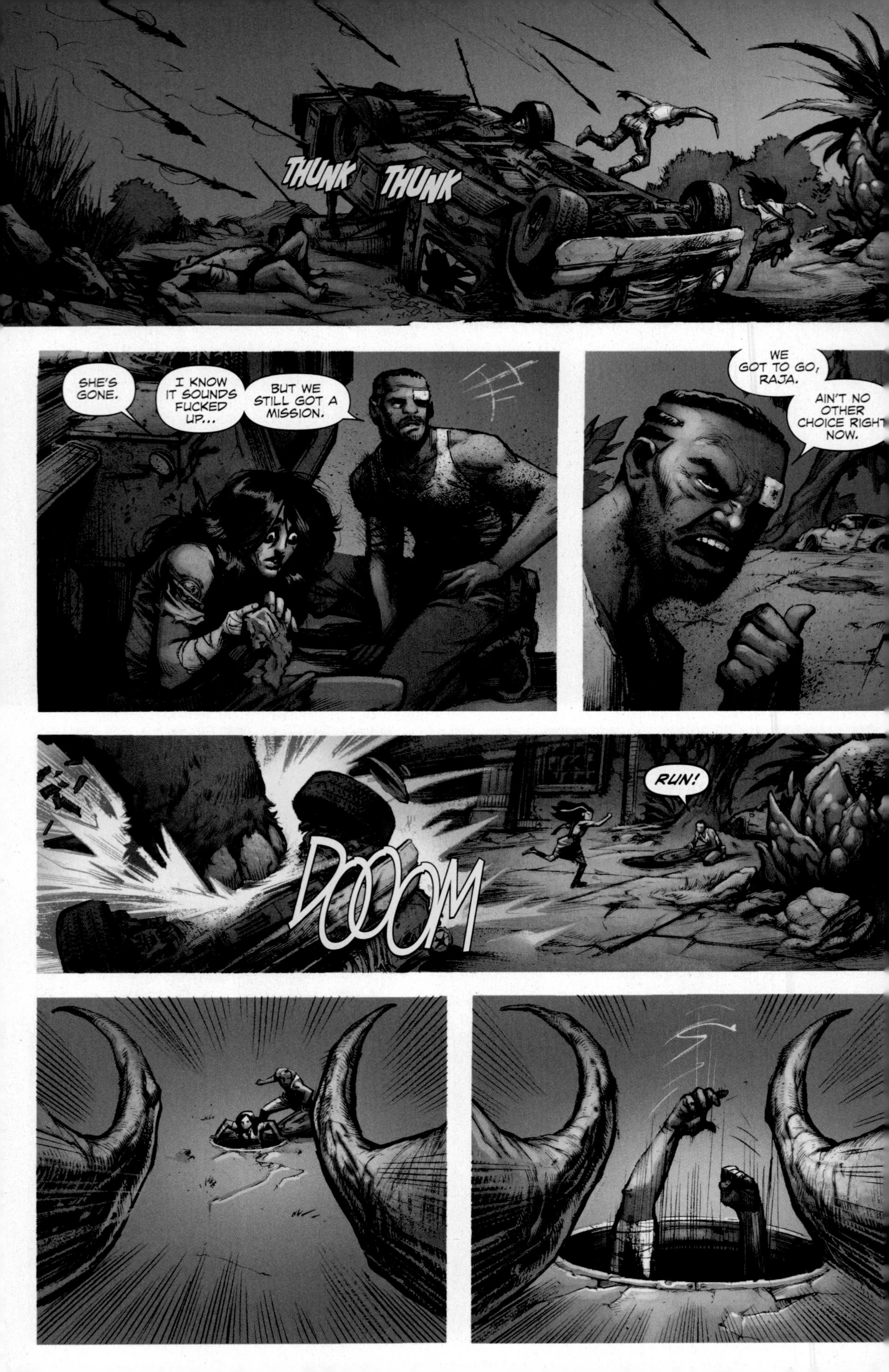

THUNK
THUNK
SHE'S GONE.
I KNOW IT SOUNDS FUCKED UP...
BUT WE STILL GOT A MISSION.
WE GOT TO GO, RAJA.
AIN'T NO OTHER CHOICE RIGHT NOW.
DOOOM
RUN!

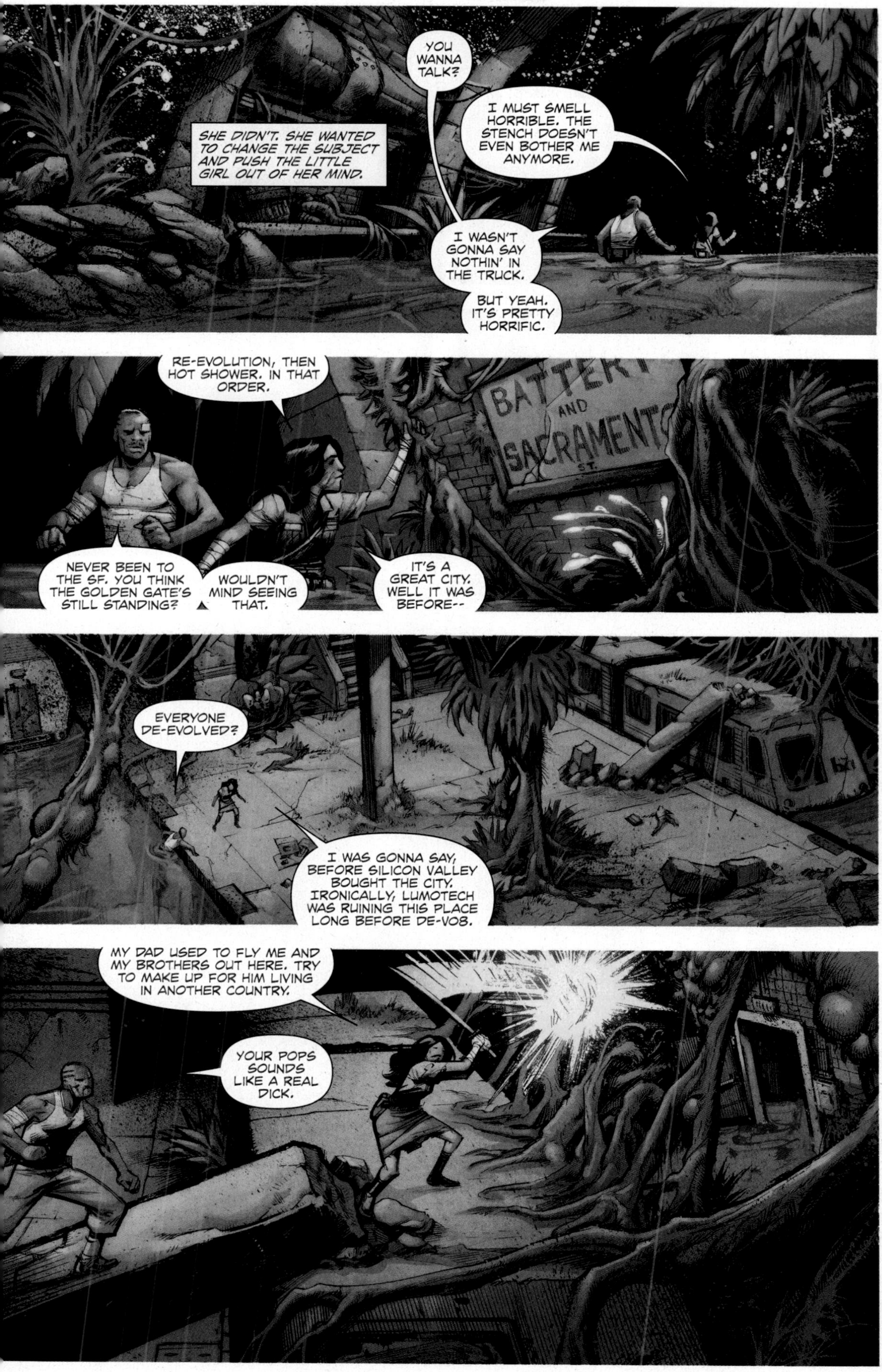
SHE DIDN'T. SHE WANTED TO CHANGE THE SUBJECT AND PUSH THE LITTLE GIRL OUT OF HER MIND.
YOU WANNA TALK?
I MUST SMELL HORRIBLE. THE STENCH DOESN'T EVEN BOTHER ME ANYMORE.
I WASN'T GONNA SAY NOTHIN' IN THE TRUCK.
BUT YEAH. IT'S PRETTY HORRIFIC.
RE-EVOLUTION, THEN HOT SHOWER. IN THAT ORDER.
BATTERY AND SACRAMENTO ST.
NEVER BEEN TO THE SF. YOU THINK THE GOLDEN GATE'S STILL STANDING?
WOULDN'T MIND SEEING THAT.
IT'S A GREAT CITY. WELL IT WAS BEFORE--
EVERYONE DE-EVOLVED?
I WAS GONNA SAY, BEFORE SILICON VALLEY BOUGHT THE CITY. IRONICALLY, LUMOTECH WAS RUINING THIS PLACE LONG BEFORE DE-VO8.
MY DAD USED TO FLY ME AND MY BROTHERS OUT HERE. TRY TO MAKE UP FOR HIM LIVING IN ANOTHER COUNTRY.
YOUR POPS SOUNDS LIKE A REAL DICK.

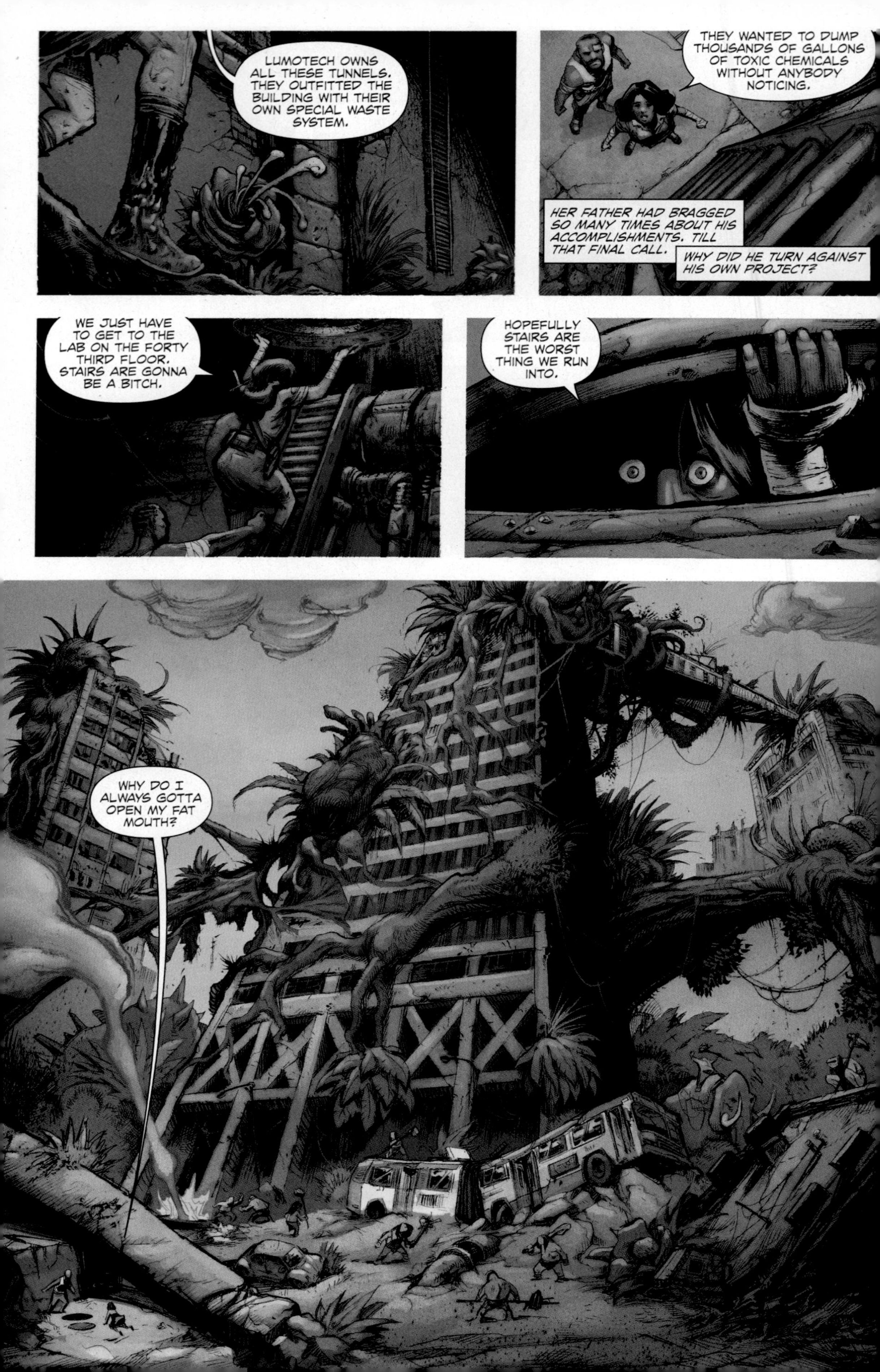
LUMOTECH OWNS ALL THESE TUNNELS. THEY OUTFITTED THE BUILDING WITH THEIR OWN SPECIAL WASTE SYSTEM.
THEY WANTED TO DUMP THOUSANDS OF GALLONS OF TOXIC CHEMICALS WITHOUT ANYBODY NOTICING.
HER FATHER HAD BRAGGED SO MANY TIMES ABOUT HIS ACCOMPLISHMENTS. TILL THAT FINAL CALL.
WHY DID HE TURN AGAINST HIS OWN PROJECT?
WE JUST HAVE TO GET TO THE LAB ON THE FORTY THIRD FLOOR. STAIRS ARE GONNA BE A BITCH.
HOPEFULLY STAIRS ARE THE WORST THING WE RUN INTO.
WHY DO I ALWAYS GOTTA OPEN MY FAT MOUTH?

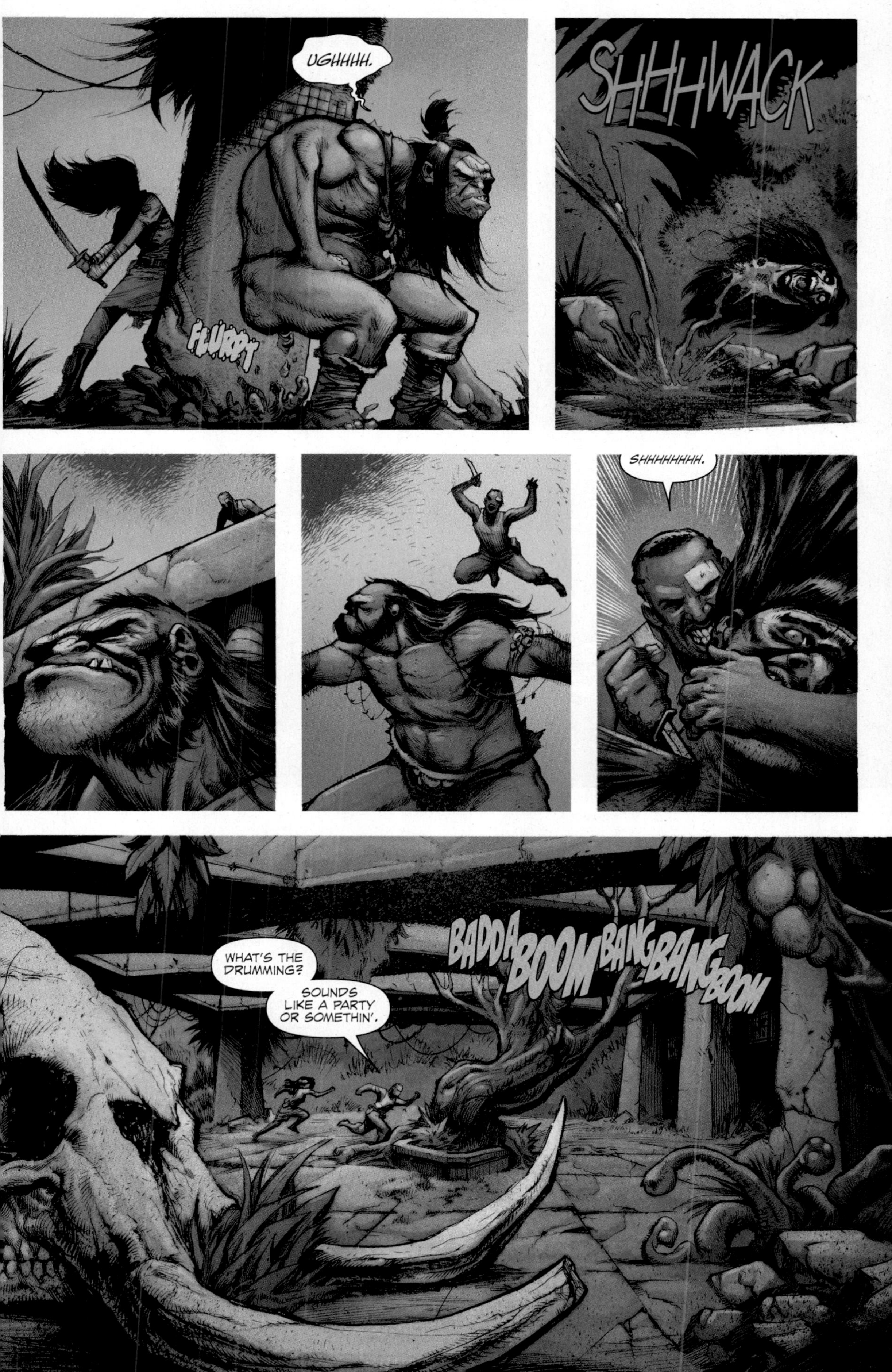
UGHHHH.
FLURPT
SHHHWACK
SHHHHHHHH.
BADDA BOOM BANG BANG BOOM
WHAT'S THE DRUMMING?
SOUNDS LIKE A PARTY OR SOMETHIN'.

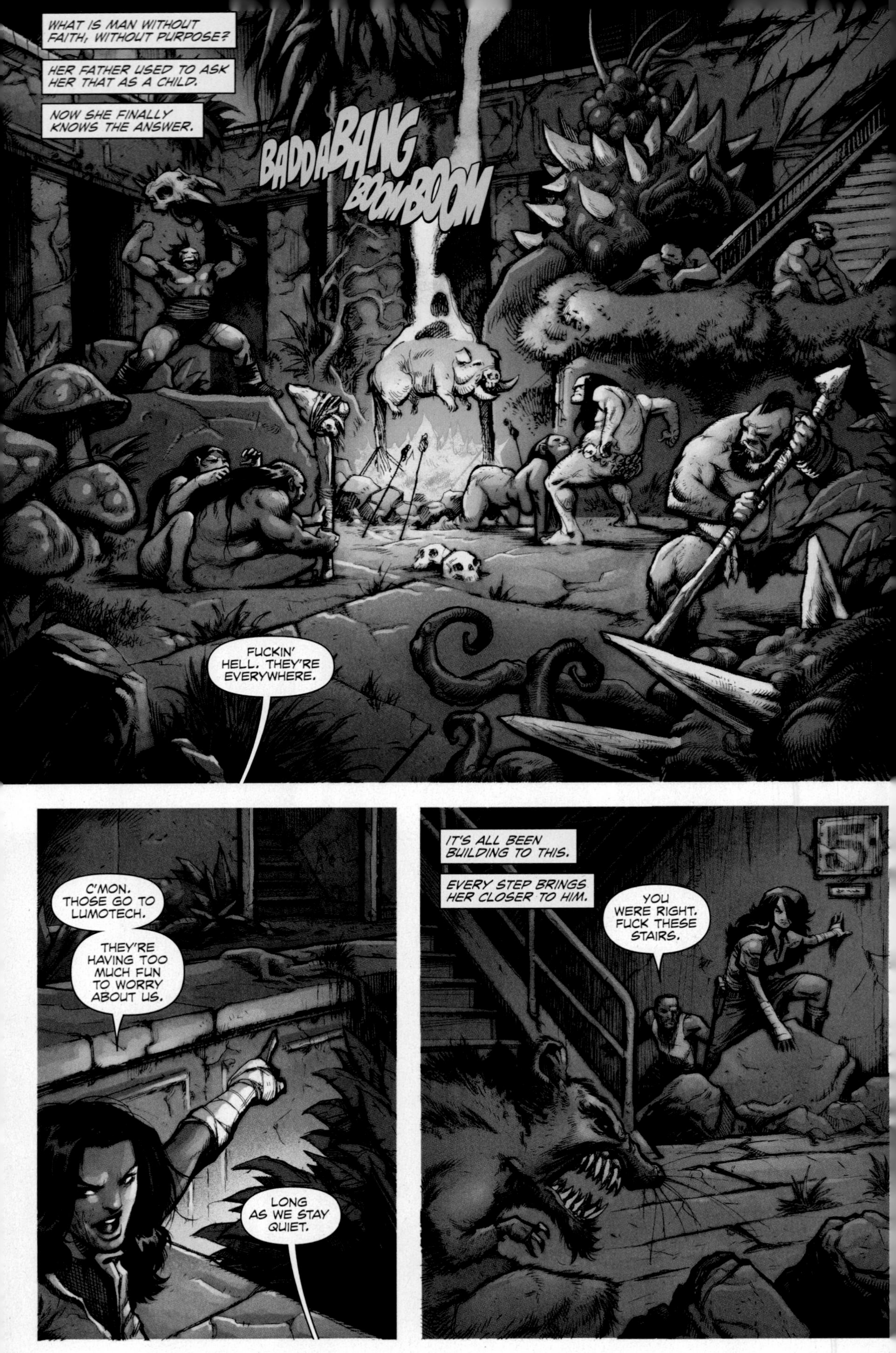
WHAT IS MAN WITHOUT FAITH, WITHOUT PURPOSE?
HER FATHER USED TO ASK HER THAT AS A CHILD.
NOW SHE FINALLY KNOWS THE ANSWER.
BADDABANG BOOMBOOM
FUCKIN' HELL. THEY'RE EVERYWHERE.
C'MON. THOSE GO TO LUMOTECH.
THEY'RE HAVING TOO MUCH FUN TO WORRY ABOUT US.
LONG AS WE STAY QUIET.
IT'S ALL BEEN BUILDING TO THIS.
EVERY STEP BRINGS HER CLOSER TO HIM.
YOU WERE RIGHT. FUCK THESE STAIRS.

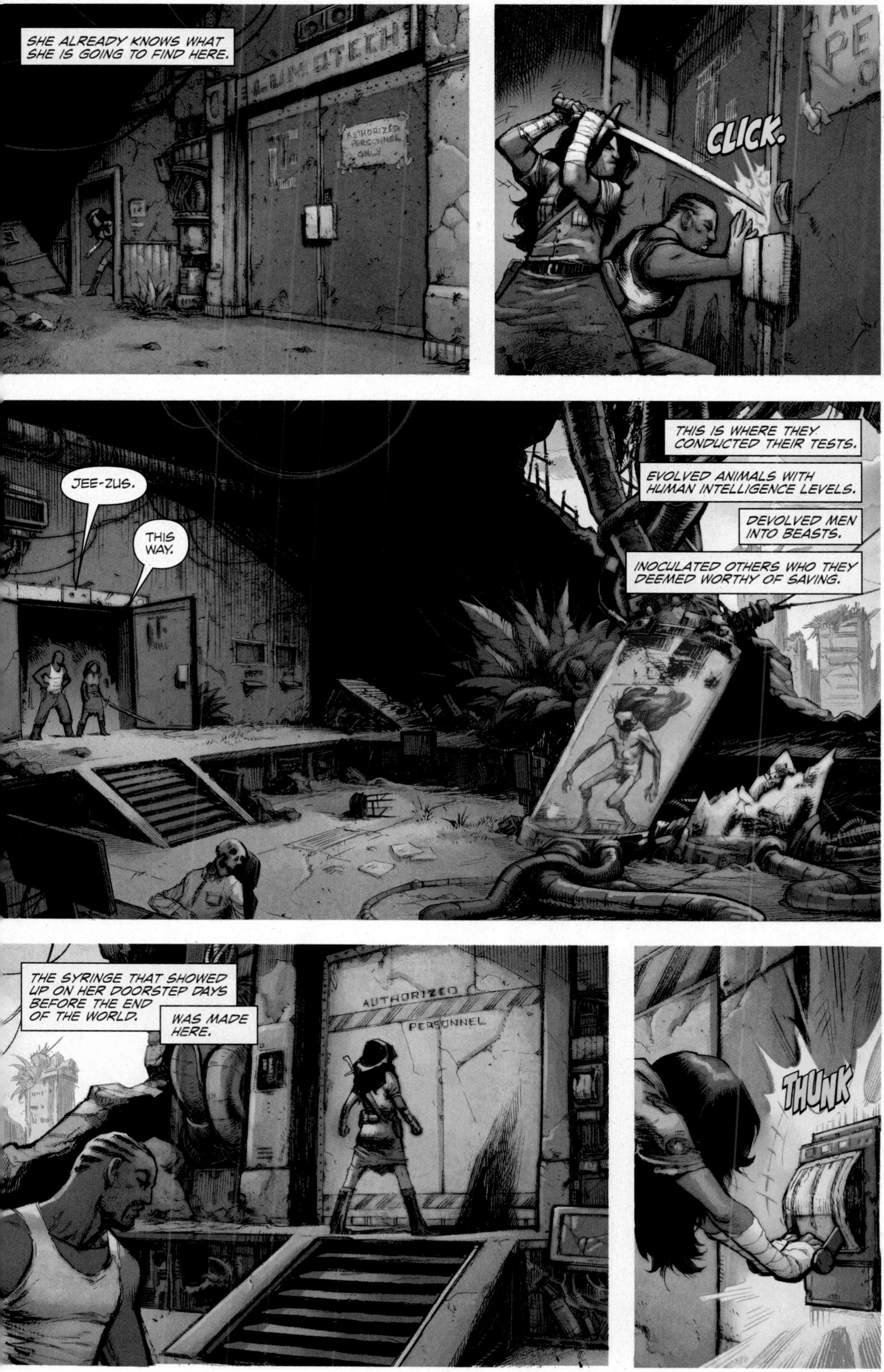
SHE ALREADY KNOWS WHAT SHE IS GOING TO FIND HERE.
AUTHORIZED PERSONNEL ONLY
CLICK.
JEE-ZUS.
THIS WAY.
THIS IS WHERE THEY CONDUCTED THEIR TESTS.
EVOLVED ANIMALS WITH HUMAN INTELLIGENCE LEVELS.
DEVOLVED MEN INTO BEASTS.
INOCULATED OTHERS WHO THEY DEEMED WORTHY OF SAVING.
THE SYRINGE THAT SHOWED UP ON HER DOORSTEP DAYS BEFORE THE END OF THE WORLD.
WAS MADE HERE.
AUTHORIZED
PERSONNEL
THUNK

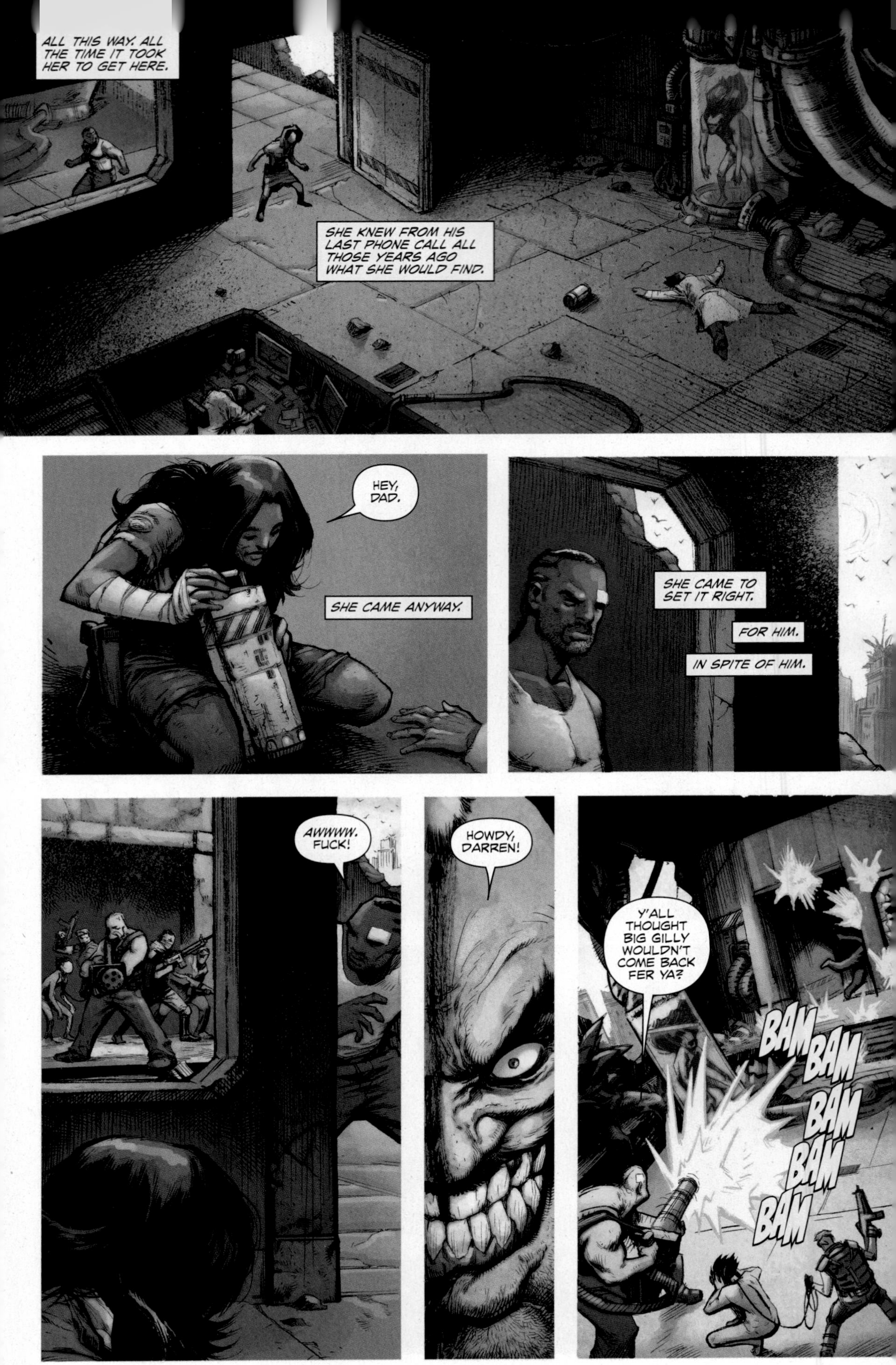
ALL THIS WAY. ALL THE TIME IT TOOK HER TO GET HERE.
SHE KNEW FROM HIS LAST PHONE CALL ALL THOSE YEARS AGO WHAT SHE WOULD FIND.
HEY, DAD.
SHE CAME ANYWAY.
SHE CAME TO SET IT RIGHT.
FOR HIM.
IN SPITE OF HIM.
AWWWW. FUCK!
HOWDY, DARREN!
Y'ALL THOUGHT BIG GILLY WOULDN'T COME BACK FER YA?
BAM BAM BAM BAM BAM

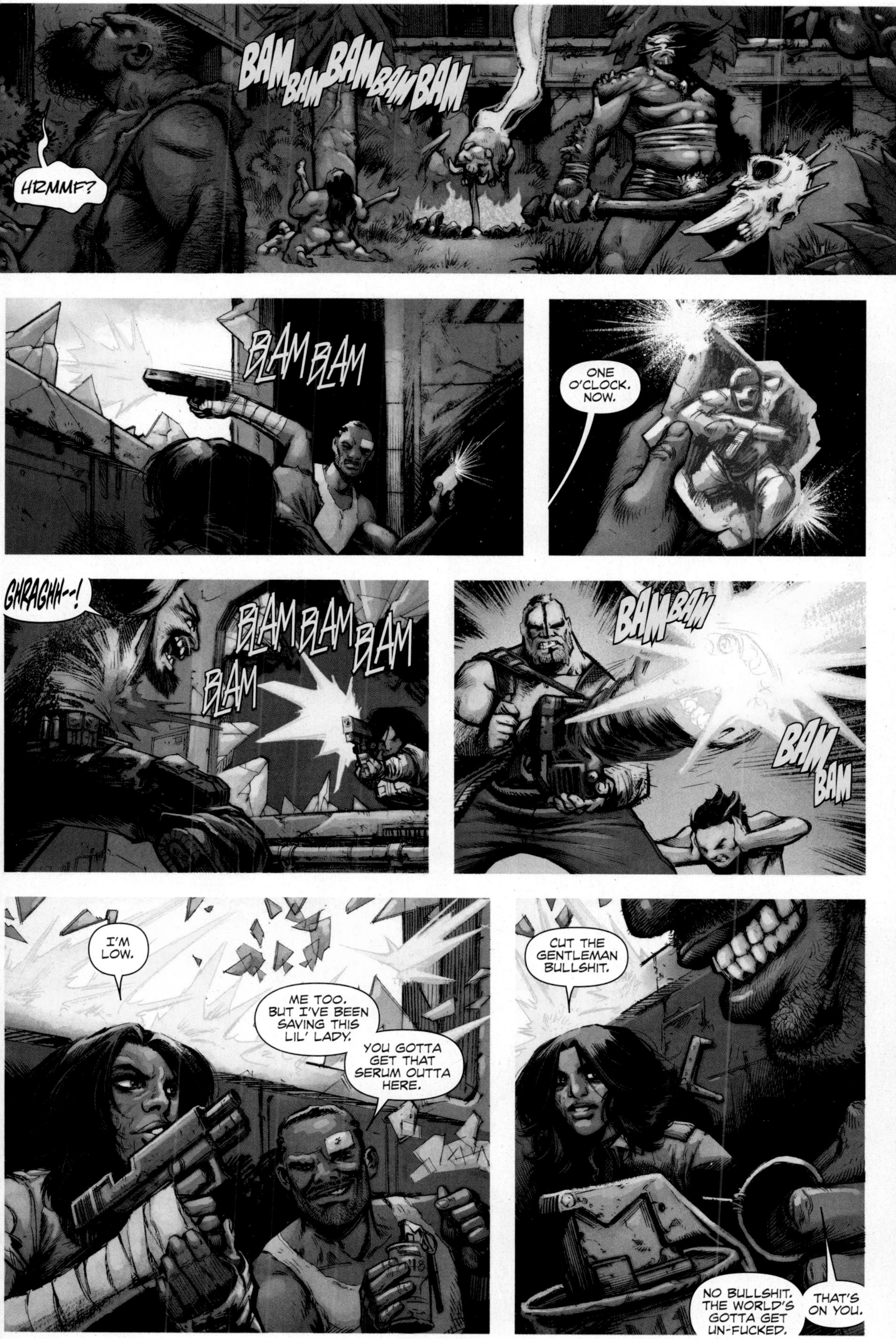

HRMMF?
BAM BAM BAM BAM BAM
BLAM BLAM
ONE O'CLOCK. NOW.
GHRAGHH--!
BLAM BLAM BLAM BLAM
BAM BAM
BAM BAM
I'M LOW.
ME TOO. BUT I'VE BEEN SAVING THIS LIL' LADY.
YOU GOTTA GET THAT SERUM OUTTA HERE.
CUT THE GENTLEMAN BULLSHIT.
NO BULLSHIT. THE WORLD'S GOTTA GET UN-FUCKED.
THAT'S ON YOU.

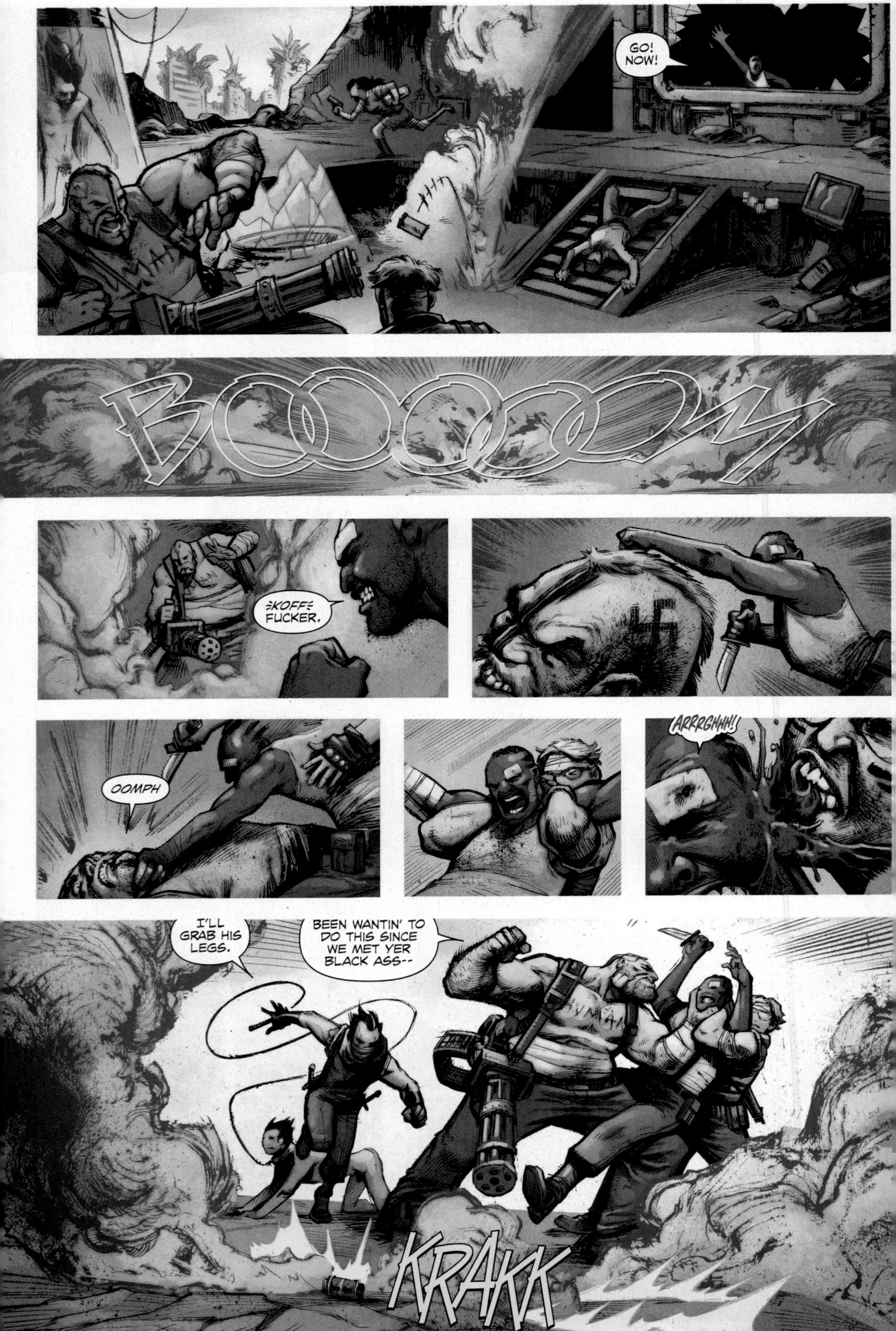
GO! NOW!
BOOOOOM
=KOFF= FUCKER.
OOMPH
ARRRGHHH!!
I'LL GRAB HIS LEGS.
BEEN WANTIN' TO DO THIS SINCE WE MET YER BLACK ASS--
KRAKK

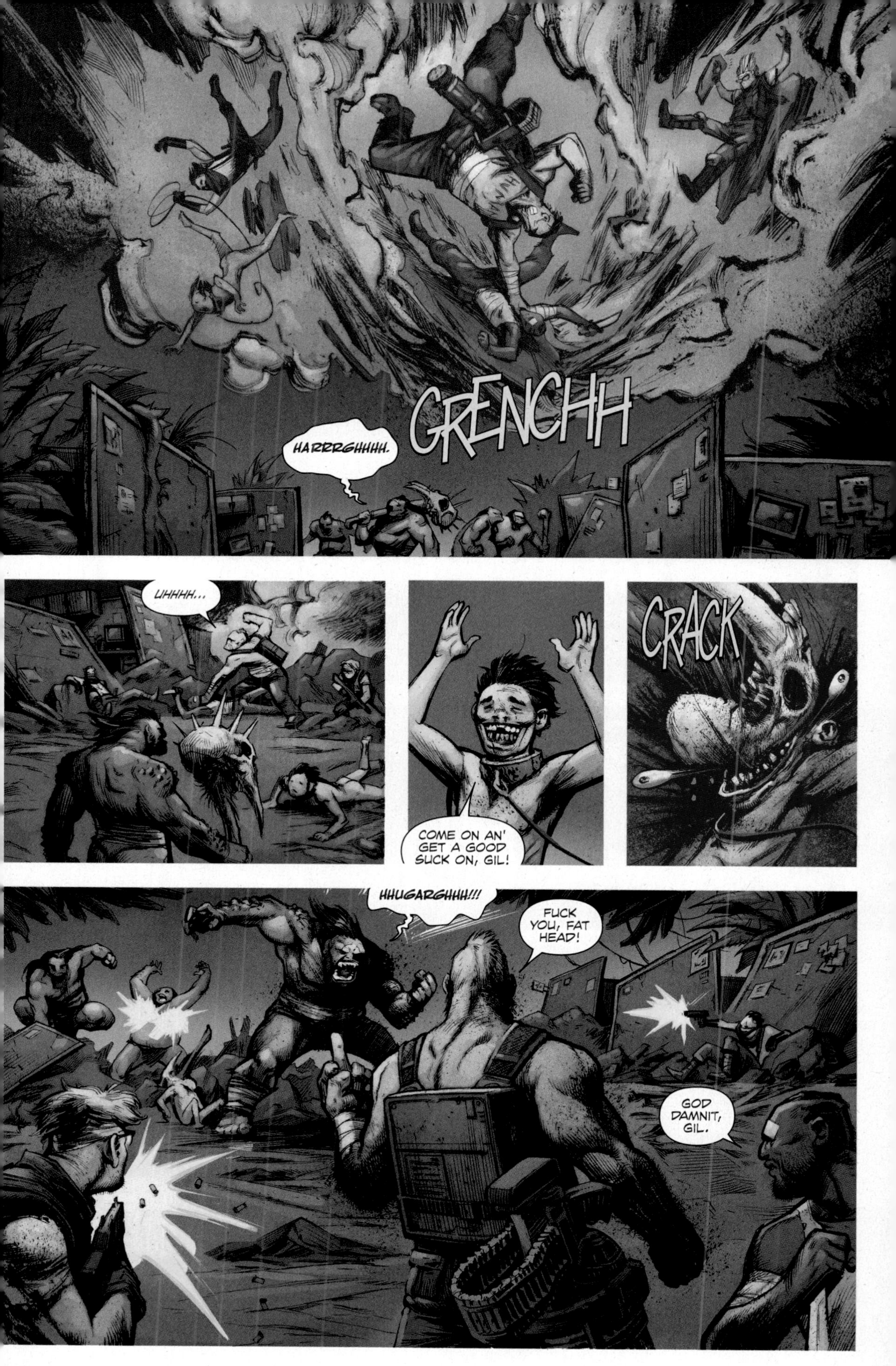
GRENCHH
HARRRGHHHH.
UHHHH...
COME ON AN' GET A GOOD SUCK ON, GIL!
CRACK
HHUGARGHHH!!!
FUCK YOU, FAT HEAD!
GOD DAMNIT, GIL.

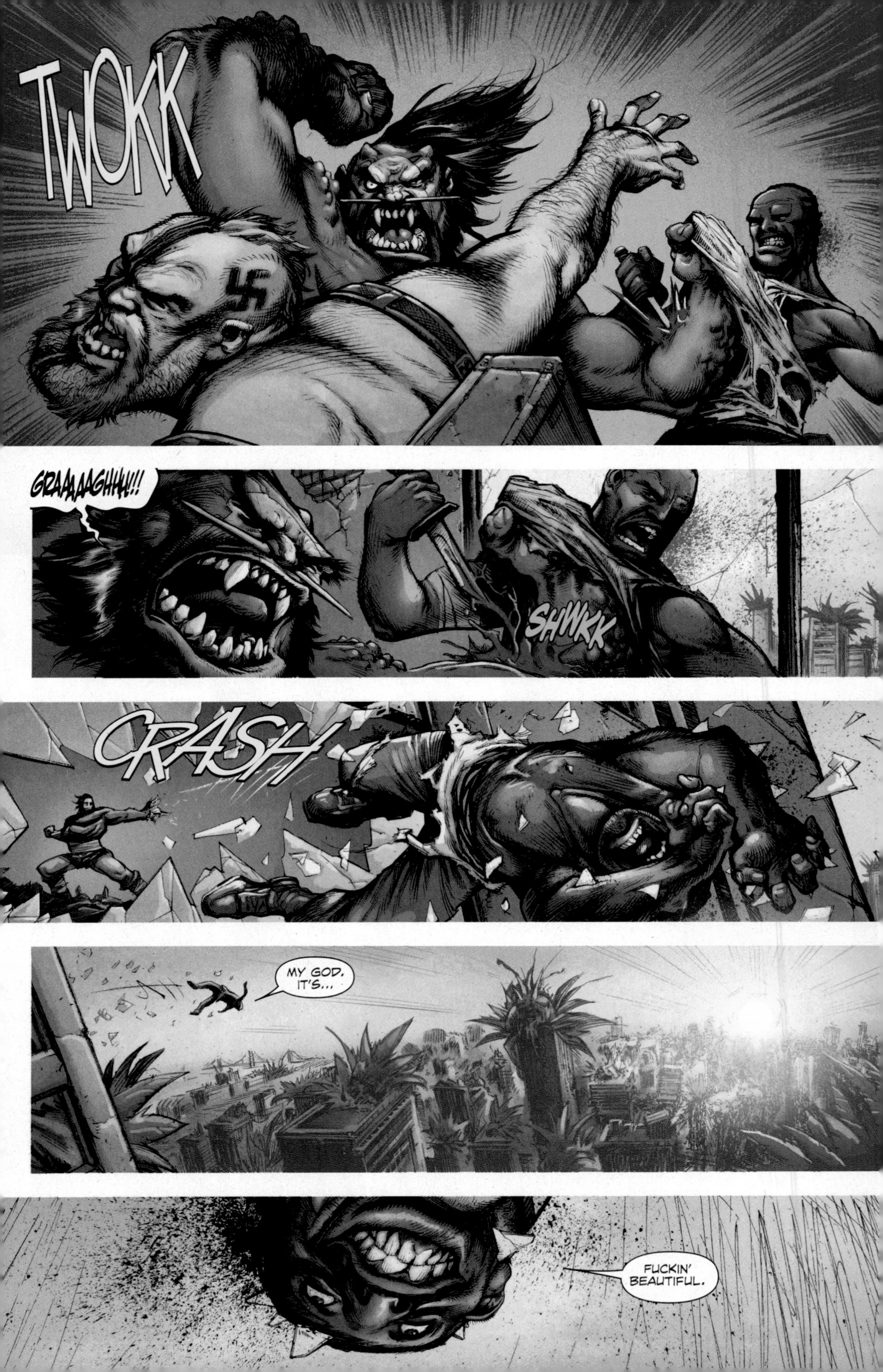
TWOKK
GRAAAAAGHHH!!!
SHWKK
CRASH
MY GOD. IT'S...
FUCKIN' BEAUTIFUL.

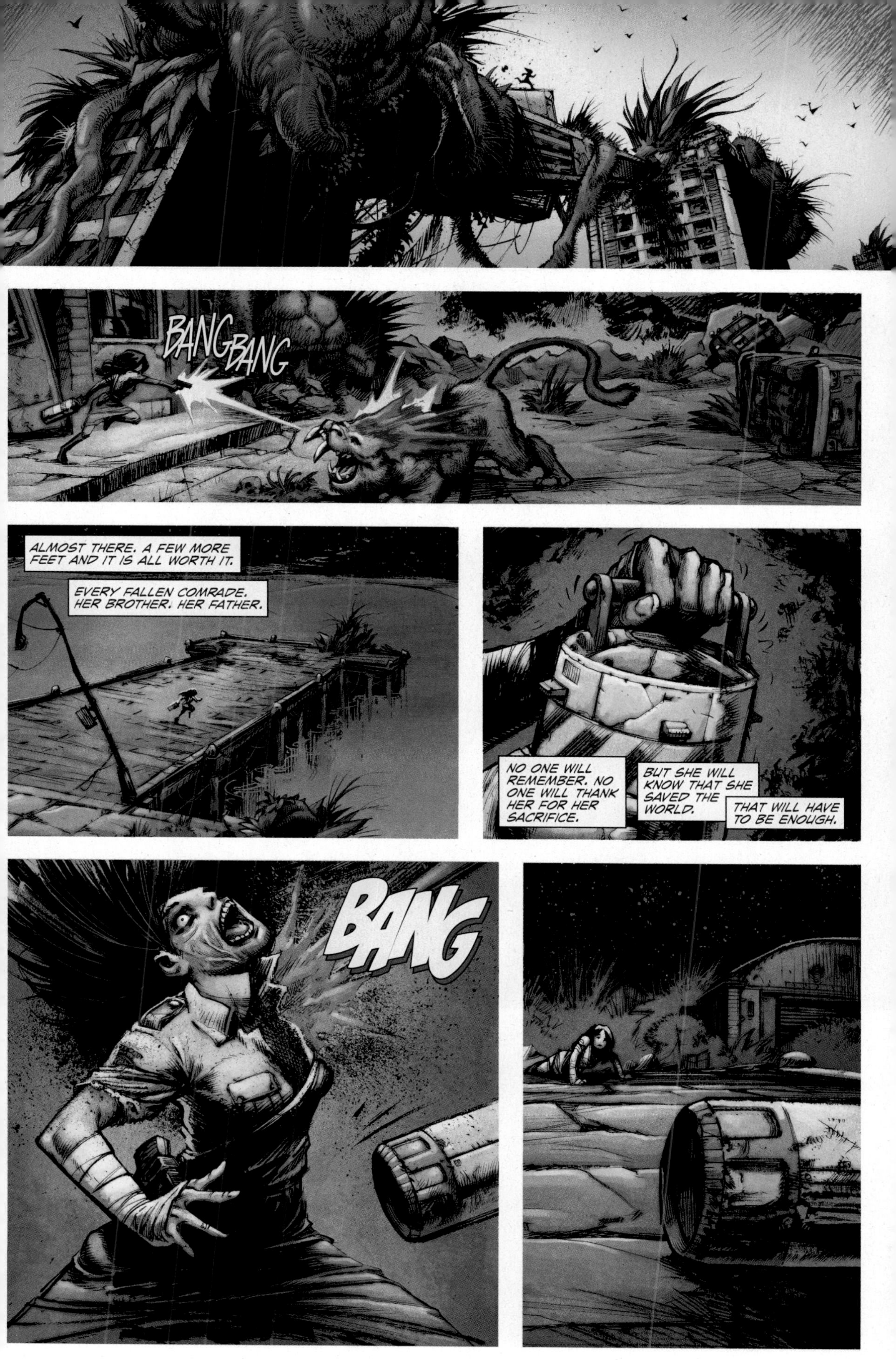
BANG BANG
ALMOST THERE. A FEW MORE FEET AND IT IS ALL WORTH IT.
EVERY FALLEN COMRADE. HER BROTHER. HER FATHER.
NO ONE WILL REMEMBER. NO ONE WILL THANK HER FOR HER SACRIFICE.
BUT SHE WILL KNOW THAT SHE SAVED THE WORLD.
THAT WILL HAVE TO BE ENOUGH.
BANG

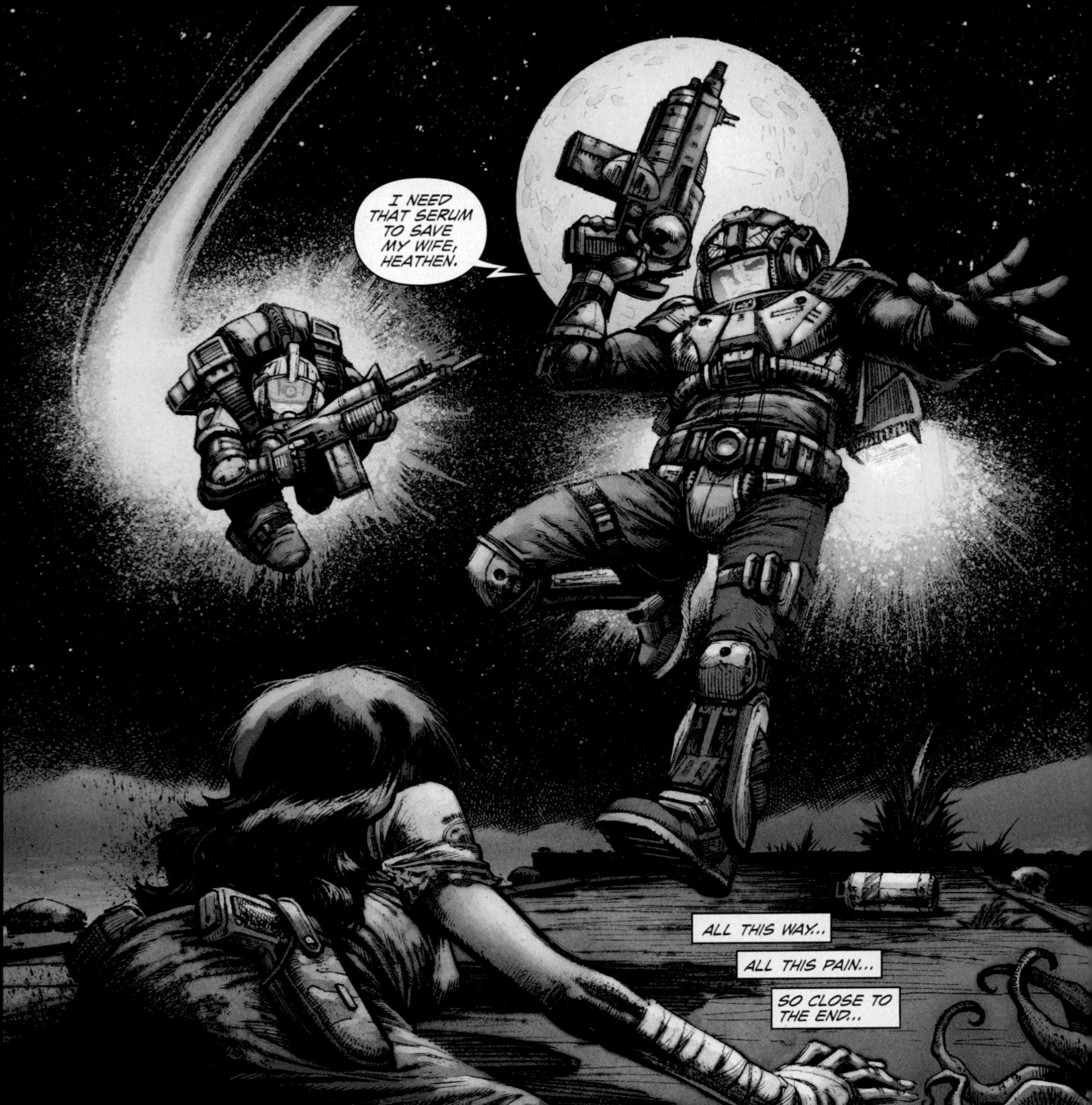
I NEED THAT SERUM TO SAVE MY WIFE, HEATHEN.
ALL THIS WAY...
ALL THIS PAIN...
SO CLOSE TO THE END...
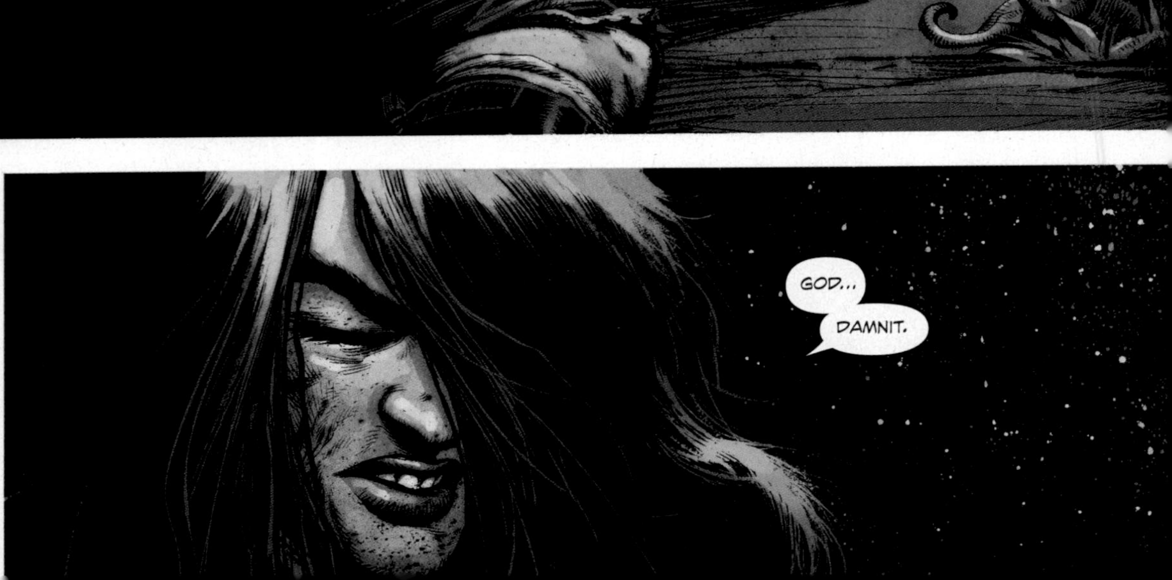
GOD...
DAMNIT.

Issue 5 Cover by JAE LEE With Colors by JUNE CHUNG

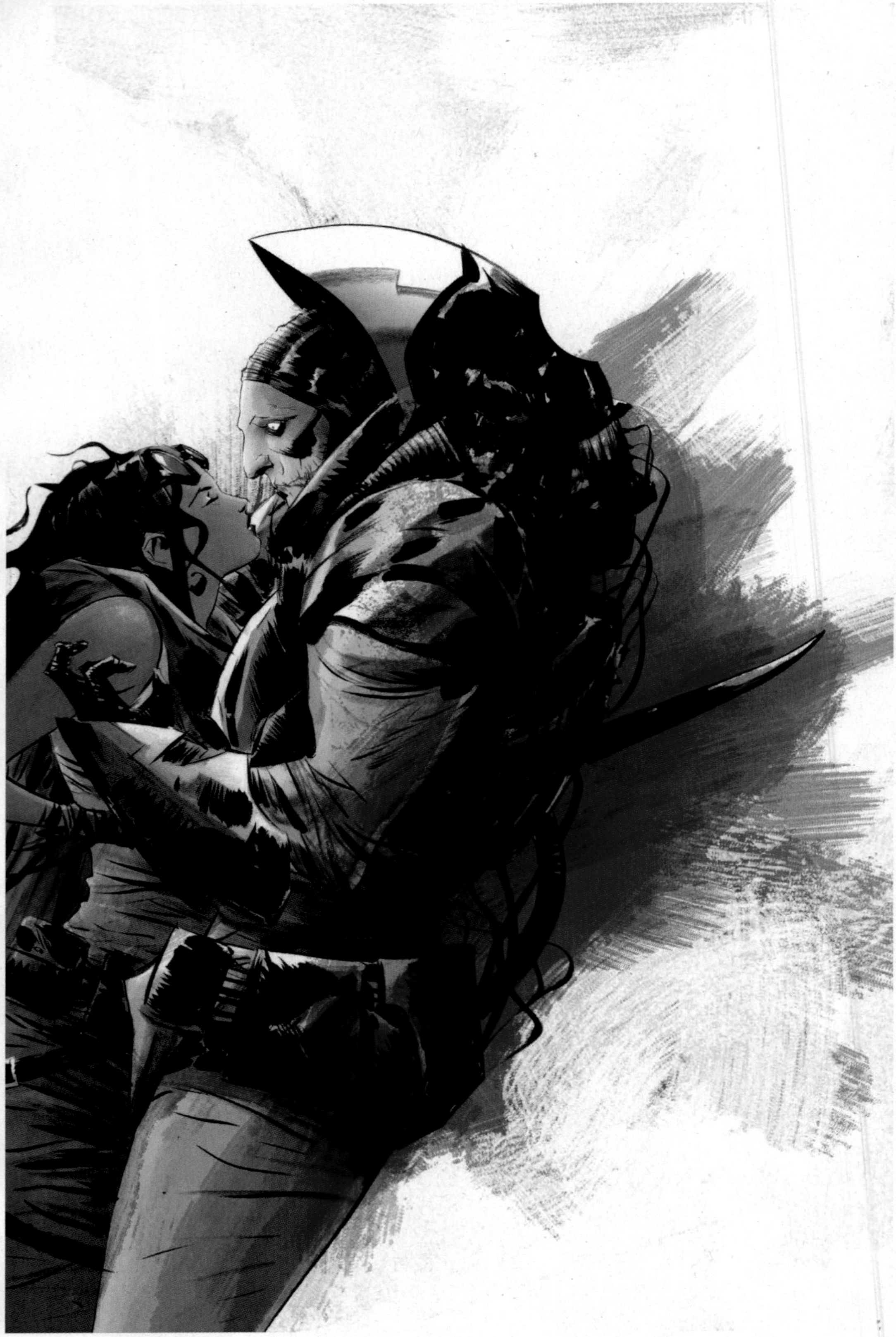

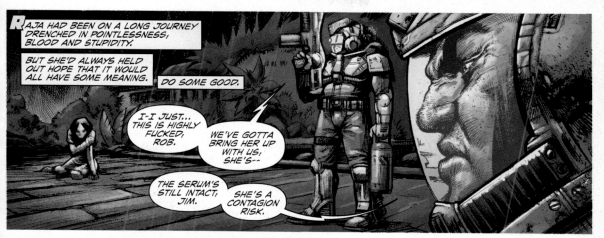

RAJA HAD BEEN ON A LONG JOURNEY DRENCHED IN POINTLESSNESS, BLOOD AND STUPIDITY.

BUT SHE'D ALWAYS HELD OUT HOPE THAT IT WOULD ALL HAVE SOME MEANING.

DO SOME GOOD.

I-I JUST... THIS IS HIGHLY FUCKED, ROB.

WE'VE GOTTA BRING HER UP WITH US, SHE'S--

THE SERUM'S STILL INTACT, JIM.

SHE'S A CONTAGION RISK.

DIP. DIP.

YOUR WIFE WENT DEVO FROM JUST ONE DROP.

PLIP PLOP PLOOP

AND I WANT TO GO RE-EVOLVE HER BEFORE THE BOSS FINDS OUT. I'M NOT TAKING ANY OTHER RISKS.

SORRY, LADY, I KNOW THIS IS A BAD END.

THERE'S JUST NOTHING WE CAN DO.

BEEP BEEPBEEP

NO SAVING EARTH TODAY--BUT I CAN STILL SAVE MY WIFE.

THE MIND CREATES A NARRATIVE, IMAGINES LOGIC TO THINGS.

IT TELLS US 'IF WE DO X WE CAN EXPECT Y.'

BUT REALITY ISN'T A STORY.

AFTER ALL THESE YEARS OF HOLDING ONTO HOPE, THE ONLY THING SHE KNOWS FOR SURE...

ZZERROOOM

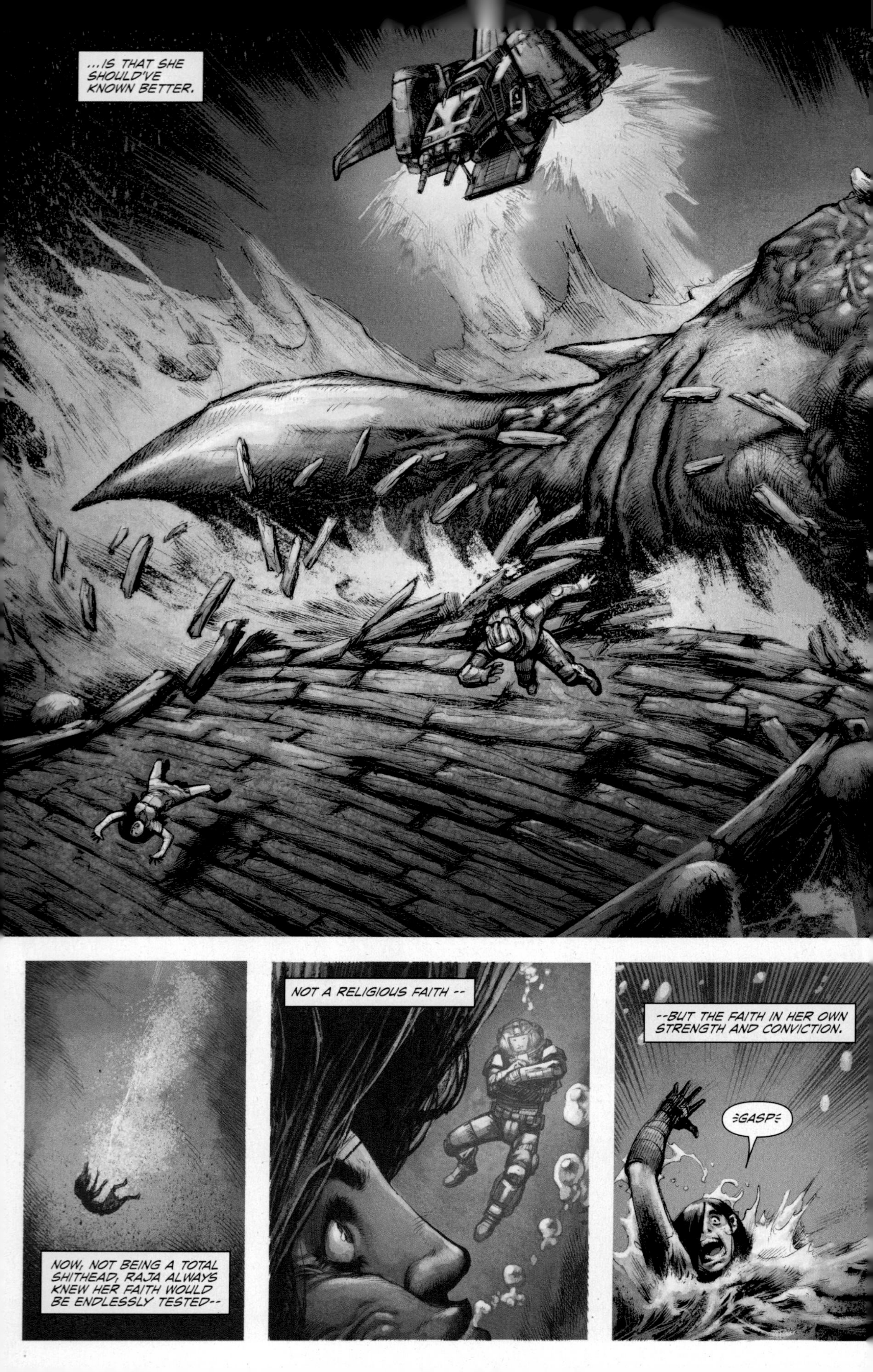
...IS THAT SHE SHOULD'VE KNOWN BETTER.
NOW, NOT BEING A TOTAL SHITHEAD, RAJA ALWAYS KNEW HER FAITH WOULD BE ENDLESSLY TESTED--
NOT A RELIGIOUS FAITH --
--BUT THE FAITH IN HER OWN STRENGTH AND CONVICTION.
GASP

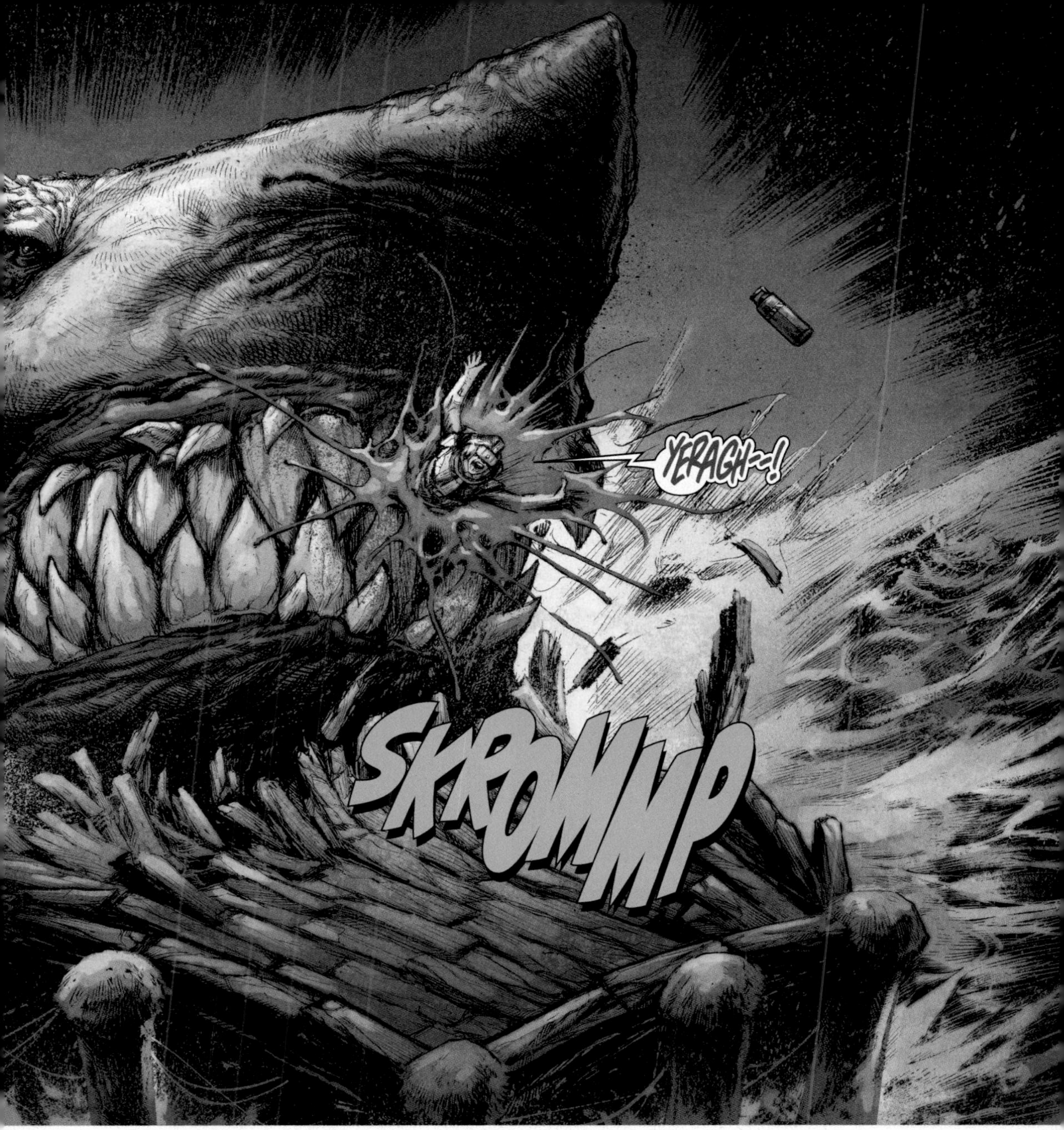
YERAGH--!
SKROMMMP

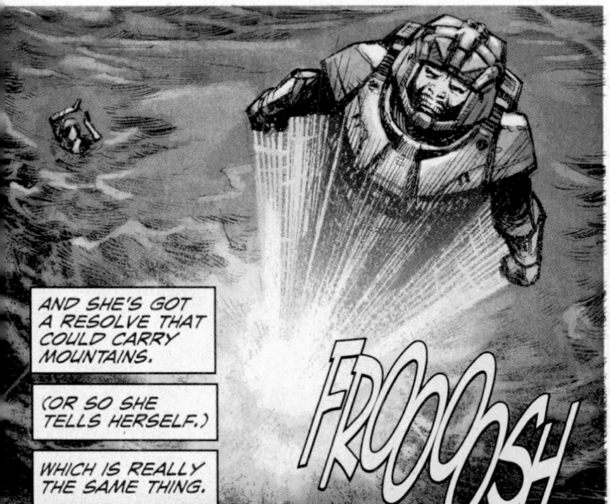
AND SHE'S GOT A RESOLVE THAT COULD CARRY MOUNTAINS.
(OR SO SHE TELLS HERSELF.)
WHICH IS REALLY THE SAME THING.
FROOOOSH

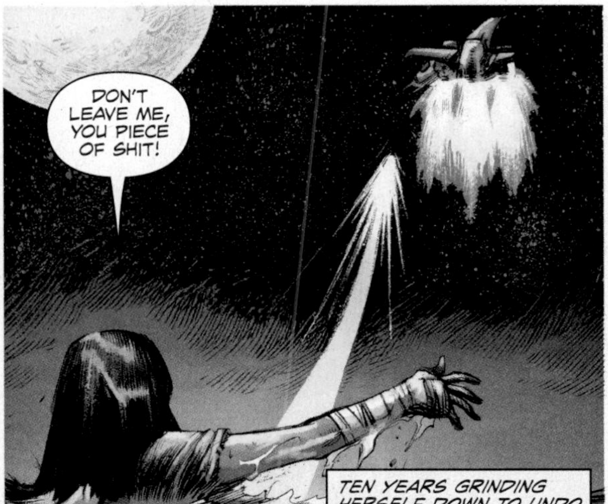
DON'T LEAVE ME, YOU PIECE OF SHIT!
TEN YEARS GRINDING HERSELF DOWN TO UNDO HER FATHER'S MESS--

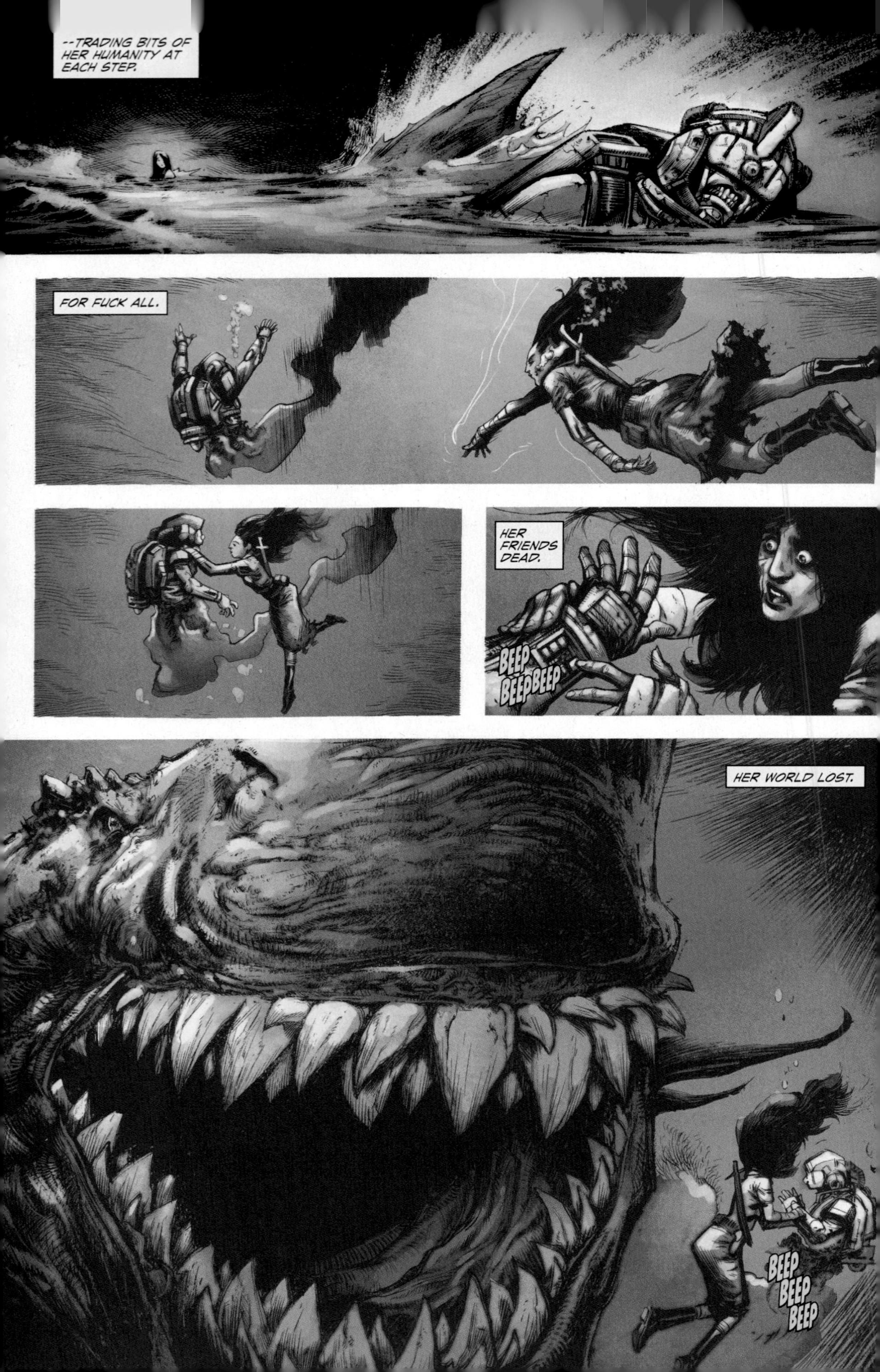
--TRADING BITS OF HER HUMANITY AT EACH STEP.
FOR FUCK ALL.
HER FRIENDS DEAD.
BEEP BEEPBEEP
HER WORLD LOST.
BEEP BEEP BEEP

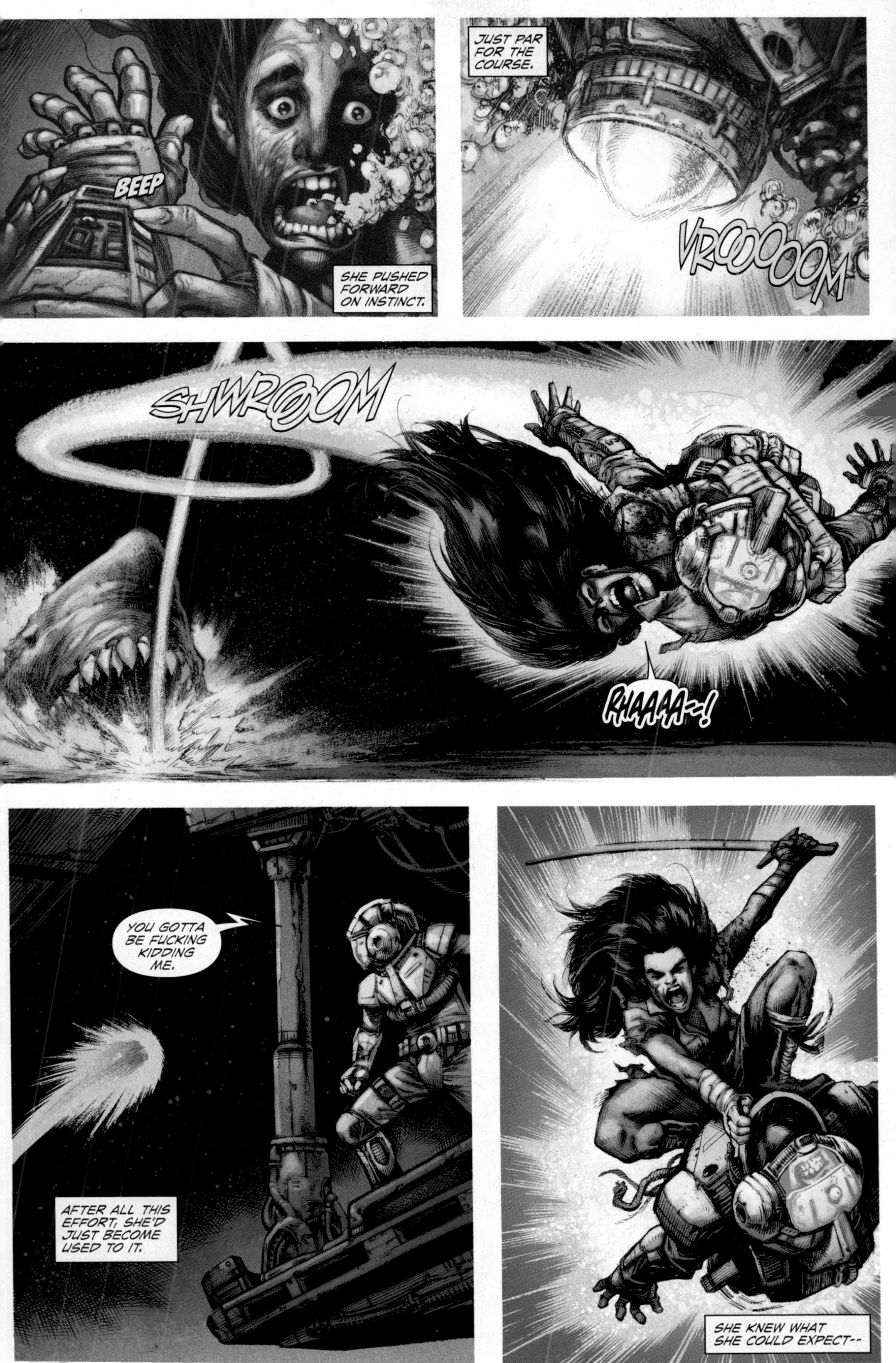

BEEP
SHE PUSHED FORWARD ON INSTINCT.
JUST PAR FOR THE COURSE.
VROOOOOM
SHWROOM
RHAAAA--!
YOU GOTTA BE FUCKING KIDDING ME.
AFTER ALL THIS EFFORT, SHE'D JUST BECOME USED TO IT.
SHE KNEW WHAT SHE COULD EXPECT--

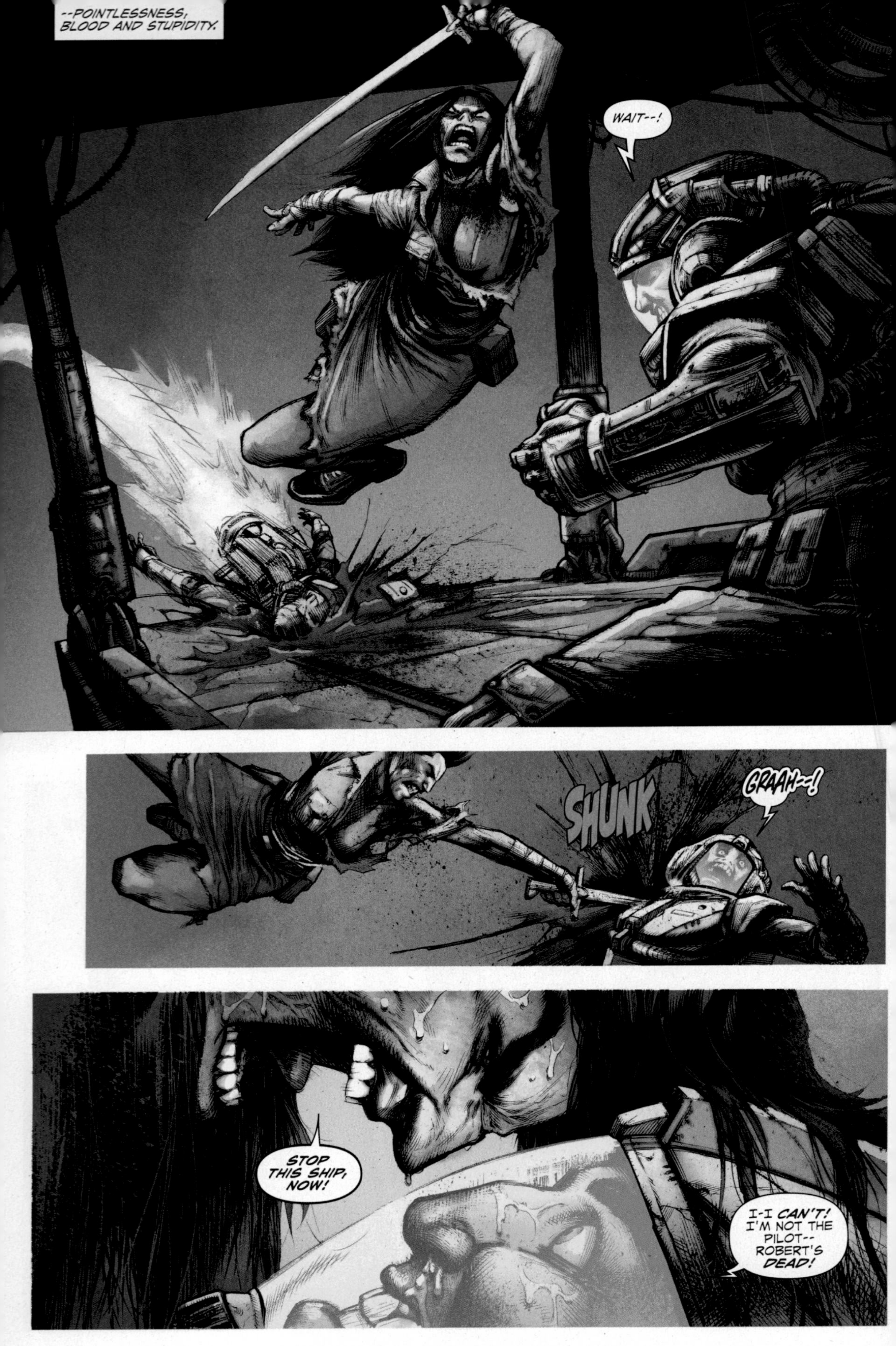
--POINTLESSNESS, BLOOD AND STUPIDITY.
WAIT--!
SHUNK
GRAAH--!
STOP THIS SHIP, NOW!
I-I CAN'T! I'M NOT THE PILOT-- ROBERT'S DEAD!

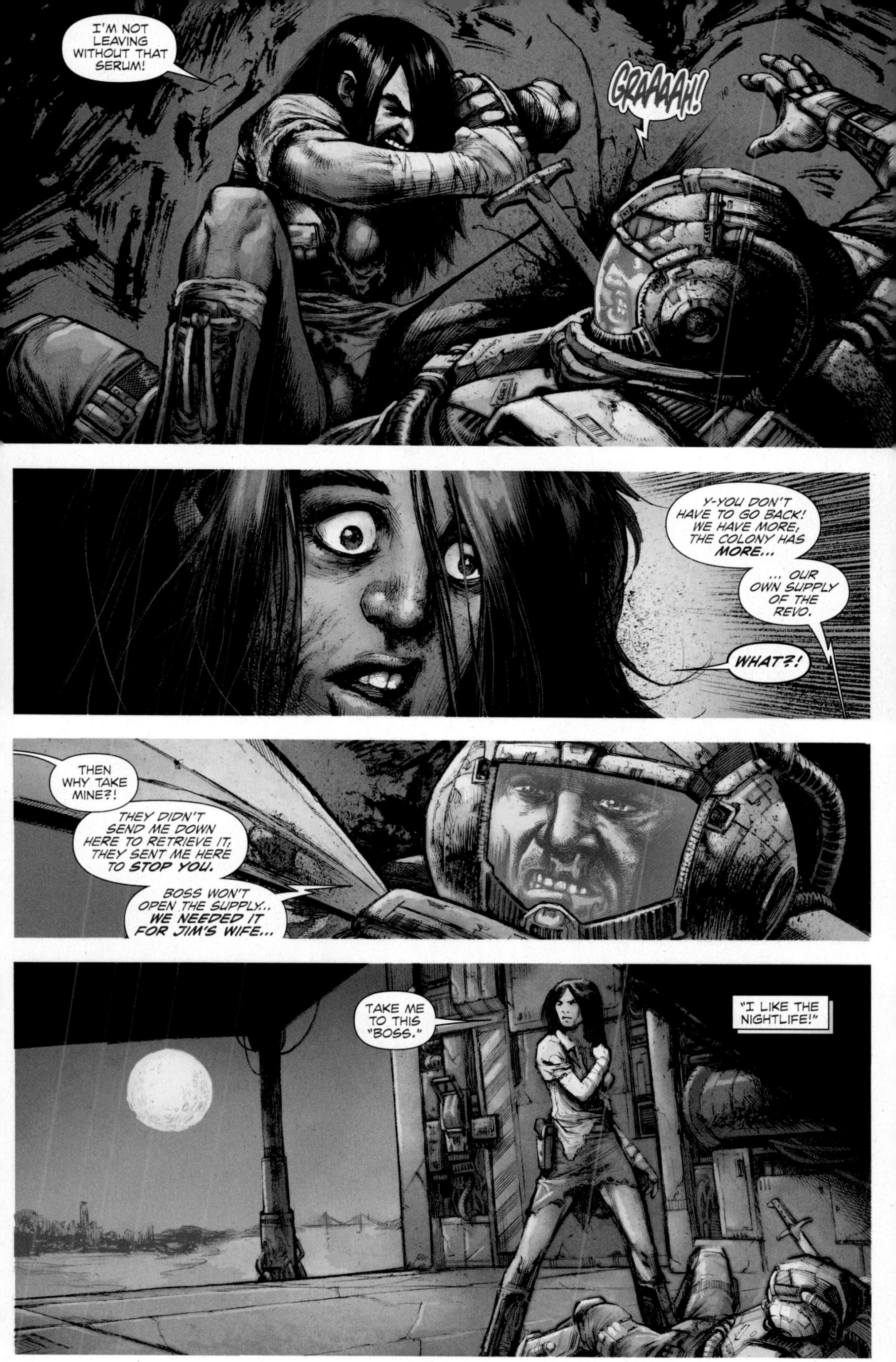
I'M NOT LEAVING WITHOUT THAT SERUM!
GRAAAAH!
Y-YOU DON'T HAVE TO GO BACK! WE HAVE MORE, THE COLONY HAS MORE...
... OUR OWN SUPPLY OF THE REVO.
WHAT?!
THEN WHY TAKE MINE?!
THEY DIDN'T SEND ME DOWN HERE TO RETRIEVE IT, THEY SENT ME HERE TO STOP YOU.
BOSS WON'T OPEN THE SUPPLY... WE NEEDED IT FOR JIM'S WIFE...
TAKE ME TO THIS "BOSS."
"I LIKE THE NIGHTLIFE!"

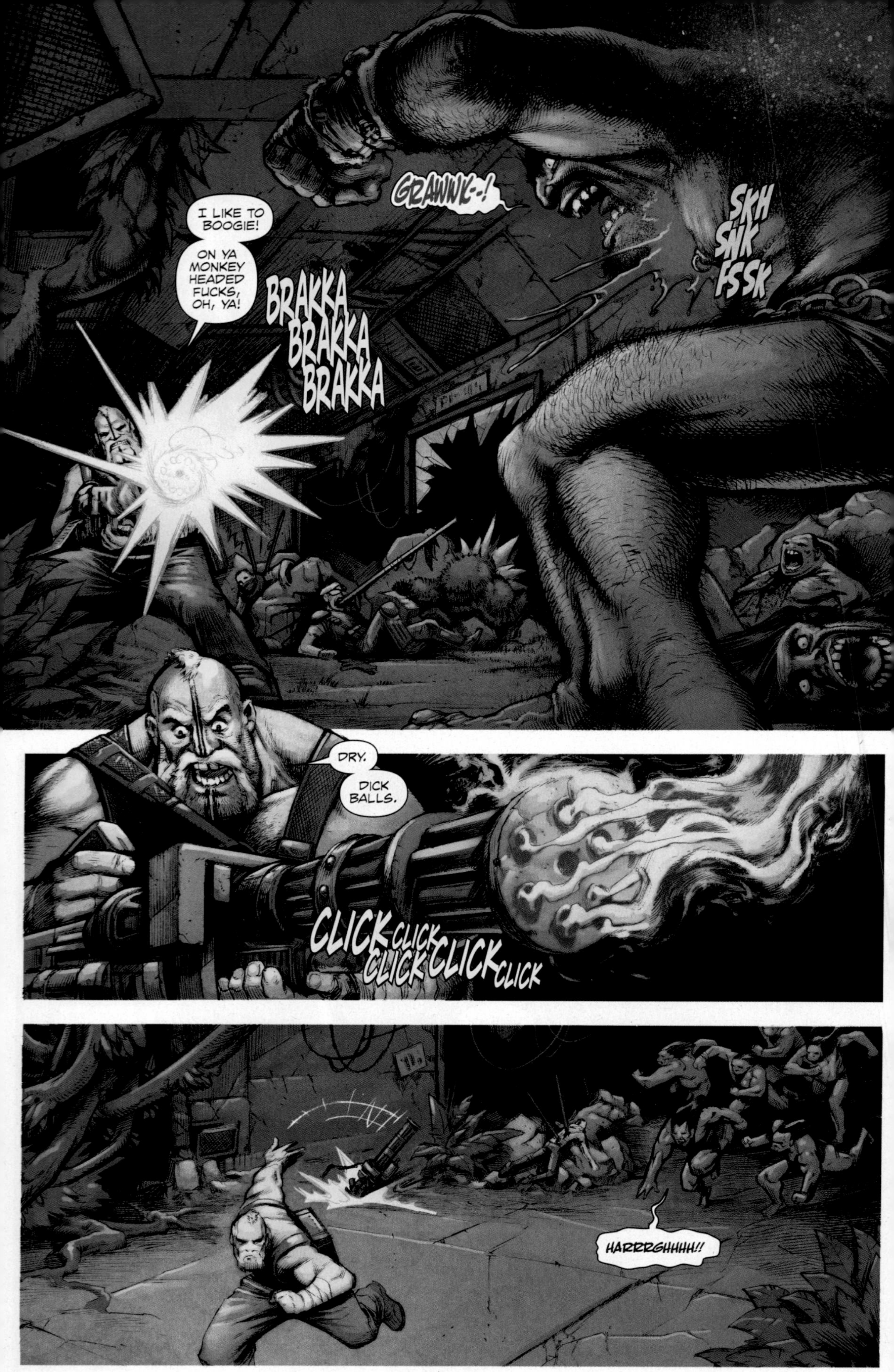
GRAWWK-!
SKH SNK FSSK
I LIKE TO BOOGIE!
ON YA MONKEY HEADED FUCKS, OH, YA!
BRAKKA BRAKKA BRAKKA
DRY.
DICK BALLS.
CLICK CLICK CLICK CLICK CLICK
HARRRGHHHH!!

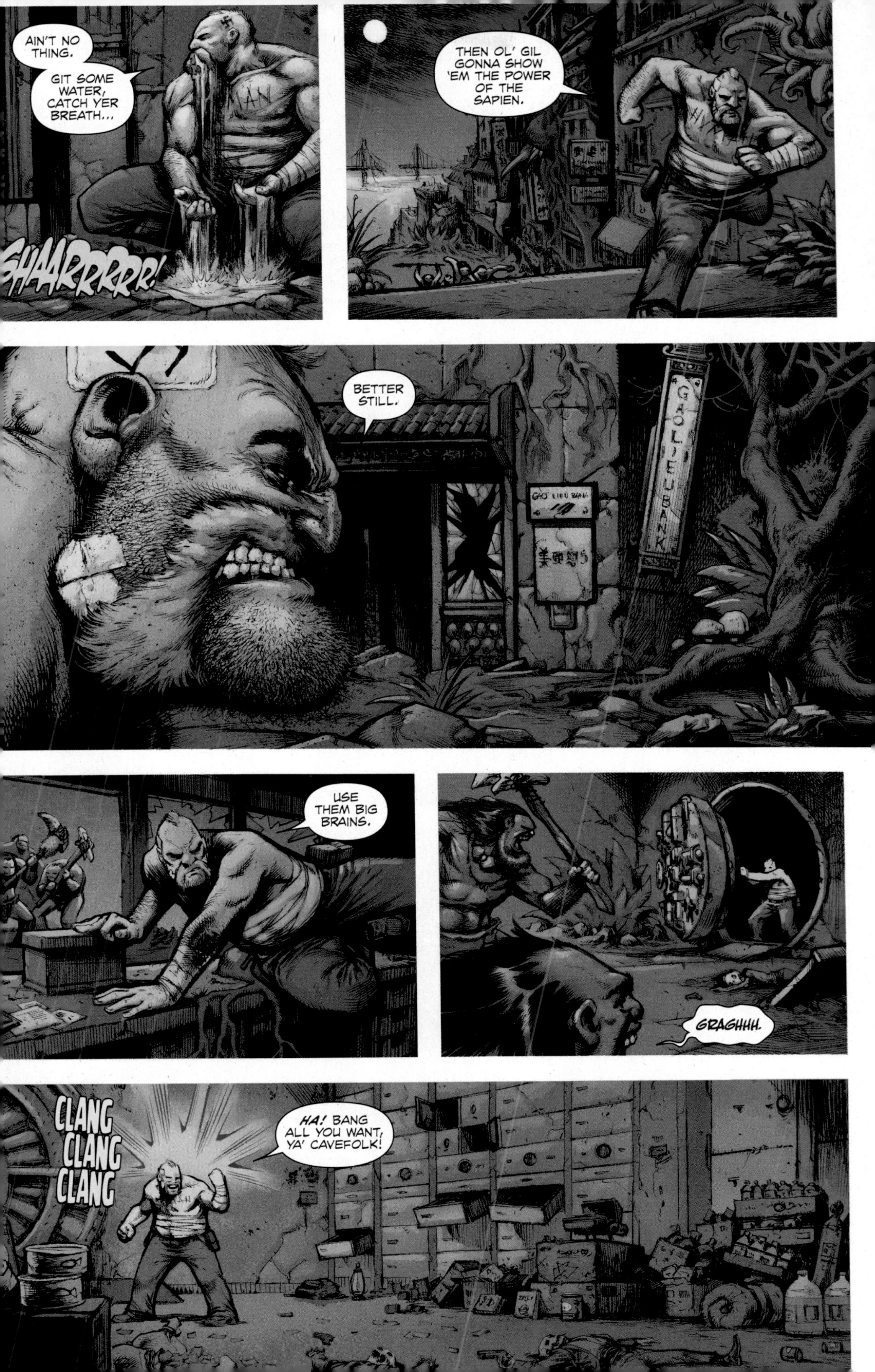

AIN'T NO THING.
GIT SOME WATER, CATCH YER BREATH...
SHAARRRRR!
THEN OL' GIL GONNA SHOW 'EM THE POWER OF THE SAPIEN.
BETTER STILL.
GAOLIEUBANK
USE THEM BIG BRAINS.
GRAGHHH.
CLANG CLANG CLANG
HA! BANG ALL YOU WANT, YA' CAVEFOLK!

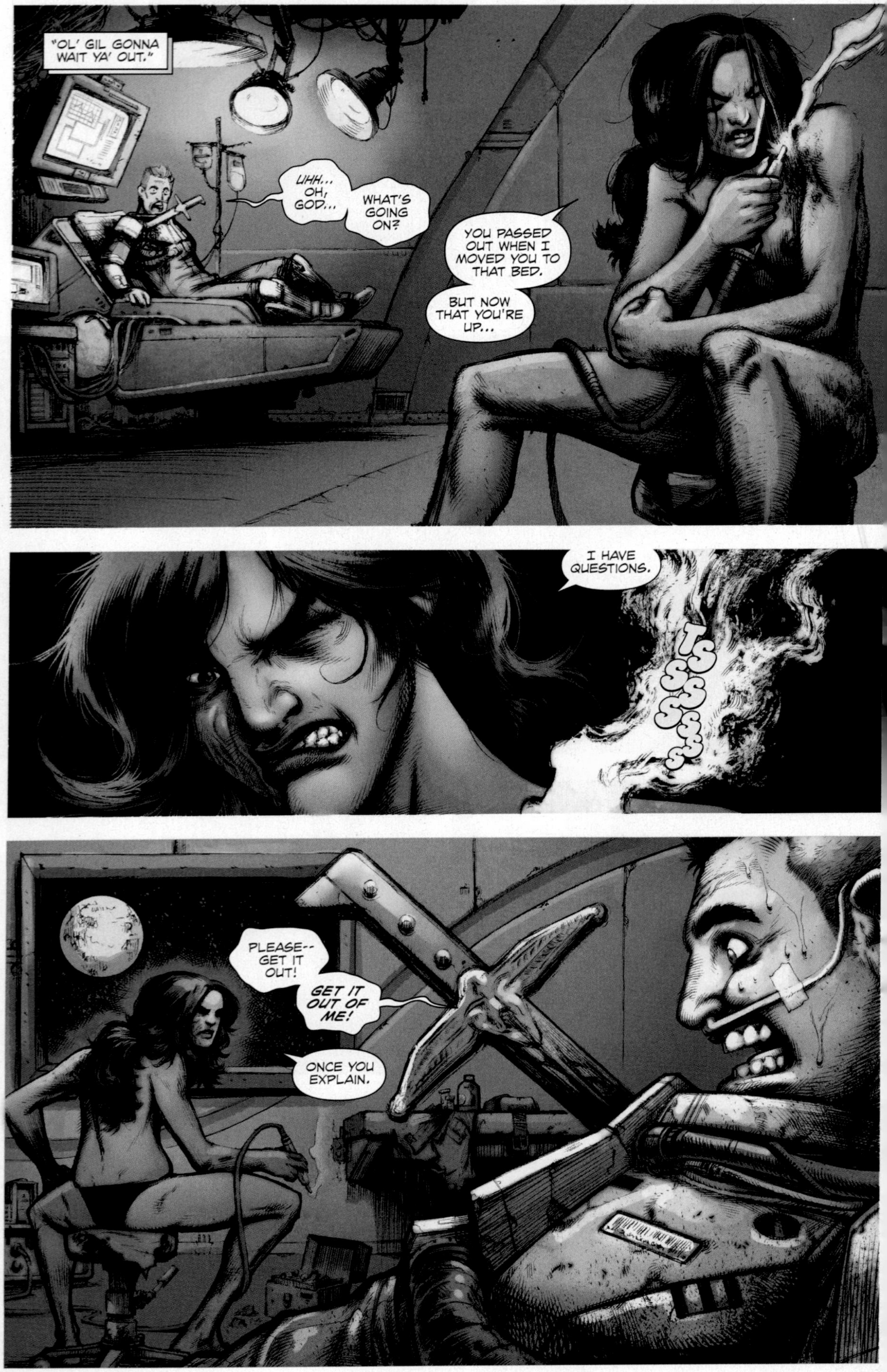
"OL' GIL GONNA WAIT YA' OUT."
UHH... OH, GOD...
WHAT'S GOING ON?
YOU PASSED OUT WHEN I MOVED YOU TO THAT BED.
BUT NOW THAT YOU'RE UP...
I HAVE QUESTIONS.
TSSSSSS
PLEASE-- GET IT OUT!
GET IT OUT OF ME!
ONCE YOU EXPLAIN.

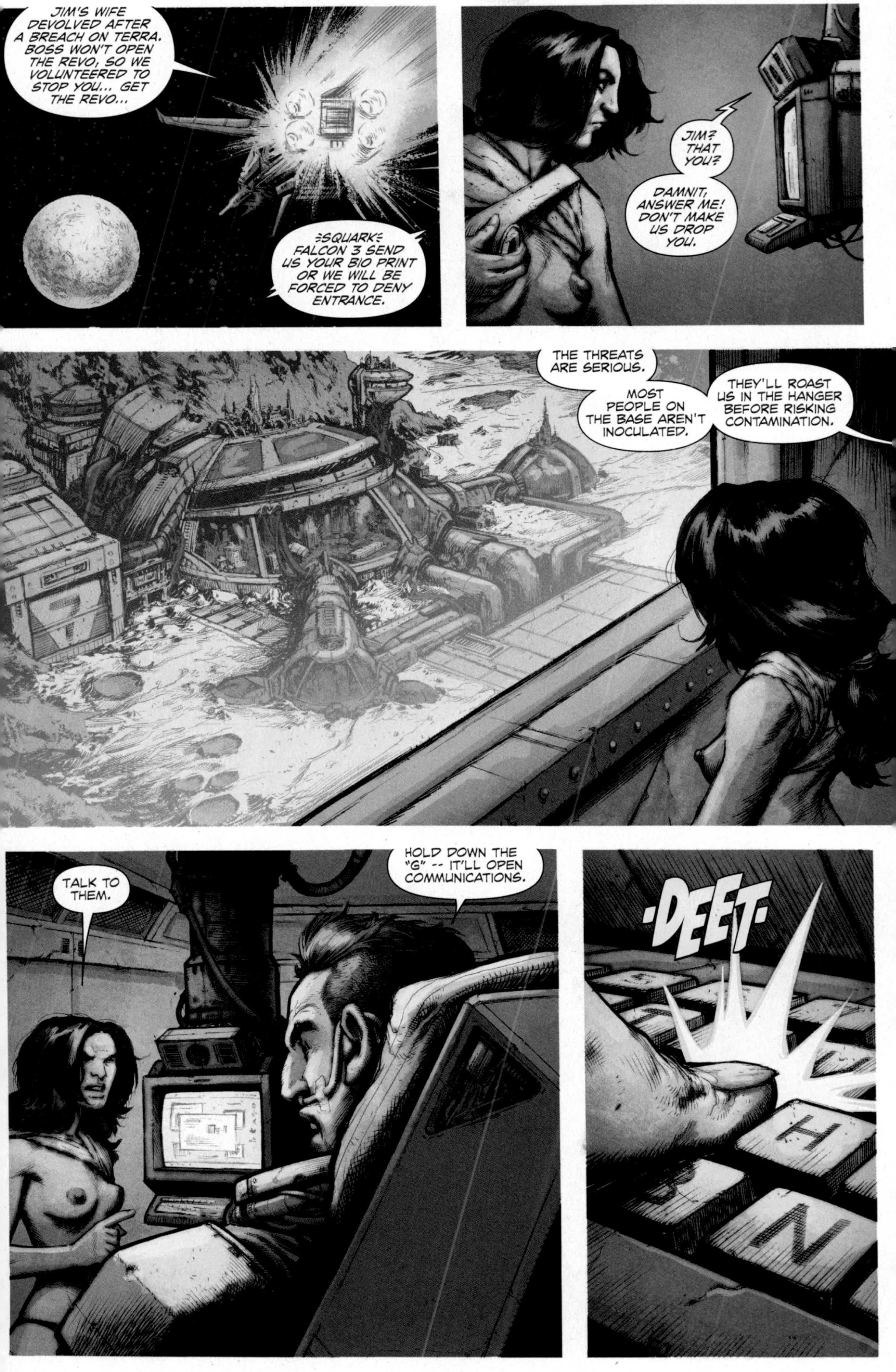
JIM'S WIFE DEVOLVED AFTER A BREACH ON TERRA. BOSS WON'T OPEN THE REVO, SO WE VOLUNTEERED TO STOP YOU... GET THE REVO...
SQUARK FALCON 3 SEND US YOUR BIO PRINT OR WE WILL BE FORCED TO DENY ENTRANCE.
JIM? THAT YOU?
DAMNIT, ANSWER ME! DON'T MAKE US DROP YOU.
THE THREATS ARE SERIOUS.
MOST PEOPLE ON THE BASE AREN'T INOCULATED.
THEY'LL ROAST US IN THE HANGER BEFORE RISKING CONTAMINATION.
TALK TO THEM.
HOLD DOWN THE "G" -- IT'LL OPEN COMMUNICATIONS.
-DEET-

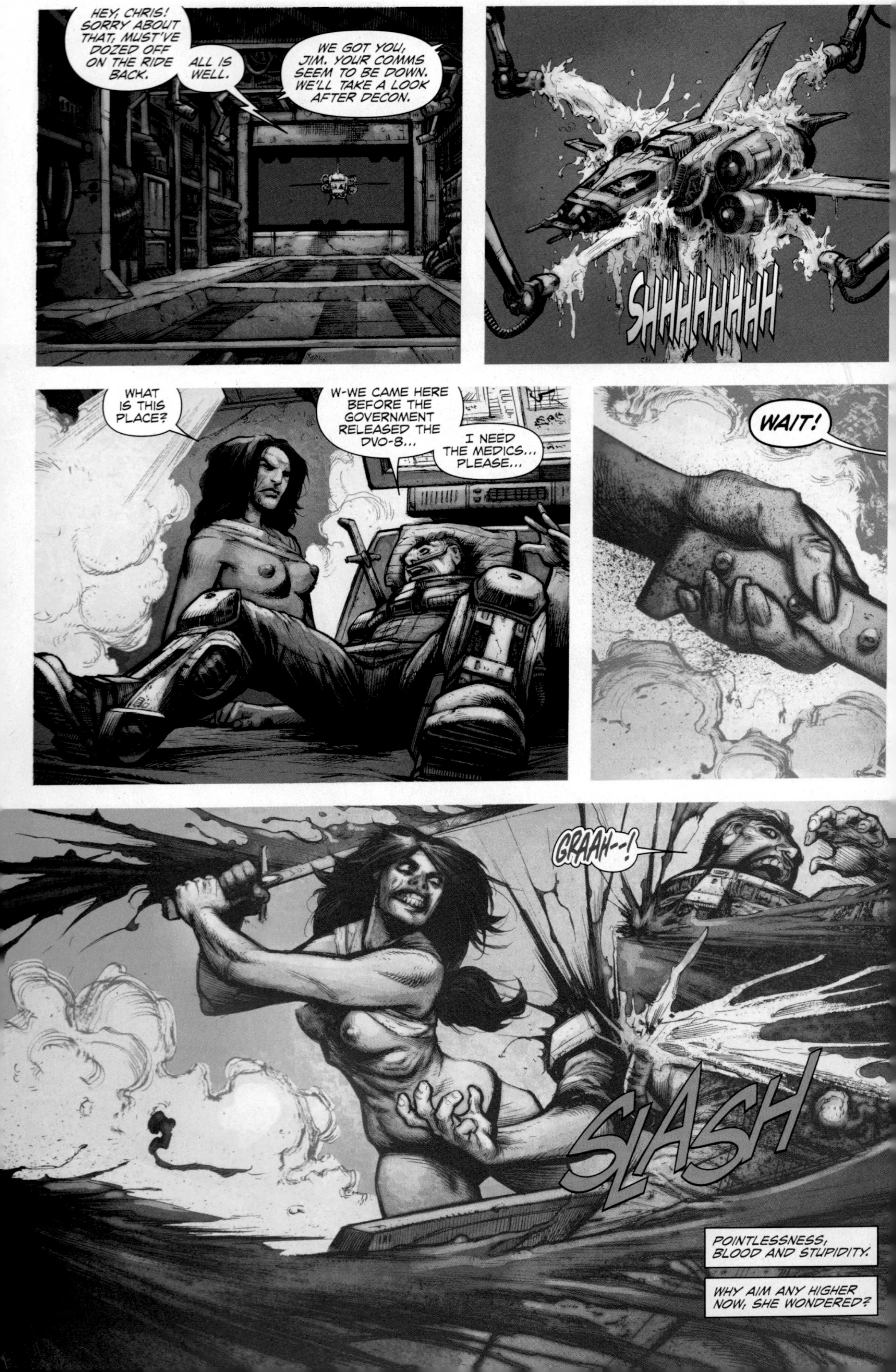
HEY, CHRIS! SORRY ABOUT THAT, MUST'VE DOZED OFF ON THE RIDE BACK.
ALL IS WELL.
WE GOT YOU, JIM. YOUR COMMS SEEM TO BE DOWN. WE'LL TAKE A LOOK AFTER DECON.
SHHHHHHHH
WHAT IS THIS PLACE?
W-WE CAME HERE BEFORE THE GOVERNMENT RELEASED THE DVO-8...
I NEED THE MEDICS... PLEASE...
WAIT!
GRAAH--!
SLASH
POINTLESSNESS, BLOOD AND STUPIDITY.
WHY AIM ANY HIGHER NOW, SHE WONDERED?

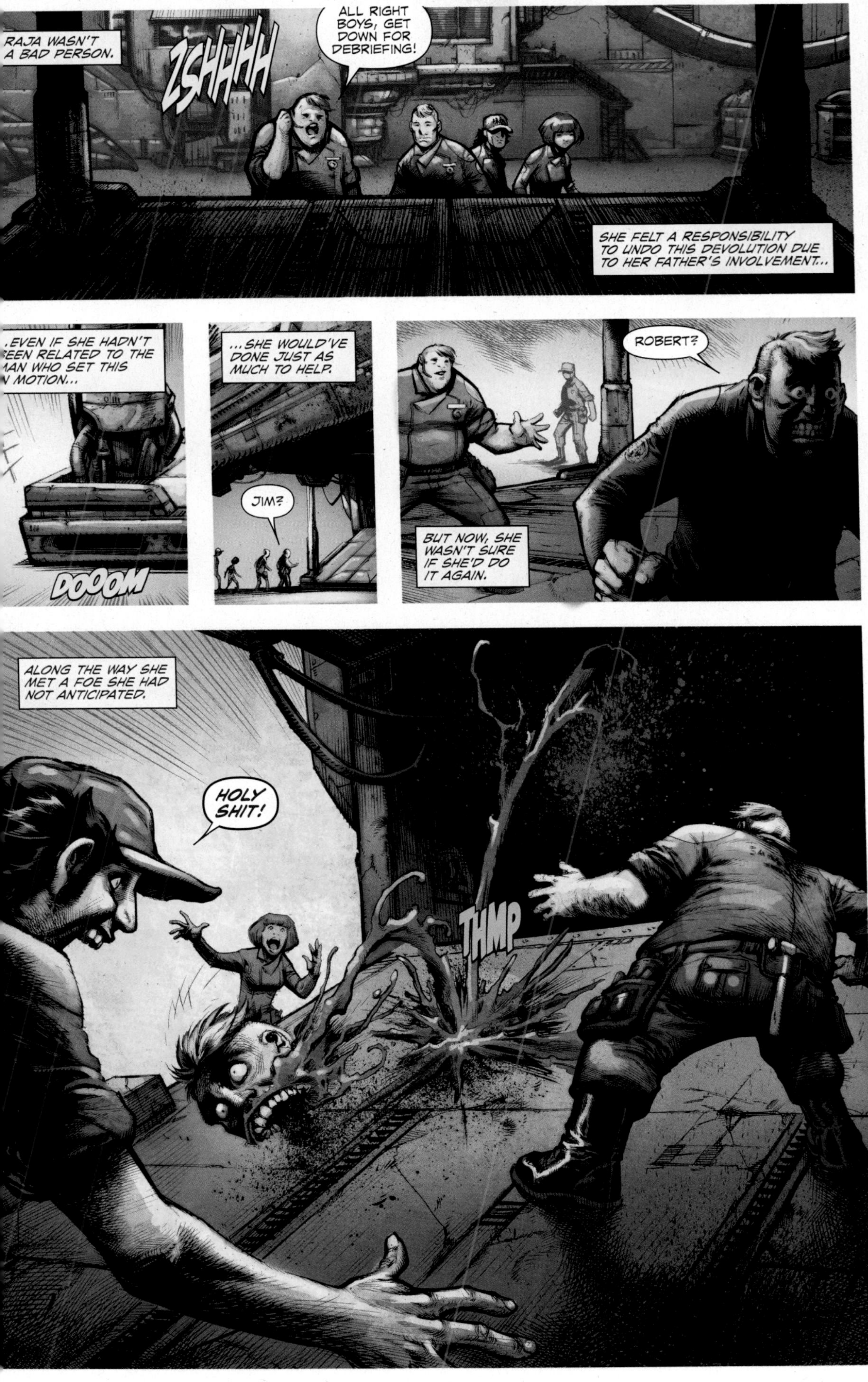
RAJA WASN'T A BAD PERSON.
ZSHHHH
ALL RIGHT BOYS, GET DOWN FOR DEBRIEFING!
SHE FELT A RESPONSIBILITY TO UNDO THIS DEVOLUTION DUE TO HER FATHER'S INVOLVEMENT...
...EVEN IF SHE HADN'T BEEN RELATED TO THE MAN WHO SET THIS IN MOTION...
DOOOM
...SHE WOULD'VE DONE JUST AS MUCH TO HELP.
JIM?
ROBERT?
BUT NOW, SHE WASN'T SURE IF SHE'D DO IT AGAIN.
ALONG THE WAY SHE MET A FOE SHE HAD NOT ANTICIPATED.
HOLY SHIT!
THMP

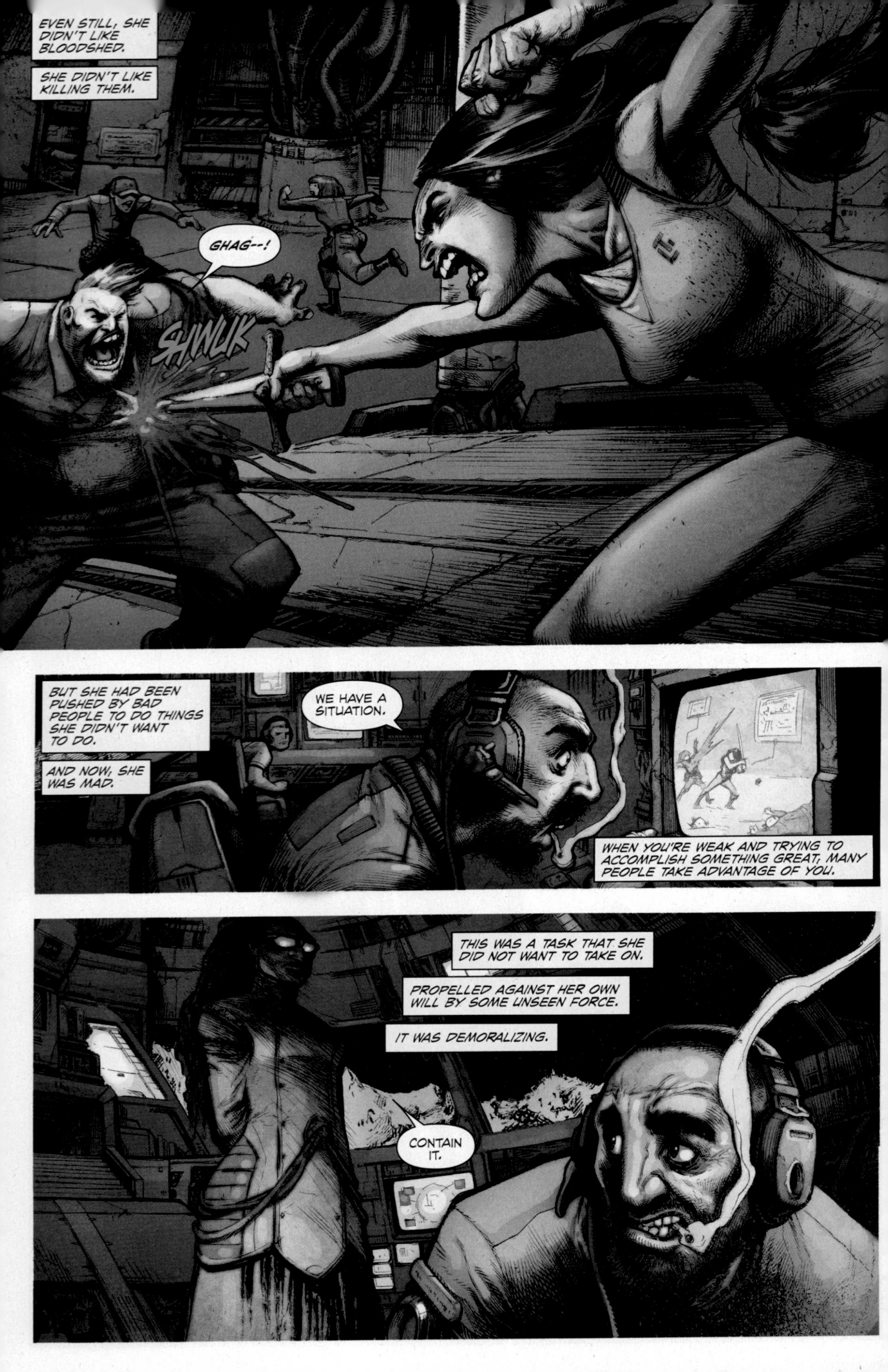
EVEN STILL, SHE DIDN'T LIKE BLOODSHED.
SHE DIDN'T LIKE KILLING THEM.
GHAG--!
SHWUK
BUT SHE HAD BEEN PUSHED BY BAD PEOPLE TO DO THINGS SHE DIDN'T WANT TO DO.
AND NOW, SHE WAS MAD.
WE HAVE A SITUATION.
WHEN YOU'RE WEAK AND TRYING TO ACCOMPLISH SOMETHING GREAT, MANY PEOPLE TAKE ADVANTAGE OF YOU.
THIS WAS A TASK THAT SHE DID NOT WANT TO TAKE ON.
PROPELLED AGAINST HER OWN WILL BY SOME UNSEEN FORCE.
IT WAS DEMORALIZING.
CONTAIN IT.

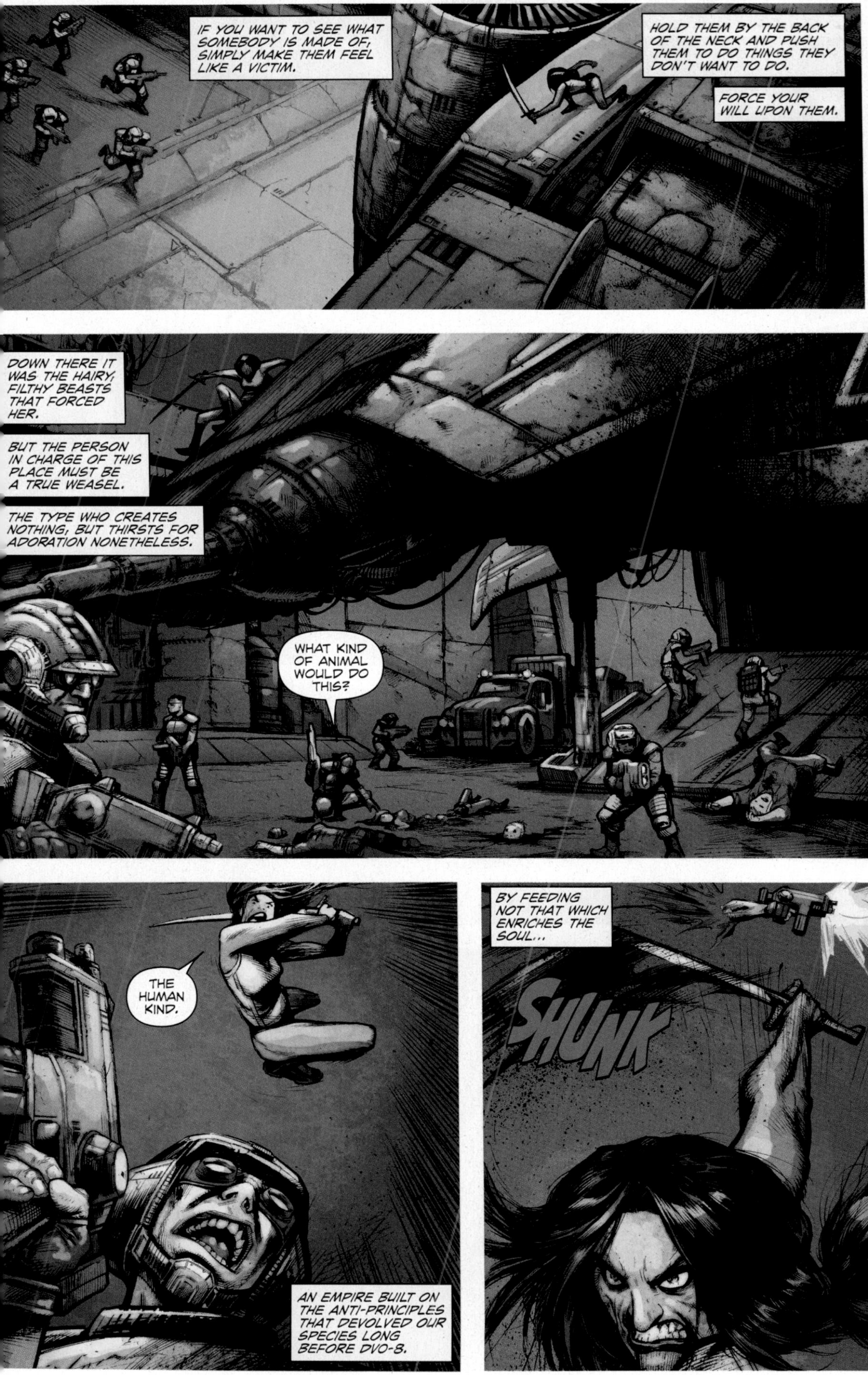
IF YOU WANT TO SEE WHAT SOMEBODY IS MADE OF, SIMPLY MAKE THEM FEEL LIKE A VICTIM.
HOLD THEM BY THE BACK OF THE NECK AND PUSH THEM TO DO THINGS THEY DON'T WANT TO DO.
FORCE YOUR WILL UPON THEM.
DOWN THERE IT WAS THE HAIRY, FILTHY BEASTS THAT FORCED HER.
BUT THE PERSON IN CHARGE OF THIS PLACE MUST BE A TRUE WEASEL.
THE TYPE WHO CREATES NOTHING, BUT THIRSTS FOR ADORATION NONETHELESS.
WHAT KIND OF ANIMAL WOULD DO THIS?
THE HUMAN KIND.
AN EMPIRE BUILT ON THE ANTI-PRINCIPLES THAT DEVOLVED OUR SPECIES LONG BEFORE DVO-8.
BY FEEDING NOT THAT WHICH ENRICHES THE SOUL...
SHUNK

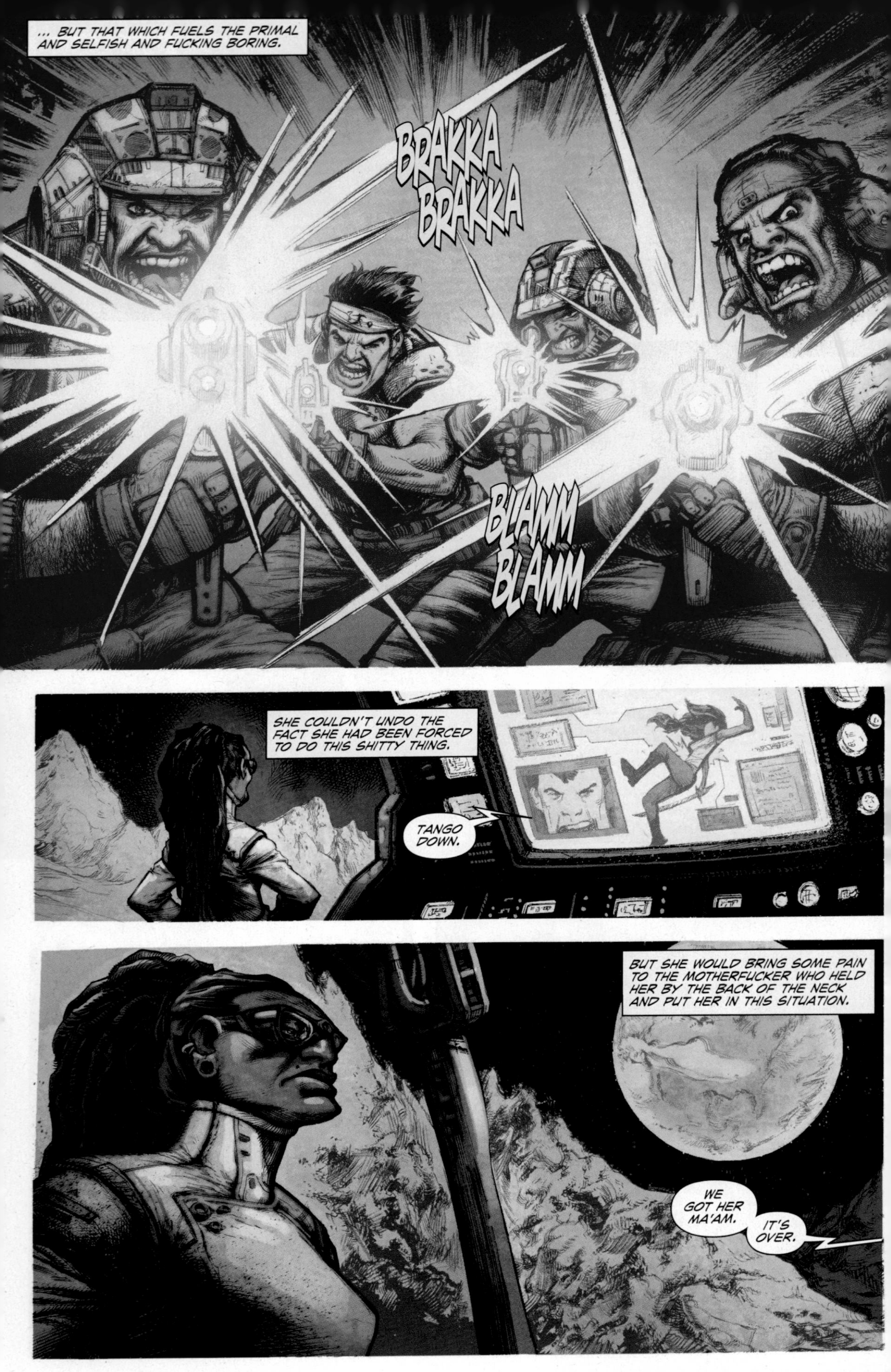
... BUT THAT WHICH FUELS THE PRIMAL AND SELFISH AND FUCKING BORING.
BRAKKA BRAKKA
BLAMM BLAMM
SHE COULDN'T UNDO THE FACT SHE HAD BEEN FORCED TO DO THIS SHITTY THING.
TANGO DOWN.
BUT SHE WOULD BRING SOME PAIN TO THE MOTHERFUCKER WHO HELD HER BY THE BACK OF THE NECK AND PUT HER IN THIS SITUATION.
WE GOT HER MA'AM.
IT'S OVER.

"DO YOU REMEMBER THE STORY OF THE FARMER AND THE SNAKE, LITTLE JEWEL?"

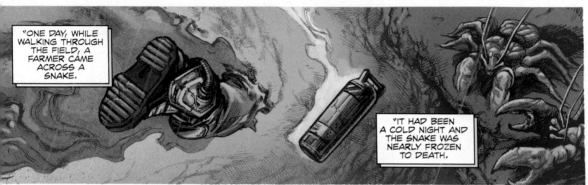

"ONE DAY, WHILE WALKING THROUGH THE FIELD, A FARMER CAME ACROSS A SNAKE.

"IT HAD BEEN A COLD NIGHT AND THE SNAKE WAS NEARLY FROZEN TO DEATH.

"THE FARMER WAS KINDHEARTED AND BROUGHT THE SNAKE HOME AND LAID THE SERPENT BY THE FIRE TO WARM.

"THE FARMER SAVED THE SNAKE'S LIFE. BUT INSTEAD OF SAYING THANK YOU...

"THE SNAKE BIT THE FARMER. A DEADLY STRIKE.

"AS THE FARMER GASPED HIS LAST BREATH, HE ASKED THE SNAKE, 'WHY BITE THE MAN WHO SAVED YOU?'

"AND THE SNAKE REPLIED, 'BECAUSE I AM A SNAKE.'"

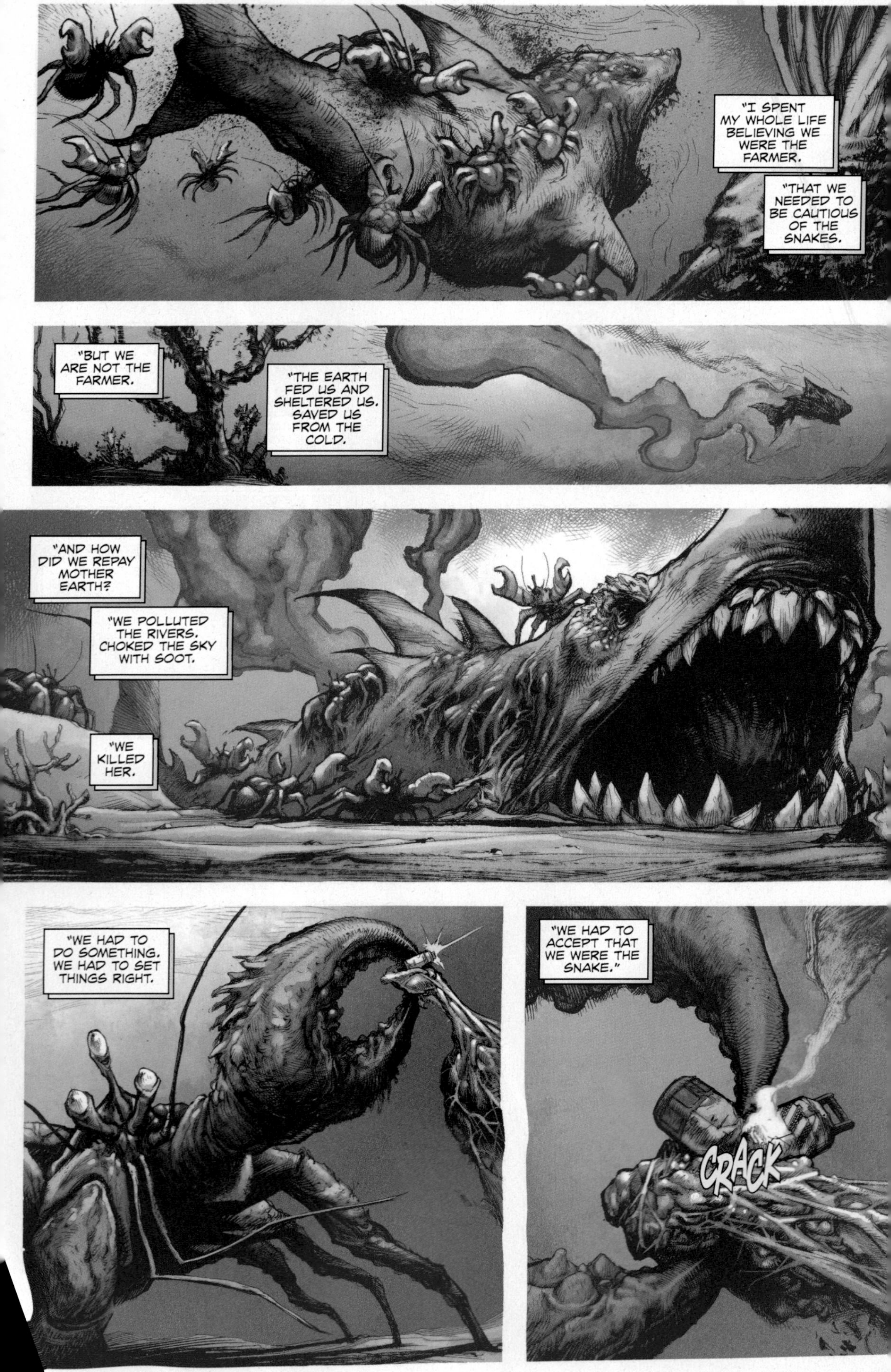
"I SPENT MY WHOLE LIFE BELIEVING WE WERE THE FARMER.
"THAT WE NEEDED TO BE CAUTIOUS OF THE SNAKES.
"BUT WE ARE NOT THE FARMER.
"THE EARTH FED US AND SHELTERED US. SAVED US FROM THE COLD.
"AND HOW DID WE REPAY MOTHER EARTH?
"WE POLLUTED THE RIVERS. CHOKED THE SKY WITH SOOT.
"WE KILLED HER.
"WE HAD TO DO SOMETHING. WE HAD TO SET THINGS RIGHT.
"WE HAD TO ACCEPT THAT WE WERE THE SNAKE."
CRACK

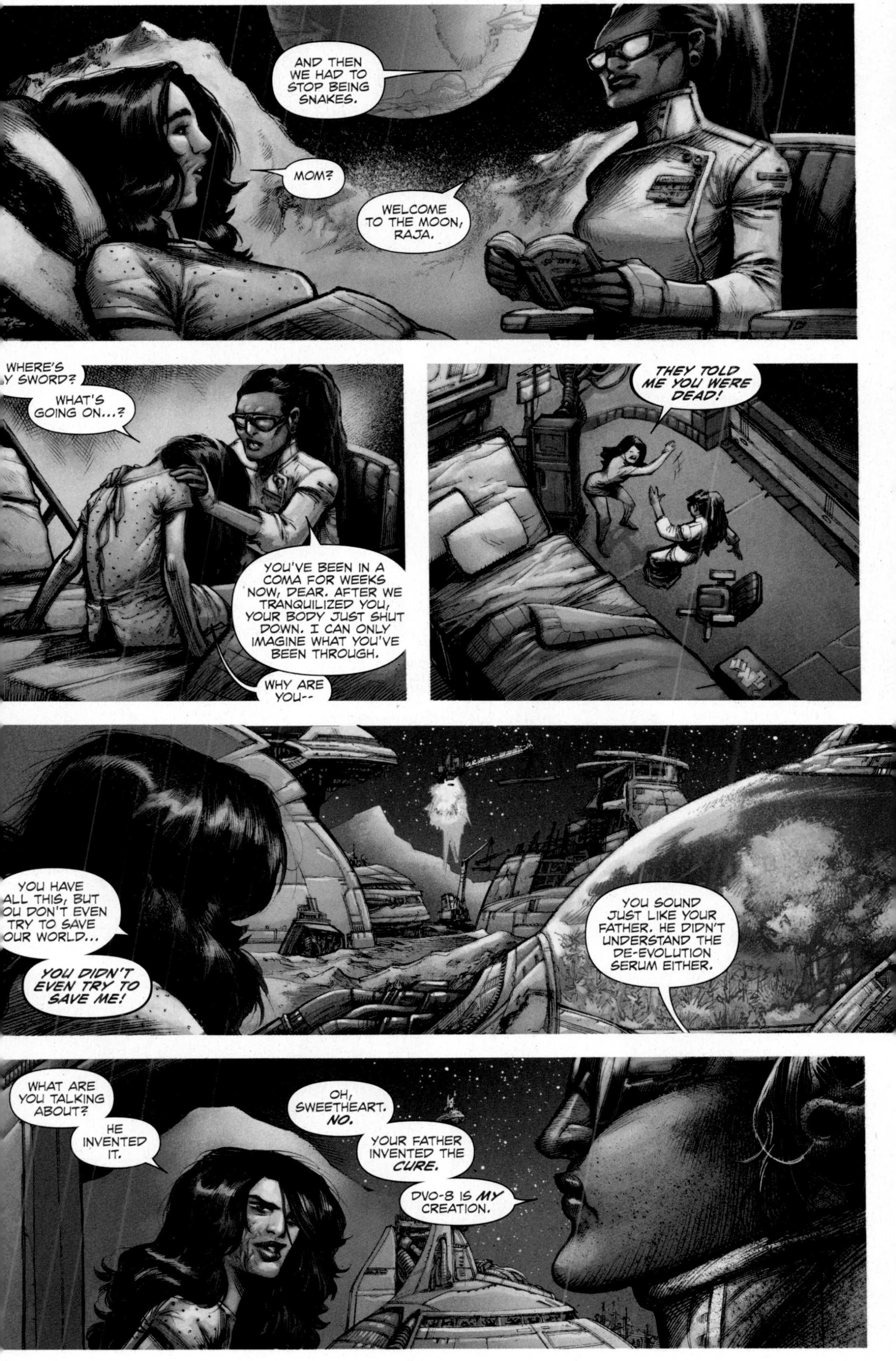
AND THEN WE HAD TO STOP BEING SNAKES.
MOM?
WELCOME TO THE MOON, RAJA.
WHERE'S Y SWORD?
WHAT'S GOING ON...?
YOU'VE BEEN IN A COMA FOR WEEKS NOW, DEAR. AFTER WE TRANQUILIZED YOU, YOUR BODY JUST SHUT DOWN. I CAN ONLY IMAGINE WHAT YOU'VE BEEN THROUGH.
WHY ARE YOU--
THEY TOLD ME YOU WERE DEAD!
YOU HAVE ALL THIS, BUT OU DON'T EVEN TRY TO SAVE OUR WORLD...
YOU DIDN'T EVEN TRY TO SAVE ME!
YOU SOUND JUST LIKE YOUR FATHER. HE DIDN'T UNDERSTAND THE DE-EVOLUTION SERUM EITHER.
WHAT ARE YOU TALKING ABOUT?
HE INVENTED IT.
OH, SWEETHEART. NO.
YOUR FATHER INVENTED THE CURE.
DVO-8 IS MY CREATION.

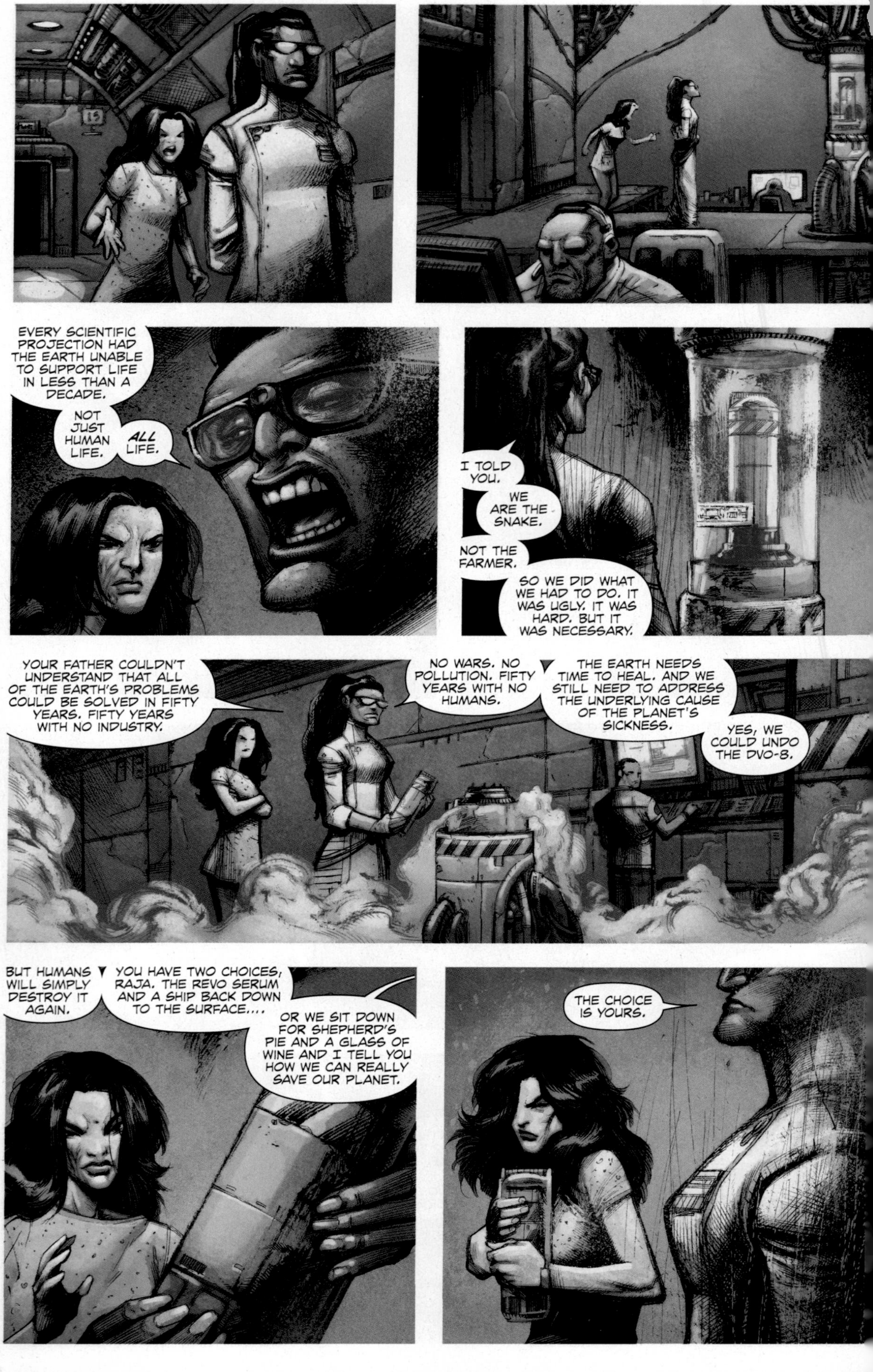
EVERY SCIENTIFIC PROJECTION HAD THE EARTH UNABLE TO SUPPORT LIFE IN LESS THAN A DECADE.
NOT JUST HUMAN LIFE.
ALL LIFE.
I TOLD YOU.
WE ARE THE SNAKE.
NOT THE FARMER.
SO WE DID WHAT WE HAD TO DO. IT WAS UGLY. IT WAS HARD. BUT IT WAS NECESSARY.
YOUR FATHER COULDN'T UNDERSTAND THAT ALL OF THE EARTH'S PROBLEMS COULD BE SOLVED IN FIFTY YEARS. FIFTY YEARS WITH NO INDUSTRY.
NO WARS. NO POLLUTION. FIFTY YEARS WITH NO HUMANS.
THE EARTH NEEDS TIME TO HEAL. AND WE STILL NEED TO ADDRESS THE UNDERLYING CAUSE OF THE PLANET'S SICKNESS.
YES, WE COULD UNDO THE DVO-8.
BUT HUMANS WILL SIMPLY DESTROY IT AGAIN.
YOU HAVE TWO CHOICES, RAJA. THE REVO SERUM AND A SHIP BACK DOWN TO THE SURFACE....
OR WE SIT DOWN FOR SHEPHERD'S PIE AND A GLASS OF WINE AND I TELL YOU HOW WE CAN REALLY SAVE OUR PLANET.
THE CHOICE IS YOURS.

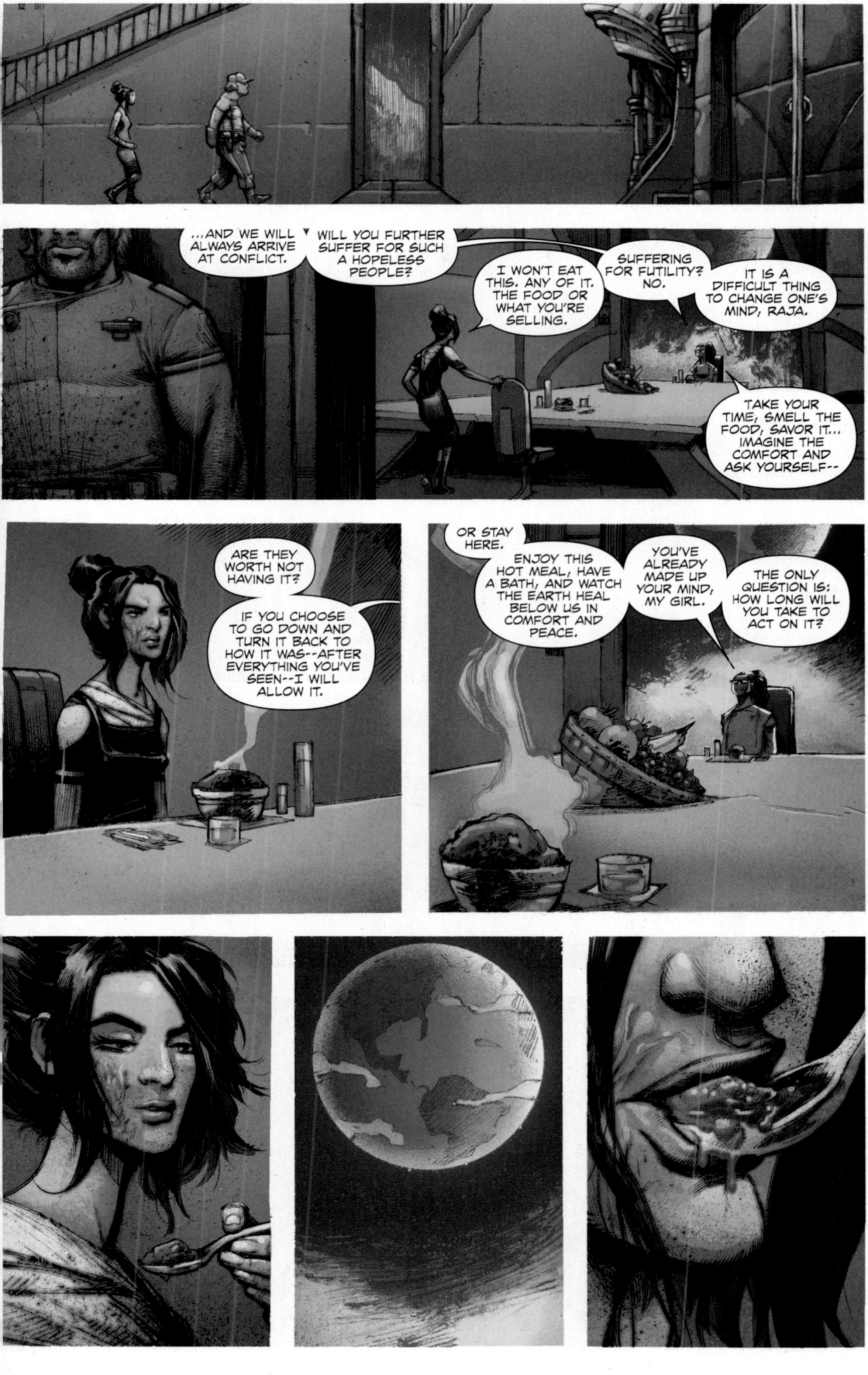
...AND WE WILL ALWAYS ARRIVE AT CONFLICT.
WILL YOU FURTHER SUFFER FOR SUCH A HOPELESS PEOPLE?
I WON'T EAT THIS. ANY OF IT. THE FOOD OR WHAT YOU'RE SELLING.
SUFFERING FOR FUTILITY? NO.
IT IS A DIFFICULT THING TO CHANGE ONE'S MIND, RAJA.
TAKE YOUR TIME, SMELL THE FOOD, SAVOR IT... IMAGINE THE COMFORT AND ASK YOURSELF--
ARE THEY WORTH NOT HAVING IT?
IF YOU CHOOSE TO GO DOWN AND TURN IT BACK TO HOW IT WAS--AFTER EVERYTHING YOU'VE SEEN--I WILL ALLOW IT.
OR STAY HERE.
ENJOY THIS HOT MEAL, HAVE A BATH, AND WATCH THE EARTH HEAL BELOW US IN COMFORT AND PEACE.
YOU'VE ALREADY MADE UP YOUR MIND, MY GIRL.
THE ONLY QUESTION IS: HOW LONG WILL YOU TAKE TO ACT ON IT?

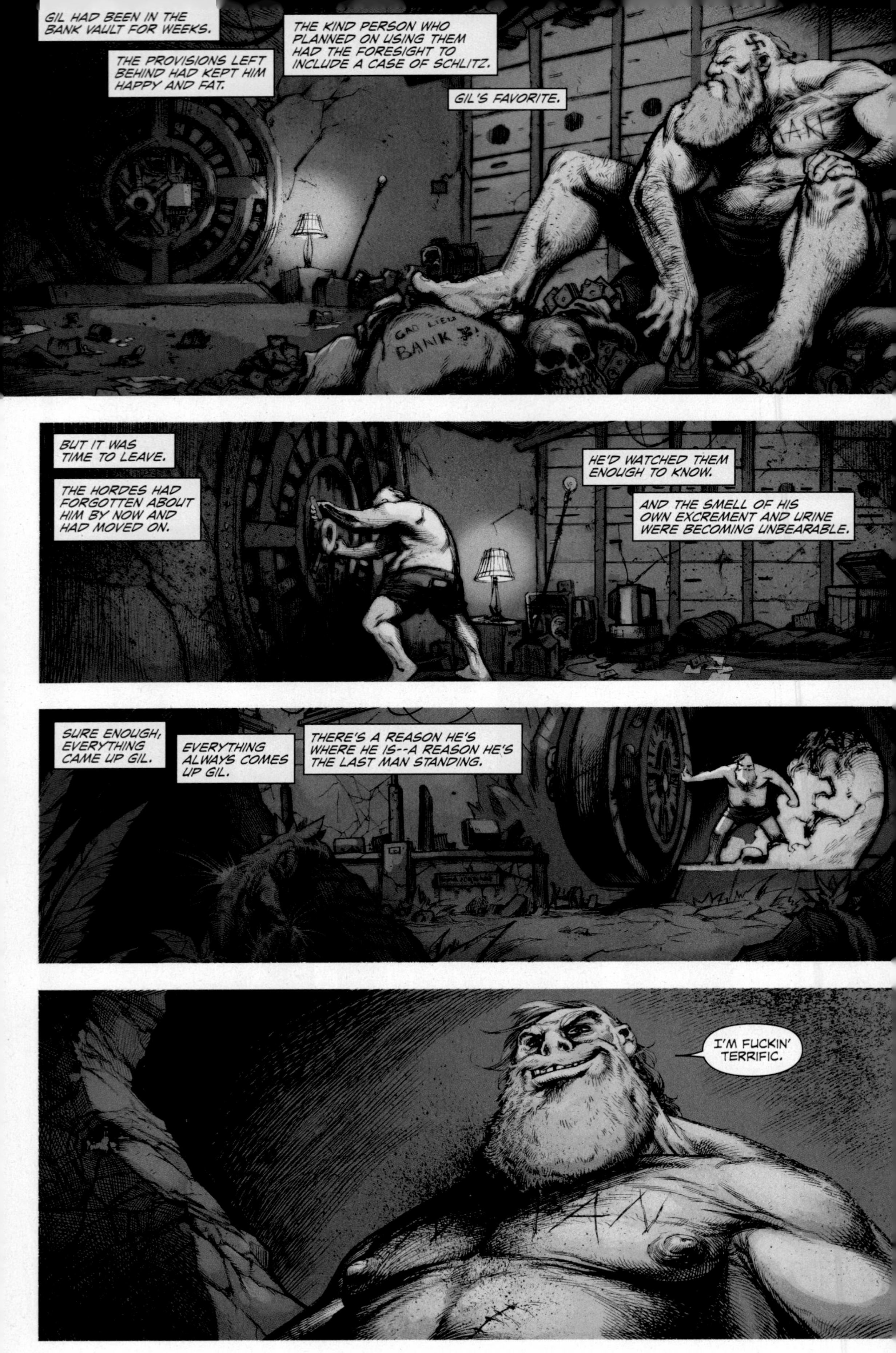
GIL HAD BEEN IN THE BANK VAULT FOR WEEKS.
THE PROVISIONS LEFT BEHIND HAD KEPT HIM HAPPY AND FAT.
THE KIND PERSON WHO PLANNED ON USING THEM HAD THE FORESIGHT TO INCLUDE A CASE OF SCHLITZ.
GIL'S FAVORITE.
BUT IT WAS TIME TO LEAVE.
THE HORDES HAD FORGOTTEN ABOUT HIM BY NOW AND HAD MOVED ON.
HE'D WATCHED THEM ENOUGH TO KNOW.
AND THE SMELL OF HIS OWN EXCREMENT AND URINE WERE BECOMING UNBEARABLE.
SURE ENOUGH, EVERYTHING CAME UP GIL.
EVERYTHING ALWAYS COMES UP GIL.
THERE'S A REASON HE'S WHERE HE IS--A REASON HE'S THE LAST MAN STANDING.
I'M FUCKIN' TERRIFIC.

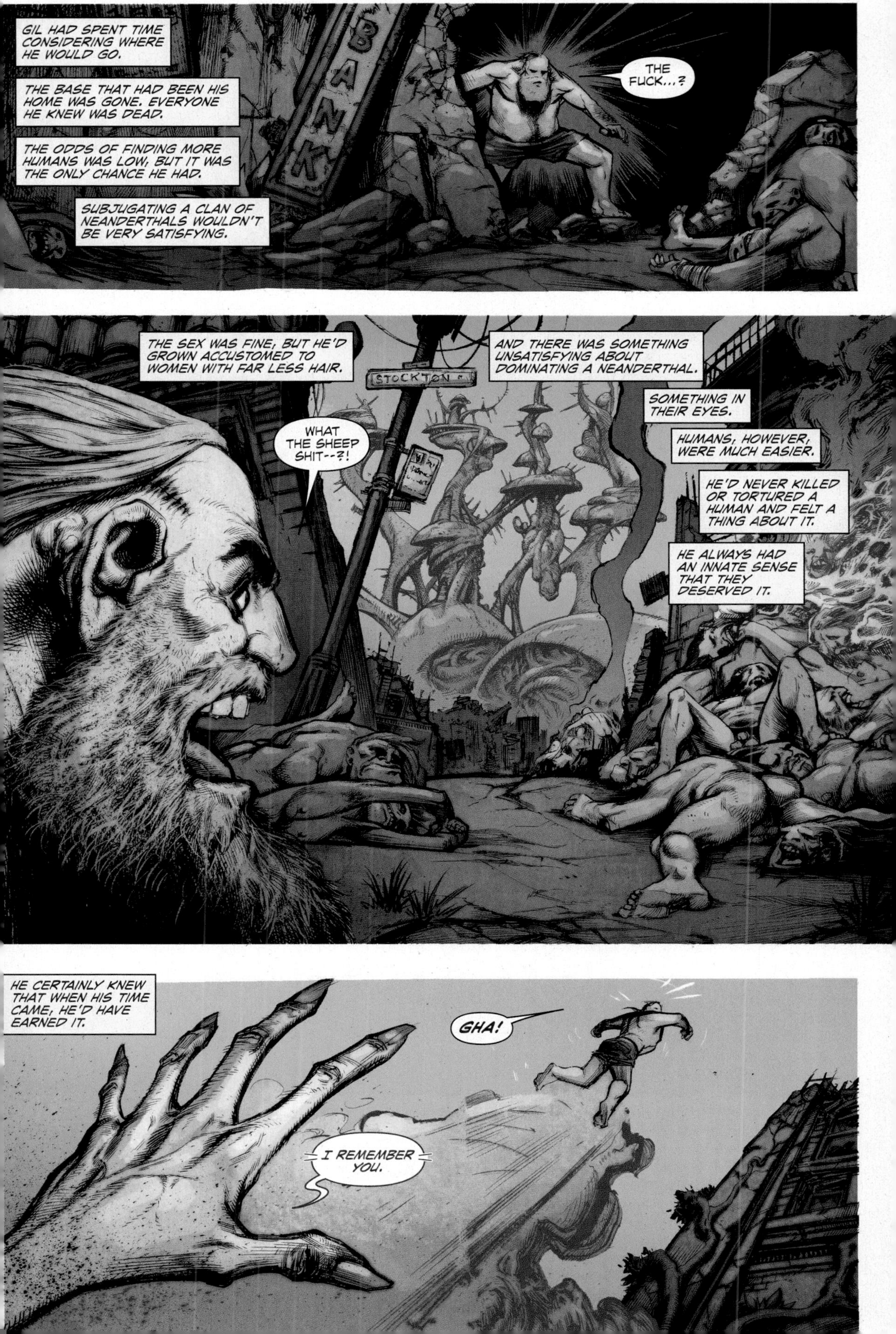
GIL HAD SPENT TIME CONSIDERING WHERE HE WOULD GO.
THE BASE THAT HAD BEEN HIS HOME WAS GONE. EVERYONE HE KNEW WAS DEAD.
THE ODDS OF FINDING MORE HUMANS WAS LOW, BUT IT WAS THE ONLY CHANCE HE HAD.
SUBJUGATING A CLAN OF NEANDERTHALS WOULDN'T BE VERY SATISFYING.
BANK
THE FUCK...?
THE SEX WAS FINE, BUT HE'D GROWN ACCUSTOMED TO WOMEN WITH FAR LESS HAIR.
AND THERE WAS SOMETHING UNSATISFYING ABOUT DOMINATING A NEANDERTHAL.
STOCKTON
SOMETHING IN THEIR EYES.
HUMANS, HOWEVER, WERE MUCH EASIER.
HE'D NEVER KILLED OR TORTURED A HUMAN AND FELT A THING ABOUT IT.
HE ALWAYS HAD AN INNATE SENSE THAT THEY DESERVED IT.
WHAT THE SHEEP SHIT--?!
HE CERTAINLY KNEW THAT WHEN HIS TIME CAME, HE'D HAVE EARNED IT.
GHA!
I REMEMBER YOU.

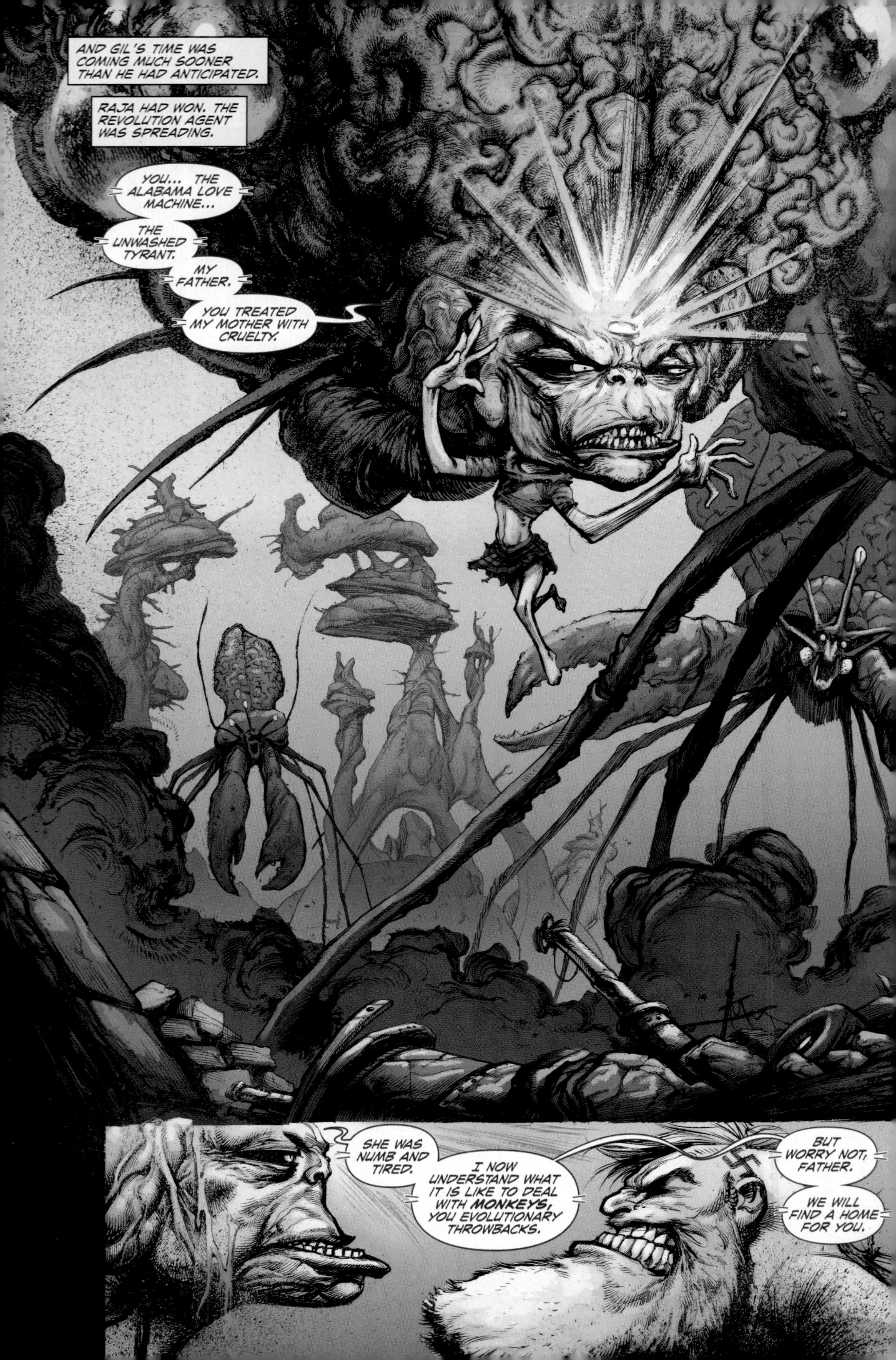

AND GIL'S TIME WAS COMING MUCH SOONER THAN HE HAD ANTICIPATED.
RAJA HAD WON. THE REVOLUTION AGENT WAS SPREADING.
YOU... THE ALABAMA LOVE MACHINE...
THE UNWASHED TYRANT.
MY FATHER.
YOU TREATED MY MOTHER WITH CRUELTY.
SHE WAS NUMB AND TIRED.
I NOW UNDERSTAND WHAT IT IS LIKE TO DEAL WITH MONKEYS, YOU EVOLUTIONARY THROWBACKS.
BUT WORRY NOT, FATHER.
WE WILL FIND A HOME FOR YOU.

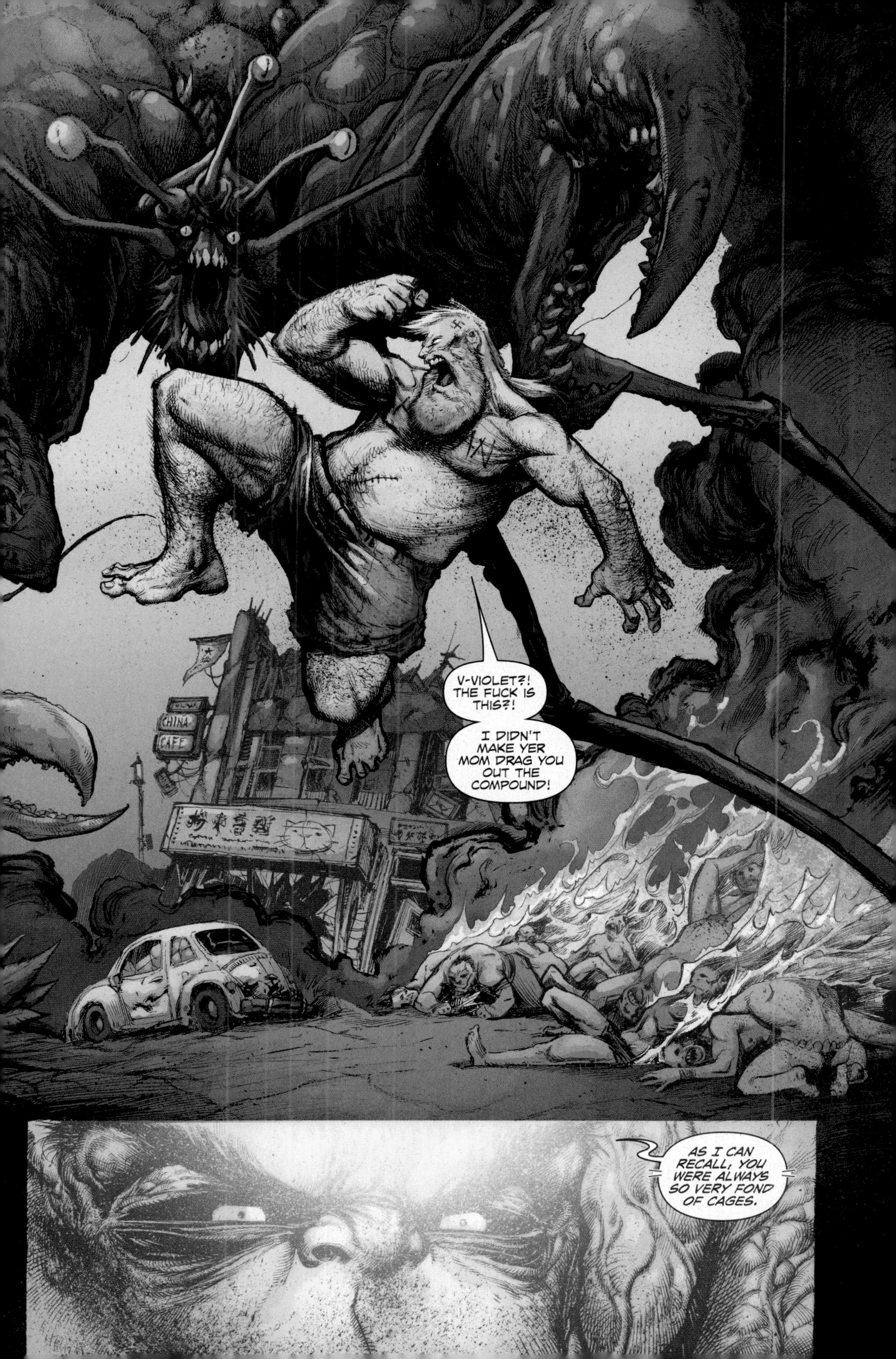
V-VIOLET?! THE FUCK IS THIS?!
I DIDN'T MAKE YER MOM DRAG YOU OUT THE COMPOUND!
CHINA CAFE
AS I CAN RECALL, YOU WERE ALWAYS SO VERY FOND OF CAGES.

DEVOLUTION

RICK REMENDER
WRITER

JONATHAN WAYSHAK
ARTIST

JORDAN BOYD
COLORIST

RUS WOOTON
LETTERER

JOSEPH RYBANDT
EDITOR

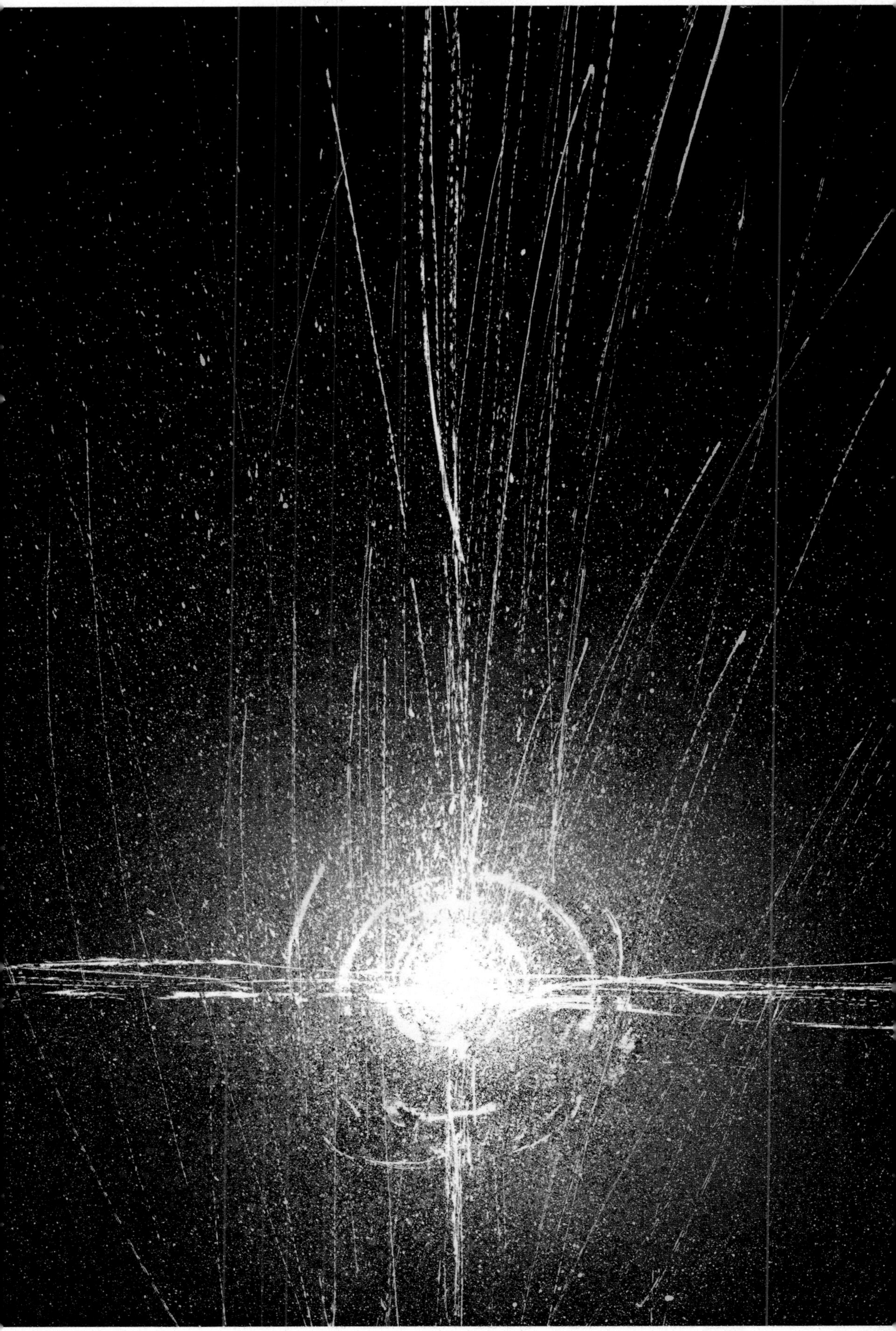

Issue 1 Cover by JAE LEE With Colors by JUNE CHUNG

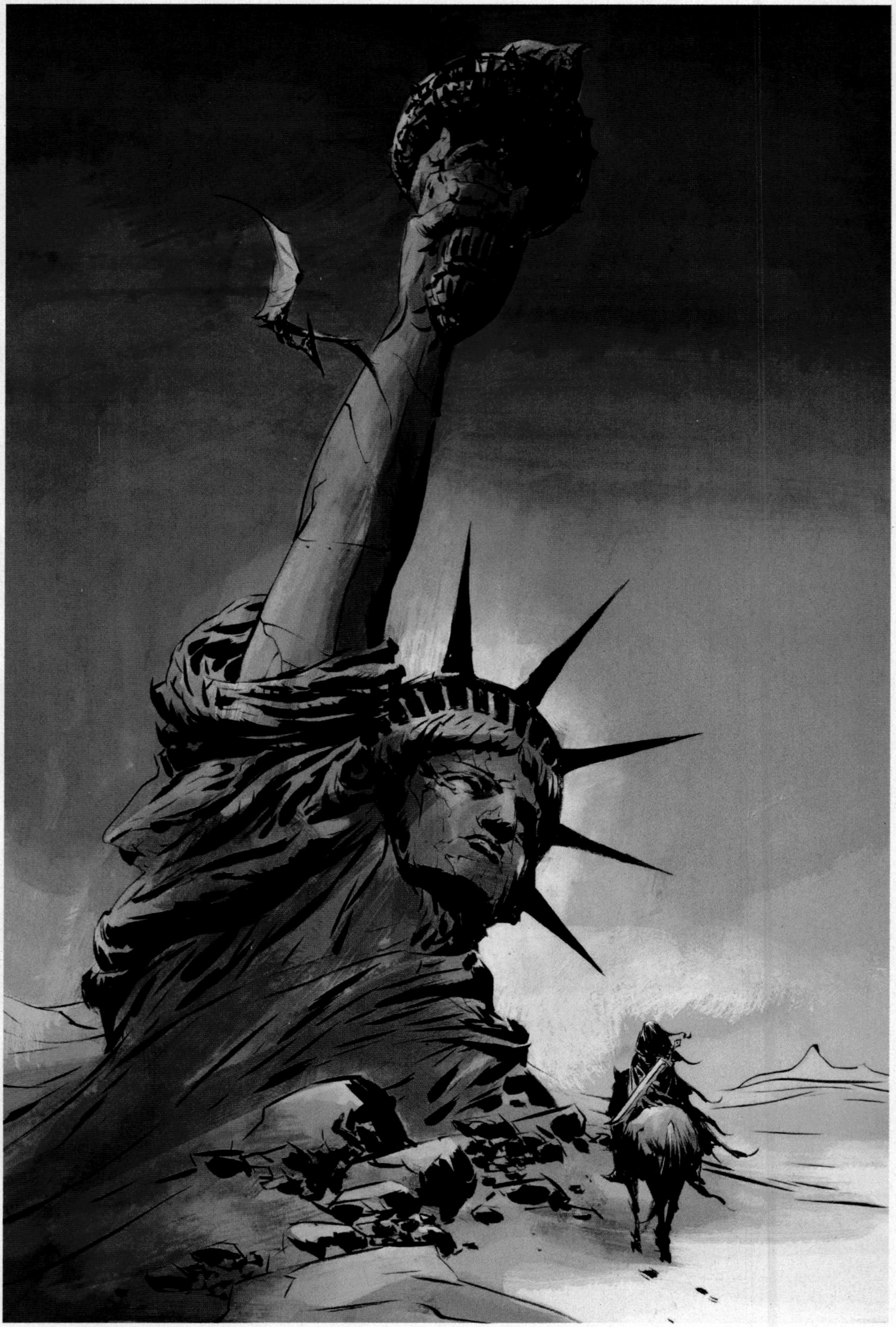

Blind Box Comics exclusive

BONUS MATERIAL

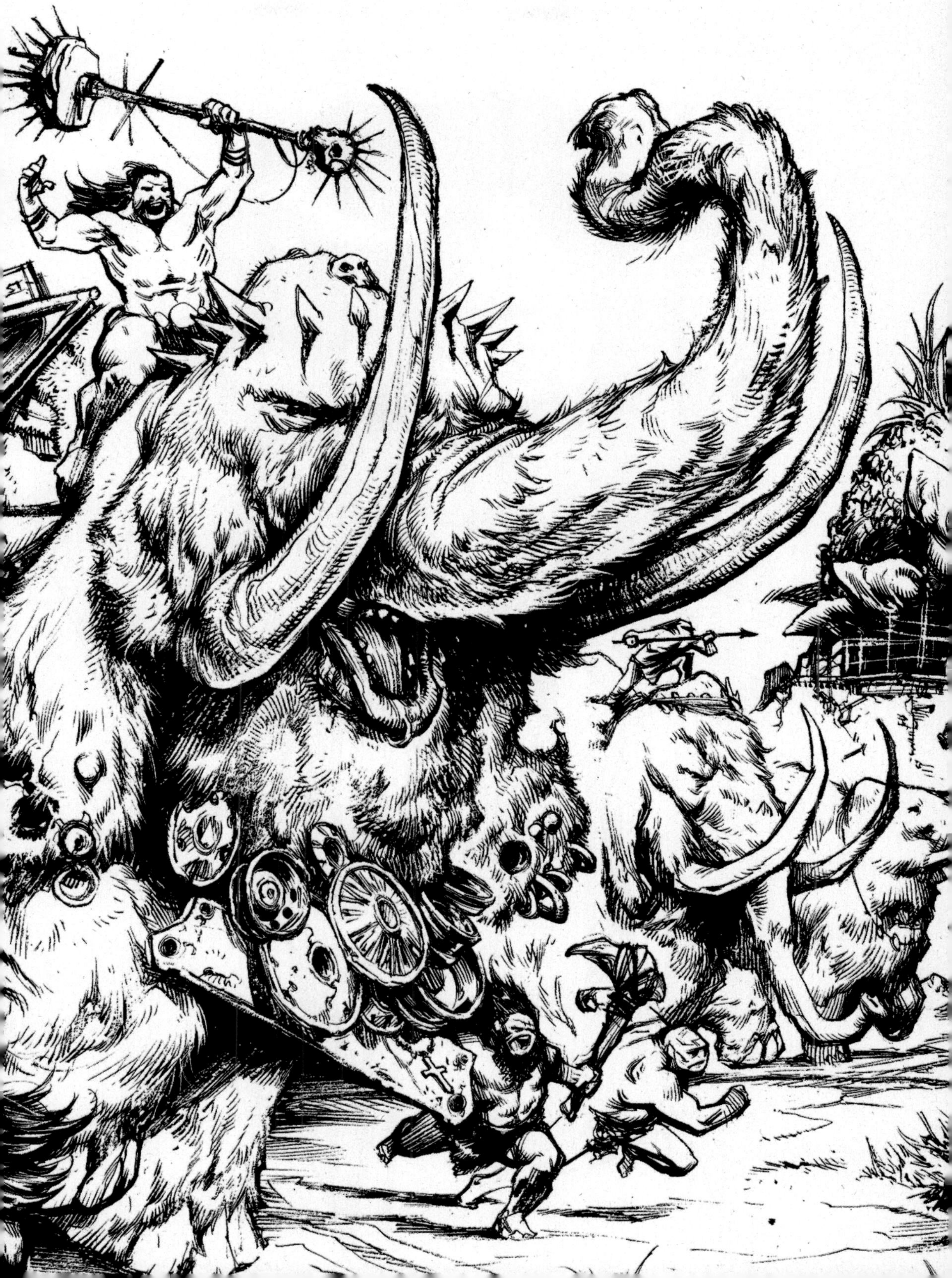

Original Character Sketches
by JONATHAN WAYSHAK

RAJA

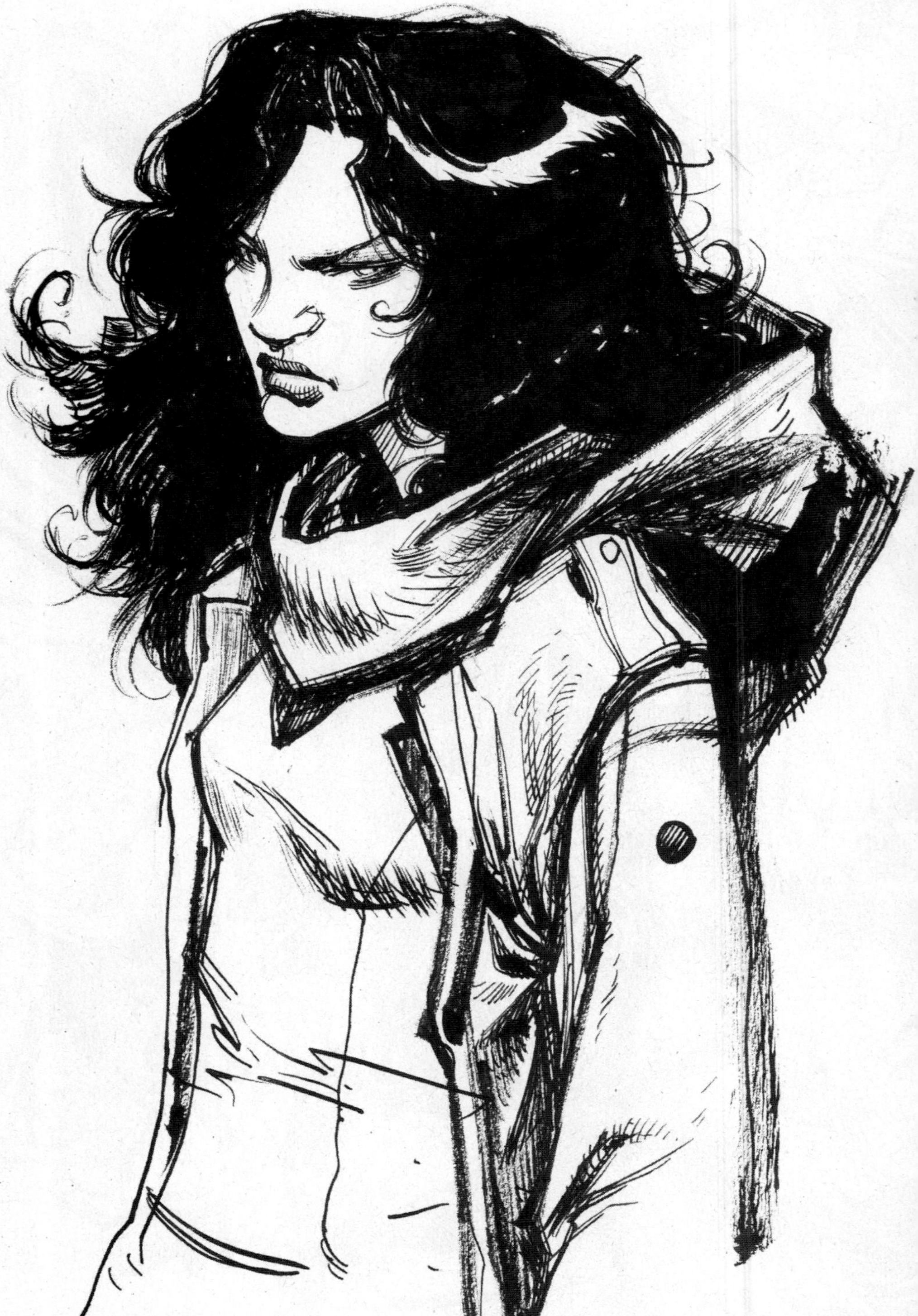

Original Character Sketches
by JONATHAN WAYSHAK

DARREN

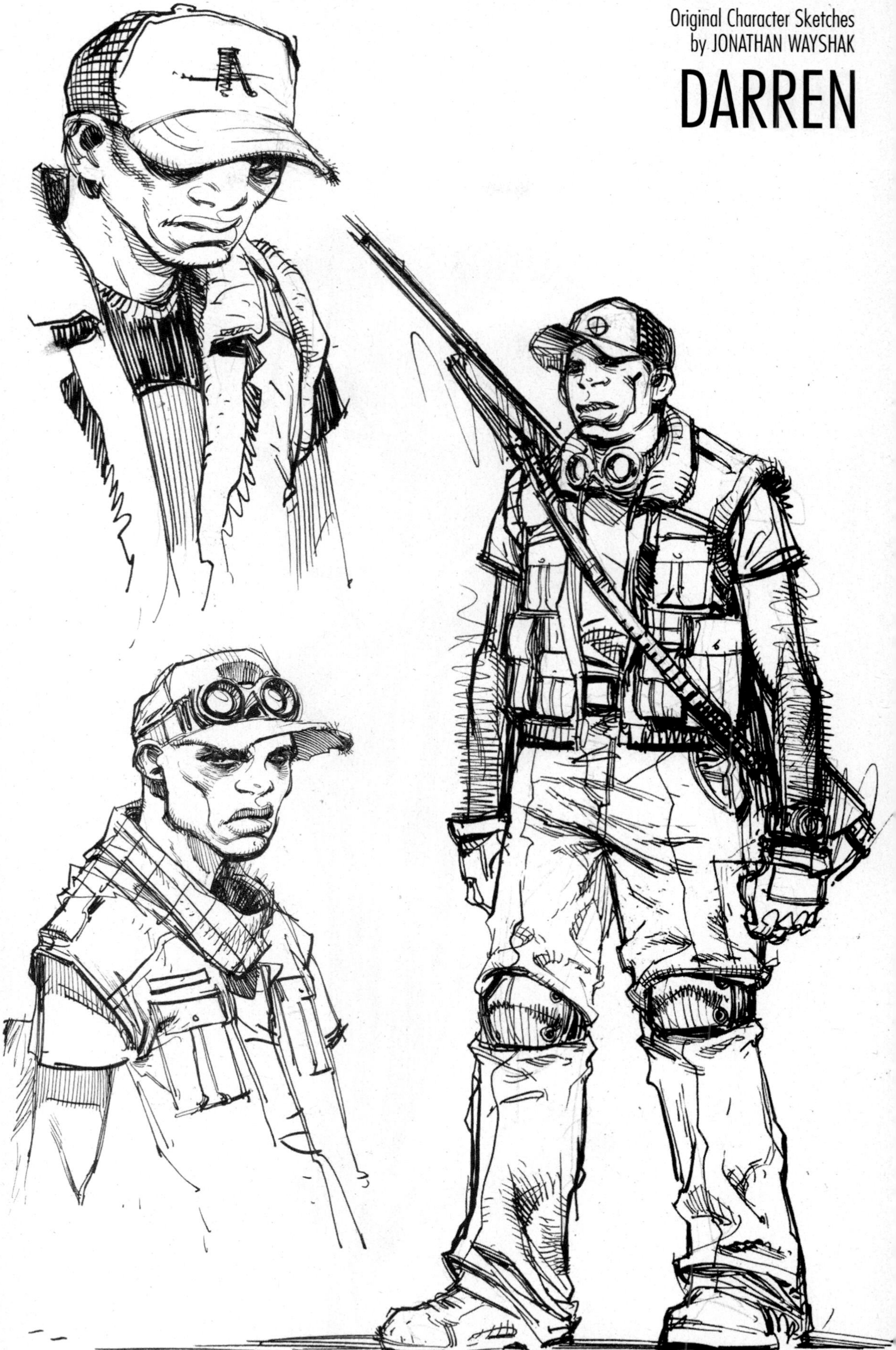

Original Character Sketches
by JONATHAN WAYSHAK

SCOTT

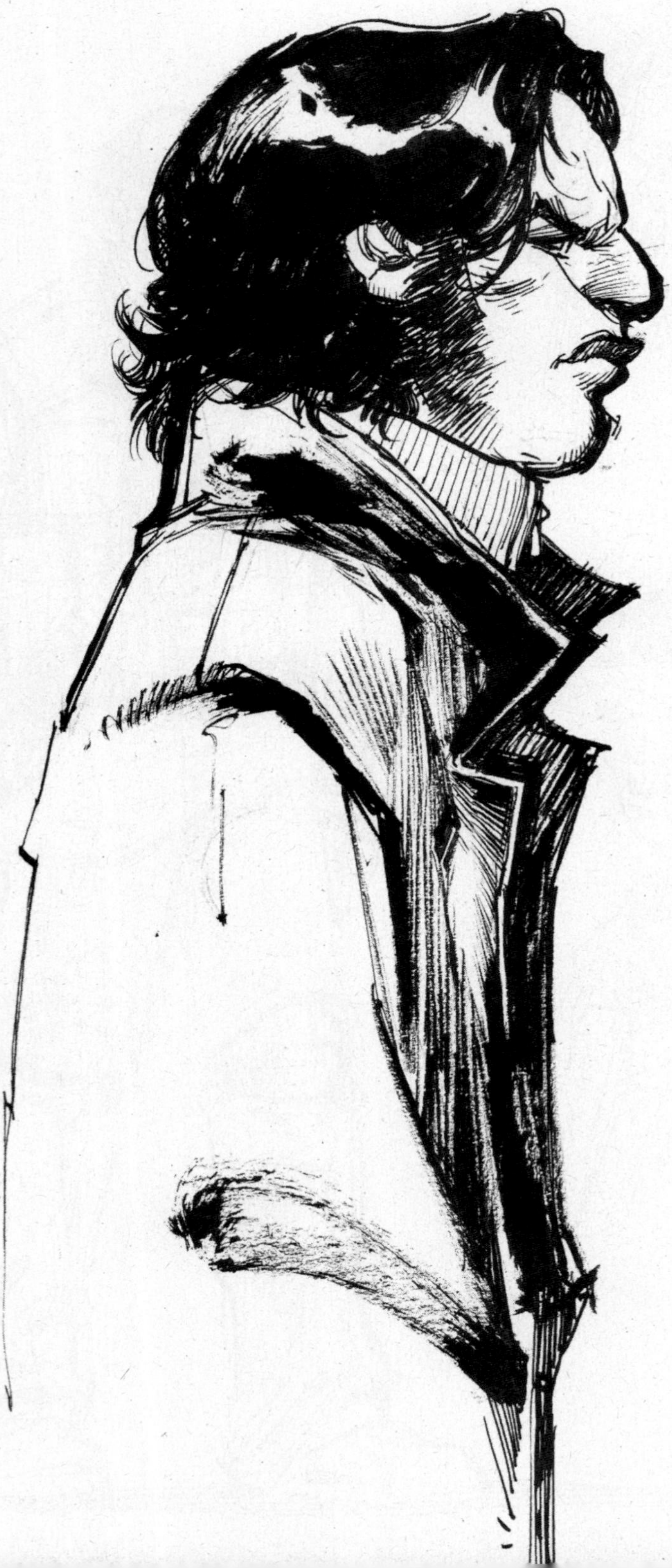

Original Character Sketches
by JONATHAN WAYSHAK

HENCHMAN

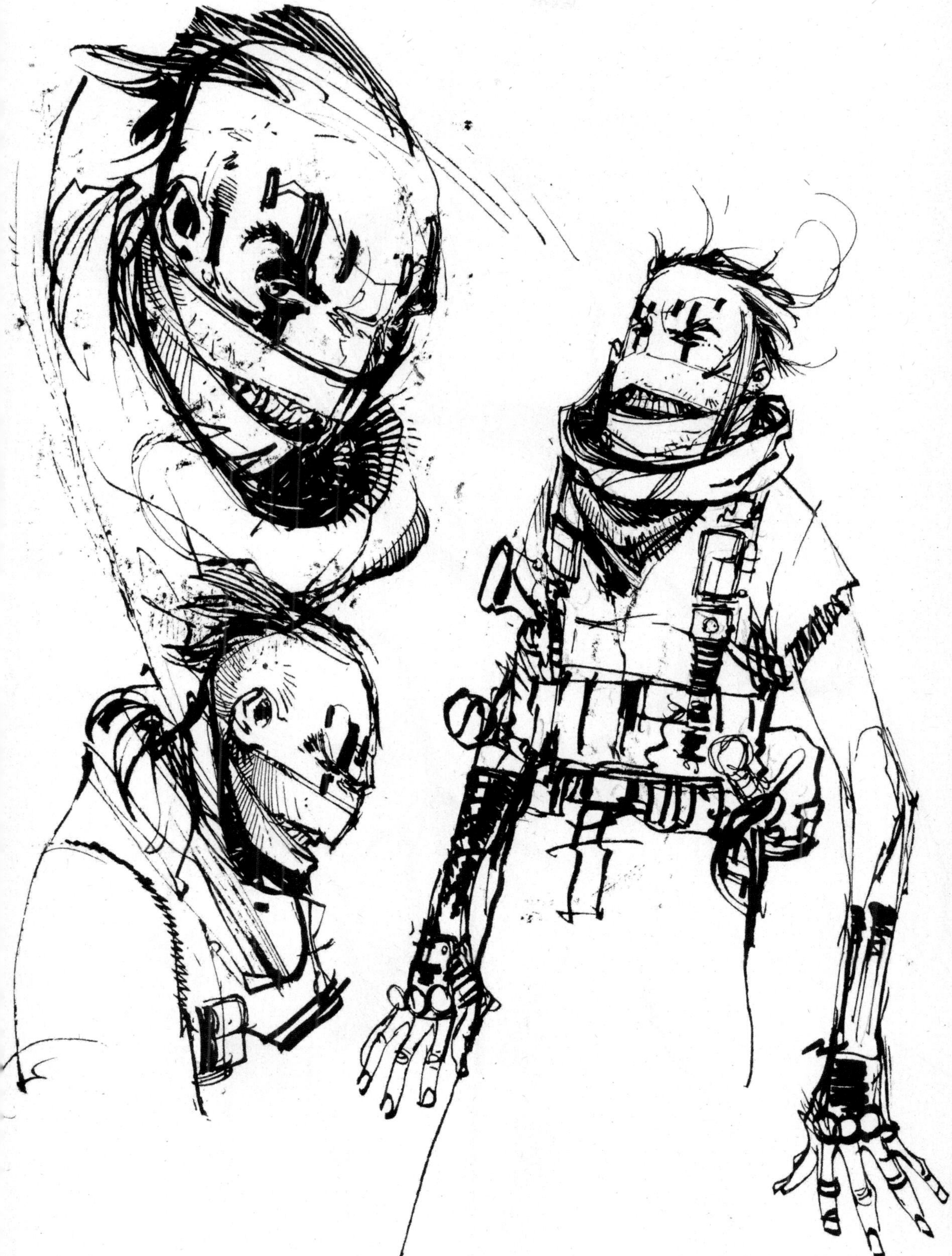

Original Character Sketches
by JONATHAN WAYSHAK

GIL

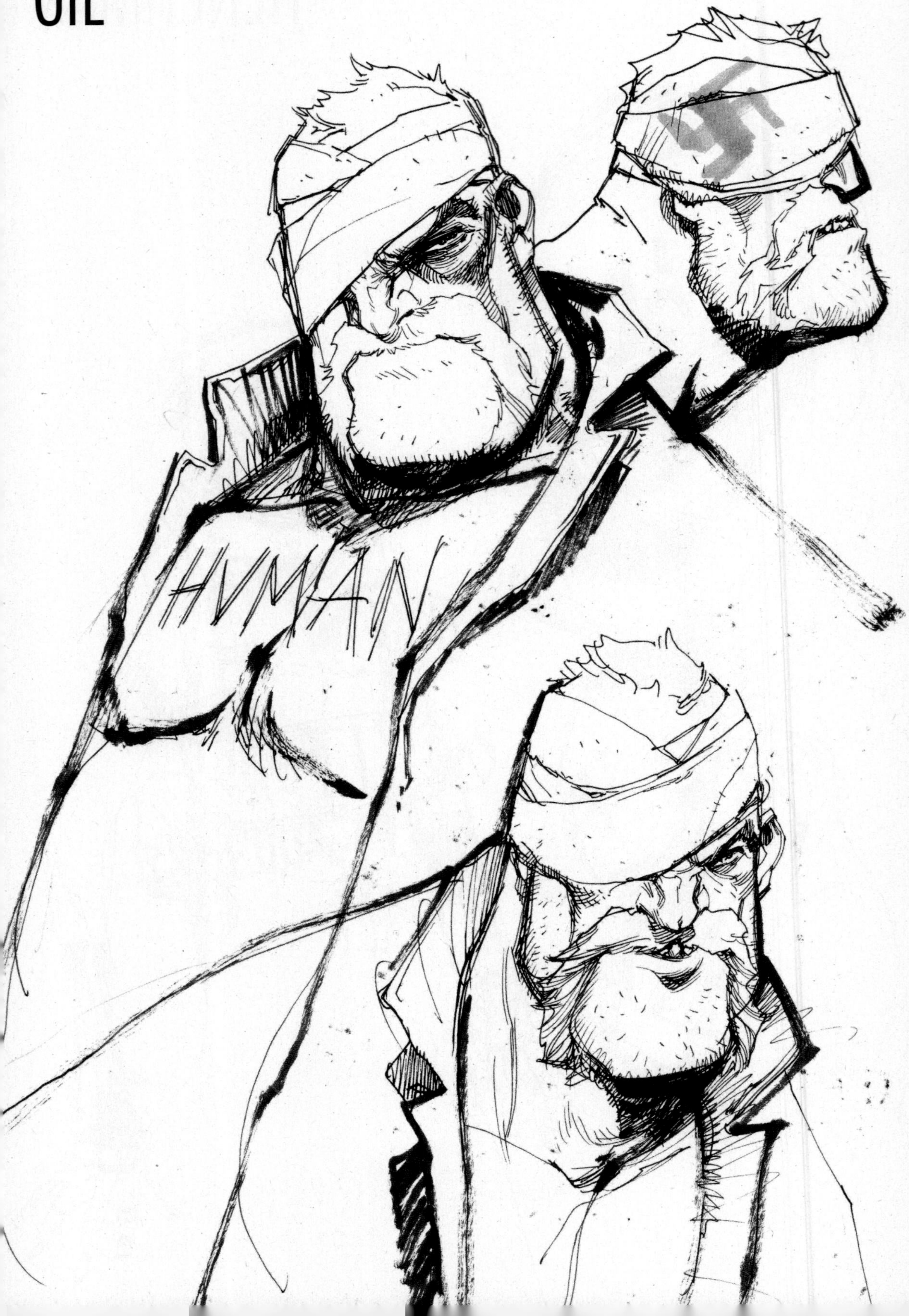
HUMAN

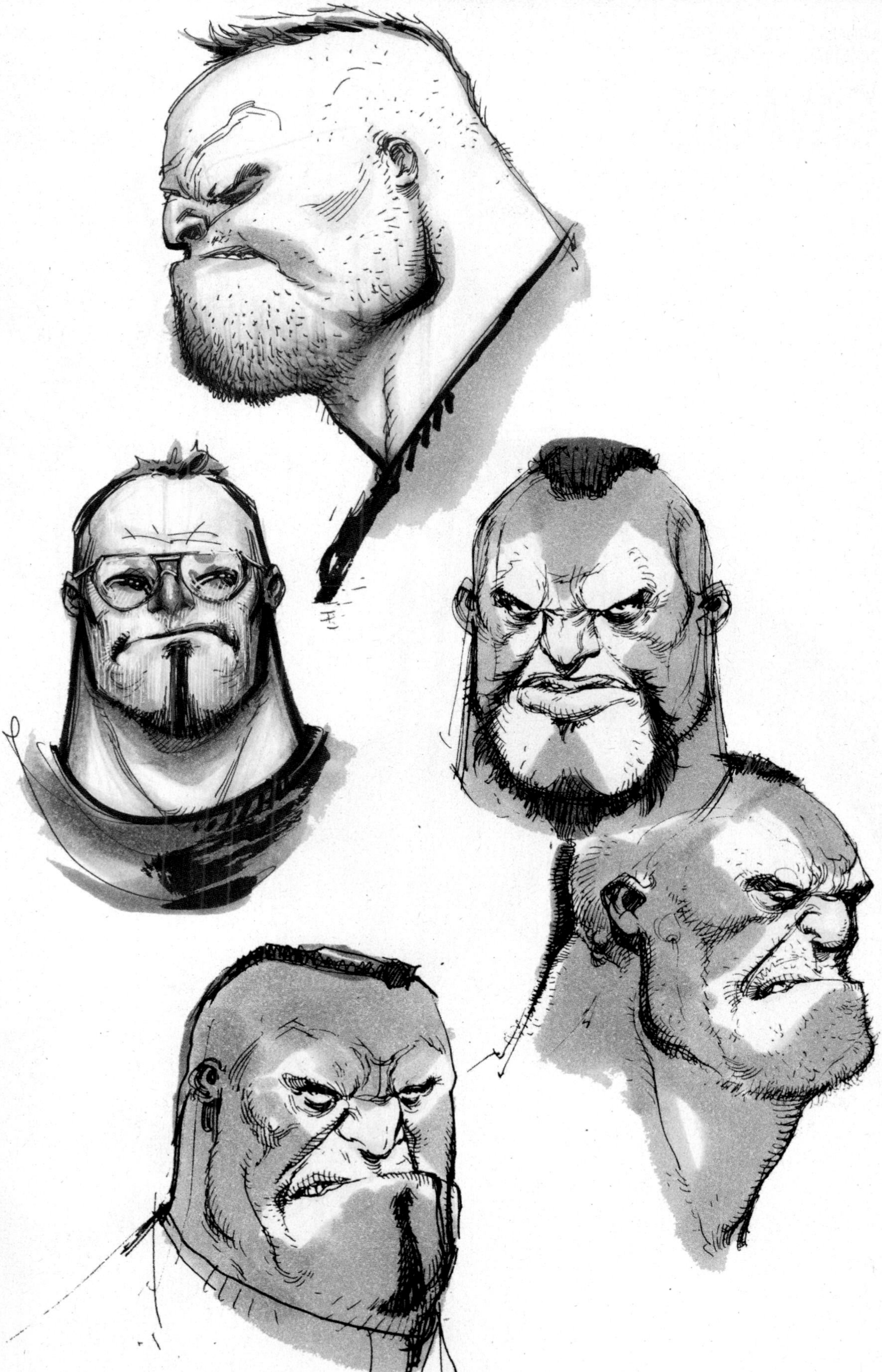

Original Character Sketches
by JONATHAN WAYSHAK

SAVAGES

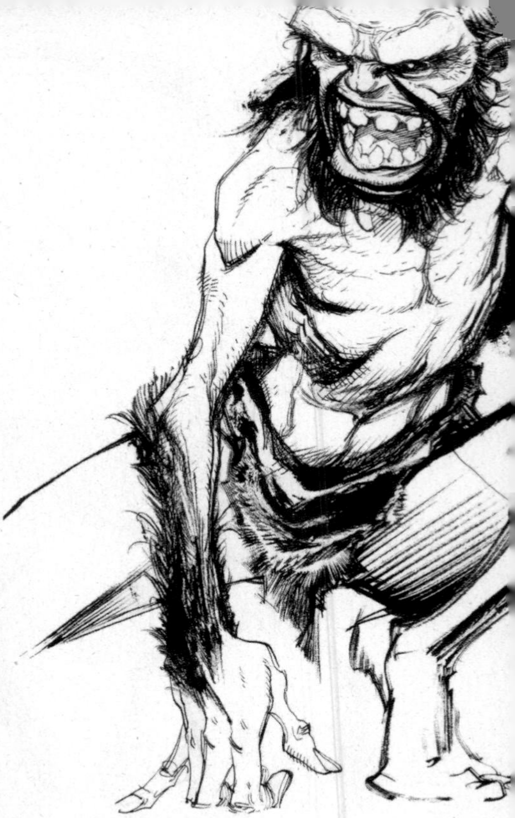

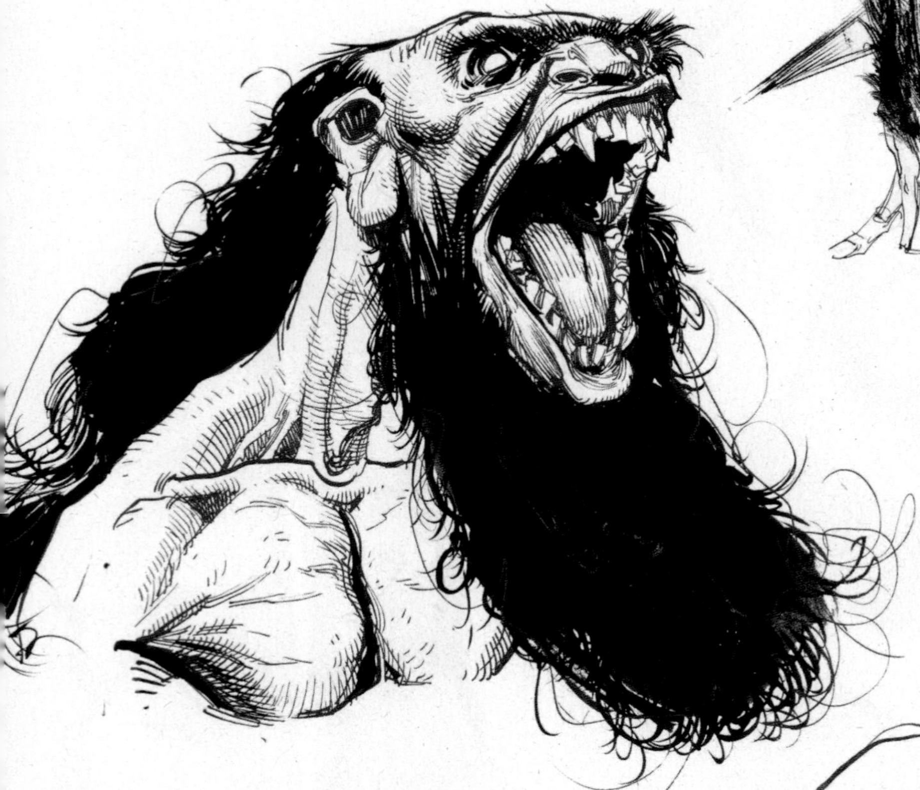

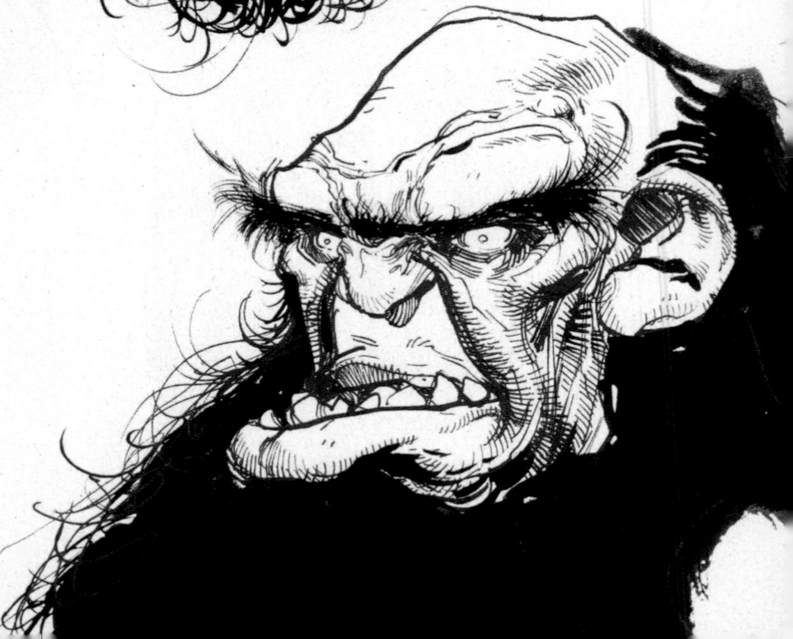

(Opposite) Original Rough Pencils for
Issue 1, Page 1 by JONATHAN WAYSHAK

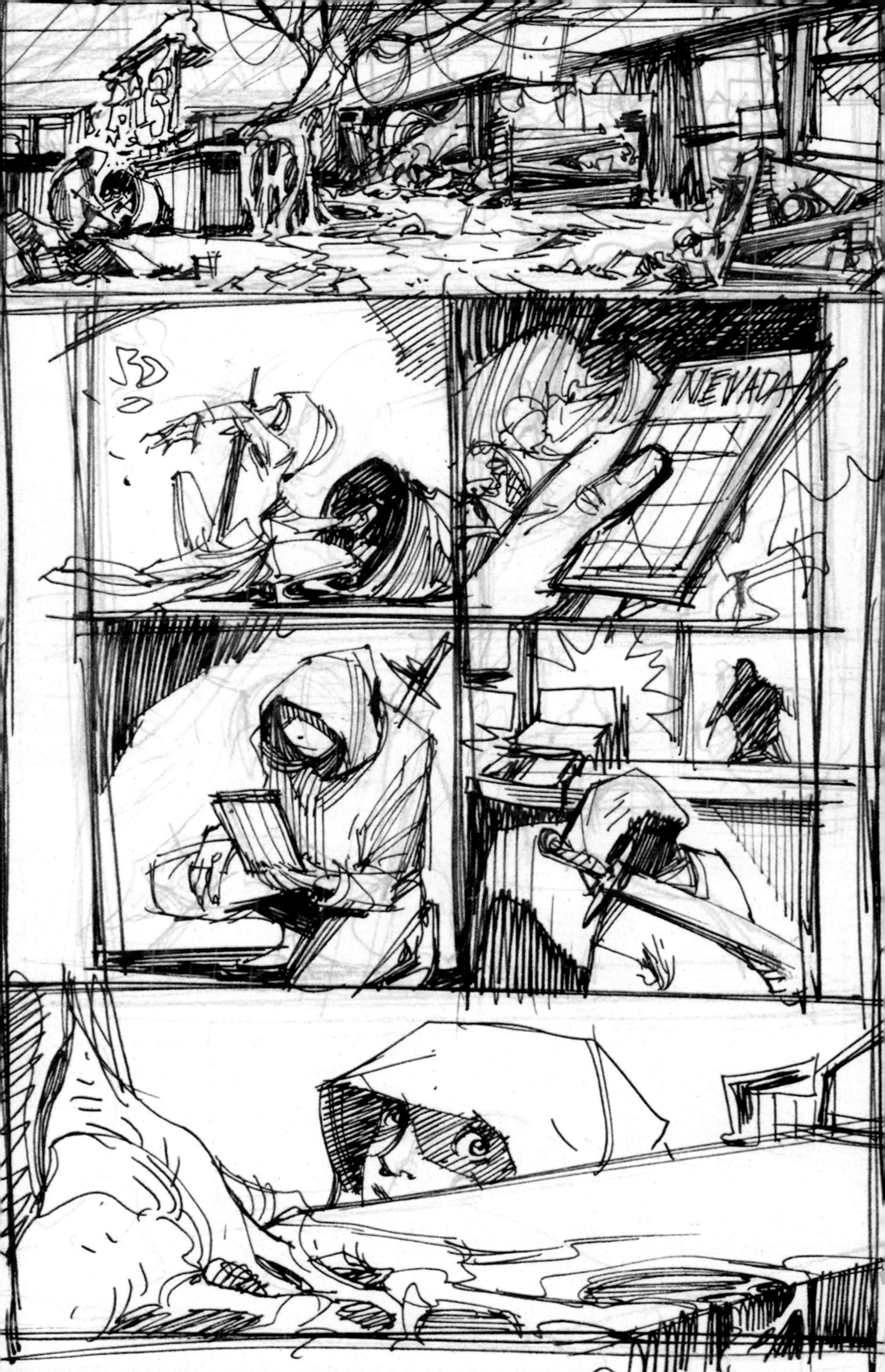
NEVADA

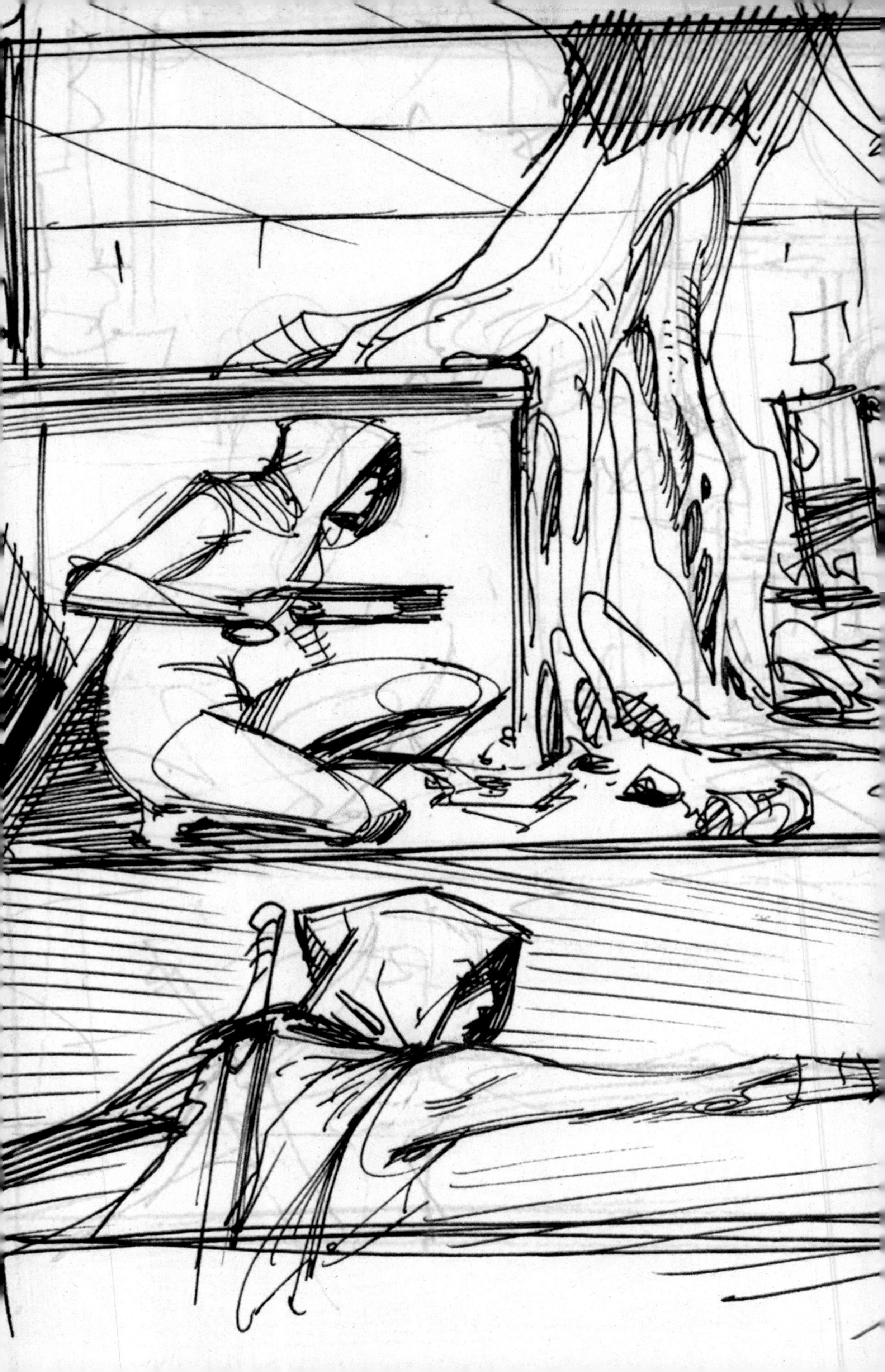

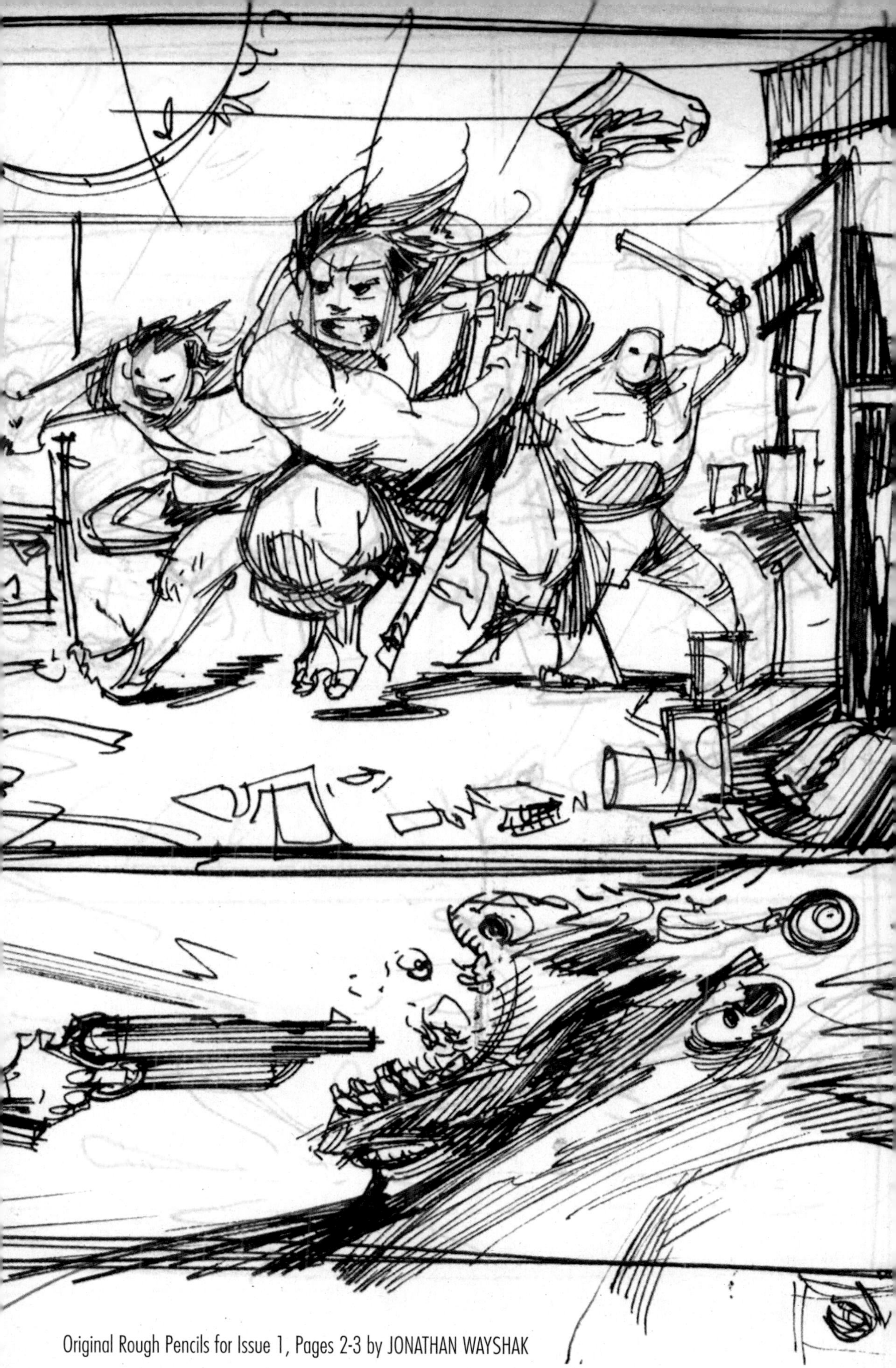

Original Rough Pencils for Issue 1, Pages 2-3 by JONATHAN WAYSHAK

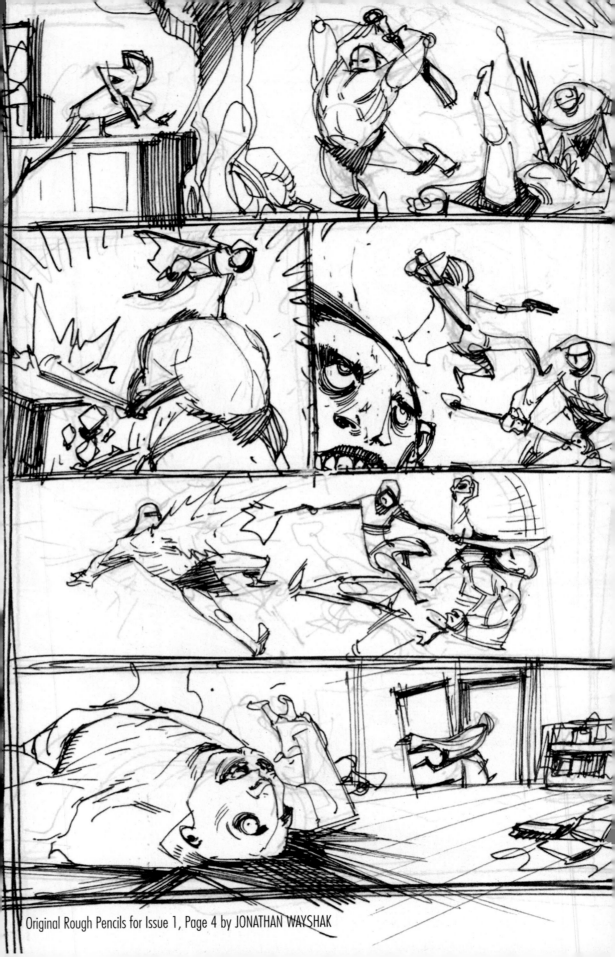

Original Rough Pencils for Issue 1, Page 4 by JONATHAN WAYSHAK

Original Rough Pencils for Issue 1, Page 5
by JONATHAN WAYSHAK

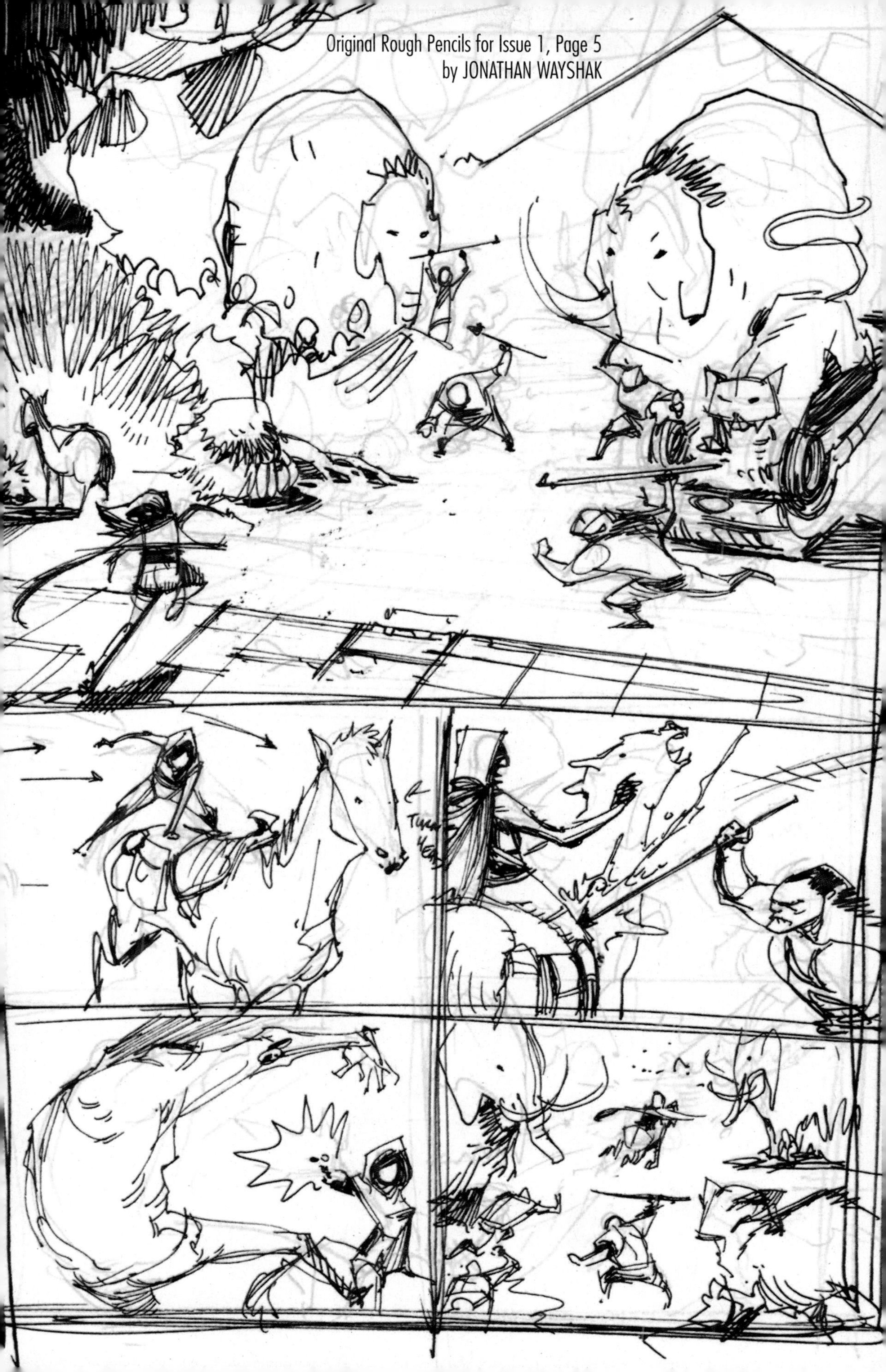

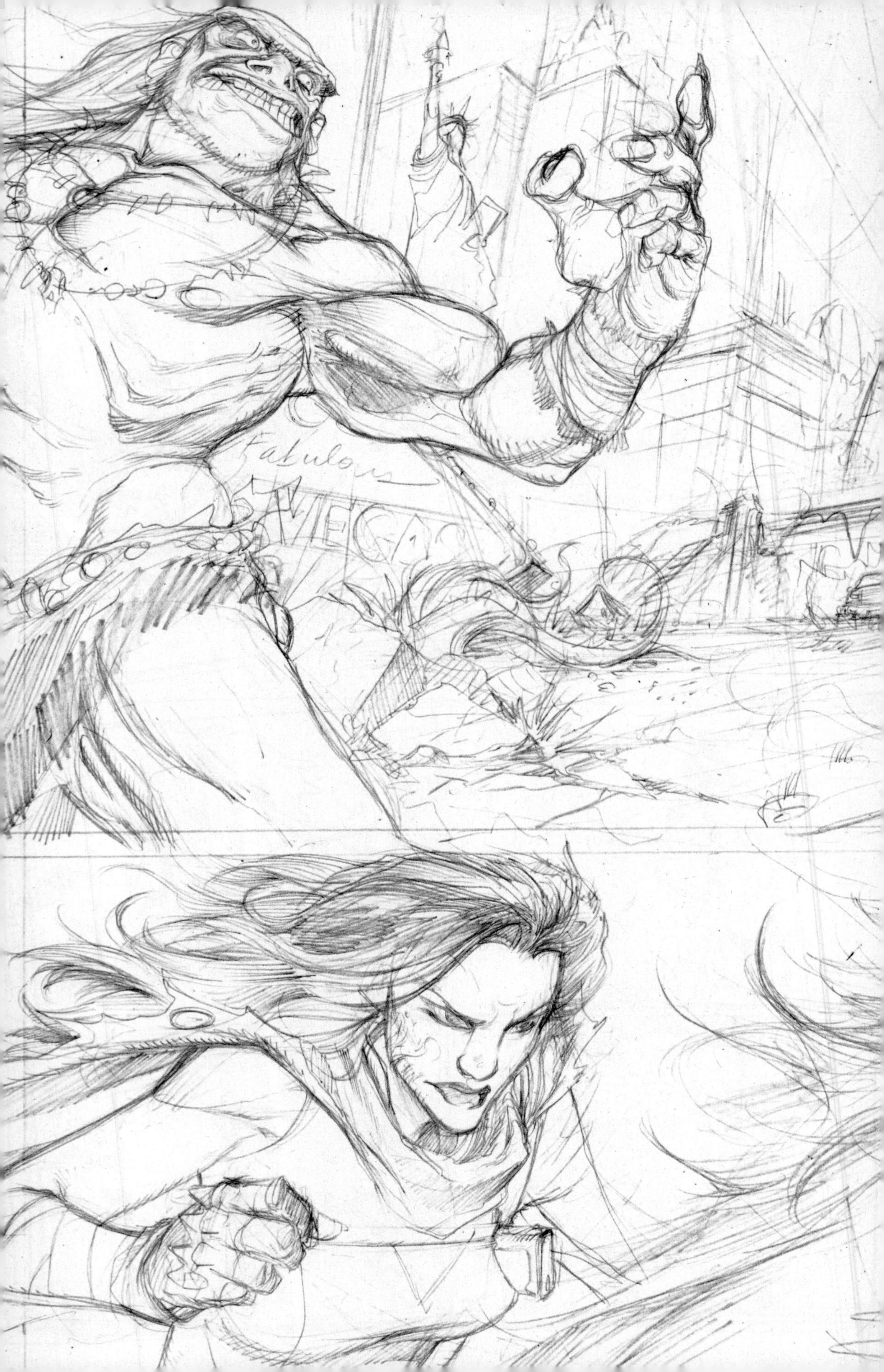

Fabulous

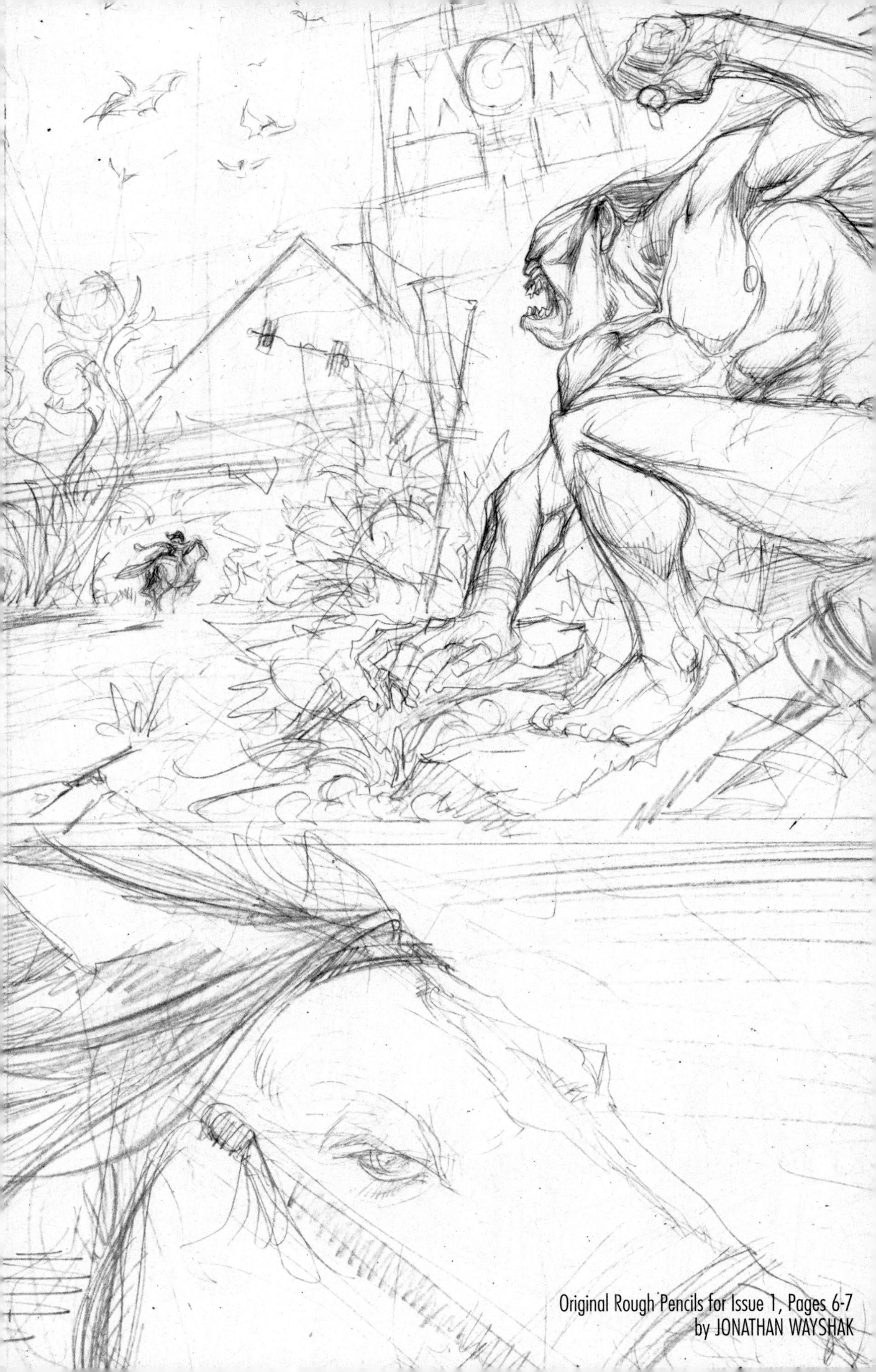
AGM

Original Rough Pencils for Issue 1, Pages 6-7
by JONATHAN WAYSHAK

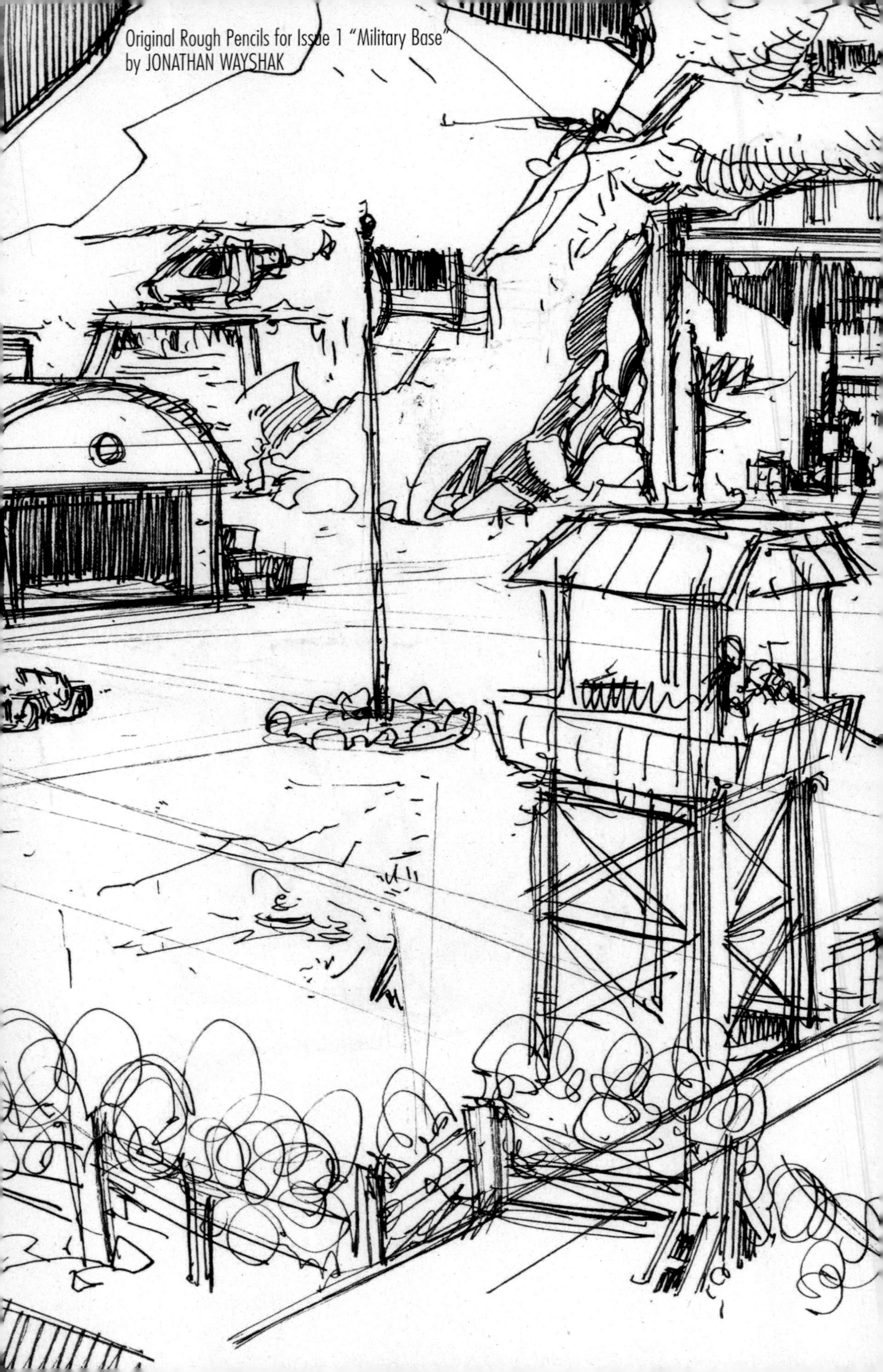

Original Rough Pencils for Issue 1 "Military Base"
by JONATHAN WAYSHAK

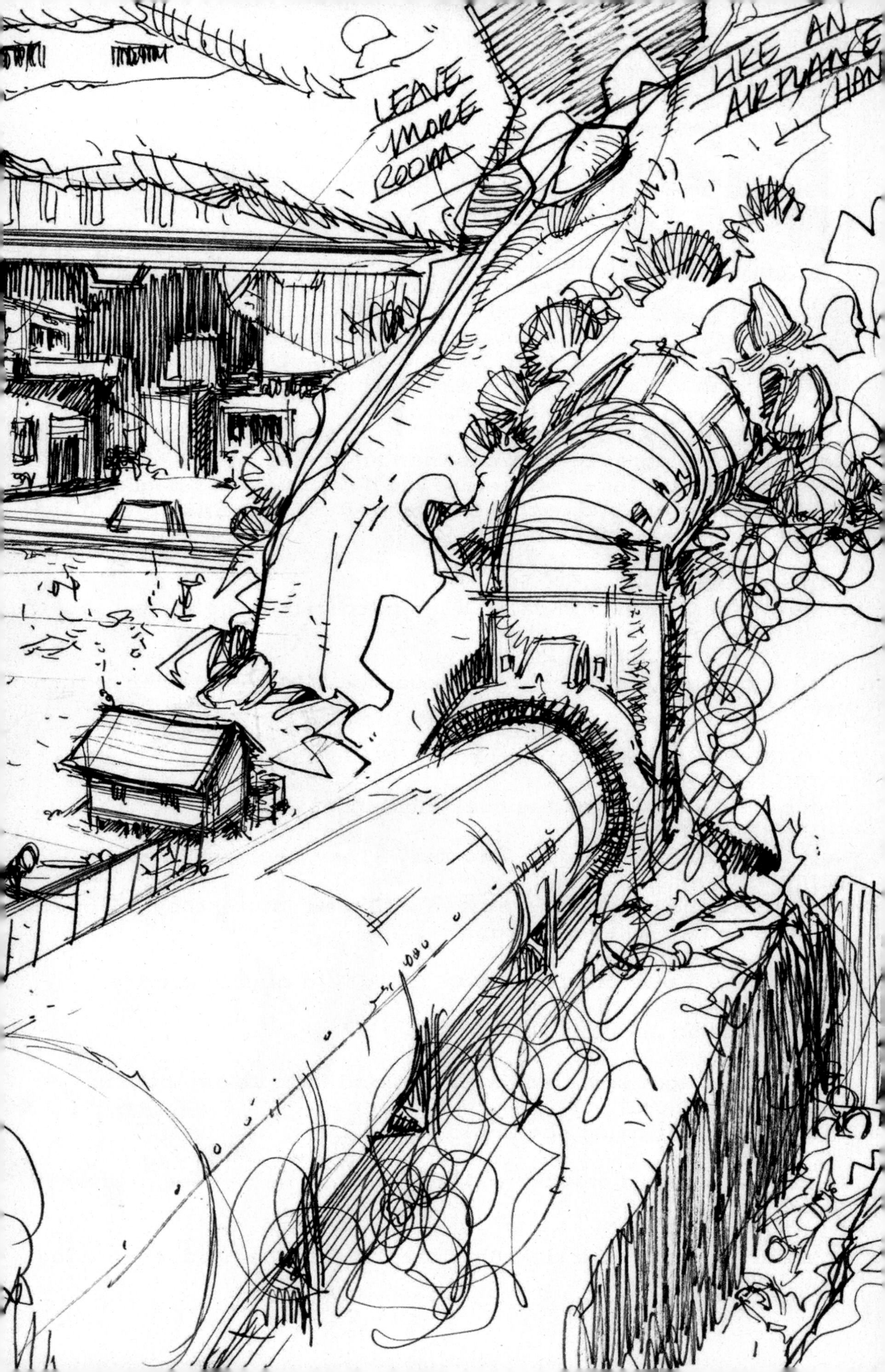
LEAVE MORE ROOM
LIKE AN AIRPLANE HAN

DEVOLUTION
ISSUE 1

PAGE 1

1 - NEVADA, THE FUTURE - EST. INT. A LONG SINCE DILAPIDATED 7-11 CONVENIENCE MART - The store is totally RANSACKED and gone through, strange alien plants, moss, and vines grow in from the shattered windows. RAJA, hood up, HIDING HER FACE, is behind the counter, desperately looking for something. On Raja's back is an ARABIAN SCIMITAR SWORD sheathed, on her thigh a SAWED OFF SHOTGUN in a holster.

THIRD PERSON (CAP)
This area was more treacherous than any other in her long journey. She couldn't remember before the devolution had began she couldn't remember a time that she wasn't flush with anxiety and living in constant peril

THIRD PERSON (CAP)
It wasn't the heat, which paled when compared to the summers in Saudi Arabia.

THIRD PERSON (CAP)
Food and water, normally a rare resource, had been easier to turn up.

2 - CLOSER - Raja is digging through TRASH, frantically.

THIRD PERSON (CAP)
Which likely explained the great number of Thals.

THIRD PERSON (CAP)
Never before had she seen this many--They flourished here--

THIRD PERSON (CAP)
And unlike the others, these lived with a structure; they followed leaders and attacked in groups.

3 - She sees a pile of OLD MAPS OF NEVADA in plastic wrap.

THIRD PERSON (CAP)
But she was on God's mission.

THIRD PERSON (CAP)
She was an angel sent to deliver mankind from its own hubris.

THIRD PERSON (CAP)
She knew in her heart she would not fail.

4 - She is cleaning one map with her hand so we can see clearly it is a MAP OF NEVADA.

THIRD PERSON (CAP)
The map was worth the risk. She learned that the hard way coming up the Gulf of Mexico.

THIRD PERSON (CAP)

Without the map you could wander for days.

5 - She turns towards one of the windows a SHAPE MOVES OUTSIDE, and a sound outside has her terrified.
THIRD PERSON (CAP)
Could end up cornered in a canyon again... but that was better not to think about.
THIRD PERSON (CAP)
As were the companions she'd lost there.
THIRD PERSON (CAP)
Her brother had been torn to pieces--the devils were savage and took no mercy.

6 - LOW ANGLE - We are behind the counter with her. She is crouched low behind the counter, pulling her sawed-off shotgun. We can't see what's on the other side of the counter.
THIRD PERSON (CAP)
Mankind turned backwards into primates.
THIRD PERSON (CAP)
Punishment for their hubris and sinful nature.
THIRD PERSON (CAP)
A reminder from God that there is no way forward without him...

PAGES 2-3

1 - 3/4 TALL - IMPACT - DOUBLE PAGE SPREAD - Raja stand up to see FOUR NEANDERTHALS bursting into the convenience mart from the main door and the shattered windows. Big power chord shots as they rush he location, ready too kill. These Neanderthals are
savage, feral; they have WHITE "X" painted across their faces. They each hold different weapons, each found items bent and turned into clubs.
THIRD PERSON (CAP)
...only devolution.

2 - DOUBLE WIDE - SIDE ANGLE - CLOSE ON RAJA, her arm is lifted, in front of her and BLOWS AN APPROACHING NEANDER-THAL'S HEAD OPEN. Plenty of brains and gore and skull pieces, an eye hangs mid-air in the goop.
SFX
GLADOOOM

PAGE 4

1 - Raja leaps up gracefully onto the counter avoiding the second Neanderthal's club, he comes from the side, smashing the area she was just standing. Two more Neanderthals approach from the door, where the body of the headless one slumps to the ground

2 - She flips up, and over, the Neanderthal coming at her from the doorway missing an attack.

3 - BEAT PANEL - She hovers, mid-air, between the two devils, PULLING HER SWORD in her free hand.

4 - She lands between the two, and in one move she swings her sword down, sinking it into one Neanderthal's head as she shoots the other one entering through the door in the chest.

5 - She runs towards the door, leaping over the Neanderthal falling dead to the ground in her way.

PAGE 5

1 - IMPACT - EXT. CONVENIENCE MART - Raja comes out to see a CLAN OF NEANDERTHALS all with the same mark on their faces. Two ride on top of WOOLLY MAMMOTHS; one has a SABERTOOTH TIGER on a chain leash. HER HORSE is roped to an old bike wrack peeking through the strange alien brush that covers the area. The Mammoths are painted with war paint, their hair braided, decorated. Some foot soldiers prepare to hurl spears.

2 - She hops on the hose as one spear whizzes by, just missing her, and another STICKS INTO HER LEG.

3 - She spins, and shoots apart the chest of an approaching Neanderthal with a sledgehammer over its head about to attack.

4 - She kicks her horse and it sprints, galloping right between the two Mammoths. They are too slow to attack it.

PAGES 6-7

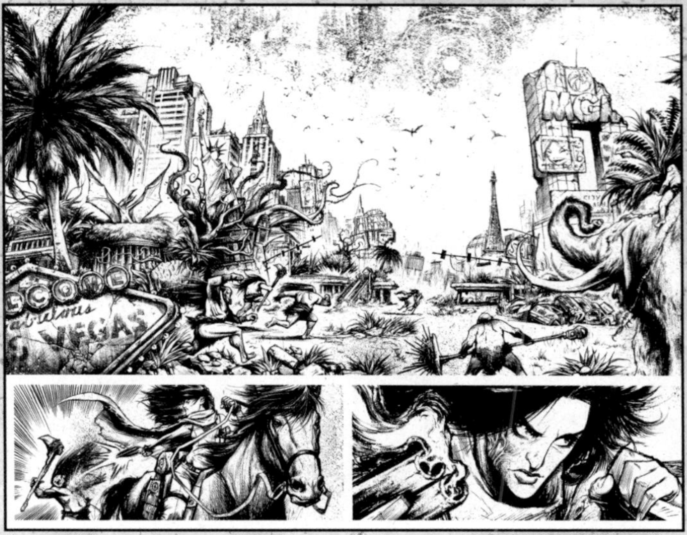

1 - 3/4 SPLASH - WIDE ANGLE, EST. SHOT OF THE VEGAS STRIP - Raja rides her horse hard and down the CENTER OF THE STRIP, no time to remove the spear in her leg, the strip is congested with RUSTING, and long since ABANDONED, CARS. PTERODACTYLS circle in the sky. This is where we show people what is happened to the world, though we can see the buildings and famous casinos and hotels they are overgrown with strange plant life. In the windows of the Hotels have all been smashed out and inside them live Neanderthal families, hundreds. Many have campfires burning by the smashed windows, smoke rises from dozens of windows. On the streets we see many other Neanderthals going wild as Raja passes them. They hang from street signs, leer from windows and rooftops, one looks up form a dead dog it eats, whatever you can think up, this is where we first sell what has happened.
THIRD PERSON (CAP)
She was on God's mission.
THIRD PERSON (CAP)
She was an angel sent to deliver mankind from its own hubris.

2 - PAGE WIDE HORIZONTAL - TIGHT FRONT ON RAJA'S FACE, she's hunched over, riding her horse as fast as he'll go, HER HOOD PULLED BACK SHOWING US HER FACE FOR THE FIRST TIME. She is scarred up, stunning but scarred. She has clearly seen MANY battles.
THIRD PERSON (CAP)
She knew in her heart she would not fail.

PAGE 8

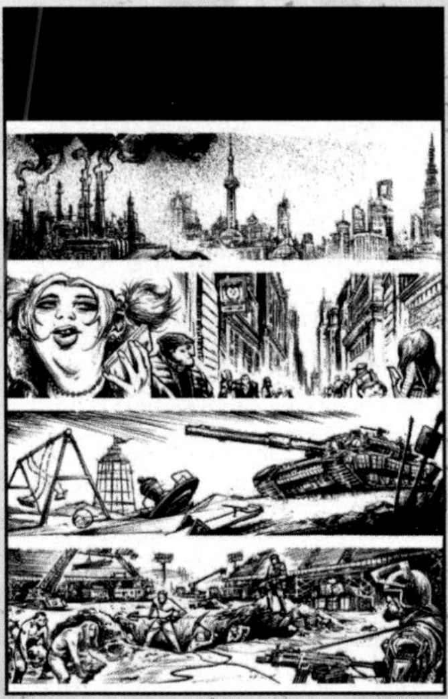

ALL PAGE WIDE HORIZONTAL PANELS, GIVE IT A WIDESCREEN FILM FEEL

1 - PAGE WIDE HORIZONTAL PNAEL - ALL BLACK.
RAJA (CAP)
Mankind had been devolving long before H1J.

2 - CUT TO - PAGE WIDE HORIZONTAL SHOT THE SKYLINE OF SHANGHAI - BEFORE THE DEVOLUTION - The sky is hazy with POLLUTION smoke-

stacks in the foreground admit plumes of white pollutants into the air. The city streets are so filled with smog that we can barely see anything beyond a few people walking to work wearing masks.

RAJA (CAP)
We polluted our world--all temp talk about the devolution of thought and culture here. 9 years prior Homo sapiens dominated the Earth.

RAJA (CAP)
A golden era, blessed with technology and medical advancements.

3 - CUT TO - CUT TO MIDTOWN MANHATTAN - A busy NY day, people hustle and bustle. Many people are fat. Most are drinking coffee drinks. The air is polluted.

THIRD PERSON (CAP)
Our ranks swelled to 7 billion.

The planet was sick from trying to sustain them.

4 - CUT TO - UKRAINE - A Russian tank is rolling over a playground, destroying it, as the Russians invade.

RAJA (CAP)
We waged war.

Killed for territory-- (go deeper, this is surface level and boring)

5 - CUT TO - BRAZIL STADIUM - We are looking at the stadium as it is being built by slave labor. These people are overworked, bleeding and miserable. To the side we see armed guards ensuring these men keep working.

RAJA (CAP)
--And built modern day pyramids with the suffering of others.

PAGE 9

ALL PAGE WIDE HORIZONTAL PANELS
1 - CUT TO - WAL-MART - A super fat man in a scooter is buying Twinkies and cookies as a poor looking other holds a fat baby in one hand, a bottle of cheap baby formula in the other.

RAJA (CAP)
We were calorie junkies, addicted to sugar from birth--

2 - CUT TO - A GIANT MEGA CHURCH - This church is a monument to capitalism, the kind of disgusting televised church that is made only to draw in money.

RAJA (CAP)
--True believers too busy awaiting the rapture to help our fellow
man--

3 - CUT TO - AN IMPOVERISHED APARTMENT CHINA -- A man walks
in to his large family, clearly exhausted. This one or two room
apartment needs to sell the poverty they excerpting.
RAJA (CAP)
Or honest workers, too busy to think beyond their families next
meal.

An entire species made indifferent to the world around us.

And that indifference was our bane.
4 - CUT TO - MIDDLE EAST DESERT - Armed ISIS troops march vil-
lagers to a mass grave, other soldiers are shooting men already
lined up for execution. In the background we see men carrying
off young and old women. This is a TERRIBLE scene, little girls
crying, bodies filling a ditch, every terrible thing you can cook
up.
RAJA (CAP)
From the middle east rose a terrible conflict.

Ethnic cleansing, casual rape, abolished
education, public executions and kidnapping--

5 - CUT TO - WAR FOOTAGE FROM IRAQ - US
TROOPS ARE IN A FIREFIGHT.
RAJA (CAP)
An endless war erupted in the Middle East.

PAGE 10

ALL PAGE WIDE HORIZONTAL PANELS

1 - CUT TO - ISRAEL - A small nuclear explo-
sion is wiping out a prosperous city.
RAJA (CAP)
The atrocities immeasurable.

But it wasn't until the first nuclear explosion that we woke from
our stupor.

2 - CUT TO - UNITED NATIONS - Speakers point and scream at each
other, their panic clear.
RAJA (CAP)
Politicians debated, each blocking the others solution, fueled by
a petty need to stand out.

The west raced for a solution--
RAJA (CA)

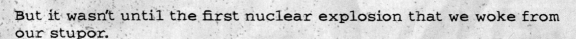

--And in our desperation created a viral agent designed to alter men--

3 - CUT TO - INT. A HIGH TECH LABORATORY - We see Muneef, Raja's father, working over a man in a cage as he turns into a Thrall. We see SHARRON, in a lab coat, working among other scientists.
RAJA (CA)
--to make them docile.
RAJA (CAP)
Band of scientists, Scott among them, were put together to devise a chemical agent that would neuro-inhibit religious fervor and neuter the part of their brain that believed in God.

It would devolve what was scene as a hyper active

4 - CUT TO - GOVERNMENT MEETING ROOM - MUNEEF and SHARRON and FELLOW SCIENTISTS stand in their lab coats giving a presentation to a long meeting table full of the UNITED STATES GEN'S And TOP OFFICIALS. SHARRON uses a pointer to indicate the section of the human brain that they were shrinking on a monitor.
THIRD PERSON (CAP)
And they were successful, they not only isolated the section of the brain most associated with belief in a higher power and they devolve this, reducing it in size which in turn turned off the recipients belief in God.

5 - CUT TO - A US MILITARY BASE IN AFGHANISTAN - SHARRON and MUNEEF stand watching as DARREN AND GIL load missiles that are marked with the INTERNATIONAL SYMBOL FOR CHEMICAL AGENT. At this point Gil DOES NOT have the swastika on the side of his head.
THIRD PERSON (CAP)
Of course there were side effects, but nothing severe enough to preclude its use on the field.
THIRD PERSON (CAP)
Scott oversaw a special band of Marines who were charged with the task of handling the Devo agent and deploying it in the field.

PAGE 11

ALL PAGE WIDE HORIZONTAL PANELS

1 - CUT TO - A TALIBAN STRONGHOLD - MUSLIM MILITANTS run in a panic gasping and holding their throats as white mist fills the area.
THIRD PERSON (CAP)
These were among some of the only people to receive the antidote to the chemical agent.

2 - CUT TO - THE SAME SHOT OF THE SAME VILLAGE but it is a YEAR LATER and the Muslim extremists are replaced with NEANDERTHALS. The plant life has grown wild covering their

hearts and were there were no trees before there is now a jungle of strange prehistoric plant life.

THIRD PERSON (CAP)
But things didn't go according to plan, as they seldom do, and the chemical agent had unexpected consequences in the real world.

3 - CUT TO - PRESENT DAY - Raja and her brothers are fighting crazy animal demons with parasitic plants growing out of them. They are just normal citizens of Saudi Arabia, not warriors, not yet.
RAJA (CAP) (CONT'D)
The Devo was far more virulent,
more volatile than we ever anticipated. Within a few short generations it was jumping between species, infected every living thing with catastrophic results. Mutant birds carried Devo across the planet faster than humanity could react. It was the end of civilization"

4 - The battle is over. Raja stands, triumphant, looking down at her dead brothers.
RAJA (CAP)
But the chemicals made it into the ground water and spread.

humanity fell--
RAJA (CAP) (CONT'D)
Mankind may have earned its punishment--
RAJA (CAP) (CONT'D)
But we will earn their salvation.

5 - CUT TO - NEW YORK - SAME EXACT SHOT FROM THE OPENING - New York the same thing has occurred. We should see DOZENS OF NEANDERTHALS in the street, eating rats, fucking, fighting, a grand metaphor.
THIRD PERSON (CAP)
It began to reverse devolution process and it began to devolve in reverse mutate all life on earth. The live cultures were airborne...

THIRD PERSON (CAP)
Within one year everything on earth had suffered the effects of--

Page 12 - 13

Double page spread, all black.
TITLE
Devolution.

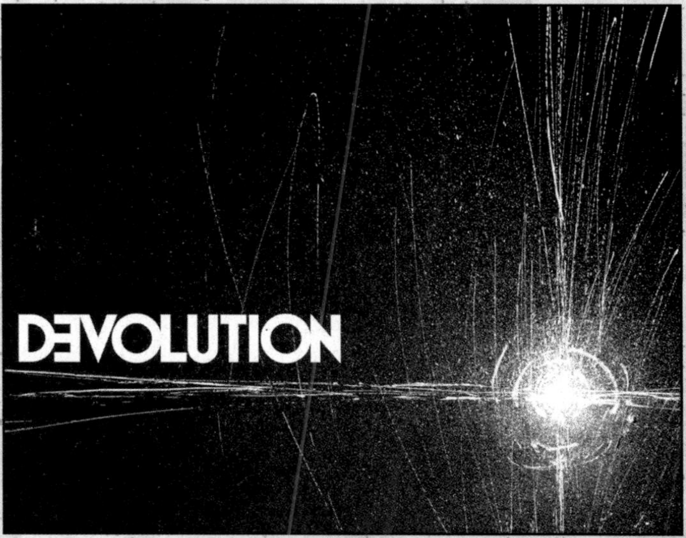
DEVOLUTION

PAGE 14

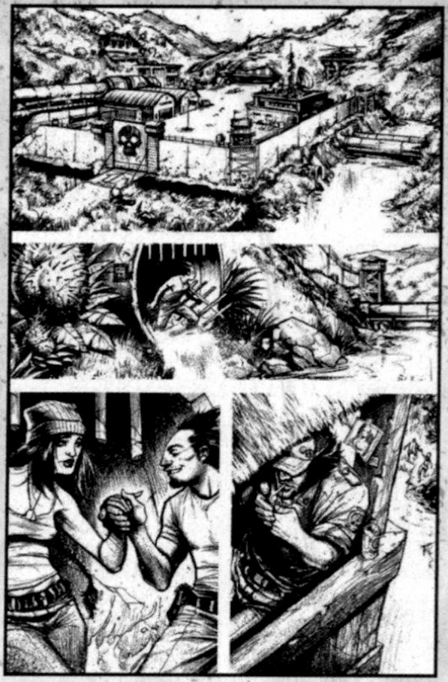

1 - 1/2 PAGE - WIDE EST. On an old military base built into the side of a tall and lush mountain - This area is deep prehistoric jungle, with strange plants unlike anything we've ever seen. The base is covered by a wall with numerous nests for turret gunners. Inside there are a few all terrain vehicles.
2 - Pull in on the outside the gate, closest to the side of the mountain the base is dug into, away from eyes. Angle on a duct under the gate for water runoff. DR. SCOTT LYNCH has removed the metal bars, he holds them open for his lady JANA--
3 - PULL IN CLOSER - HIS LADY JANA EMERGES, CLIMBS THROUGH. Scott Lynch is a slim Asian man, in his 30s, good looking but weathered, he has a pistol on his hip in a holster. She is in her twenties, Latino, very attractive, dressed in military garb, green slacks, white tee shirt. They look scared.
4 - Having grabbed cover behind a lip in the mountain, Scott peeks to see the UNAWARE WATCH TOWERS GUARDS; they are looking in the other direction.

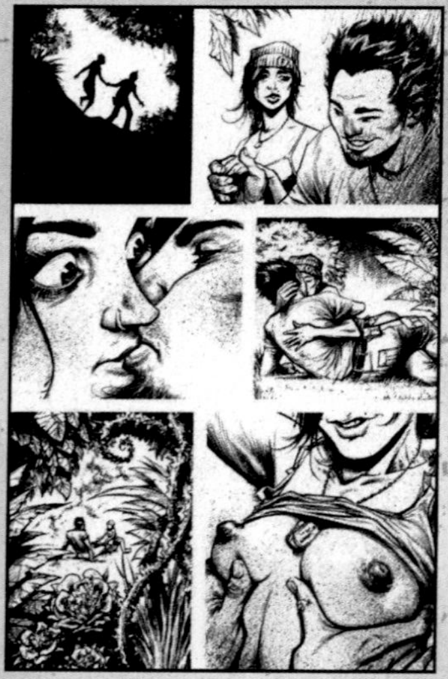

PAGE 15

1 - They run down the side of the mountain,
SCOTT
This is the only way. Gil has camera all over the base, he'd know otherwise.

2 - At a clearing he stops her.
SCOTT
It's safe. No Thralls come this close.

3 - Turns her around and kisses her.

4 - He pushes her to the ground, kissing her.

5 - POV from the jungle, the POV of someone else watching - they begin to make love in the strange jungle clearing. She kisses him back and rolls over on top of him.

6 - She takes off her top. Boobs!

PAGE 16

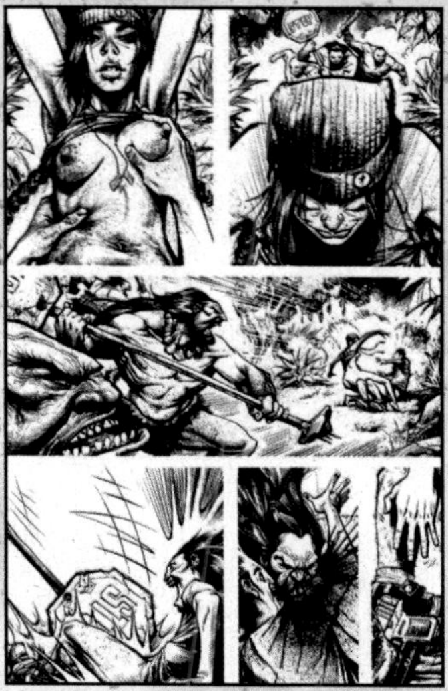

1 - Closer on the couple, having sex. Scott holds her breasts as she rides him. Pants around ankles, the whole bit.
2 - She bends down to kiss his neck, REVEALING THREE NEANDERTHALS APPROACHING BEHIND HER. One, the leader, holds the METAL POST from a street stop sign.

3 - Scott pushes her off, as the Neanderthals rush, at them. The leader about to bring down the METAL POST he uses for a club.

4 - Scott scotches backwards, the metal item comes down right between his legs, just missing his exposed manhood. Obviously we don't want to show his junk, but stage it so we can see he narrowly avoided a bad time.

5 - The Neanderthal leaps on Scott, biting down deep into his shoulder.

6 - Scott reaches for his gun holster around his ankles as the Neanderthal gnaws on his shoulder.

PAGE 17

1 - Scott shoots the NEANDERTHAL in the stomach three times, the slug blow out the beasts back.

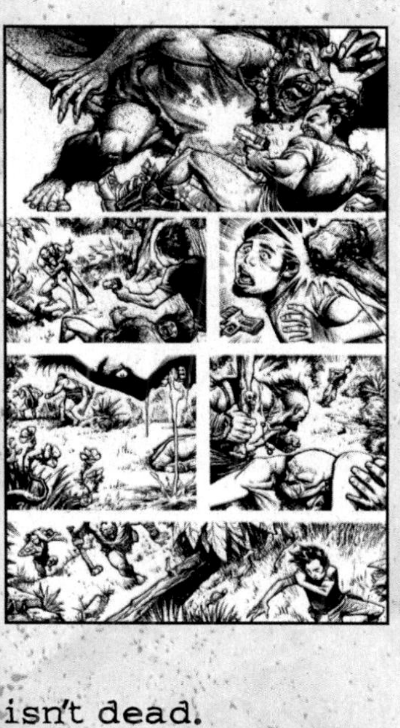

2 - Scott turns, pointing his gun to the screams of Jana as THREE NEANDERTHALS GRAB HER. She is terrified, exposed breasts, classic horror film from the 70s vibe.

3 - Before he can fire the gun HE IS HIT in the side of the head with a wooden plank.

4 - Scott is on the ground, bloody head, face in the dirt, his GUN NOW OUT OF REACH, he's looking up from the ground to see THE NEANDERTHALS DRAGGING JANA INTO THE JUNGLE, kicking and screaming.

5 - Scott stumbles to his feet, pulling his pants on as the leader takes notice that he isn't dead.

6 - Scott running, sprinting, through the thick alien jungle. Two Neanderthals brandishing found items as clubs rush behind him.

PAGE 18

1 - Vista shot - He comes out of the dense jungle and off a cliff. He's literally airborne here, ran himself right off the ledge. We see the Hoover Dam in the distance, grown over with thick brush, alien flowers, and thick vines the size of buildings. Pterodactyls circle overhead. Strange critters in the trees.

2 - He falls down through the trees and strange plants, about to hit a steep incline below.

3 - He breaks his leg as he lands, badly. He screams loudly.

4 - He falls rolling forward, hands out in front of him.

5 - ALL BLACK as he's knocked out.

PAGE 19

1 - NOW - 1/2 SPLASH - ANGLE BEHIND RAJA ON HER HORSE, SCOTT slung over the back is out cold. In front of her is "THE TOILET" THE BASE our Marines live in. The GUN NESTS are manned and TURRET GUNS ARE AIMED AT US AS WE APPROACH.  Maybe go with a low angel here to sell the scope and sell the fear as this lone horse slowly rides up to town. Outside of the base around the gates we see dead Neanderthals decomposing as well as a dead giant beetle. Victims of the turret gun now trained on out hero.
THIRD PERSON (CAP)
She'd heard the Neanderthals going wild and turned away. Until she heard the woman.

The first human she'd heard in years, and she was screaming.
THIRD PERSON (CAP)
A scream that was suddenly cut short.

Raja's mission is too important to compromise it, even to help another homosapien.

2 - CUT TO - INT. CROWS NEST on the wall of the military base. THE GUNNER FOLLOWS RAJA AND SCOTT as they come riding into the base, the giant front gate being opening for them, numerous guards, mean looking mother fuckers, watch the horse and its

rider.

THIRD PERSON (CAP)

But she couldn't allow the woman to die, what good a mission from God if one ignore those in need.

THIRD PERSON (CAP)

By the time she'd discovered the woman it was too late, she'd been savaged.

3 - The front gates close behind her. We still haven't seen inside.

THIRD PERSON (CAP)

She'd seen the military base but known to stay away, she'd find supplies somewhere else.

PAGES 20-21

1 - DOUBLE PAGE WIDE BIG EST. SHOT - INSIDE MAIN CAMP COURTYARD - RAJA LEAPS OFF THE HORSE, marines approaching with guns on her, the gates closed behind her, Scott slung over the back of the horse still. Soldiers, MEAN LOOKING AMERICAN MARINES, surround them. Darren is not visible here. The courtyard is what used to be a military base, but is now a mix between ROAD WARRIOR and CONAN THE BARBARIAN. There are no innocent civilians here though. Only marines, and only men have weapons. The Women are for cooking and fucking to these men, they are not allowed guns. SIX DEAD PEOPLE HANG FROM THE GALLOWS, birds head on them. The marines are ferocious, they bark at her.

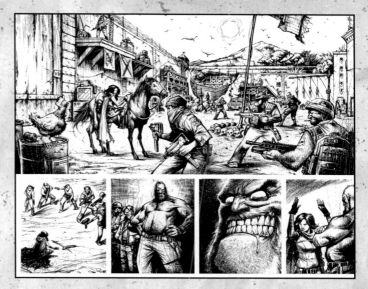

THIRD PERSON (CAP)

But the sign of the attack saw a trail break off in two directions. The second lead her to Scott.

THIRD PERSON (CAP)

His military grab let her know he was a part of whoever was within the base.

THIRD PERSON (CAP)

They might reward her for his return.

2 - ANGLE BEHIND RAJA - SHE HANDS OVER HER SWORD AND SHOTGUN TO A MEAN MARINE. Many others have guns fixed on her.

THIRD PERSON (CAP)

But that was beginning to look less and less likely.

GIL (CAP)

What we got here?

3 - RAJA LOOKS UP TO SEE THE LOUD MAN; DIRTY GIL makes his way

towards her through the guards who part for their leader. Gil's bitch crony DAN CASSIDY is following behind him, a loyal dog.
GIL
Good lord sendin' me another wife?

4 - RAJA'S POV - ANGLE OVER GIL'S SHOULDER AND RIGHT ON THE SIX DEAD PEOPLE HANGING FROM THE GALLOWS, birds feed on them.
THIRD PERSON
But she quick sees that these men are not to be trifled with. She'll accept the insult, the mission was the only thing that mattered.

5 - RAJA LIFTS HER ARMS IN A SIGN OF SURRENDER. Gil is giant, not a fight she wants. What she sees in front of her is more savage than what she saw outside. Six people hang from the gallows, birds feed on them. The marines are ferocious, skulls painted on their helmets. Gil, eyes on her breasts.
GIL
Arms up, showin' ol' Gil what she got ta trade fer.

PAGE 22

1 - The leader of the base, Dirty Gil, a giant man with a tree trunk neck walks past Raja and towards Scott.
GIL
I'll get up at them titties in a bit darlin'

2 - Gil holds Scott by the back of his neck like a disobedient puppy.
GIL
Where's Dana?
SCOTT
I-I was on m-my own, Gil. I was--

3 - Gil goes fucking insane! HE GRABS SCOTT AROUND THE NECK AND BEGINS CHOKING HIM TIGHTLY. Scott is in terror.
GIL
WHERE IS MY MOTHER FUCKIN' WIFE!

4 - GIL JERKS SCOTT OFF OF THE HORSE LIKE A RAG DOLL AND SEND HIM FACE FIRST INTO THE MUD. Raja doesn't give a fuck. She thought she was doing them a favor bringing this man here, but boy was she wrong.
GIL
You filthy yellow chink cunt.

5 - GIL PULLS OUT A MACHETE! He's going to cut Scott's head off.
GIL
You took my girl out to fuck in the jungle and you got here killed.

You took my WIFE for a jungle time party fuckin' an some thralls got up in that party, 'm I right?

PAGE 23

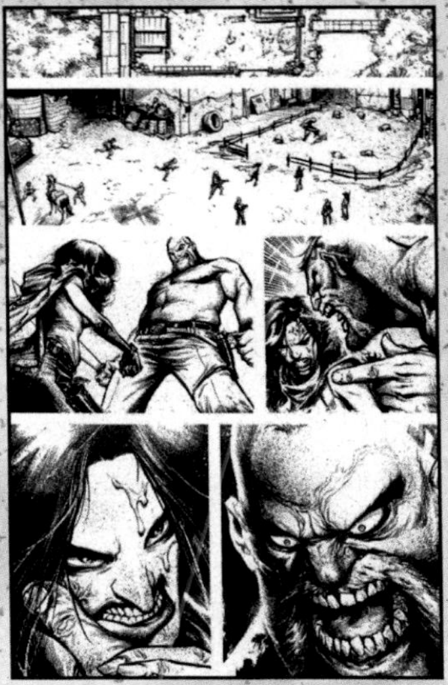

1 - CUT TO - A SATELLITE DIGITAL SHOT OF THE TOP OF THE SCENE WE ARE WATCHING IN THE MILITARY BASE. Someone in a satellite is taking pictures of this.
VOICE (ELECTRIC)
We have a visitor. A human.

Same one caused the upset in Vegas.
VOICE 2 (ELECTRIC)
Stay on her.

2 - CUT BACK TO THE BASE - Gil turns to Raja, sniffing her out.
RAJA
›STOP!‹
MARINE #2
The fuck is she saying? What language is that?
GIL
Guess there's an upshot. Scott got my ol' lady killed--brought me a new lady.

Dune coon, but still Sapien. Still sapien"ish" anyway.

3 - Gil look at her body like a piece of meat. She remains motionless.
GIL
I like to marry you. You want to marry? That's why you come here is it?

You were lookin' high an' low fer one American drill fuckin' redneck.

Here I am. Alabama party machine.
RAJA
›I serve the will of God. I am come to save man from his hubris

4 - Gil is a pig, he grabs her face, gets close, crazy. Her arms still up. Chewing tobacco dribbling down his face.
GIL
I don't speak sand nigger, girl.

My cock speaks all kinds o' language though. We don't we gonna let ol' Johnny translate.

5 - On Raja, defiled but powerless. Pissed but she doesn't move.
RAJA
›I know the cure to this world's illness.

›I came only to deliver this man to trade for food.

>I must not linger here.<

6 - GIL YELLS IN HER FACE AGAIN. He's a big dumb savage and when he barks chewing tobacco sprays out of his mouth and onto Raja's face.
GIL
Stop talkin' stupid.

Stop runnin' yer stupid mouth!
SCOTT (OP)
She's telling you she knows how to save the world.

PAGE 24

1 - GIL, COLD AND ANGRY, TURNS TO SCOTT ON THE GROUND. Gil's right hand man DAN "THE SHITHEAD" is running over to kick Scott.
SCOTT
She speaks Arabic--

2 - Dan kicks Scott in the face, blood erupts.
DAN
Why'ncho shut yer fuckin' gook trap Tokyo rose!
SFX
PLOKK

3 - Dumb Dan is about to stomp in Scott's head.

DARREN (OP)
Stop.

4 - Angle on Darren, calm, smoking a cigar, sitting on the top of the gate, no expression on his face. He's a bad ass, and one of our heroes.
DARREN
What happens if you kill, Scott?

5 - Gil turns to see Darren walking over, he's calm, smoking a cigar.
GIL
The fuck you think yer talkin' to, monkey?
DARREN
Scott. Our only doctor, right?

What happens if he dies?

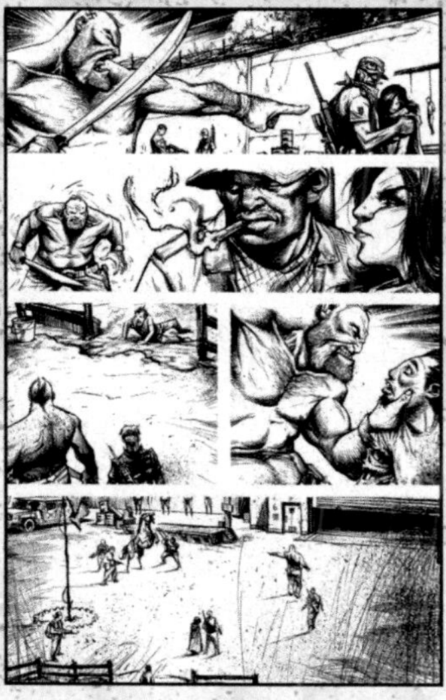

PAGE 25

1 - DARREN doesn't wait for an answer, he just TURNS AND WALKS AWAY WITH RAJA, Gil looks up at him contemptuously. Darren looks back; we sell a lot of hatred between these two.
GIL
I don't like yer' tone, monkey.
DARREN
Like it or not--She's coming with me.

You hurt her we'll never get anything out of her.

Who she is, where she came from, what she's doing here.

2 - MEDIUM TWO SHOT - SHARON AND RAJA, EYES LOCKED AS DARREN WALKS RAJA AWAY. In the background we can see Gil, hand on his rifle, looking at Darren with murder on his face.
DARREN
I'm sorry you came here, sister.

3 - Gil walks over to Scott.
GIL
How did you understand our mongrel guest?
SCOTT
Six years as a field medic in the Middle East.

I speak Arabic.

4 - Gil kneels down and looks Scott in the face.
SCOTT
Well, alright, Scott. You got some uses still.

So I ain't gonna kill ya.

But it'll be bad for ya here. Life gonna be hard.

5 - Gil turns to go inside, he waves for the others to kill the horse.
SCOTT
Bring 'em in. Let's have a pow-wow.

Slaughter 'er horse fer food.

PAGE 26

1 - we see Gil yelling at his living wives Linda (new character) and Tanisha are washing clothes. NOTE: The total population of the base is only going to be like 30 total.

GIL
Scott got yer sister wife killed while out o' the base fuckin'

You two gonna have ta double time yer chores.

2 - Darren walking towards the main building with Raja. Behind her a marine shoots her horse in the head.

DARREN (WHISPER)
Oh sister, I'm so sorry you came here.

3 - Follow behind them now as they enter the blackness of the ominous base, bad times ahead. Dead bodies dangle from the gallows, BEING FED ON BY PTERODACTYLS.

THIRD PERSON (CAP)
She had been on this mission of more years than she could count.

4 - ANGLE ON THE DEAD BODIES HANGING, BEING FED ON BY PTERODACTYLS.

THIRD PERSON (CAP)
During all her travels she'd not seen a single human being.

5 - CLOSER ON THE DEAD BODIES, THEIR DECOMPOSING FACES BEING PICKED AWAY BY PTERODACTYLS.

THIRD PERSON (CAP)
And she now wished it had stayed that way.

PAGE 27

1 - EXT. MOONBASE - TWO 2 ASTRONAUTS, BOTH ARABS, ONE MAN AND ONE WOMAN, wearing VERY COOL ASTRONAUT SUITS are approaching the VACUUM LOCKED DOOR leading into a MOON BASE. Let's not show the entire moon base, let's save that reveal for later.

2 - INT. THE VACUUM-SEALED COMPARTMENT - ASTRONAUT NUMBER 1 stands inside the sealed compartment. A BLUE LASER SENSOR traces up-and-down him.

3 - A LIGHT ABOVE A DOOR LEADING into the moon base proper turns GREEN, this man is

clean.

4 - The first astronaut now stands inside the base looking through a glass porthole as the 2ND ASTRONAUT, the woman, enters the vacuum compartment.

5 - A blue laser sensor traces up-and-down the female astronaut.

PAGE 28

1 - The light above the door turns RED; she is detected to be CONTAMINATED. She freaks out.

2 - The man inside the base pounds on the door as the woman stands, realizing she has to get away from them. This man is watching his wife in the final moments of her life.

3 - She holds up a hand, waving goodbye to her husband as the door behind her opens up.

4 - EXT. MOON BASE - THE FEMALE ASTRONAUT IGNITES ROCKET THRUSTERS on the bottom of her feet and is flying away from the moon base, it is suicide but she does it for the good of others.

5 - She rockets away from the moon base and towards space, tears streaming, in a bit of pain.

PAGE 29

1 - INT. MOONBASE - THE MALE ASTRONAUT IS ON HIS KNEES in front of a large PICTURE WINDOW he's looking up as the FEMALE ASTRO-NAUT FLOATS AWAY, her body contorts she begins the transforma-tion she is now floating above the moon earth in the far background.

2 - SPACE - On the female astronaut she is in great pain grasping at the rim of her helmet. She is floating away from the moon and in the space having been shot out from the moon base.

3 - She coughs up DARK YELLOW MUCUS onto the front of her helmet, she is in TERRIBLE AGONY.

4 - On the female astronaut as she BEGINS TO TRANSFORM INTO A NEANDERTHAL. Think about the transformation of an American werewolf

in London, this should look horrific and painful.

5 - She continues to transform, she is now grunting and screaming.

PAGE 30

1 - Close on the Neanderthal woman's face, terrified and confused. The transformation is complete she has devolved into a Neander-thal, a confused Neanderthal now floating in space.

2 - She drifts away from the moon, A rocket boots turned off she is no longer in control of the space suit, just a confused primate wearing an astronaut suit floating through space.

3 - She floats away from us and towards Earth.

4 - She continues to float away from us.

5 - She continues to float away from us getting smaller and smaller beautiful blue earth in the background.

END ISSUE 1.